Confronting Cyber-Bullying

WHAT SCHOOLS NEED TO KNOW
TO CONTROL MISCONDUCT AND
AVOID LEGAL CONSEQUENCES

Shaheen Shariff, Ph.D.
McGill University

CAMBRIDGE
UNIVERSITY PRESS

CAMBRIDGE UNIVERSITY PRESS
Cambridge, New York, Melbourne, Madrid, Cape Town, Singapore, São Paulo, Delhi

Cambridge University Press
32 Avenue of the Americas, New York, NY 10013-2473, USA

www.cambridge.org
Information on this title: www.cambridge.org/9780521700795

First published 2009

Printed in the United States of America

A catalog record for this publication is available from the British Library.

Library of Congress Cataloging in Publication Data

Shariff, Shaheen.
Confronting cyber-bullying : what schools need to know to control misconduct and avoid legal
consequences / Shaheen Shariff.
    p.   cm.
Includes bibliographical references and index.
ISBN 978-0-521-87723-7 (hardback) – ISBN 978-0-521-70079-5 (pbk.)
 1. Cyber-bullying. 2. Bullying in schools – Automation. 3. Computer crimes.
4. Internet and teenagers. 5. Internet and children. I. Title.
K5210.S53 2009
371.5'8–dc22   2007045665

ISBN   978-0-521-87723-7 hardback
ISBN   978-0-521-70079-5 paperback

**7 – DAY
LOAN**

CONF

This b   olicy
maker   anti-
author   iolo-
gies. T   legal
respon   hool
hours   Students,   uthor
analyz   ed in
legally   judicial de   rects
attenti   iools
balanc

Dr. Sh   n at
McGil   *ion?:*
Confr   *yber-*
Bullyi

I dedicate this book to my parents, Ramzan and Gulshan Dedhar, for their continued love

*   *   *

To my sister, Shahira Clemens, for being an exemplary mum to my gifted and beautiful nieces, Saffia and Suraya

*   *   *

And, last but not least, to my loving husband and children, Zahir, Farhana, and Hanif, for your patience and love always

Contents

Figures

Tables

Preface

My interest in the intersection of law and education began with my return to graduate school in Vancouver, Canada, as a mature student. I had worked at law firms for about twenty years while raising two children. As they reached their teens, I returned to university to pursue an academic career. The Centre of Education, Law and Society at Simon Fraser University, spearheaded by Professor Michael Manley-Casimir, provided an opportunity, under his mentorship and that of Dr. Roland Case, an active member of the centre, to study the range of ways in which the law (normative, legislative, and judicial) affects every aspect of school life and ultimately shapes policy decisions and educational practices resulting from those decisions.

As my children went through school, there were several incidents in which they were bullied by peers but received little intervention on the part of school administrators and teachers. This led me to study, as part of my doctoral work, the legal obligations of schools to address bullying. At that time, the Internet was not as powerful as it is now, and cyber-bullying did not exist. However, I had already learned about the challenges schools face in navigating stakeholder rights and interests relating to freedom of expression, equality, and safety. These challenges became evident during my master's degree study of a controversial court case involving the banning of three children's books recommended for discussion of same-sex parents in kindergarten classrooms. I learned that school officials and teachers need guidance in navigating and balancing stakeholder claims to control of knowledge, learning, and expression in school contexts.

My subsequent doctoral work on the legal obligations of schools comprised an in-depth review of tort law cases on negligence of supervision in the school context, of constitutional obligations such as equality and freedom of expression rights of children, and of human and civil rights to learn in environments free from discrimination and harassment. These pluralistic legal frameworks enabled me to develop a set of standards for bullying in schools, informed by comprehensive review of the research on the forms of bullying, its etymology and history, and its prevalence and impact, all of which provided a context for the legal frameworks.

Once I began my academic career at McGill University, expanding this research to identify a set of legal standards and responsibilities of schools to address cyber-bullying was a natural extension of my work. I secured two grants from the Social Sciences and Humanities Research Council of Canada to engage in national and international research on cyber-bullying in Canada, the United States, Japan, China, India, New Zealand, Australia, and Great Britain. The international work is just beginning, and hence only preliminary results could be reported in this book. Little did I realize when I embarked on this research, however, how complex and challenging it would become. Nor had I envisioned the amount of attention it would receive or the extent of the fear, controversy, and interest the topic would attract. Cyber-bullying is now at the forefront of many public policy debates and legislative initiatives and a focus of the media worldwide.

As technologies evolve and advance at rapid rates and children are immersed in them at increasingly younger ages – and as adolescents become proficient and comfortable with social networking sites, blogs, chat rooms, and mobile phones – many adults, whose use of computers is limited to e-mail and word processing, find themselves incapacitated and left behind – or as some would say, technologically challenged. With lack of familiarity comes discomfort. With discomfort comes fear of the unknown, and with fear of the unknown comes loss of a sense of control. This fuels the desire to regain control and power over the ways in which children learn and express themselves. Technologies place newfound power in the hands of young people, and cyberspace provides fluid, as opposed to rigid, boundaries within which to move. While young people test out their newfound spaces, parents, teachers, and school administrators confront a policy vacuum with regard to the extent they can be expected to supervise student expression and online interaction as the lines between freedom of expression, safety, privacy, and supervision become increasingly blurred.

Although most scholarly research and books on bullying focus on children's behavior and look for ways to treat it using behavior modification techniques or positivist modes of discipline, my book addresses an important gap in the scholarship on bullying and cyber-bullying. I provide a unique perspective that directs educators, government policy makers, and legal practitioners to reconceptualize their policy responses through critical pedagogy and legally pluralistic responses that are grounded in substantive principles of law.

This book also discloses the extent and potential of cyber-bullying to spread in countries with large populations such as India and China. The international research also discloses a tendency in Asia, like the West, to adopt a punitive rather than educational approach, although a number of interesting cultural nuances are disclosed. A profile of bullying and cyber-bullying is included in Chapter 2. Chapters 3 to 5 each address a specific aspect of law relating to cyber-bullying, such as cyber libel and defamation, freedom of expression, and human rights issues, framed within a contextual discussion of the issues and presented through analysis of case studies and research. Chapter 6 considers supervision and censorship of student spaces and expression.

Chapter 7 undertakes a discussion of positivist versus legally pluralistic perspectives and highlights proposed or emerging legislation in Europe and North America to address cyber-bullying. Finally, in Chapter 8, I present teacher education and professional development models that are grounded in substantive law, legal pluralism, and critical educational pedagogies. These are alternatives to the popular reliance on disciplinary approaches that are rooted in military models. The approaches I advocate in this book lend themselves to significantly more ethical, nonarbitrary, and legally defensible policy and practice responses than do punitive responses that enhance intolerance, criminalize children, and censor useful educational technologies.

Technologies are here to stay. The behavior of young people on the Internet is simply an extension and reflection of the attitudes and forms of discrimination adults model on a regular basis in the physical world. Although disciplinary approaches that are rooted in positivist perspectives of the law might be well intentioned and seem sensible, such responses will only serve to exacerbate an already complex phenomenon. If I can convince readers that there are intelligent and thoughtful alternatives that also reside in law but are grounded in the fundamental principles of social justice and legal pluralism, I believe we will be on our way to resolving the so-called battle in cyberspace, as the issue has been defined in the media. Ultimately, it is less a question of winning a war than of developing constructive and collaborative relationships with young people that allow us all to use technologies and engage in digital literacies to gain their maximum learning and social potential.

It will be evident to readers, commencing with the opening quote in Chapter 1, that some of the examples of cyber-bullying in this book contain lewd and obscene language. It should be noted that the language in these quotations is either taken directly from fictional texts as referenced, or represents actual examples of cyber-bullying that were detailed in judicial transcripts, using the authentic language. It is important for judges to do this for the purpose of judicial analysis as set out in their reasons for judgment. I have chosen to use the authentic words no matter how lewd to illustrate their full impact on those who are victimized as a result of such expression and to be consistent with the court transcripts. The accuracy of the words used, therefore, originates in the judicial transcripts and fictional writing.

As such, I cannot take responsibility for any misquotes.

Shaheen Shariff, Ph.D., Faculty of Education, McGill University

Acknowledgments

I begin by thanking Ms. Frances Helyar, Ph.D. candidate, without whose commitment, persistence, efficiency, thoroughness, and patience this book would not have been completed. Frances persevered with me through this book under extremely tight deadlines, taking on more than she had promised, always graciously and with a smile (yes, I can read the smiles in your e-mails at 1:00 A.M., Frances!). I am greatly indebted for your perseverance, timeliness, and perfectionism throughout this second book project.

A special thank-you to my legal research assistants; Thomas Bernard McMorrow for his brilliant paper on legal pluralism and cyber-bullying; Pavel Matrosov for help with the legal citations; and Sujith Xavier, Amar Khoday, Katy Frattina, and Sarah O'Mahoney for their valuable contributions on international legislation and case law on cyber-bullying.

To my research assistants in the Faculty of Education, who have worked on both my cyber-bullying Social Science and Humanities Research Council of Canada (SSHRC) research projects, I thank you for your conscientious commitment and dedication. In particular, I thank Andrew Churchill for his leadership, enthusiasm, and intelligent insight; Tomoya Tsutsumi for his precision in encoding the data in Quebec; and Julie d'Eon, Yasuko Senoo, and Lanxu Zhang for providing the cultural insight into the Japanese and Chinese contexts, for helping me develop collaborative networks in Japan and China, and for translating the research.

I also thank SSHRC for making possible the research that went into this book and related projects. It is encouraging to have a federal government granting agency that recognizes the need for cutting-edge research on a moving target, bringing together interdisciplinary research paradigms such as law, technology, and education in an international forum. Connected with my SSHRC projects, I thank my colleagues: Professor Colin Lankshear, who was instrumental in helping me bring together my understanding of the mind-sets people adopt with respect to digital literacies, as well as Dr. Dawn Zinga, Dr. Dianne Hoff, Mr. Roderick Flynn, Dr. Roland Case, Dr. Edward Brown, Professor Motohiro Hasegawa, Mr. Wenqi Zhang, Dr. Jaishankar Karuppannan, Dr. Patricia

Ehrensal, and Mr. John Fenaughty, all of whom are collaborators, coinvestigators, or consultants involved in the international project on its educational or legal aspects. All of your unconditional collaboration and input has helped me to gain an informed perspective on navigating the emerging complexities of cyber-bullying worldwide.

I am also indebted to Ms. Cathy Wing and Ms. Catherine Pearce of the Media Awareness Network for their invaluable support, research contributions, and joint conference presentations. I look forward to working with them to develop much-needed online professional development and teacher education programs. Thank you to Mrs. Nancy Hain, assistant director of secondary schools at the Lester B. Pearson School Board, for her support as we conducted research in the schools and for her initiative in setting up a local task force; to Myles Ellis of the Canadian Teachers' Federation for authorizing use of the federation's recent resolution; to Joyce Mason and Beatrice Schriever of the Ontario College of Teachers for getting my message out and approving use of that organization's most recent survey on cyber-bullying of teachers; and to all school administrators, teachers, and parents, too many to be named, who have contributed in some way to my research.

Thank you to the following publishers for permissions granted for use of sources and my earlier work, as follows: Sense Publishing, *Education and Law Journal, Atlantis: A Women's Issues Journal, International Journal of Cyber-Criminology, International Journal of Learning, McGill Journal of Education, The Educational Forum*, the University of Toronto Press, Trentham Books, Peter Lang, and Routledge (Taylor & Frances Group).

Thank you to my family – Zahir, Farhana, and Hanif – for believing in what I do and for your patience, despite the fact it takes me away from you for long hours.

CHAPTER ONE

Cyber Misconduct: Who Is Lord of the Bullies?

"Yo Jaysus, your ass is drippin," says Max Lechuga. He's the stocky guy in class, you know the one. Fat, to be honest, with his inflatable mouth. "Stand clear of Jaysus' ass, the fire department lost another four men up there last night." The Gurrie twins huddle around him, geeing him on. . . . The class detonates through its nose. . . . Jesus abandons his desk with a crash and runs from the room. . . . Then Max Lechuga gets out of his chair, and goes to the bank of computer terminals by the window. One by one, he activates the screen-savers. Pictures jump to the screen of Jesus naked, bent over a hospital-type gurney.

(Pierre, 2003, pp. 231–233)

. . .

The courts of law would shit their pants laughing. . . . But here's why they'd laugh: not because they couldn't see . . . but because they knew nobody else would buy it. You could stand before twelve good people . . . and they wouldn't admit it. They'd forget how things really are, and slip into TV-movie mode where everything has to be obvious.

(ibid., p. 51)

INTRODUCTION

Pierre's *Vernon God Little* illustrates the tortuous power of words and images; the anger, hate, and pain they can promote; and their transformation into depictions and online permanence for viewing by an infinite and global audience, from classroom to cyberspace. The narrative depicts peer classroom bullying and cyber-bullying at its core.

Not only does this narrative promote significant discomfort as we witness the bullying of a boy named Jesus, the symbolism of Jesus' crucifixion in a school classroom by his fellow students represents the plight of all victims of bullying and cyber-bullying. The narrative is laden with antiauthority significance – a rebellion against the institutional order of the classroom, of the church, and of the state, with schools as its agents. It also symbolizes a challenge to a well-known symbol of love, peace, and order in the world.

1

However, the Jesus in Pierre's book fights back, like Eric Harris and Dylan Klebold, who were responsible for the Columbine High School massacre in 1999 (Shariff, 2003). Jesus runs out, buys a gun, and returns to undertake a shooting rampage, killing the perpetrators of his bullying. His friend Vernon becomes singled out as having supported Jesus, although Vernon did not know what his friend was going to do. As I finalize and edit this chapter on September 11, 2007, I am painfully aware that a year ago this week in Montreal, young Kimveer Gill walked into Dawson College in the heart of Montreal and went on a shooting rampage, killing one student and injuring many others. It was later disclosed that Gill had posted photographs of himself with his guns on a vampires.com Web site and had endured years of bullying as a student in elementary and high school. Moreover, it does not escape me that on September 11, 2001, six years ago today, the World Trade Center towers were blown up in one of the most unforgettable acts of terrorism in Western history. Following that event, we have all become sensitized and desensitized to the endless media reports of U.S. military action in Iraq and Afghanistan, of suicide bombers, of more shooting rampages in schools, and of incessant news reports about the ills of the Internet, the dangers that lurk within it, and opinions on how it allows young people to run rampant without adult control.

In human society throughout history, there have always been perpetrators of bullying (whether they engage in it individually, in groups, or through state-sanctioned wars). Hence, there are always victims – those who are targeted by the perpetrators – and there are others who become "collateral damage" like Jesus' friend Vernon. In the bullying and cyber-bullying context, I contend that even the bystanders who witness, reinforce, and support bullying are victims because they learn to engage in hostile behavior, following poor leadership models and being distracted from engaging in positive social relationships and beneficial learning. Whether the bullying takes place in school or in cyberspace, the fact is that it is perpetrated by human beings who act in particular social, institutional, political, and normative contexts. What changes, therefore, are the contexts, the actors, and the specific influences that affect their actions and forms of expression.

The issue of cyber-bullying and cyber misconduct currently tops the agendas of government officials, educators, parents, civil libertarians, and legal practitioners. Enter the legal system. Laws have always been necessary to maintain a certain level of social order and compliance to agreed norms of behavior in civil societies. When the boundaries of that normative order shift, traditional modes of legal control no longer apply. The transformed order requires new applications of the law, new law, or alternative means of navigating new dilemmas. This is the challenge that has emerged for educators and policy makers in an information age driven by rapid technological advancement. Maintaining civilization and civil behavior is difficult enough in organized society, even when the rule of traditional law is supposed to prevail and order and authority exist to protect innocent citizens. What happens when traditional rules and the authority are removed, as in dystopian fiction? This is the dilemma that schools confront as they attempt to navigate the legal and moral challenges around responding to cyber-bullying and, ultimately, developing in students appropriate moral compasses for an electronic age.

This book seeks to identify legal responses to online bullying and antiauthority forms of expression that demonstrate the greatest promise to address the issues in the absence of established legal precedents related to cyber-bullying. I draw on a range of established legal frameworks and emerging judicial decisions to demonstrate that policy responses grounded in substantive law and legal pluralism, informed by critical approaches to education, show the greatest promise of success.

Peer Cyber-Bullying: A *Lord of the Flies* Syndrome?

The rapid advancement of cellular phones and Internet technologies has opened up new and infinite spaces that young people can explore with fluid boundaries that are difficult to monitor or supervise. In this regard, cyber-bullying, as I have explained elsewhere (Shariff & Hoff, 2007), is a modern-day version of Golding's (1959) *Lord of the Flies*. In this classic tale, Golding maroons a large group of schoolboys on a deserted island where no rule makers are present, compelling the boys to deal with the resulting vacuum. Their first thoughts are to look for adult authority figures:

"Where's the man with the megaphone?" . . . "Aren't there any grownups at all?"

"I don't think so." The fair boy said this solemnly; but then the delight of a realized ambition overcame him.

(Golding, 1959, p. 7)

It does not take long for relationships to deteriorate. The ruthless Jack and his gang of friends use force and intimidation to dominate the other kids on the island. Piggy, an overweight, asthmatic, bespectacled boy, becomes the natural target for these perpetrators of violence because of his perceived weaknesses. He is increasingly picked on, teased, and excluded on the basis of his shortcomings. Maligned throughout the novel, Piggy is treated as an object of derision rather than a human being. Golding builds up this objectification and brutality to an excruciating level, culminating in Piggy's violent death at the hands of his peers:

The rock struck Piggy a glancing blow from chin to knee; the conch exploded into a thousand white fragments and ceased to exist. . . . His head opened and stuff came out and turned red. Piggy's arms and legs twitched a bit, like a pig's after it has been killed. Then the sea breathed out again in a long, slow sigh, the water boiled white and pink over the rock; and when it went, sucking back again, the body of Piggy was gone.

(ibid., p. 167)

I remember this book as required reading when I was a high school student in Kenya, East Africa, and I recall particularly the quote just cited. The symbolism in the book was evident to me even at age fourteen or fifteen. I remember being deeply disturbed by Piggy's death. As an overweight, shortsighted student confined to wearing thick eyeglasses at an all-girls' boarding school, I often found myself bullied for my weight, shortsightedness, and academic proficiency at school. My closest friend and I were not very athletic. As soon as we began to study the book in class, the teasing "Piggy and Porky" began during physical education classes. I recall not being significantly affected by it until I read that paragraph. Afterward, I was frightened of being equated with Piggy. In revisiting this story, I am now reminded about the ironies and symbolism that Golding so cleverly incorporated and that are so important to a discussion of traditional and cyber-bullying. Some of the symbolism relating to power and disempowerment is highlighted proficiently in a paper by law student Thomas Bernard McMorrow (2007):

The rock loosened by Roger, one of Jack's bullying cronies, signals the ultimate stage in the sacrifice of Piggy at the altar of might. Defining might is its blindness to the dignity of the persons over whom it is exercised. The inviolable value that each human being possesses is thereby ignored, denied or overridden. As philosopher Simone Weil once noted: "Might is that which makes a thing of anybody who comes under its sway. When exercised to the full, it makes a thing of man in the most literal sense, for it makes him a corpse."[1] Throughout the novel, Piggy is increasingly treated, not as a person but as a thing. The callousness of this casual brutality thickens and hardens, rendering nearly all the boys but especially the likes of Jack and Roger, totally insensible to the respect that a human life, such as Piggy's ought to evoke.

As McMorrow notes, reading about Piggy's treatment in *Lord of the Flies* one cannot help but feel enraged, just as reading about Jesus' treatment in *Vernon God Little* is disturbing – all the more so because the portrayal of injustice hits so close to home. The scenarios are all too familiar when we recall the recent suicide deaths of fourteen-year-old Canadian teenagers Hamed Nastoh and Dawn-Marie Wesley as a result of bullying. Hamed jumped off a bridge, and Wesley hanged herself at home. Also devastating was the cold and callous murder of teenager Reena Virk by her peers, who beat and chased her over a bridge and down to the water where they burned her face with cigarettes and drowned her in the Pacific Ocean. The primary perpetrator, Kelly Ellard, held Reena's head under water with her foot while smoking a cigarette, until her victim breathed no more.

It strikes me that nothing has changed since Golding's time. These are all cases of bullying that took place within the past decade. Lawyers for Kelly Ellard's defense described Reena as dark and overweight, with hair on her back, while Kelly was depicted as a pure white girl from a middle-class neighborhood who would never do any wrong (Shariff, 2003). Just like Piggy, Reena was reduced to a thing – a subhuman and unattractive beast, thereby implying some sort of justification for the violence that befell her. As Chapter 2 demonstrates, one of the key aspects of bullying is that perpetrators gain power by defining their victims as objects – often weak, ugly, or dangerous – who deserve the punishment. This serves as justification for exclusion, ostracism, and violence in almost every case. Moreover, in Golding's boys, each of us might recognize ourselves, because at sometime in our lives, we have all put others down or made them feel excluded for a variety of reasons.

What frightens educators and policy makers is that cyber-bullying similarly puts students on a virtual island with no supervision and few rules. It might be assumed that this allows bullying to escalate to dangerous, even life-threatening levels. Further, the boys on the island realize that being "evil" is easier when they assume a different persona, and so they paint their faces for anonymity before they attack. Cyber perpetrators who bully their peers are no different. They hide behind pseudonyms and well-disguised IP (Internet protocol) addresses, making it difficult, if not impossible, for the victim to determine the source of the threat. This anonymous nature of cyber-bullying is perhaps the most troubling of all, for it leaves victims wondering which of their classmates might be a cyber aggressor.

Indeed, as the quote from *Vernon God Little* depicts, the entire class population could be involved. Yet recall from the opening narrative where the initial bullying took place: within the *supervised confines of a physical space* – the classroom. It then moved into cyberspace. Hence the argument that cyberspace might in and of itself cause students to engage in bullying does not carry significant weight. Bullying in the physical context has taken place throughout history for years. We cannot blame technology. What is disturbing when cyber-bullying is involved is that for victims, attending school and confronting unknown perpetrators is like being on an island – there is no escape unless they take the options adopted by Vernon's friend Jesus, or Harris and Klebold at Columbine High School, striking back randomly and with extreme violence. Then there are always innocent or "collateral" victims like Vernon or the victims of Klebold, Harris, and Kimveer Gill.

It is important not to overlook the following two important premises that underlie Golding's book, as reflected in his strong use of irony, because they are pertinent to the cyber-bullying context in schools.

Adults as Bullies

The first premise is that the young boys are no different from a group of adults, whose relationship might deteriorate in the same way if marooned on an island without rules. As television reality shows such as *Survivor* and *Lost* evidence, it is not the lack of maturity in children that can result in these conditions but the way in which human beings are prone to behave in conditions of depravity. In this regard, Golding is talking about survival of the fittest. Moreover, as McMorrow observes, the need for laws and rules that govern behavior comes from "[T]he idea that the vast majority of us is so beyond the pale and that it must be left to a cabal of enlightened law-makers to steer us to happiness in this world (or the next) conflicts with humanist values underpinning the liberal democratic political project"[2] (McMorrow, 2007, p. 5). In the context of bullying and cyber-bullying, this could explain the heavy reliance on zero-tolerance punishments, such as suspensions and expulsions, and, more recently, the strong calls from teachers and their unions for legislation as antiauthority forms of cyber-bullying become more prevalent online. We always believe that the law will resolve everything and that after we punish the perpetrators, all will be well. Regrettably, this is never the case. Nothing is that simple. The phenomenon of bullying in and of itself is a complex one. When we add cyber-bullying to the mix, there are no simple answers and, indeed, no one legal response that will stop it.

The second, and in my view more important, premise that underlies Golding's story is that all human beings are born with the capacity to make decisions between doing good to others and their animal capacity for committing acts of cruelty to others. If we assume that with appropriate nurturance and guidance human beings can develop a moral framework that will overcome the desire to harm others, then the focus turns to the society in which those human beings live and the extent to which its institutions and culture are able to provide that guidance and support. Whether the moral instinct to do good can survive in extreme situations such as that in which Golding's boys found themselves is dependant on the strength of their upbringing. What kind of society did these boys come from? McMorrow explains their context:

Consider the larger context in which the novel is set. While the socio-political backdrop to the story is never drawn out explicitly, the fact that there is no explanation for why all of these English lads are on a plane so far from home and how it is that British naval personnel end up "rescuing" the boys implies that something is rotten in the state of adult affairs (i.e. the affairs of states) as well.[3] If this is so, if the life of the boys on the island, brutish and nasty as it is, reflects life off the island, where global leaders guard their stash of arms as jealously as Jack clutches his wooden spear, then the shocking breakdown in social relations among the boys should come as no surprise.

(ibid., p. 6)

Accordingly, the message Golding conveys is that the boys come from a world that is just as violent and hostile to human dignity as the new one in which they are stranded; therefore, the only moral framework available to them in dire conditions is to emulate that of the world they already know, hence the camouflaging of their faces to attack their enemies and the insidious and dangerous power hierarchies that emerge on that island.

It is well known that children emulate the adults in their lives. In today's world, we simply need to read a newspaper or turn on the television to witness global political conflicts that continue to destroy the infrastructures of several countries, especially in the Middle East. We see imperialist governments that talk about collateral damage when women and children are killed in wars that make no sense. Victims of war are often reduced to objects so that there is less guilt on the part of those who extinguish lives without a thought to the fact that those who died were someone's parents, mothers, fathers, and children. On the news each day, we witness suicide bombers creating havoc in the streets of Iraq and Afghanistan and the homes of Palestinians being bulldozed. We have witnessed people living in squalid refugee camps in which generations of children live and grow up in extreme poverty with no home, school, or country – and no one who particularly seems to care. We hear about children in Uganda and Sierra Leone who were kidnapped by adults and forced to commit murder and rape or mutilate those thought to be "the enemy." We hear of children kidnapped from public playgrounds or their own backyards in Western countries, with their bodies turning up raped and murdered – by adults. We know about child pornography and its perpetration on the Internet yet are helpless to eradicate it.

We view Hollywood movies in which actor Bruce Willis, for example, callously shoots off a person's arm and makes him run for his life knowing a gun is focused on his back. We repeatedly witness school shootings in which the perpetrators are students who were bullied or adults involved in school shootings who had difficulties in their lives and learn that when those perpetrators sought help, the system failed them (Dedman, 2000).

Consider the Holocaust or the genocide in Bosnia, Rwanda, or Darfur in which powerful governments took little action to stop the violence for long periods of time. Consider, too, the mere lip service that many governments pay to constitutional and human rights, even when it comes to protecting or prosecuting their own citizens. Given such realities, it seems clear that Golding's boys could very well have come from such a world and imitate its powers on an island with no adults.

Similarly, adults fail to protect Vernon in *Vernon God Little* after his friend Jesus retaliates against his classmates. Vernon, the narrator, is scapegoated by community members who believe he supported Jesus' actions, although he is entirely innocent. Vernon is as vulnerable as he is intelligent, but he is also inexperienced. He tries to run away from it all but realizes that people's minds are already made up. The media has sensationalized his role in the tragedy, handing down a sentence that even judges cannot reverse.

The second opening quote, the "judges would shit their pants laughing," is expressed by Vernon, who becomes resigned to the fact that adults in this world are the greatest bullies of all – the worst culprits in modeling violence through television, Hollywood movies, and sensational news stories. In his opinion, although the judges and even a jury might understand his innocence, they may not be able to stand up against the public outcry for a scapegoat. Further, although judges understand that society systemically fosters and sustains the forms of violence they must adjudicate on a regular basis, they are bound by law and precedent and have less room to maneuver than people think (Case, 1997).

The most common complaint from victims of bullying and cyber-bullying is that schools generally put up a "wall of defence" (Shariff, 2003) through which they imply that the victims brought the bullying on themselves and that cyber-bullying is a parental responsibility because it takes place outside the school on personal computers and cell phones bought by parents. School officials often argue that they already have antibullying programs in place, which absolves them from doing more to protect victims. Moreover, few lawsuits reach the courts. Most are settled out of court because of the expense caused by delays school-board lawyers implement and the added difficulty of establishing tangible harm when injury from bullying is psychological rather than physical. I address all these issues in greater detail in upcoming chapters.

Antiauthority Cyber Expression

A second form of student expression, antiauthority cyber expression (which is also commonly referred to as cyber-bullying), has recently garnered substantially more attention than peer-to-peer bullying. There have been stronger calls for action from school and government officials, teachers and teachers' unions, because this form of cyber-bullying involves student postings on social networking sites where the focus of discussion is teachers or school officials. Although most young people use social networking sites to do just what the name implies – engage in enjoyable social conversations – some students use them to demean and put down their teachers or school administrators, joke about them, modify photographs, and invite insults and comments from other students. As I have mentioned, there is disagreement among students (supported by civil libertarians and some parents) and school authorities as to whether this form of online student expression constitutes cyber-bullying. For the purposes of this book, I believe it is important to discuss it as a form of cyber-bullying because it has garnered so much attention and concern from educators and policy makers that in turn affects computer use by all students. The power differential involved in this form of student online communication is reversed. The "victims" of such expression are teachers, school principles, and college and university professors (authority figures) who are disempowered because they have little control over who sees the online comments about them. Because the jury is still out as to whether this form of student expression constitutes cyber-bullying, I also refer to it as "antiauthority cyber expression" or "antiauthority online expression." The media have described teachers and their unions, as well as government and school officials, as being powerless at the mercy of such "cyber brats." The issue is increasingly, and globally, depicted in news reports as a "battle." Consider the following headlines:

- "Cyber-bullying targeting teachers: poll" (Leong, 2007)
- "A gift from the devil: Worry about on-line activities" (Soloyon, 2005);
- "Cyber-bullying: The Internet is the latest weapon in a bully's arsenal" (Leishman, 2002)
- "Internet gives teenage bullies weapons to wound from afar" (Harmon, 2004)
- "Cyber-bullying blighting our lives" (Reading Evening Post, 2006)
- "Teachers declare war on cyber-bullying" (Brown, 2007)
- "School war against the bullies brings academic success" (Asthana, 2007)
- "Regina bylaw to target cyber-bullies" (CBC News, 2006)

- "Web giants like YouTube are being urged to get tough with the cyber-bullies that use their sites to make pupils' and teachers' lives a misery" (Goff, 2007)
- "Foiling cyberbullies in the new Wild West" (Franek, 2006)

What concerns civil libertarians is that we might also sacrifice innocent students, like Vernon, who are using technology in responsible ways and, in some cases, simply stating truths, making political statements, or making their opinions known online, believing that they have the constitutional right to do this. The words Vernon uses to describe the judicial system as being part of the problem and as powerless to help him prove his innocence might be couched in vulgar terms as shown in the quote at the beginning of the chapter; however, he makes an important point that ought to be given significant weight.

As school authorities and teachers' unions call for governments to legislate suspensions and punishment for this type of expression, it is important to remember that the judiciary interprets the law within similar normative frameworks and contexts that inform societal hegemonies (Gramsci, 1971, 1975). In fact, some would argue they are part of the system that perpetuates the very hierarchies that sustain prejudices in society and that ultimately contribute to the forms of cyber-bullying that we see expressed by teenagers (Ehrensal, 2003). Judges make their rulings on the basis of the facts of each case, but in doing so, they often accept social or normative constructs that are already embedded in legal language (Ehrensal, 2005; Lankshear & Knobel, 2006). In this regard, the courts are merely another arm of the influential power base that governs public institutions such as schools. When normative constructs go unquestioned, courts might tacitly legitimate them, including taken-for-granted assumptions about children, school, free speech, and authority. Often they do this by refusing to open the floodgates to litigation. In educational matters, courts have often deferred to the expertise of educators, stating that courts do not get involved in matters of "public policy" (Jafaar, 2002). Given that cyber-bullying is an issue that has not yet been addressed to a great extent, some judiciaries may adopt such an approach to avoid inviting more lawsuits.

In this regard, the law wields power, both in terms of the decisions courts render and the constructs that they subtly endorse. To understand legal power, it is important to look at the language of law, for in law, language is power.

Hence the perspectives of critical theorists and pedagogues such as Giroux (2003), McLaren (1998), Lankshear and Knobel (2006), and Ehrensal (2003, 2005) draw attention to the way in which the courts conceptualize and describe learning and behavior in their reasons for judgment. This may apply to constructs of cyber-bullying, especially in its antiauthority forms, and how, in legal terms, it might ultimately become defined and embedded in legal precedent. Through the lens of critical theory and cultural studies of law, it is essential to examine the assumptions that judges make about educator authority and the fiduciary relationships of trust between teachers and their students and to examine how these relationships impinge on and restrict free speech and learning.

Once a landmark court decision in an emerging area such as cyber-bullying is handed down, the doctrine of *stare decises* (adherence to precedent) ensures that most future decisions adhere to the landmark precedent unless the court can distinguish a case as sufficiently different in nature to move away from precedent. In this regard, the courts have a powerful influence on shaping governmental policy and practice. Schools, as government agents, must in turn adhere to the standards set out by the courts.

There is no doubt that the landscape, as observed by one learned judge (*Hill v. Church of Scientology of Toronto*, 1995), has changed so dramatically that it is difficult to know where the boundaries of authority end.

The landscape upon which the line where the balance tips from protected speech for students to permissible punitive power for school administrators has changed dramatically. The internet marks that landscape change as dramatically as the Front Range marks the end of the Great Plains.

(*Beidler v. North Thurston School District Number 3*, 2000)

To reiterate, although many young people use technologies in what adults perceive to be a responsible manner, some take advantage of this seemingly unsupervised space as license to say and do what they want. Yet this is where the crux of the dilemma resides. *What* constitutes *responsible* discourse or expression (online or otherwise), and *who* decides what *content and forms of online expression* ought to be limited? Further, once there is agreement (which is a challenge in itself), *how* and *to what extent* can such speech be limited? What criteria exist to determine these invisible boundaries in a cyber society? Moreover, as rapidly evolving technologies are increasingly integrated into our everyday lives, our children are growing up with a range of technological tools and resources that were not available to the baby boomer generation when we grew up. Consequently, although some adults and corporations are in the business of creating, building, and making available such tools, online social networking tools popular with young people are less easily embraced or understood by the average parent, teacher, or lawmaker.

With adult discomfort in the use of technologies comes suspicion, a feeling of exclusion, fear of change, and fear of a loss of control over the normative status quo. There is a yearning to return to the "good old days" when children did what they were told in manageable physical spaces because the consequences (including even corporal punishment) were clear. As this fear takes hold, it becomes easier to blame the tools – technologies ironically created by adults – and to blame the kids for the way they use these tools, incorporating forms of expression that are offensive and disturbing to a public audience of adults (Churchill, 2007).

It is no wonder that antiauthority forms of expression continue to become increasingly lewd and obscene. Such expression is a call that society ought to heed. Although one could argue, as in the Golding's first premise and Neil Boyd's (2000) book *The Beast Within*, that people are naturally aggressive, there is also substantial evidence, as I show in Chapter 5, that people can be socialized to identify and act in different ways. Hence, as McMorrow (2007) observes, the world of *Lord of the Flies* is an *extension*, not a breakdown, of the adult world from which the children come. Similarly, I argue in this book that student behavior in cyberspace is simply an extension of the physical world in which children live:

> Thus, the world of the *Lord of the Flies* does not represent the utter breakdown in the legal normative framework of the adult world from which the children come; on the contrary, it is its logical extension. A normative order centred on the idea that *might* makes *right* prevails not because it is the only type of normative order possible but because it resonates most with the boys' experience and expectations of the world. *In contrasting the actions of characters like Piggy and Simon with the other boys on the island, the fact that certain boys subject their behaviour to a different set of norms than others attests to this normative plurality and heterogeneity among the group. Piggy and Simon serve as living examples that other worlds are possible, even if those other normative worlds intersect and interact with the predominate normative worlds to which the other boys subscribe.*[4]
>
> (ibid., emphasis added)

It is this diverse nature of children, people, normative structures, global societies, and ultimately the law that I focus on in this book. I want to illustrate that the calls at national and global levels for positivist approaches are misguided because none of them considers the broad range of social, political, economic, biological, and normative influences that come into play. What is more, I emphasize that a pluralistic legal approach is feasible, and in fact desirable, because it provides the best possible opportunities to address the roots of the issues that reside in deeply embedded forms of discrimination and power hierarchies in every society. Moreover, I proffer that there are ethical, educational, and legally defensible approaches that show greater promise in addressing the disturbing forms of bullying in which human beings are capable of engaging, both in the physical world and in cyberspace.

Hence, one of my objectives is to illustrate a larger context for the dilemma of controlling students in cyberspace. Substantial pieces of this puzzle are missing. These gaps are represented by our lack of attention to student perspectives – to students' autonomy, identity formation, socialization, and their capacity to take responsibility and contribute to lawmaking. Moreover, it is important to raise awareness of the range of stakeholder influences and power hierarchies that inform, contain, and attempt to control the forms of knowledge to which children are exposed, as well as *how* and *what* children in turn express as knowledge or normative discourses. As most high school teachers and parents of teenagers would acknowledge, the vocabulary of popular discourse among adolescents and teens has evolved to incorporate numerous racial, homophobic, and sexist slurs. These are embedded to such an extent in young people's music and interaction that although adults may roll their eyes in frustration, they reluctantly ignore and accept them as part of normative interaction among youth. This does not always have to be the case. There is a point at which such discourse can cross the fine line to become bullying or cyber-bullying. I address this issue in greater detail in Chapter 2.

A Global Issue

Cyber-bullying is not restricted to North America. Governments and schools globally are grappling with the issue of how to address it. Consider the following online forms of expression and their devastating impact on students and teachers. As the examples show clearly, few countries are exempt. In Japan, a young girl was murdered after receiving a threat on a contentious Web site (Associated Press, 2004). Satomi Mitarai, twelve, bled to death in a study room after her neck was cut open with a cutter knife in 2004 by her closest eleven-year-old friend, who informed police that the dispute arose on instant messaging. The accused admitted to summoning Satomi out of their homeroom classroom with the intention of killing her. The *Japan Times* reported that the girls each had a Web site and often used their personal computers to communicate via text messaging. Two years later, on November 6, 2006, the minister of Education, Culture, Sports, Science, and Technology (MEXT) in Japan received an anonymous e-mail warning him of a potential suicide due to *netto ijime* (cyber-bullying). This incident made the government aware for the first time that cyber-bullying was alive and well in Japan. The suicide note had an enormous impact on the Japanese administration because there had been many previous suicides from traditional bullying (Senoo, 2007).

In China, a middle-school teacher in Foshan Guangdong reported that three photographs of his face with a naked human body, the body of a monkey and the body of a chicken respectively had been posted online, in the *Foshan Daily Forum*. It took the police forty-eight hours to find the perpetrator, a second-year high school student who went by the name of Xiaorong. The student admitted to downloading his teacher's pictures from school's Web site. He searched pornography and animal pictures online and used Photoshop software to combine several photographs. He claimed that he did not know he had broken the law, and like some of the North American and British cases that I discuss later, perceived that his actions would be received as a joke. He argued the photographs were not meant to harm his teacher at all. He simply wanted to make his friends laugh (Zhang & Wei, 2007).

In Canada, David Knight, a student who had endured traditional bullying throughout his elementary and secondary school years, was told to check a certain Web site originating in Thailand. To his horror, the Web site was titled, "Welcome to the page that makes fun of Dave Knight." This was a clone of a Web site created by his peers in Canada that described him as a pedophile and sexual predator, inviting online viewers to post derogatory insults next to his photograph.

In India, students sent the following e-mail to a rival school team: "If u think they r hot... Well, let me tell u they're not They're ugly, they're fat, they look like ratz!!!! Even alienz look better dan dat!!!!!"

In March 2007, a group of Australian schoolboys filmed themselves sexually abusing and degrading a female classmate. Their film was uploaded onto the YouTube Web site. The film showed twelve youths surrounding a seventeen-year-old girl, who has a mild mental disability, bullying her to perform sex acts, urinating on her, and setting her hair alight. The education minister in southern Victoria, the state where the attack took place, decided that the state's 1,600 public schools would block access to YouTube. Her comments are reported to say, "The government has never tolerated bullying in schools and this zero tolerance approach extends to the online world" (Bartlett, 2007).

In England, a teacher's life was threatened on YouTube, resulting in demands by Britain's largest teachers' union for the government to ban YouTube. Moreover, in Canada, there has been enormous public outcry relating to student comments about teachers on social networking sites such as Facebook. Students posted online comments about their teachers masturbating in class; teachers were described as pedophiles, having didactic teaching styles, being homosexual and lesbian, and having bad hygiene and unusual dressing habits. In response, the offending students were suspended from schools, banned from field trips, and banned from using technologies at school. In Ontario, the result was a heated student protest supporting freedom of expression. The protest turned violent and had to be quelled by police (Chung, 2007). These incidents resulted in a resolution by the Canadian Teachers' Federation to develop a task force to understand the issues (Canadian Teachers' Federation, 2007).

In each case, Canadian, American, and British students, like their Chinese counterpart Xiaorong, insisted their comments, even those that included graphic sexual detail, were not meant to hurt teachers but were posted to amuse friends. In Canada, a recent survey by the Ontario College of Teachers disclosed that 84 percent of Ontario teachers believe they have been cyber-bullied or made fun of online (Ontario College of Teachers, 2007).

CONCLUSION

Although some legal considerations relating to cyber-bullying are discussed briefly in Chapter 7 of my book *Cyber-Bullying: Issues and Solutions for the School, the Classroom, and the Home* (Shariff, 2008), this book undertakes a more in-depth examination of legal principles and doctrines that might affect educational policy decisions and practice. That said, however, I limit the legal technicalities to engage in contextual analysis and explanations that ensure the discussion is not too legal for educational policy makers and practitioners. I want those educational professionals to gain the greatest benefit from learning their legal rights and responsibilities, and the rights of their students in cyberspace.

I also believe that legal practitioners and anyone interested in the impact of law and technologies on educational policy and practice and on the way we construct and interpret education in a knowledge society will find significant value in this book. If I can help readers approach the issues with a new or sufficiently adjusted lens through which to conceptualize the legal and policy issues, I will have succeeded in my quest.

Given that my research has expanded to international levels, I provide case examples and emerging information on legal responses that are being implemented in various countries such as Japan, China, India, European nations, Australia, New Zealand, Britain, the United States, the United Kingdom, and Canada. By way of caveat, however, I caution readers that we are currently in the early stages of legal research on cyber-bullying. Many countries have only recently become aware of the fact that cyber-bullying exists. Some are only just beginning to recognize the enormous potential of online expression (when not redirected in positive ways) to undermine learning and social development among children and youth. Although this ought to raise concerns, I do not want to raise fears in the minds of educators and policy makers. I strongly believe that the study of cyber-bullying using a more substantive legal approach will demonstrate educational and ethical opportunities that allow all of us to transform negative student online expressions into collaborative and proactive learning and social initiatives. Proactive responses can help us take advantage of the infinite resources such technologies provide. It is therefore incumbent on us as educators to seize these opportunities instead of focusing too heavily on the dark side of student online communication.

I believe this is important not only from the perspective of reducing or curtailing cyber-bullying, but also because it will help educators, government policy makers, and legal practitioners realize that the Internet and communications technologies are here to stay and that education will inevitably be increasingly delivered through the use of these technologies. If we cannot "control it" we will need to ensure that technologies do not control us. To that end, I believe it is important to draw attention to the opposing mind-sets that adults, compared with young people, bring to their conceptions and use of the Internet. I address these mind-sets in upcoming chapters to highlight the ways in which governments and schools continue to apply outdated approaches to controlling cyberspace. My use of the plural "technologies" compared with the use of the singular "it" is purposeful and will make sense to readers when I discuss the differences between adult and student mind-sets in conceptualizing and working with new technologies.

Cyberspace cannot be controlled, and traditional school management techniques no longer work. Technologies can, however, provide many useful and collaborative avenues for educators and their students to engage in rule making and learning. It is for these reasons that I place greater attention on institutional and educator responsibilities that reside in substantive law than positivist and punitive approaches that reside in criminal law. Hence I argue against knee-jerk reactions to cyber-bullying (or online antiauthority student expression), no matter how insulting and defamatory they might be. Although many aspects of cyber-bullying are clearly criminal in nature and would most likely be subject to prosecution if brought before the courts (such as threats of violence, criminal coercion, terrorist threats, stalking, hate crimes, child pornography, and sexual exploitation), I have focused greater attention on the institutional responsibilities of schools to educate students to become contributing and civic-minded citizens. I advocate avoidance of legal avenues that put young people through the criminal justice system, along the lines of Robert DiGuilio's (2001) frustration that we "medicate" and "litigate" students far too much instead of educating and caring for them.

Policy Guidelines

By reviewing established and emerging law, I draw attention to a need for guidelines that will help schools adopt educational means to prevent and reduce cyber-bullying. Early indications suggest that zero-tolerance suspensions and school and governmental responses tacitly condone cyber-bullying and perpetuate the problem by removing the focus from its underlying systemic causes and attempting to control its symptoms. I propose a policy approach grounded in substantive law, legal pluralism, and critical pedagogy that supports dialogue, preventative and proactive measures that will better enable children to learn and communicate in inclusive and nondiscriminatory school environments (physical and virtual).

   Accordingly, my goal is to raise awareness of the key dilemmas that confront schools, students, and their parents, with a view to encourage reconceptualization of cyber-bullying toward the development of proactive and educationally and legally defensible responses. The Internet and digital literacies have become part of young people's lives, their social relationships, and their learning. I present approaches in this book that I hope will facilitate this learning in school environments – both physical and virtual – that are conducive to children's well-being and development as civil-minded and socially responsible, contributing citizens of a global society. It is of crucial importance that children and adults become familiar with their rights and their legal responsibilities to engage in democratic society. I propose that we engage young people to develop the rules, codes of conduct, and legislation to meet constitutional, human rights, and legally pluralistic frames of reference. More specifically, the policy guidelines are informed by the following legal considerations.

Legal Considerations

Within the context of two forms of cyber-bullying, peer-to-peer and antiauthority cyber expression, this book joins a body of emerging work on legal issues relevant to cyber misconduct and its impact on student safety and learning in the school context. Most cases are from the United States and Canada (Balfour, 2005; Servance, 2003; Willard, 2003), although I also bring in specific examples of responses (legal or policy) that are beginning to surface in various countries. As already mentioned, at this stage, my legal research in other countries is just beginning. It builds on my own previous work that examines the legal considerations relating to defamation and cyber libel; freedom of expression and safety under the Canadian *Charter of Rights and Freedoms*; Canadian human rights law and American civil rights law (Title IX) on Internet sexual harassment; potential school liability under Canadian and American tort law; and finally international conventions relating to children's rights (Shariff, 2004; Shariff & Gouin, 2005; Shariff & Strong-Wilson, 2005).

North American laws are largely derived from British common law, which continues to be applied in most postcolonial countries across the globe. Therefore, although I rely for the most part on the North American jurisprudence and legislation in this book, the policy guidelines that I develop to inform solutions to these issues are pertinent to the international context. Countries such as India, Japan, Britain, Australia, South Korea, and New Zealand work within similar legal frameworks and can also benefit from an appreciation of applicable legal frameworks and judicial trends. Research projects are emerging worldwide to examine how young citizens in various countries are adapting to and using technology. The way in which schools as institutional agents of the political and social orders of each country respond also has yet to be assessed. As far as my own international research project on cyber-bullying is concerned (http://www.cyberbullying.co.nr) I will, subsequent to publication of this book, be working with international collaborators to compile a separate and updated publication. Our publication, to be launched in 2008–9, will contain focused chapters on the profile, extent, and responses taking place in each country involved in our project. Our edited publication will include academic papers to be delivered at an international conference to be held jointly with NetSafe, a nonprofit organization in New Zealand, in July 2008.

In the meantime, it is nonetheless important to consider how North American and British courts have addressed the complexities of free expression, privacy, cyber libel, and responses to student expression, especially in terms of the legal obligations to supervise expression on and off campus. Given that so few cases on traditional bullying have been settled out of court without going to trial, even fewer precedents on cyber-bullying exist at the time this book was written. Murphy's Law might dictate that as soon as this book hits the presses, a landmark case on cyber-bullying will surface and set a legal precedent. If that happens, the new decision will be reported in journals or book chapters that follow and will add to the foundation that I provide here. For now it is possible to seek guidance from thousands of cases involving negligence in supervision on school playgrounds and field trips and cyber-libel cases involving adults and Internet use (tort law); sexual and homophobic harassment and other forms of discrimination under civil and human rights law; and freedom of expression and privacy considerations under constitutional law, particularly in cases in which the fostering of a positive school environment is concerned. These court rulings, under established and emerging law, make it possible to extrapolate and gauge the legal boundaries (or extent of authority and responsibilities) that can be expected of educational stakeholders when dealing with cyber-bullying or cyber misconduct. If we can find consistencies or trends in judicial decisions regarding the institutional and professional responsibilities of adults in school contexts and detect shifts in judicial approaches to assessing on- and off-campus technology use and supervision, we can inform the development of a framework of standards to address the existing policy vacuum.

Tort Law

The first of these legal frameworks is tort law (or the law to correct "wrongs" committed intentionally or unintentionally; Linden & Klar, 1994). There are two areas of tort law relevant to cyber-bullying of peers and authority figures: libel and negligence. Given that there is so much concern among school authorities about the antiauthority version of cyber-bullying on social communication networks, I begin my legal review in Chapter 3 by taking a look at the issue of libel as a tort – or wrong committed intentionally or unintentionally – and the impact of libelous comments on targets of such expression (teachers and school authorities).

As seen from the international case examples earlier in this chapter, students who post such comments insist that they have no intention of hurting or directly communicating with the teachers and school officials whom they discuss online. They explain that these comments were not meant to be read by school officials – and constituted private conversations between friends. In that context, students do not consider their actions to be cyber-bullying because the teachers are not the direct targets of harassment. Unlike peer-to-peer cyber-bullying, for which Web sites are intentionally set up for the purpose of drawing victim's attention to his or her flaws, the expression posted about teachers are not directed to them – and therefore any harm done is unintentional. It is plausible to argue under tort law, however, that depending on a variety of circumstances, a wrong can be done to someone unintentionally (negligently) and that this can lead to liability – or a claim for compensation of the harm done. Clearly, most young people are not aware that they risk legal liability in this way, which suggests the need to educate them about how the law of torts can be applied. Few adults, with the exception of those who work in law-related fields, are aware of the liability issues involved in tort law. Upcoming chapters present the judicial perspective as it relates to the extent of school supervision responsibilities and what this might mean for supervision in cyberspace.

Constitutional Law: Freedom of Expression versus Safety and Privacy

My research to date has not disclosed any known cases specifically relating to cyber-bullying in the school context in Great Britain or in other parts of the world. Not surprisingly, however, courts in the United States, a highly litigious country, have already heard cases on cyber-bullying and applied a triumvirate of well-established U.S. judicial decisions relating to student freedom of expression, in the absence of legal precedents relating to cyberspace. I highlight the key standards that have emerged from the judicial scrutiny of cyber-bullying in terms of the debate relating to student expression and limits on school supervision in Chapter 4. As I explain in that chapter, there have been a number of mixed court rulings on the extent of school responsibilities or expectations to interfere when students engage in forms of cyber-bullying from home computers.

Human and Civil Rights Jurisprudence: School Environment

It may be some time before the Supreme Court of Canada rules on the censorship issues involved in cyber-bullying because such cases are generally brought under tort law for negligence and under human rights law. This does not suggest that constitutional or quasi-constitutional considerations are not implied or expected. A number of Canadian human rights and American civil law cases on sexual harassment – for example, *Robichaud v. Canada (Treasury Board)* – have ruled that institutions are responsible for providing safe environments for their employees even if the sexual harassment by a coworker occurs outside of the workplace. These are discussed in Chapter 5.

One of the points I make in support of my arguments for an improved understanding of law in education, particularly as it relates to cyber-bullying, is that just because law may not be obvious does not mean that legal rules do not inform every aspect of social life and learning. As I work through and present the range of applicable legal frameworks in this book, I provide evidence to show why a singular, legally positivist approach to addressing cyber-bullying ignores the fact that various legal principles and normative rules work together to influence how people act or express themselves in certain contexts. Hence, there is the need to pay attention to young people's notion of identity, how that identity changes on the Internet, and the agency that they use to communicate and express themselves online compared with in cyberspace.

I argue that to change the way children behave online toward one another and toward their authority figures, we are engaging in a law reform practice. In doing so, it is essential to ask which existing laws and policies work best to address considerations of agency, context, and identity. What we must ask ourselves is which policies are workable and how do we implement them? At the end of the day, any policies grounding laws on the issue of cyber-bullying must be informed by the interactions of students themselves. At the same time, such laws ought to respect students' autonomy but, more fundamentally, respect their inherent human dignity. To that end, I present in my concluding chapter a combination of legal standards and models that inform a critical legal literacy and legally pluralistic approach to teacher education and professional development that I argue show greater promise to help educators navigate the policy vacuum of cyber-bullying.

Before we turn to these issues, I would like to introduce readers to a general understanding of the nature of traditional bullying, its forms and profile, and the conditions under which it occurs, as it has been studied within the paradigms of developmental psychology and sociology. The profiles of traditional and cyber-bullying that I present in Chapter 2 establish the devastating impact of bullying and cyber-bullying, which have tragically taken the lives of many young people through suicide and even murder. I have researched the subject sufficiently to understand the deep and lasting psychological consequences of bullying and cyber-bullying on children and adults who are victimized, especially at the hands of large groups of peers or unknown individuals on the Internet.

Although I fully support a need for some form of consequences for those who engage in cyber-bullying, I contend that we place too much emphasis on positivist legal forms of discipline and punishment after the fact. I would like us to think about long-term proactive responses that are rooted in the fundamental principles of democracy. These might not have immediate impact but over time should make their mark more permanently. This approach will make better sense to readers after they have an improved understanding of bullying and its discriminatory nature. I proffer that in many educational institutions, what some scholars describe as "systems of oppression" sustain racism, sexism, homophobia, and ableism and intersect and interlock (Razack, 1998) to perpetuate bullying and marginalize some students more than others. When considered in these terms, it becomes easier to appreciate why constitutional and human rights considerations are more important to policy responses than legally positivist responses that are generally rooted in criminal law. It is to this profile of bullying and cyber-bullying that I now turn.

REFERENCES

Associated Press. (2004, June 2). Japanese girl fatally stabs a classmate. *New York Times*, p. 12.

Asthana, A. (2007, June 3). School war against the bullies brings academic success [Electronic version]. *Guardian Unlimited*. Retrieved August 13, 2007, from http://education.guardian.co.uk/pupilbehaviour/story/0,,2094886,00.html.

Balfour, C. (2005). *A journey of social change: Turning government digital strategy into cybersafe local school practices*. Paper presented at Safety & Security in a Networked World: Balancing Cyber-Rights & Responsibilities, Oxford Internet Institute, University of Oxford, England. Retrieved August 10, 2007, from http://www.oii.ox.ac.uk/microsites/cybersafety/?view=papers.

Bartlett, L. (2007, March 29). Cyber bully concern grows [Electronic version]. *cooltech.iafrica.com*. Retrieved March 29, 2007, from http://cooltech.iafrica.com/features/729468.htm.

Boyd, N. (2000). *The beast within: Why men are violent*. Vancouver, Canada: Greystone Books.

Brown, L. (2007, July 13). Teachers declare war on cyber-bullying [Electronic version]. *TheStar.com*. Retrieved August 13, 2007, from http://www.thestar.com/article/235675.

Canadian Teachers' Federation. (2007). Communications technology concern resolution. Toronto: Author.

Case, R. (1997). *Understanding judicial reasoning: Controversies, concepts and cases*. Toronto: Thompson Educational.

CBC News. (2006, April 25). Regina bylaw to target cyber-bullies [Electronic version]. *CBC News*. Retrieved August 13, 2007, from http://www.cbc.ca/canada/saskatchewan/story/2006/04/25/bullying-regina060425.html.

Chung, M. (2007, March 25). Online comments were "inside joke." Posts meant for friends only, teen says [Electronic version]. *TheStar.com*. Retrieved August 15, 2007, from http://www.thestar.com/article/195823.

Churchill, A. (2007). Don't blame the Internet for cyberbullying [Electronic version]. *The Gazette*. Retrieved September 12, 2007, from http://www.canada.com/montrealgazette/news/editorial/story.html?id=62b8e6a4-256f-457c-831b-9166b9583809.

Dedman, B. (2000, October 16). Schools may miss mark on preventing violence [Electronic version]. *Chicago Sun-Times*. Retrieved August 12, 2007, from http://www.ustreas.gov/usss/ntac/chicago_sun/shoot16.htm.

DiGiulio, R. C. (2001). *Educate, mediate, or litigate? What teachers, parents, and administrators must do about student behavior*. Thousand Oaks, CA: Corwin Press.

Ehrensal, P. A. L. (2003). The three faces of power: U.S. Supreme Court's legitimization of school authority's parental, police, and pedagogic roles. *Educational Administration Quarterly, 39*(2), 145–163.

Ehrensal, P. A. L. (2005). *Law, legislation, policy and power: A critical discourse analysis approach to school law*. Paper presented at the First Congress of Qualitative Inquiry, University of Illinois, Urbana–Champagne.

Franek, M. (2006). Foiling cyberbullies in the new Wild West. *Educational Leadership, 63*(4), 39–43.

Giroux, H. (2003). *The abandoned generation: Democracy beyond the culture of fear*. New York: Palgrave Macmillan.

Goff, H. (2007, April 16). Websites urged to act on bullies [Electronic version]. *BBC News Online*. Retrieved August 13, 2007, from http://news.bbc.co.uk/2/hi/uk_news/education/6539989.stm.

Golding, W. (1959). *Lord of the Flies*. New York: Capricorn Books.

Gramsci, A. (1971). *Selections from the prison notebooks of Antonio Gramsci*. London: Lawrence Wishart.

Gramsci, A. (1975). *Letters from prison* (L. Lawner, trans.). London: Jonathan Cape.

Harmon, A. (2004, August 24). Internet gives teenage bullies weapons to wound from afar [Electronic version]. *New York Times*. Retrieved August 26, 2004, from http://www.nytimes.com./2004/08/26/education.

Jafaar, S. B. (2002). Fertile ground: Instructional negligence and the tort of educational malpractice. *Education & Law Journal, 12*(1), 1–132 at 131–132.

Lankshear, C., & Knobel, M. (2006). *New literacies: Everyday practices and classroom learning* (2nd ed.). Maidenhead, England/New York: Open University Press.

Leishman, J. (2002, October 10). Cyber-bullying: The Internet is the latest weapon in a bully's arsenal [Electronic version]. *CBC News. The National*. Retrieved January 27, 2003, from http://cbc.ca/news/national/news/cyberbullying/index.html.

Leong, M. (2007, August 27). Cyber-bullying targeting teachers: Poll [Electronic version]. *National Post*. Retrieved August 28, 2007, from http://www.canada.com/nationalpost/news/story.html?id=53ff8165-4cd8-4d1b-bc18-39da4d9e82b8&k=0.

Linden, A. M., & Klar, L. N. (Eds.). (1994). *Canadian tort law: Cases, notes & materials* (10th ed.). Markam and Vancouver, Canada: Butterworths Canada.

Macdonald, R. A., & Sandomierski, D. (2006). Against nomopolies. *Northern Ireland Legal Quarterly, 57*, 610–633.

McLaren, P. (1998). *Life in schools: An introduction to critical pedagogy in the foundations of education* (3rd ed.). New York: Longman.

McMorrow, T. (2007). Lord of the bullies: Advocating a student-centred approach to legal research into cyber-bullying. Unpublished paper submitted for graduate course at McGill University, Montreal, Canada.

Ontario College of Teachers. (2007). COMPAS State of the Teaching Profession [Electronic version]. *Professionally Speaking, the Magazine of the Ontario College of Teachers*. Retrieved August 28, 2007, from http://www.oct.ca/publications/PDF/survey07_e.pdf.

Pierre, D. B. C. (2003). *Vernon God Little*. London: Faber & Faber.

Razack, S. (1998). *Looking white people in the eye: Gender, race, and culture in court-rooms and classrooms*. Toronto: University of Toronto Press.

Reading Evening Post. (2006, June 1). Cyber bullying blighting our lives [Electronic version]. *getreading*. Retrieved August 13, 2007, from http://www.getreading.co.uk/news/2001/2001939/cyber-bullying blighting our_lives.

Senoo, Y. (2007). Netto-ijime (cyber-bullying): Bullying moves to cyberspace. Unpublished term paper for EDEM 609 Issues in Education Masters course, Department of Integrated Studies in Education, Faculty of Education, McGill University, Montreal, Canada.

Servance, R. L. (2003). Cyber-bullying, cyber-harassment and the conflict between schools and the First Amendment. *Wisconsin Law Review*, 6, 2003, 1213 at 1244.

Shariff, S. (2003). *A system on trial: Identifying legal standards for educational, ethical and legally defensible approaches to bullying in schools*. Unpublished doctoral dissertation, Simon Fraser University, Burnaby, Canada.

Shariff, S. (2004). Keeping schools out of court: Legally defensible models of leadership to reduce cyber-bullying. Educational Forum. *Delta Kappa Pi*, 68(3), 222–223.

Shariff, S. (2008). *Cyber bullying: Issues and solutions for the school, the classroom, and the home*. Abington, England: Routledge (Taylor and Francis Group).

Shariff, S., & Gouin, R. (2005). *Cyber-dilemmas: Gendered hierarchies, free expression and cyber-safety in schools*. Paper presented at the Safety & Security in a Networked World: Balancing Cyber-rights & Responsibilities, Oxford Internet Institute, University of Oxford, England. Retrieved August 9, 2007, from http://www.oii.ox.ac.uk/microsites/cybersafety/?view=papers.

Shariff, S., & Hoff, D. L. (2007). Cyber-bullying: Clarifying legal boundaries for school supervision in cyberspace [Electronic version]. *International Journal of Cyber Criminology*. Retrieved August 9, 2007, from http://www40.brinkster.com/ccjournal/Shaheen&Hoffjcc.htm.

Shariff, S., & Strong-Wilson, T. (2005). Bullying and new technologies: What can teachers do to foster socially responsible discourse in the physical and virtual school environments? In J. Kincheloe (Ed.), *Classroom teaching: An introduction* (pp. 219–240). New York: Peter Lang.

Soloyon, C. (2005, February 2). A gift from the devil: Worry about on-line activities. *Gazette*, p. A2.

Willard, N. (2003). Off-campus, harmful online student speech. *Journal of School Violence*, 1(2), 65–93.

Zhang, W., & Wei, J.-Y. (2007, July 22). *The cyber-bullying research (China II)*. Hangzhou, China: Zhejiang University, funded by the Social Science and Humanities Research Council of Canada (SSHRC). Shaheen Shariff, Principal Investigator, McGill University, Montreal.

CHAPTER TWO

Profile of Traditional and Cyber-Bullying

SNERT... That's what some call the trouble-makers of cyberspace. Attributed to Kurt Vonnegut, the term stands out for "Snot-Nosed Eros-Ridden Teenager." It concisely captures much of what many cyberspace deviants are all about. They thumb their noses at authority figures and smear their discontent all over themselves and others.

(Suler & Philips, 1998)

INTRODUCTION.

This chapter is a reiteration of the background on bullying that I have provided in my book on teaching and parenting issues (Shariff, 2008). It is important that readers who are interested in the law and policy aspects gain insight into the forms and complexities of bullying and cyber-bullying. This is especially important for legal practitioners, academics, and judges, because their understanding of its nuances could make an enormous difference in adjudicating cases of cyber-bullying, or even in negotiating settlements with parents and victims.

WHAT IS BULLYING?

Bullying among school children is certainly an old phenomenon, although it was not until the early 1970s that it was made the object of systematic research. In schools, bullying usually occurs in areas with minimal or no adult supervision. It can occur within or around school buildings, although it more often occurs in physical education classes, hallways, bathrooms, or classes that require group work, as well as during after-school activities. Bullying in school sometimes consists of a group of students taking advantage of or isolating one student in particular and outnumbering him or her. Targets of bullying in school are often pupils who are considered strange or different by their peers, making the situation harder for them to deal with. Bullying can also be perpetrated by teachers or instigated against them.

/ Historically bullying was not seen as a problem that needed attention but rather has been accepted as a fundamental and normal part of childhood (Campbell, 2005; Limber & Small, 2003). In the last two decades, however, this view has changed, and schoolyard bullying and cyber-bullying are seen as serious problems that warrant attention. /

In the 1990s, the United States saw an epidemic of school shootings (the most notorious of which was the Columbine High School massacre in Colorado). This continued into 2006, when in Virginia and in Montreal, Canada, in separate incidents, two young men went on shooting sprees at two postsecondary institutions, taking in their wake their own lives and those of peers and teachers. Although most of the youth who carry out these shootings take their own lives, a commonality is that all of the perpetrators were, at some point in their lives, victims of bullying by peers (Dedman, 2000).

In most cases, it was discovered that they resorted to violence only after the school administration repeatedly failed to intervene, as in the case of the shootings in Virginia and Columbine. As a result of these trends, numerous antibullying programs and zero-tolerance policies have proliferated as schools attempt to reduce and control bullying. According to Hoover and Olsen (2001), up to 15 percent of students in U.S. schools are frequently or severely harassed by their peers. They add that only a slim majority of fourth through twelfth graders (55.2 percent) reported neither having been picked on nor picking on others. Furthermore, bully–victim cycles are found in which individuals are both bullies and victims (Ma, 2001; Pellegrini & Bartini, 2000; Schwartz, Dodge, & Coie, 1993; Schwartz, Dodge, Pettit, & Bates, 1997).

Numerous surveys of students have found that face-to-face bullying by peers in school is a frequent experience for many children (Genta, Menesini, Fonzi, Costabile, & Smith, 1996; Kumpulainen et al., 1998; Whitney & Smith, 1993). One in six children report being bullied at least once a week (Rigby, 1997; Zubrick et al., 1997), although that figure was as high as 50 percent if the duration of the bullying is taken as lasting only one week (P. K. Smith & Shu, 2000). In another study, 40 percent of adolescents reported having been bullied at some time during their schooling (Mynard, Joseph, & Alexander, 2000). However, the percentage of students who report longer-term bullying of six months or more decreases to between 15 percent and 17 percent (Slee, 1995; Slee & Rigby, 1993).

Bullying has been understood and defined as an age-old societal problem, beginning in the schoolyard and often progressing to the boardroom (Campbell, 2005; McCarthy, Rylance, Bennet, & Zimmermann, 2001). "Bullying" is often defined by developmental psychologists as an aggressive, intentional act or behavior that is carried out by a group or an individual repeatedly and over time against a victim who cannot easily defend himself or herself (Campbell, 2005; Olweus, 2001; Whitney & Smith, 1993). Bullying is a form of abuse that is based on an imbalance of power; it can be defined as a systematic abuse of power (Rigby, 2002; P. K. Smith & Sharp, 1994). Bullying may be physical, including behaviors such as hitting, punching, and spitting, or it may involve browbeating language using verbal assault, teasing, ridicule, sarcasm, and scapegoating (Campbell, 2005; DiGiulio, 2001; Slee & Rigby, 1993). It involves a minimum of two people, a perpetrator and a victim. However, a large number of people may be involved in an indirect manner as an audience. These bystanders may be other students who witness the bullying event but remain uninvolved. They are frequently afraid of becoming the next victim if they do interfere. They often feel powerless and show a loss of self-respect and self-confidence (Campbell, 2005; S. Harris & Petrie, 2002).

Canadian studies tell us that approximately 10 percent to 15 percent of children are bullied or engage in bullying at least once a week.[1] Bullying begins in kindergarten, involves various degrees of violence, and comprises various forms of harassment. Bullying can be physical or psychological, overt or covert, random (indiscriminate) or discriminatory. For a variety of reasons, educators may not recognize bullying for what it is, and victims sometimes find it difficult to substantiate covert or psychological forms of bullying. This is because such behavior is easily confused with teasing and generally occurs on playgrounds, in hallways, and now most frequently in cyberspace (e-mail, text messaging, Web sites), away from the watchful eyes of teachers or other supervisors.

Emerging litigation against schools indicates that victims and their parents are prepared to sue schools for failing to protect them from bullying and cyber-bullying. If schools are to keep students safe and avoid litigation, the first step is to learn how to recognize the various forms of bullying in the physical school environment and, in particular, the conditions under which it occurs.

The Etymology of Bullying

Ironically, bullying began as a term of endearment. The *Oxford University Press* dictionary notes that it originated in the 1600s as *boel*, meaning "lover of either sex" (Simpson & Weiner, 1989, p. 645). The dictionary also references a 1721 edition of *Bailey* that contains the word *boolie*, meaning "beloved." The word was also used to describe one's "brother" (ibid.). From lover to brother, the word eventually took on the meaning of close friendship as between good buddies and companions. Implicit in this relationship was amiable teasing, cajoling, and joking among friends. For example, Shakespeare prefixed "bully" as a title – for example, "Blesse thee, bully doctor" (ibid.).

British coalminers described coworkers as bullies and thus began an association with bullies as "rowdies" or "ruffians." By the late 1800s, bullying began to refer to cowardice, weakness, tyranny, and violence.[2] It also began to be associated with gangs: "A gang of bullies was secretly sent to slit the nose of the offender" (ibid., p. 646). By 1883, to act as a bully was "to treat in an overbearing manner; to intimidate, overawe" (ibid.) or to "drive or force by bullying; to frighten into a certain course" (ibid.).

The etymology says much about the problem of recognizing bullying. Its transition from general roughhousing to hostile treatment highlights interesting parallels between the historical evolution of the word and bullying in contemporary schools. First, many researchers (Glover, Cartwright, & Gleeson,

1998; Roher, 1997; P. K. Smith & Sharp, 1994; Tattum, 1997) acknowledge that until the last twenty years or so, bullying in schools was widely accepted as an unavoidable part of growing up. Smith and Sharp (1994) point out that although the topic was addressed in novels such as *Tom Brown's Schooldays*, almost no research on it was published outside Norway and Sweden until the late 1970s when the Norwegian bullying expert Olweus (1978) published an English version of his book *Aggression in the Schools: Bullies and Whipping Boys*. As the etymology discloses, this is around the time that notions of bullying shifted to incorporate negative characteristics.

Bullying was not recognized as problematic in Britain and North America, however, until the 1980s. In the army and university fraternities, bullying took the form of "hazing" of new recruits. In the British boarding schools I attended, new students were often put through a form of bullying known as "squashing" by their prefects. Authorities were well aware that this took place but tolerated it as a "toughening up" that rookies needed to build character. Similarly, with playground bullying, there was an underlying assumption among teachers that such behavior was acceptable because it forced quieter children to learn to assert themselves.

Bullying or Teasing?

In the context of the etymology, it is important to explain why teachers may not recognize teasing as bullying. Bullying has two forms: physical and psychological (which includes verbal teasing). Curiously, verbal bullying in contemporary schools fluctuates between terms of endearment and hostile treatment. For example, a significant amount of adolescent discourse occurs in the electronic medium and is often influenced by lyrics in rap and grunge music (Ashford, 1996). Drawing from such lyrics, teens might greet each other by saying, "What's up, dawg?"(derived from African American rap lyrics). They may chide a friend, "I'm going to kick your ass." They may tell a friend he's "bad" (meaning he's "cool"). They may challenge a friend to roughhouse by saying, "Bring it on F...Face" ("let's fight").

Much of this language, when directed at friends, is meant without harmful intentions. Take, for example, a recent human rights bullying case, *Jubran v. North Vancouver School Distr. No. 44*, in which Azmi Jubran, a high school student of Iranian descent, suffered four years of incessant bullying at his North Vancouver high school in British Columbia. After graduating, Jubran brought a human rights claim against the school for failing to protect him from the homophobic discrimination that comprised a large part of the bullying. He insisted he was not homosexual but was harassed on the basis of his appearance. One of Jubran's persecutors, referred to as "Mr. Richardson," testified that, in high school, taunts that adults might interpret as homophobic are not always meant that way when directed toward friends:

Mr. Richardson testified that the words used by the students were "part of the high school vocabulary," and words like "gay" were used to describe someone, something, or a situation that a student didn't like. Mr. Richardson testified that he himself used those words "all the time." He testified it would be common for a student to say: "that shirt is so gay" or the "long jump is so gay" if the student didn't like it. He also said that the words "queer," "faggot" and "homo" were commonly used as part of normal conversation, even among friends, *as terms of endearment*. He further testified that he still has a friend who says to him "what's up homo?" and that those words are used without reference to sexual orientation.

(C. Roberts, *Jubran v. North Vancouver School Distr. No. 44*, p. 7, emphasis added)

This discourse emulates the amicable teasing among buddies in the early 1800s, such as "My over jolly bully-boy, let be" (Simpson & Weiner, 1989, p. 645). Bullying begins to reflect the shift in its etymology from a "buddy" relationship to its more hostile and overbearing character when identical words and actions are directed toward someone who is not a friend. For example, the words "homo" and "gay" make the transition from being terms of endearment between friends to hostile words intended to harm. The testimony from *Jubran* is again useful to illustrate how this happens. A number of his perpetrators, referred to by their last names in the tribunal transcripts, gave the following testimony:

Mr. Howard, Mr. Higgins, Mr. Kai and Mr. White all testified that when the words were spoken by someone who was not a friend, the terms "dork," "geek," "gay," and "faggot," were used interchangeably as words of insult or as a put-down. Their evidence was that the words were not intended to imply that Mr. Jubran was homosexual, and that neither they nor others who called Mr. Jubran those names were of the view that Mr. Jubran was homosexual. Mr. Howard and Mr. Kai denied that any of the "sting" of the words resulted from the fact that they related to homosexuality; they testified that the word were simply used as another form of insult.

(Judge Robertson, *Jubran v. North Vancouver School Distr. No. 44*, p.7)

This language used in two entirely different ways might explain why teachers continue to tolerate verbal bullying. Although teachers try to stop students using swear words and sexist language, they cannot monitor every word or conversation.

Glover et al. (1998) report Boulton and Hawker's (1997) British study that found teachers commonly look for physical injury and generally ignore verbal bullying. In keeping with the popular adage "sticks and stones will break my bones but words will never hurt me," they found many teachers turn a blind eye to verbal bullying. Middle school students reported that teasing was the most common aspect of the bullying they experienced (90 percent of the time), and their responses suggest various reasons as to why teachers might tolerate bullying. One student noted that "Teachers turn a blind eye to name calling because they believe it doesn't hurt you" (Boulton & Hawker, 1997, p. 32). Another observed, "It seems that action is only taken if someone is really hurt [physically]," and a third complained, "Teachers want a school with no bullying and so they pretend it doesn't exist" (ibid.).

Other studies support similar findings,[3] and although most researchers have moved away from stereotypical views about bullying as simply a physical assault,[4] many teachers and students apparently still perceive bullying as physical and not verbal. For example, Glover et al. (1998) studied the responses of British teachers and students in junior and secondary schools who were provided with a list of behaviors (including a range of physical activities such as kicking, hitting, and shoving and verbal behaviors such as teasing, name-calling, and threatening). In their study, a significantly higher proportion of responses by teachers (90 percent) described physical behaviors as bullying compared to verbal behaviors. Students also identified physical bullying as being more serious than verbal bullying, but to a lesser extent than teachers did.

Moreover, most of the teachers who were interviewed believed children should cope with teasing on their own. One teacher responded, "It happens so much that I just tell them [the children] to get on with it. It's no good encouraging them to be too sensitive, they should learn to ignore it" (Glover et al., 1998, p. 55). These results are significant, because teachers' perceptions of bullying affect how they respond to complaints, and students' perceptions of verbal bullying as harmless may encourage them to participate in it.

These findings illustrate how important it is to ensure that educators and the courts understand the complexities of bullying well enough to recognize and appreciate the range of bullying behaviors and their effects. This is also important to bear in mind when we turn to the profile of cyber-bullying because a significant amount is verbal with greater psychological ramifications than physical bullying.

General Characteristics

Bullying entails overt or covert behavior and takes verbal or physical forms. Good-natured horseplay and teasing escalate into bullying when victim(s) and perpetrator(s) cease to agree when the behavior should stop and when a power imbalance is created between them. Bullying generally involves a range of hostile behaviors instigated by certain perpetrators to gain power and dominance over others.

Girls and boys display similar levels of bullying. However, boys report bullying more often and generally engage in overt physical forms of bullying, whereas girls tend to engage in covert psychological bullying (Crick, Grotpeter, & Bigbee, 2002; Hall, 1999; Pepler & Craig, 1997; Rauste-Von Wright, 1992). Nonetheless, there is now evidence of a trend in increased physical bullying and violence by females.[5] Tremblay (1991) suggests that the disparity between genders is due to extensive focus on male aggression and lack of focus on female aggression.[6] The disparity in rates could also be explained by changes in the way girls are socialized and how females are depicted in the media and in society – another point to remember when we go to a discussion of gender differences and cyber-bullying.

Research suggests that male students are more likely to carry a weapon onto school property and constitute 83 percent of all victims of school-related homicides or suicides. In addition, boys are more likely to fight among themselves, whereas girls fight with either sex. After extended periods of relentless bullying, victims of both sexes are more likely than students who are not bullied to bring weapons to school for protection (DiGiulio, 2001; Olweus, 1993).

Current research identifies a broad consensus that the following general factors contribute to bullying in schools. Take note of these conditions because they also exist in cyberspace and inform the profile of cyber-bullying:

- There is always a power imbalance that favors the perpetrator(s) over the victim.
- The perpetrators are often supported by a group of peers, some of whom actively encourage the bully and others who watch but do nothing to help peers who are targeted.
- Targeted students draw the negative attention of their peers and are actively pushed out of the group and isolated (Crick et al., 2002; Schuster, 2001).
- Exclusion and isolation from the larger peer group fortify the power of the perpetrator(s).
- The perpetrators' behavior is uninvited and unwanted by the victim.
- The perpetrators' actions are deliberate, repeated, and often relentless.

Why is the combination of power and exclusion so characteristic of school bullying? Other types of violence may involve power but not necessarily exclusion. Take war, for example. War between countries or tribes involves power, and prisoners of war might be isolated from their people, but that is not a primary objective of war. In bullying, the perpetrator's primary objective is the isolation and exclusion of certain peers, and as we will see in the profile of cyber-bullying, in cyberspace, teachers and other authority figures are also isolated and demeaned. The perpetrator's actions draw the support of the larger peer group, increasing the victim's vulnerability. In addition, although not all members of the group will support bullying, the frightening reality is that a larger number of peers (an average of 30 percent; Olweus, 2001; Salmivalli, Lagerspetz, Björqvist, Österman, & Kaukiainen, 1996) will support individual bullies rather than help the victim. This is a key consideration to bear in mind when we move to the profile of cyber-bullying.

Other researchers agree that the most lethal aspect of bullying is the group effect, which perpetuates and sustains abuse of individual victims (Bukowksi & Sippola, 2001; Crick et al., 2002; Juvonen & Graham, 2001; Perry, Willard, & Perry, 1990; Salmivalli, 2001; Schuster, 2001). Perpetrators are generally driven by the need for power and recognition to make up for a lack of confidence and self-assurance. They crave acceptance. Recruiting the support of the peer group by isolating and demeaning someone satisfies that need. Note at this stage that I prefer to use the word "perpetrator" rather than the label of "bully" because a perpetrator initiates a certain action or actions in a specific context, whereas labeling an individual as a "bully" gives the perception that such an individual is a bad or "evil" person at all times – it connotes a negative flaw in the person's character, whereas a perpetrator may only engage in bullying once – he or she may, as research has found, also be a victim of bullying. Hence for me it is important that we move away from labels. Although I use "victim" and "target" interchangeably throughout this book, their use depends on the context of the discussion. Suffice it to say that labels such as "disruptive," "aggressive," "evil," and "terrorist" essentialize and justify blame-laying and scapegoating.

Perpetrators and Targets
People often ask about the characteristics of kids who engage in bullying. Are they the popular kids or the so-called losers? There is a discrepancy in the research on this question. The National Crime Prevention Council (NCPC) (1997) reported that perpetrators are generally unpopular, whereas a number of more recent studies have confirmed that perpetrators exhibit high levels of leadership and confidence and are often popular with peers and teachers (DiGiulio, 2001; Katch, 2001; Olweus, 2001). DiGuilio (2001),[7] for example, contends that the instigators are popular with teachers because of their leadership skills and academic abilities. Unlike the stereotypical "bully" who is perceived to be dejected and unpopular, perpetrators are often classroom leaders and peer tutors (Salmivalli et al., 1996) – those whom teachers might assume would defend victims rather than instigate or reinforce bullying. It is plausible, however, that peer leaders who engage in bullying may not be as self-assured as they seem. They may crave attention and take on peer leadership roles as a way to gain prestige and power.

Targets may thus be chosen on the basis of whether they are perceived to advance or hinder the effective functioning of the peer group. Individuals who are perceived as "different" are singled out for exclusion, which then triggers the bullying (Artz & Riecken, 1997; Katch, 2001; Olweus, 2001; Salmivalli, 2001).

To obtain more specific information on children's motivation to single out and bully certain victims, Glover, Cartwright, and Gleeson (1998) interviewed 3,417 elementary and high school students in Britain. The students were asked if and why they had engaged in specific antisocial behaviors, without having to admit they had "bullied." The researchers were also assessing the reasons children gave for discrimination. The greatest justification to bully someone (14 percent for boys and 12 percent for girls) was based on whether the victim was perceived as "too clever"(Glover et al., 1998, p. 27). A victim's looks were another motivator (14 percent for boys and 13 percent for girls). Other responses included the following: "I hadn't got on with her ever since primary school. . . . I don't know why . . . it's the way he looks at me and makes me feel I don't like him" (Glover et al., 1998). Parental or peer pressure provided another motivation for victim exclusion: "we weren't allowed to mix with them"(Glover et al., 1998). The author summarized his findings as follows:

- Ethnic background and religion are more frequently mentioned among older males as reasons for bullying, whereas gender is more frequently the reason for discrimination by adolescent males as a male taunt (sexual harassment).
- Perceptions of being rich or poor and family background are of limited concern, but the way people look and dress is a significant motivation to bully, especially for girls.
- Boys attack hard workers more than girls in adolescence, but victim "cleverness" motivates students of both genders to bully until Grade 11. Learning problems and lack of sporting aptitude are also motivations for boys to bully until Grade 11.
- Being different causes 10 percent to discriminate with little reduction until grade 11. This is especially true for students who are new to a school and speak with different accents.

Once targets are identified, they are presumed to deserve the punishment and "get what is coming to them." This justifies the exclusion that is a ubiquitous aspect of bullying. Katch (2001) inadvertently discovered that children's motivation to blame, exclude, and victimize begins as early as kindergarten:

When I first started audio-taping the children's play and talk, I cut out every discussion about exclusion. I thought it did not relate to my subject of violence. But when exclusion kept coming up, I decided to listen to those discussions, and I found that exclusion and violence seemed to be inextricably intertwined. Excluding someone from the group seemed to justify violence, both by the excluded child and by those who exclude him, just as when Seth and Patrick called Joel a baby before knocking him down and when Caleb called Nate a girl before punching him. On the other hand, ... as we learned from the killers at Columbine, the excluded child can feel justified in using violence to hurt those who exclude him. I wish I could just tell the children to be more inclusive, but it's never that easy.

(Katch, 2001, pp. 129–130)

Wason-Ellam (1996) believes that race, combined with class, is often a reason for exclusion, although girls tend to exclude on race more than boys do. She also notes that toys, such as Barbie dolls, can reinforce negative stereotypes that contribute to bullying. Barbie is still popular with young girls, and Wason-Ellam observes how it became a tool of privilege and race that girls used to exclude a Punjabi student who did not own the doll. The girls dressed their Barbies and shared lip gloss, makeup, and hair clips in "gestures of intimacy" (ibid., p. 97), but when the student, Surinder, would try to join in, she was dismissed with, "Go away, we don't want you in the group" (ibid., p. 96) and "I'm going to Renee's house after school to play with make-up because we are best friends. I am not going to invite you, 'cos your clothes are funny and you're a paki dot" (ibid.). Wason-Ellam recalls Surinder's response when she called her a "princess": "I inadvertently address Surinder as a 'princess' as she arrives in school in a fancy dress. Soulfully, she looks up at me and says, 'I can't be a princess because I don't look like a princess, Linda'" (ibid., p. 97).

Surinder's response illustrates how this type of exclusion negatively affects students' self-image. These findings also suggest that perpetrators bully to fill an emotional void resulting from a lack of confidence or self-worth. Victimizing others on the basis of their differences allows the bully to gain status and recognition (whether positive or negative) within the peer group. The finding that gender is an important motivator, especially for boys, is not surprising. What is surprising is that gifted students, or those with a strong work ethic, appear to invite bullying – perhaps because young people subconsciously want to achieve academic success when they realize the career success and social status it brings. Chapter 4 expands on some of these socializing and attitudinal influences in greater detail.

Types of Bullying
As I have noted, there are two principal types of bullying: physical and psychological. Both can be carried out in overt or covert ways and may involve indiscriminate or discriminatory forms of behaviour.

Physical Bullying
Physical bullying is generally described as "overt" because it usually involves open attacks on a victim (Olweus, 1993) that often grow worse if others are watching. Studies have found that the longer the perpetrators are encouraged, the more serious the physical abuse (Salmivalli et al., 1996).

Extreme physical bullying can take many forms, including beating, locking peers in school lockers, strangling, shooting, or using other weapons or objects to cause harm. Other methods of harassment include flicking rubber bands at the victim's face, throwing nails and wood chips in the eyes, spraying victims with harmful substances, pouring acid or gasoline on the person's body, tying him or her up, or blindfolding (National Crime Prevention Council, 1997; Olweus, 1993). These are only a few of the many examples of the kinds of activities students engage in to enforce a power relationship in which victims are overwhelmed and helpless.

Physical bullying can also be "covert." This kind of bullying takes place in the absence of supervisors or adults and might involve actions such as locking a victim in a school locker – or rape. A well-known example of covert bullying resulted in the murder of a South Indian teenager. Reena Virk (see Jiwani, 1997) was tricked into meeting peers by a grocery store and later beaten to death and drowned. She was accused of stealing a friend's diary and calling all the boys who were listed in it. Indiscriminate forms of physical bullying do not identify the victim on the basis of an enduring prejudice such as race, sex, gender, or ability but may be triggered on a whim or a spontaneous sense of annoyance or discomfort. A victim's look or body language, if misinterpreted as hostile, can trigger bullying, or a perpetrator may identify a suitable victim as someone who seems vulnerable (Artz, 1998).

More often than not, physical bullying takes on discriminatory forms, such as sexual or racial harassment of a physical nature or physical attacks on children with special needs. The pervasiveness of sexual bullying and harassment in schools is well documented, and updated studies on sexual cyber-bullying in Chapter 4 confirm that it continues to persist. For example, Stein (1991, 1995, 1999) disclosed that approximately 80 percent of girls and 60 percent of boys report they have been victims of sexual harassment.[8] Sexual harassment incorporates at least four of the characteristics of bullying described here: (1) there is usually a power imbalance between the perpetrator(s) and victim, (2) the harassment is unwanted, (3) it is deliberate and relentless, and (4) it is based on the victim's gender.

Sexual harassment is included in the Canadian National Crime Prevention Council's (1997) description of types of bullying. Although kissing and hugging are gestures of care, they become bullying when they are unwanted and imposed on victims against their will. This kind of bullying could include pulling down someone's pants, flipping up girls' skirts or snapping or unhooking bras, crude gestures, exposing genitals, or forcing someone to commit a sexual act against his or her will (all of which can also be defined as sexual assault; Stein, 1995, 1999; Welsh, 1997–1998). This type of sexual harassment is discriminatory because the victim is selected according to gender (with girls generally victimized more than boys).

Homophobic physical bullying incorporates random forms of physical bullying just described, combined with verbal insults about the individual's sexual orientation. Tolman, Spencer, Rosen-Reynoso, and Porches (2001) found that adolescent boys in Grade 9 are most susceptible to homophobic bullying, and this is based on their appearance. If they are not strong athletes or are physically smaller than others, boys may become targets. However, it is important not to oversimplify the reasons for this kind of bullying, because research suggests that victim identification depends as well on the self-assurance, relational attitudes, and emotional well-being of victims.

Racial attacks include the forms of physical bullying described here, or they can be combined with sexual harassment or other forms of discrimination. The difference is that they are either directed by mainstream students toward victims from visible ethnic groups on the basis of skin color, appearance, manner of dress, manner of speech, or cultural background (Dei, 1997; Janoviček, 2001; Jiwani, 2001; Razack, 1998) or by students from visible ethnic groups against each other. For example, in her study of immigrant and refugee girls, Janoviček (2001) reports that students of Iranian lineage bullied Iraqi students, Koreans bullied Philippinos, Hispanic and African American students conflicted, and so on. This illustrates how complex racial attacks can be and reminds us that it is not always mainstream students who instigate racial bullying.

It has been suggested that race was most certainly a factor in the case of Reena Virk, whose brutal murder was noted earlier and in more detail in Chapter 1 (Jiwani, 2001). The initial assault was overt: she was attacked on an open bridge and later under a tree by a group of adolescents. However, after most of the adolescents left, Kelly Ellard and Warren Glowatski followed her to the water and continued the "covert" beating and drowning. Ellard, smoking a cigarette, held Reena's head under the water with her foot until she no longer surfaced. Significantly, even though word spread that Reena had been killed, none of the many students who knew about the murder reported it for at least a week. Another alert for the reader as it relates to cyber-bullying: the code of silence and the sense of entitlement to privacy among perpetrators, bystanders, and reenforcers. These examples illustrate how covert physical bullying can be harder to substantiate than overt bullying, particularly if perpetrators and witnesses have a code of silence. Researchers (Glover et al., 1998; P. K. Smith & Sharp, 1994) report that observers are afraid to "rat" or "grass" on the offenders in case they become the next victim.

This network of covert support for perpetrators was also evident in the Jubran case. Covert bullying was part of the homophobic bullying Jubran endured for four years at Handsworth Secondary School in North Vancouver, British Columbia. Friends shielded a classmate who set fire to Azmi Jubran's shirt, and although each boy owned up to the abuse, each also later denied it. School administrators had difficulty identifying the individual who carried out the assault, making it difficult to discipline him.

Children with special needs are also highly susceptible to physical bullying because they may have difficulty with speech or mobility and as such are already in a position of vulnerability. P. K. Smith and Sharp (1994) report that physically disabled children, for example, may not be strong or fast enough to protect themselves or retaliate. They found that approximately two-thirds of the special needs children interviewed reported being bullied, compared with one-quarter of mainstream students. One special needs student complained, "They kick me and punch me and they are horrible to me. They smack me and spit on my back" (P. K. Smith & Sharp, 1994, p. 222). Another stated that because he had difficulty carrying his lunch tray, his friend always carried it for him, but then he was challenged to a fight because other students accused him of being lazy.

Finally, as DiGuilio (2001) observes, students in contemporary schools are raised in a commercial- and media-driven society that tells them how they should look and dress to be "cool" or acceptable. Children who cannot afford the latest fashions or may simply refuse to conform to the popular dress code may be physically attacked. At the other end of the spectrum, affluent children who wear desirable clothes are also vulnerable to physical attacks in which their clothes and watches are stolen from them. This form of bullying is also known as "taxing." A government survey in Quebec, Canada (Séguin, 2002) found that 11 percent of 16,600 young people in the province reported being victimized this way.

Psychological Bullying

Psychological bullying generally involves either inflicting mental anguish to cause their targets to fear for their physical safety, or breaking down self-esteem and confidence. This is obviously an integral aspect of cyber-bullying. Again, at least three or more of the characteristics of bullying are always present: (1) the harassment is unwanted and uninvited, (2) it is relentless, and (3) the victim is singled out for the abuse. Verbal psychological bullying is "overt" in the sense that joking and insults can be heard or read by witnesses and substantiated by victims.

Covert (nonverbal) psychological bullying is intended to exclude and isolate by stalking or ostracizing the victim. It is the most difficult form of bullying for victims to substantiate because teachers cannot see it or prove that it has occurred. Perpetrators might suddenly ignore victims or refuse to work with them on class projects or other activities. They may spread unsubstantiated rumors that embarrass the victim or make him or her appear dishonest or untrustworthy to peers.

Psychological bullying, like physical bullying, can also be indiscriminate or discriminatory. Indiscriminate psychological bullying might involve teasing, making repeated derogatory statements about the victim, or other kinds of verbal harassment. For example, a boy might be called a "loser" because he does not have a girlfriend or cannot afford clothes that help him fit in with the "cool" crowd. He may be called "cry baby" if the pressure from the bullying gets to him and "four eyes" or "geek" or "dork" if he wears glasses (National Crime Prevention Council, 1997; Olweus, 1991).

Bullying often stems from the social inequities that adult society creates, fosters, and sustains – and with which it continues to grapple. Research confirms that a significant amount of psychological bullying is discriminatory (Dei, 1997; Glover et al., 1998; Janoviček, 2001; Wason-Ellam, 1996). Students are excluded and purposely isolated through covert psychological bullying because of race, gender, sexual orientation, disability, accent, or because they are good students and do well in class. Children from these categories are already marginalized because of their differences, which are then exacerbated through bullying. Peers may not pick them for sports teams or class projects, and they may be ignored, stalked, or stared at. Scholars observe that not only are such children marginalized by one form of discrimination, they often face a combination of discriminatory factors (for example, they might experience covert bullying through exclusion because of their race as well as their gender or sexual orientation, and possibly a learning disability or giftedness) (Jiwani, 2001). This results in intersecting and interlocking barriers of discrimination that victims find difficult to overcome, understand, or explain. They know they are isolated but may not understand why.

Covert psychological bullying makes it difficult for teachers to support the victim. For example, teachers cannot punish someone simply for staring and may not be able to establish for certain that it was done with malicious intent.

Alleged stalkers, for example, could defend their actions by saying they simply happened to be walking the same way as the victim. Similarly, children cannot be disciplined for laughing unless the teacher overhears inappropriate language or unfair innuendoes. And students will undoubtedly be embarrassed to have a teacher insist that they be accepted into a group or sports team when they are clearly unwanted.

Psychological sexual harassment can also be overt or covert, comprising sexual proposals and threats, name-calling, or repeated demands for sexual acts, among other demands. Girls may be called "bitch," "hoe" (whore), "dyke," "butch," or "lesbian," whereas boys will be called "gay," "homo," "sissy," or "girl." As with physical bullying, children from visible ethnic groups are especially vulnerable to psychological bullying. Studies on refugee and immigrant students from these groups disclose that these students are subjected to significantly more bullying than mainstream students. Racial slurs include comments such as "go home to India (or China, or Iran)" and taunts about appearance and manner of dress. Refugee and immigrant students are often referred to as "FOBs" ("fresh off the boat") and are sometimes also harassed by peers from their own communities who were born here and see them as an embarrassment (Handa, 1997).

Finally, children with special needs are particularly vulnerable to verbal bullying because of their disabilities. D. J. Smith (1995) explores how devastating this bullying is for these children; children reported being called "cabbage," "maggot," and "whale" (pp. 223–224) and having their peers jeer at their low marks in class. At the other end of the spectrum, gifted children are also subjected to harassment as "teacher's pet," "dork," "geek," or "walking encyclopaedia."

Boulton and Hawker (1997) explain that because teasing is characterized by a combination of irritating and lighthearted qualities and often contains hidden messages, it can be difficult for teachers and students to recognize it as bullying. Indeed, what one child finds upsetting, another may find playful, and what one child finds funny on one occasion may not be appreciated when it becomes persistent. It can therefore be difficult for the victim as well as adult observers to determine the teaser's intention and for the perpetrators to appreciate fully the effect of their words and actions.

Changing Roles

Adding to the difficulty in identifying and addressing bullying is the fact that the roles of perpetrator and victim can be interchangeable. The National Crime Prevention Council (1997) reports that children who find themselves victimized can also perpetrate violence and are often perceived as "bullies." Studies conducted in Scandinavia by Salmivalli (1999, 2001; Salmivalli et al., 1996) identified six distinct participant roles that children take in bully–victim situations: bully, victim, assistant (joins the bully), reenforcer (encourages the bully by observing and laughing), defender (assists the victim by siding with him or her or trying to stop others), and outsiders (students unaware of the bullying or who avoid such situations by staying away). The researchers studied 573 sixth-grade students and found they represented six participant roles in the following proportions:

Bullies	8.2%
Victims	11.7%
Assistants	19.5%
Reenforcers	17.3%
Defend victims	23.7%
Outsiders	12.7%

Although they found that 23.7 percent of students said they would defend the victim, a larger percentage (an aggregate of 36 percent of the children in this sample) exhibited some level of support for the behaviour.

Pepler and Craig (1997) found that although 83 percent of students report discomfort in watching someone being bullied, their actual observations showed that 25 percent of bystanders supported the perpetrators. Henderson, Hymel, Bonanno, and Davidson (2002) note that peer bystanders who watch but do nothing contribute significantly to the problem. Equally disturbing is the fact that bystanders are often friendlier toward the instigators after such episodes, which increases their excitement and aggression.

O'Connell, Pepler, and Craig (1999)[9] identified three major reasons for peer inaction:

1. the personal responsibility is diffused because of the presence of others,
2. children are intimidated by the power differential between themselves and the perpetrator and are afraid of becoming victims themselves, and
3. children may not have strategies for dealing with bullying and opt not to intervene.

Notably, another group of studies confirms that peer witnesses lack the courage to report bullying because they are not confident of receiving assistance and protection from teachers or administrators (Besag, 1989; O'Moore & Hillery, 1991; Tattum & Herbert, 1993). In sum, peer inaction contributes to a negative school environment in which victims cannot rely on their peers for support, and as the next chapter shows, in cyberspace, peer support for perpetrators can multiply to millions of onlookers and bystanders. Their inaction adds significantly to the victim's humiliation and creates a negative online and in-school environment for them.

Henderson, Hymel, Bonanno, and Davidson (2002) also report that the greater number of children present, the longer the behavior continues, and, concomitantly, the abuse intensifies. Again, this should be noted because it is especially true of cyber-bullying when large numbers of kids can get involved at any time of the day or night. These studies support Boulton and Hawker's (1997) findings that a greater proportion of students, like their teachers, did not perceive verbal harassment as bullying. It is possible that the bystanders do not see themselves as actual participants, even though they watch and may verbally contribute to the harassment.

Effects of Bullying

As Hamed Nastoh's story in Chapter 1 illustrates, the tragic consequences of extreme bullying, as witnessed in cases involving suicide and murder,[10] are well known. The impact of bullying on children in the normal course of school life is not as well recognized but can also be devastating. Mental anguish from the social exclusion caused by physical and psychological bullying is sufficient to destroy the confidence of any adult, let alone a child on whom it can have lifelong effects. As the evidence illustrates, the impact of bullying (on victims *and* perpetrators) should not be taken lightly.

Researchers (Haynie et al., 2001; Hodges & Perry, 1996; Juvonen & Graham, 2001; Kochenderfer-Ladd & Wardrop, 2001; Rigby, 2001) find that victims and bullies experience greater psychosomatic problems, including depression, anxiety, low self-esteem, and poorer overall mental and physical health than those not involved in bullying. Interestingly, children who are both victims and bullies are at even greater psychological risk than those who are one or the other (Haynie et al., 2001; Kumpulainen, Rasanen, & Henttonen, 1999; Nansel, Overpeck, Pilla, Simons-Morton, & Scheidt, 2001). They demonstrate greater psychological problems, tend to seek out deviant peers, and perform more poorly in their schoolwork. They also report poorer self-concept and greater social dissatisfaction. Boulton and Hawker (1997) point to a growing body of research that shows that teasing and exclusion in particular can have devastating consequences, including school avoidance and poor school functioning. These findings are corroborated by victims' own descriptions in their legal claims against schools and by parents of students who committed suicide (*Dufour v. Howe Sound Board of Education, 2001- case abandoned*; *Jubran v. North Vancouver Distr. No. 44*, 2002).[11]

Bullying and bystander support for perpetrators have serious consequences for students from marginalized groups, such as immigrants or refugees. These students are less likely to complain to authorities because they are new to the school system, do not speak English well, and may be too shy to build a rapport with their teachers. They may not understand the role of school counselors, or their own cultural protocols may require them to maintain deference to authority (Handa, 1997). Similarly, disabled students, gays and lesbians, and heterosexual children of same-sex parents may exhibit poor school performance and related depression (Sears, 1993).

It is important to point out that the effects of bullying can be profound – and lifelong. Devlin's (1997) study of British prison inmates is instructive here. Devlin found that most of the inmates had experienced severe bullying during their lives, and although much of the bullying was probably physical, the psychological impact clearly affected them long after the physical scars had healed.

Many became hardened criminals because of pent up anger and frustration and lack of trust in peers, as well as in teachers and other adults in their lives.

The consequences of most physical bullying are easily recognizable. Teachers can easily see when a student has bruises, a black eye, or broken bones. Internal injuries such as bleeding or broken ribs, however, are more difficult to detect and may be dismissed as whining until external signs make it clear that the student is in pain. For example, Hamed Nastoh was sent home with a stomachache two days before he killed himself, and his mother noted that he did not tell either her or school officials that he had been kicked in the stomach. The stress and anxiety of bullying can also cause physical conditions such as headaches, stomach upset, and lethargy, but teachers and parents might reasonably assume that the child has a physical illness. Not surprisingly, perpetrators also sustain serious physical injuries and tend to become involved in substance abuse and criminality (National Crime Prevention Council, 1997; Olweus, 1991). Those who fluctuate between bullying and being victimized show the greatest tendency for serious aggression and criminality in adulthood (physical fighting, weapon use, and theft; DiGiulio, 2001; Hall, 1999).

It is clear that bullying is a serious problem in schools that needs to be addressed by schools and parents. The day-to-day victimization of students is as important to ameliorate as the extreme cases. It is not only the safety, health, and well-being of victims that is affected, but also that of all students at a school where bullying occurs – and that is virtually all schools – because it creates a chill and poisons the entire school environment. I come back to the issue of school environment in later chapters because this is one of the primary areas where schools and parents can work together. It is also and an aspect of school responsibility that the courts have highlighted as paramount to learning.

BULLYING TODAY

In the wake of the Columbine, Montreal (Dawson College), and the mass random shootings at Virginia Polytechnic University (Agence France Presse, 2007) and the media attention to those and other serious bullying cases, many parents and stakeholders are concerned that school violence is on the rise[12] and possibly even out of control. Easy access to guns and the high population in the United States might contribute to the current rates of violence there. Students in Canada, Australia, China, Japan, or Britain, for example, may not experience cases of extreme violence as often because there is less ready access to guns. This does not mean, however, that bullying is not prevalent in schools in those countries or that it is not a serious concern. It is an issue in many countries, but it usually does not involve extreme violence or result in death. Yet given the media attention to bullying, it is important to consider it in context.

Canadian and U.S. researchers (Dolmage, 2000; Roher, 1997; Tanner, 1996) concur that a small number of young people (4 to 6 percent) actually engage in serious acts of violence.[13] DiGuilio, in fact, contends that schools are the "safest places in the world" (2001, p. 23). He notes that violent deaths from murder and suicide in U.S. schools declined by 40 percent between 1995 and 2001, whereas the risk of violent death for students who dropped out of school, were expelled, or were suspended increased "several hundredfold" (ibid.).[14] These statistics, although less recent than those I provide on cyber-bullying in the next chapter, are crucial. Let me repeat the fact that the risk of violent death for students who were expelled or suspended increased "several hundredfold" (ibid.). When we consider school and government responses to bullying and cyber-bullying in later chapters, these statistics will play an important role. DiGuilio also provides data that disclose a 14 percent reduction in physical fights in U.S. schools between 1991 and 1997 – another positive finding; however, as we will see in Chapter 2, it maybe simply that the physical bullying has moved into the covert realm of cyberspace with far wider reach.

In the meantime, it is notable that typically only extreme bullying cases are reported by the media, thus giving an inaccurate picture of its frequency and seriousness. According to Dolmage (2000), media-reported statistics that reflect a rise in youth violence are rarely presented in context. The numbers may instead reflect higher rates of overall violence because of a growing population[15] or because schools now report incidents of a less serious nature to police more frequently.[16] Put another way, it is important to question critically the statistics presented by the media, which are often geared to sensationalize and draw attention to aspects of a story without attention to the context. This in turn has significant impact on the policy and practice response by schools and education ministries.

I spend considerable time addressing the influence of the media in creating fear and shaping the public's perceptions about bullying, cyber-bullying, and the dangers of communication technologies in later chapters. For now, it is notable that a lot of bullying is psychological – both in terms of how it is carried out and its effects. In contemporary society, much of it flows between physical and cyberspace as "cyber-bullying" and it is to this form of bullying that I now turn.

DEFINITIONS OF CYBER-BULLYING

One of the problems I have always had with definitions of "bullying" is that they are too simplistic and therefore invited reactions, policy, and program-matic responses that failed to recognize its nuances and complexities. In the case of cyberspace, because of the range of possibilities, the fluidity with which it is possible to move from one form of technology such as e-mail, MSN, Face-book, MySpace, blogs, chat rooms, and so on to another, and the capacity for millions of people to read and participate in various forms of communication, any definition of cyber-bullying must be applied with a caveat. Cyber-bullying must be understood in the specific paradigmatic context in which it is presented.

More important, when we define a behavior, it is important to remember it as an action that takes place in a particular context, at a particular time, with various influences operating on the individual(s) who take the action. Moreover, it is the particular lens or conceptual approach that we bring to our understanding of bullying or cyber-bullying that will determine our response. I began to hint in my introduction to Chapter 1 that descriptions and definitions of reality can be deliberately framed to develop people's understanding of an issue by the words that are used to define it. So, for example, consider describing the Internet as a "Gift from the Devil" (Soloyon, 2005) or saying that the "Web ensnares teens up to eight hours a day" (Schmidt, 2006). If use of communications technology by young people is consistently described in this way, it follows that no matter how they use it, there will be a negative connotation attached to it. For example, I gave the example of the teenage boys who testified at the Azmi Jubran human rights tribunal and explained that when they call someone "gay" or a "homo" and if the expression is directed toward someone they like, then they mean it as a term of endearment. When it is against someone they dislike, then it is meant to hurt.

With so much of popular teenage discourse infiltrated with words such as "hoe" (whore) and "bitch" and quick communication codes such as "omg" ("Oh my God") that have developed using instant messaging and text messaging, teenagers are increasingly blocking out the adults in their lives. Moreover, as Lankshear and Knobel (2006) point out, kids approach cyberspace with a very different understanding of its fluidity or capacity, whereas adults tend to see cyberspace as something that can be controlled in the same way as physical space.

For example, adults might perceive that online firewalls are like brick walls that cannot be hacked through. Because adults have always had some kind of "control" over the spaces that kids occupy and over forms of knowledge young people access at home and school, they might define cyber-bullying as "antiauthority," "rampant," and "out of control." Although in the last five years, numerous studies have reported on the forms, extent, and impact of cyber-bullying, it is important to bear in mind that that these findings may help us understand only one part of the puzzle and that we ought to look at the range of influences that might tacitly condone cyber-bullying through the behavior and responses we ourselves model.

We should also be cognizant of the very fine line between youth expression that we generally accept when they interact among themselves and those that are truly harmful and offensive. Here are some definitions of cyber-bullying that illustrate the forms it takes, the tools that are used to engage in it, and ways in which it is understood to differ from traditional bullying.

It is not clear whether the term "cyber-bullying" was first coined by Canadian Bill Belsey (2005) or American lawyer Nancy Willard (2003). Belsey defined cyber-bullying as follows:

Cyber bullying involves the use of information and communication technologies such as email, cell phone and pager text messages, instant messaging, defamatory personal Web sites, and defamatory online personal polling Web sites, to support deliberate, repeated, and hostile behavior by an individual or group that is intended to harm others.

(Belsey, 2005, n. p.)

A more comprehensive, although shorter definition, is presented by Nancy Willard, director for the Center for Safe and Responsible Internet Use, who describes cyber-bullying as speech that is "defamatory, constitutes bullying, harassment, or discrimination, discloses personal information, or contains offensive, vulgar or derogatory comments" (Willard, 2003, p. 66). Remember that if we adopt this definition, the defamatory nature of the expression would have to be first established in a court of law. According to Willard, other forms of cyber-bullying can include flaming [sending derogatory messages to a person(s)], harassing and denigrating (put-downs), masquerading, outing, and excluding (Willard, 2005).

The term "cyber-bullying" describes forms of bullying that use technology. According to some reports, it is a phenomenon that children and adolescents seem increasingly to be using to harm others (Campbell, 2005), although there is also significant evidence (Media Awareness Network, 2005) that many adults are equally guilty of engaging in cyber-bullying. I provide examples of adult cyber-bullying as the discussion progresses.

There is no dearth of definitions of cyber-bullying. Elsewhere, and within the context of certain articles, I have defined peer-to-peer cyber-bullying (Shariff & Strong-Wilson, 2005) as comprising covert, psychological bullying, conveyed through the electronic mediums such as cell phones, blogs and Web sites, online chat rooms, MUD rooms (multiuser domains where individuals take on different characters), and Xangas (online personal profiles where some adolescents create lists of people they do not like).

In 2007, I would add to that definition to include social communications networks such as Facebook, YouTube, Orkut, LinkdIn, MySpace, and countless others that are surfacing on the Internet. Other researchers have defined cyber-bullying as "willful and repeated harm inflicted through the medium of electronic text" (Patchin & Hinduja, 2006). Other researchers define it as an "an aggressive, intentional act carried out by a group or individual, using electronic forms of contact, repeatedly and over time against a victim who can not easily defend him or herself" (W. J. Smith, 2004).

It might be a good idea to check the description of cyber-bullying on Wikipedia. The definitions and explanation of cyber-bullying are comprehensive and helpful because they cover a range, although not all, of cyber actions that could be included as cyber-bullying:

Cyberbullying (also spelled Cyber-bullying, Cyber bullying, or online bullying) is the term used to refer to bullying and harassment by use of electronic devises through means of e-mail, instant messaging, text messages, blogs, mobile phones, pagers, and

websites. Other terms for cyberbullying are "electronic bullying", "e-bullying," "SMS bullying," mobile bullying," "online bullying," digital bullying," or "Internet bullying."
("Wikipedia description of cyber-bullying," 2007)

Wikipedia goes on to explain that in some countries, provinces, and states, cyber-bullying is defined as a crime. As with the profile of traditional bullying presented earlier, cyber-bullying is described as follows:

[W]illful and involves recurring or repeated harm inflicted through the medium of electronic text. According to R.B. Standler, bullying intends to cause emotional distress and has no legitimate purpose to the choice of communications. Cyberbullying can be as simple as continuing to send e-mail to someone who has said they want no further contact with the sender. Cyberbullying may also include threats, sexual remarks, pejorative labels (i.e. hate speech). Cyber-bullies may publish personal contact information for their victims at websites. They may attempt to assume the identity of a victim for the purpose of publishing material in their name that defames or ridicules them.
("Wikipedia description of cyber-bullying," 2007)

These definitions all state in common the fact that communications technology tools and media are being used to engage in online bullying and that the communication is, as with general bullying, deliberate and willful, repeated and exclusionary. So the question that arises is this: Do we blame the medium or the message (McLuhan, 1964)? I would argue that the medium of cyberspace simply provides an avenue for expression of the message. As Campbell asks, "is cyber-bullying, an old problem in a new guise?" (2005, p. 68). The message is no different from that which is often expressed when bullying occurs in physical space (overtly or covertly). If we are to effectively carry out the goal of one fourteen-year-old suicide victim, Hamed Nastoh, who left a note asking his mother to educate schools and students about why bullying can be so devastating after his death, then it is critical to focus on the message, but it is also important to understand the medium so that it, too, can be used to empower learning and convey an altogether different message.

Methods used in cyber-bullying include text messaging of derogatory insults on mobile phones, with students showing the message to others before sending it to the target, sending threatening e-mails, and forwarding a confidential e-mail to all address book contacts, thus publicly humiliating the first sender. Others gang up on one student and bombard him or her with "flame" e-mails or set up a derogatory Web site dedicated to a targeted student and e-mailing others the address, inviting their comments.

In Canada, high school student David Knight lived this nightmare. David had been teased, taunted, kicked, threatened, and punched for most of his years in high school. In an interview with CBC National News (Leishman, 2002), David explained that the most devastating aspect of the bullying was the humiliation he suffered every time he logged onto the Internet. Students from his school had set up a Web site about him where they continued the threats, insults, and gossip. The derision against David spread quickly and globally. He was told by peers to check out a certain Web site originating in Thailand. To his horror, the Web site was titled, "Welcome to the page that makes fun of Dave Knight" – an extension of the Web site that was set up by his Canadian peers. David described the experience:

Rather than just some people, say 30 in a cafeteria, hearing them all yell insults at you, it's up there for 6 billion people to see. Anyone with a computer can see it... and you can't get away from it. It doesn't go away when you come home from school. It made me feel even more trapped.

(Leishman, 2002)

It took the threat of litigation against the Internet provider and David's school before the Web site was finally taken down – approximately six months after his family's initial request for removal (Leishman, 2002).

In addition, Web sites can be set up for others to vote on the biggest geek or sluttiest girl in the school (Campbell, 2005; Snider, 2004). In one instance, a video of a teenager masturbating for her boyfriend was uploaded and e-mailed to her entire class when the relationship soured (Harmon, 2004).

The previous section presented a profile of traditional bullying as either physical or psychological, and overt or covert. Although I have described it as primarily "covert," cyber-bullying can be as open, aggressive, and "overt" as other forms of psychological bullying – especially now that comments derogating teachers and persons in authority can be loaded on the Internet for everyone to see. Cyber-bullying generally takes the form of verbal and written bullying. Written forms of communication, especially online, can often be saved and reproduced, and have an element of permanence, whereas the spoken word, if not recorded, is difficult to reproduce.

As I have mentioned several times and continue to emphasize and expand on throughout this book, cyber-bullying is not restricted to children and youth. The Internet and e-mail, for example, have provided a medium for many adults to vent their anger and frustration, harass, threaten, and exploit the reputations of other adults. Some take on virtual personalities in MUD rooms and sexually harass other players. In Chapter 7, I also highlight cases involving online harassment and cyber libel against teachers by parents and introduce examples of Internet Web sites created by adults that perpetuate hate and violence.

Before presenting statistics drawing from a range of international studies to gauge the extent of technology use and cyber-bullying in various parts of the world, it is important to highlight some of the key characteristics of cyber-bullying that are not aspects of traditional bullying.

Characteristics of Cyber-Bullying

Electronic media by their nature allow for traditional forms of bullying to take on characteristics that are specific to cyberspace. Following is an overview of the various concerns related to cyber-bullying.

Anonymity

The anonymous nature of cyberspace first made it attractive to young people, especially when there is a nexus to the school, because it allows for the targeting of classmates or teachers without being easily detected (unless they are using social networking sites on which is it easier to identify those who post comments). Most cyber-bullying is anonymous because perpetrators are shielded by screen names that protect their identity. Anonymity in cyberspace adds to the challenges for schools (Harmon, 2004). Furthermore, although cyber-bullying begins anonymously in the virtual environment, it affects learning in the physical school environment. The consequences can be psychologically devastating for victims and socially detrimental for all students (Gáti, Tényi, Túry, & Wildmann, 2002). Fear of unknown cyber perpetrators among classmates and bullying that continues at school distracts all students (victims, bystanders, and perpetrators) from schoolwork. It creates a hostile physical school environment in which students feel unwelcome and unsafe. In such an atmosphere, equal opportunities to learn are greatly reduced (Devlin, 1997; Shariff & Strong-Wilson, 2005).

An Infinite Audience

A second concern, as I mentioned earlier in this chapter, is that research on general bullying finds that 30 percent of onlookers and bystanders support perpetrators instead of victims (Boulton, 1993; Salmivalli, 2001). The longer it persists, the more bystanders join in the abuse (Henderson, Hymel, Bonanno, & Davidson, 2002), creating a power imbalance between victim and perpetrators. Isolation renders victims vulnerable to continued abuse, and the cycle repeats itself. What might begin in the physical school environment as friendly banter can quickly turn into verbal bullying that continues in cyberspace as covert psychological bullying. The difference in cyberspace is that hundreds of perpetrators can get involved in the abuse, and classmates who may not engage in the bullying at school can hide behind technology to inflict the most serious abuse.

I have already used the well-known example of an abusive Web site designed to insult David Knight, which found its way into Thailand. A similar situation occurred with a Trois Rivières, Québec teenager, Ghyslain Reza, who became known worldwide as the "Star Wars Kid." Ghyslain had taped himself playing a *Star Wars* character and doing a dance with the "force be with you" sabre. He mistakenly left the tape in the media room at his school. The tape was stolen by two classmates, who uploaded the video onto a Web site. The Web site received approximately 15 million hits and more than 106 clones of the video were made. This resulted in Ghyslain becoming known as the "Star Wars Kid." He was teased everywhere he went at school. The Hollywood director of the *Star Wars* movies, George Lucas, heard about Ghyslain. The American corporate mentality kicked in, and some entrepreneurs began to produce "Star Wars Kid" memorabilia and souvenirs. At his school, students would jump up on tables and dance chanting "Star Wars Kid!" everywhere he went. His parents eventually sued the two classmates who uploaded the tape and settled out of court for approximately $360,000 Canadian in April 2006. Ghyslain had to move to another school to avoid the teasing. Although the settlement was good for Ghyslain because it took him out of the public eye, if the case had proceeded to trial, it would have been the first of its kind on cyber-bullying. Most of the court cases that are instigated for bullying and cyber-bullying seem to get settled out of court because legal costs are generally too high for parents, and school insurance companies use all kinds of delay tactics to avoid trial. Moreover, courts are reluctant to hear cases of cyber-bullying because of the definitional challenges and their concern of opening up the floodgates to litigation. David Knight's situation is a case in point. His claim was delayed for at least three years by the schools' insurers and is now under settlement negotiations.

Prevalent Sexual and Homophobic Harassment

A third concern is that sexual and homophobic harassment is emerging as a prevalent aspect of cyber-bullying, and this may be related to the gender differences in the way that males and females use the Internet and cell phone technologies. Certainly, the international findings that I discuss later are interesting in this regard.

Permanence of Expression

Fourth, online communications have a permanence and inseparability that is difficult to erase. Cellular phones are generally carried all the time, making it difficult for victims to ignore, and computers are generally used every day. Although a cell phone can be ignored, text messages and e-mails can be sent so that every time the phone or computer is turned on, the nasty messages are waiting. Many people have cell phones and need their computer for learning and work activities. Moreover, e-mails and defamatory material or modified photographs about a person on the Internet are extremely difficult to remove once posted because millions of people can download and save it immediately. These forms of expression can then be forwarded to hundreds of other people and saved on computers.

Online Social Communication Tools

Online social communications tools for preteens and teenagers such as MySpace began to surface near the beginning of the 2000s and caught on like wildfire. Especially for girls, who engage in more social and verbal forms of communication, MySpace was the perfect way to connect with friends but also exclude, harass, and demean peers. Disney has recently created a MySpace of its own to capitalize on its popularity. Until this year, incidents of cyber-bullying involving MySpace were generally restricted to peer-to-peer cases. However, with the advent of Facebook and YouTube, the world of social networking entered entirely new realms.

Facebook was launched on February 4, 2004, at Harvard University, by twenty-two-year-old Mark Zuckerberg. It was developed to be a social networking tool for Ivy League university students; within two weeks, half of Harvard students were members. By May 30, 2004, students at Stanford and Yale had joined, and by September 2005, Facebook was opened to high school students. By June 2006, the site was opened to business networks with more than 20,000 networks of employees. Within a span of three years, Facebook gained more than 19 million registered users. It is the sixth most trafficked site in the United States and 1 percent of all Internet time is spent on Facebook. com (Roher, 2007). One of its attractions is that it is a photo-sharing site on the Web. Six million photographs are uploaded daily and expected to bring Zuckerman $100 million in revenue in 2007. Yahoo offered to purchase Facebook for $1 billion and was turned down.

According to a California ethnographer, danah boyd (her legal name is in lowercase), the competition between Facebook and MySpace is based on class. In an article titled "Facebook is for 'good' kids – MySpace is for freaks" (Harris, 2007), *The Gazette* reports boyd's research that Facebook teens tend to be from families who are wealthier and emphasize a college education, are predominantly white, take honors classes, and "live in a world dictated by after school activities," whereas the young people who communicate on MySpace are described as "geeks, freaks, or queers" from lower-income families and are expected to get jobs after graduating from Grade 12. The reasons for this divide according to boyd is that people tend to gravitate to social groups where they feel most comfortable. This was verified in a survey by Comscore (an Internet data collection company) that found almost 50 percent of Facebook users – compared with the overall Web average of 40 percent – live in households in which the annual income is higher than $75,000 U.S. The media article notes that although boyd's findings were presented as a "blog essay" rather than an academic article, her reputation as a leading analyst of online behavior makes her study convincing.

I agree with other academics who found boyd's study interesting because it identifies the online subtleties of discrimination that are difficult to recognize. In light of this study, it is not surprising that the U.S. military prevented their soldiers from accessing MySpace but allowed access to Facebook, which is preferred by officers.

In a recent interview, boyd described MySpace and Facebook as follows:

MySpace and Facebook are social network sites where individuals create profiles and link to others ("friends") within the system. The profile serves as an individual's digital representation (similar to homepages) of their tastes, fashion, and identity. In crafting this profile, individuals upload photos, indicate interests, list favorite musicians and describe themselves textually and through associated media. The social network feature allows participants to link themselves to others within the system, revealing their affiliations and peer group. These sites also allow friends to comment on each other's profiles. Structurally, social network sites are a cross between a year book and a community website.

These sites also provide numerous communication tools. Both have a messaging system similar to email; MySpace also has a bulletin board where people can post messages that all friends can read and a blogging service where people can post entries for either friends or the public at large. When youth login, their first task is typically to check messages in order to see who has written to them. While email is still used to communicate with adults and authorities, MySpace is the primary asynchronous communication tool for teens. After checking personal messages, youth check friend additions, bulletins board posts, event announcements and new blog posts by friends. They visit their friends' pages to see new photos or check out each other's comments. The vast majority of social network site use amongst youth does not involve surfing to strangers' profiles, but engaging more locally with known friends and acquaintances.

(boyd & Jenkins, 2006)

According to boyd, MySpace has more than 78 million registered accounts, whereas Facebook has approximately 8 million. Although more than 85 percent of college students participate on Facebook if it exists on their campus, she explains that MySpace is a cultural requirement for American high school students. She quotes one teenager as saying, "If you're not on MySpace, you don't exist" (boyd & Jenkins, 2006). Not all MySpace users are teenagers, but most American teenagers have MySpace accounts.

boyd explains that these sites play a key role in contemporary youth culture:

These sites play a key role in youth culture because they give youth a space to hang out amongst friends and peers, share cultural artifacts (like links to funny websites, comments about TV shows) and work out an image of how they see themselves. They also serve as digital publics, substituting for the types of publics that most adults took for granted growing up, but are now inaccessible for many people – neighborhood basketball courts, malls, parks, etc. and allow them spaces *where they can escape adult culture.*

(boyd & Jenkins, 2006; emphasis added)

I ask readers to make note of boyd's remarks because they are important to my discussion of how we supervise student spaces in Chapter 5.

Because of its more elitist status and the fact that its enrollment is popular with so-called brighter and more educated youngsters, prospective employers have begun to check applicant's profiles on Facebook to see what kinds of friends they have, how much they drink (as evidenced by photographs of themselves either posted or tagged by friends), what kinds of personal conversations they have with friends on their walls, how they generally dress and behave, and so on (Sankey, 2007).

As more teens join Facebook, this social networking Web site has run into problems relating to high school and middle school students posting antiauthority cyber expression about teachers and school officials. What is surprising is that many of the kids who post the online comments argue that their conversations should not be accessed by adults (even if those adults are on Facebook and can see their postings through other people's profiles). This fuels the debate about private and public spaces, and students' arguments that they are not "willfully bullying" their teachers but simply having conversations among themselves that are not meant for their teachers' or school officials' eyes. They argue that they do not intend to harass, threaten, and generally bully their teachers and that they have every right to a free conversation. I return to an analysis of these issues later on in the book. In the meantime, other networks, such as YouTube, are also drawing their share of problems.

YouTube allows for the downloading of videos for all to see. Internationally, YouTube has caught on as a site where all kinds of videotapes can be taken of teachers and other victims. In some cases, videotapes are modified and placed on YouTube. Examples include videotaping student fights, filming peers undressing in gym locker rooms and washrooms, filming angry teachers in classrooms, and students dancing at a school dance (Roher, 1997).

Other social networking tools include Orkut, the equivalent of MySpace in India, and Freevote.com. Using Freevote.com, students can set up a Web page for an individual school that permits students to vote on issues at their school. Although the philosophy is positive, this site also allows students to make personal, degrading, and offensive anonymous comments about others. Similarly, RateMyTeacher.com and RateMyProfessor.com sometimes invite vitriolic comments when students are angry with teachers or professors for a variety of reasons. Bedo.com is popular in New Zealand, Australia, Britain, and Ireland, and contains categories such as "people search," "background check," "find friends," "find people," "chat room," "black dating," "photo album," and "on-line photo albums." Although it is important that the Web site has background checks, Bedo has also had its share of young people engaging in cyber-bullying.

These online social networking tools are both public and private to a limited extent, opening up important debates about which stakeholders have the authority (and responsibility) to intervene in cyberspace to monitor young people's social communications. The jury is still out on this issue as the courts have yet to provide clear direction on these issues. The social communications networks present an exception to the anonymity of cyber-bullying because the names of those who post comments can be made visible and accessed by others who join the same network. Because of the overwhelming global reaction to these social communication networks, I deal with them in upcoming chapters through detailed analysis, because it is through these issues that we can sift through and tease out some of the boundaries of responsibility which at present remain unclear.

Prevalence of Sexual and Homophobic Harassment

In 2005, I wrote several articles and book chapters with a graduate student, Rachel Gouin, on the prevalence of sexual and homophobic harassment in cyberspace. I reiterate here some of the findings we reported. This form of cyber-bullying is largely influenced by both biological (hormonal and prepubescent influences) and environmental (gender socialization) factors.

The research suggests that although both genders engage in cyber-bullying, there are differences between how they do so (Chu, 2005; Li, 2005). It has been argued that children who engage in any form of bullying are victims. They are influenced by biological and environmental forces, including intersecting and interlocking systemic barriers of oppression based on race, gender, sexual orientation, (dis)abilities, cultural hegemony, androcentrism, and Eurocentrism that continues to pervade many institutions including schools and courts (Razack, 1998; Shariff, 2003). I expand on these influences in Chapter 5.

Numerous scholars have written about online gender harassment (Brail, 1996; Finn, 2004; Gáti et al., 2002; Herring, 2002; McCormick & Leonard, 1996). Some have outlined categories such as gender harassment, unwanted sexual attention, and sexual coercion (Barak, 2005). Others have written about virtual rape (Dibbell, 1993; MacKinnon, 2001), cyberstalking (Adam, 2001, 2002; Spitzberg & Hoobler, 2002; Tavani & Grodzinsky, 2002), identity theft (Finn & Banach, 2000), cyber bullying (Shariff, 2004; Ybarra & Mitchell, 2004a, 2004b), and cyber violence more generally (Herring, 2002). The studies highlighted in the sections that follow illuminate ways in which gender-based cyber-bullying or violence differs from and is linked to what occurs in physical (nonvirtual) space.

Female Victims

Barak (2005) defines three categories of sexual harassment:

1. gender harassment,
2. unwanted sexual attention, and
3. sexual coercion.

She divides the first category into four subcategories:

1. active verbal sexual harassment, which includes offensive sexual messages from harasser to victim, gender-humiliating comments, and sexual remarks;
2. passive verbal sexual harassment, which includes offensive nicknames and online identities (such as wetpussy, xlargetool);
3. active graphic gender harassment, which includes unwanted erotic and pornographic content through mail or posting them in online environments; and
4. passive graphic gender harassment, including pictures and movies published on pornographic sites (such as forced pop-up windows).

The second category, unwanted sexual attention, "refers to uninvited behaviors that explicitly communicate sexual desires or intensions toward another individual" (Barak, 2005, p. 78). Finally, sexual coercion entails the use of various online means to pressure the victim into sexual cooperation. Even though the use of force is not possible online, the *threats can be perceived by the victim as being as realistic as a face to face situation.* This is illustrated by the telephone threat that caused Canadian teenager Dawn Marie Wesley to commit suicide. The words "You're f.....g dead!" by a classmate caused her to believe real harm would come to her. Her perpetrator was convicted of criminal harassment because the court observed that perceived harm by the victim amounts to the same thing as actual harm (Shariff, 2004).

This perspective that electronic threats are as real or even more frightening than those made face-to-face is supported by Herring (2002), who explains that online behavior that leads to assault against the physical, psychological, or emotional well-being of an individual or group in effect constitutes a form of violence. She distinguishes four types of cyber violence:

1. online contact leading to offline abuse (misrepresentation leading to fraud, theft, unwanted sexual contact);
2. cyber-stalking, which comprises online monitoring or tracking of users' actions with criminal intent;
3. online harassment, which consists of unwanted, repeated, and deliberate threats, abuses, and alarms; and
4. degrading online representations of women through words or images that invite disrespect or put-downs.

Adam (2001) observes that cyber violence studies disclose that the majority of perpetrators are men and the majority of victims are women. He reports that as many as one in three girls reported having been harassed online in 2001 alone. Among children, girls appear to be targeted twice as much as boys (Finkelhor, Mitchell, & Wolak, 2000).

According to Herring (2002), 25 percent of Internet users aged ten to seventeen were exposed to unwanted pornographic images in the past year. Eight percent of the images involved violence, in addition to sex and nudity. The Alberta study of middle school children referred to earlier (Li, 2005) disclosed that boys owned up to cyber-bullying more frequently and girls were more frequently victimized. Furthermore, Mitchell et al. (2001, as cited in Barak, 2005), in a survey of American teenagers, found that 19 percent of these youths (mostly older girls) had experienced at least one sexual solicitation online in the preceding year.

Female Perpetrators

Although girls may be more likely targets of cyber violence because of their location along a hierarchy of power, adolescent girls are increasingly surfacing as active instigators of cyber-bullying. Although Ybarra and Mitchell (2004a) found that males and females were equally likely to report having harassed someone online, a recent study of 3,700 adolescents (Kowalski, as cited in Chu, 2005) found that in a two-month period, 17 percent of the girls surveyed confessed to online bullying compared to 10 percent of the boys. Given that girls aged twelve to eighteen have been found to spend at least 74 percent of their time on chat rooms or instant messaging (Berson, Berson, & Ferron, 2002) this is not surprising. It is even less surprising when considered in the context of the biological and environmental (socializing) influences that are addressed in Chapter 4.

Given that preliminary research on cyber-bullying discloses a significant amount of sexual harassment and gender differences in the way Internet harassment is carried out, we cannot ignore role of gender and its manifestations of online violence. Later, I present examples and statistics that affect and motivate young men and women and how this in turn fosters affects learning environments (both physical and virtual). These examples inform my discussion relating to judicial and legislative responses to legal claims of sexual harassment in cyberspace in later chapters. For now, it is important to note that although girls and women appear to be the primary targets in cyberspace, sufficient research suggests that girls internationally are increasingly found to perpetrate cyber-bullying in groups and are more frequent users of social networking tools.

Male Targets and Perpetrators

Sexual orientation also features heavily in general and cyber-bullying. Cases of general bullying include the devastating suicide of Hamed Nastoh and the pouring of acid and four-year-long homophobic bullying of Azmi Jubran by his classmates at Handsworth High School. In Azmi's case, his perpetrators testified at the human rights tribunal that when friends are teased about being gay, it is a term of endearment; however, when the insult is directed at someone who is disliked, the words are meant to hurt. Given the persistent, drawn-out, and deliberate nature of homophobic bullying that Azmi Jubran and David Knight endured, the words were meant to hurt. In David Knight's case, he was described as a homosexual pedophile with invitations to an infinite audience to write insults and comments below his photograph.

A study conducted by Tolman et al. (2001) at the middle school level in the United States made important observations relating to sexual harassment and homophobic bullying at the adolescent level. What they found was that sexual harassment significantly increased at preadolescence and adolescence. It was largely perpetuated by male students, who also engaged in homophobic bullying of their less aggressive male peers. Tolman et al. suggest two reasons – (1) raging hormones and interest in females and (2) the male adolescents' need to prove their manhood. In doing so, they engage in sexual harassment of females and put down males who are either perceived to be competitors or perceived to have more "feminine" characteristics, resulting in the homophobic bullying.

Intersecting Forms of Discrimination

To complicate matters, in each of the cases discussed here, it is not simply sexual orientation that invites the derision. Each of the victims mentioned were teased for something else as well – in Hamed and Azmi's case, it was the fact that they were also of Iranian heritage, although both were born in Canada. In David Knight's case, his intelligence and good looks might have played a role. In Ghyslain Reza's case, his weight certainly played a role.

CONCLUSION

The nature and forms of bullying and cyber-bullying in this chapter should provide readers with a general appreciation that there are many factors to consider when we talk about bullying. These factors can affect the way that the law is interpreted and applied. I have not yet dealt with biological and socializing influences on sexual and homophobic forms of harassment. I integrate that research into my discussions of the various forms of cyber-bullying that emerge through social networking sites and student-created Web sites. It is important to remember that student expression is not invented by young people. They draw it from a social context that is largely created by adults. Children and teenagers are influenced by discriminatory attitudes, hegemonic perspectives, and androcentric and homophobic forms of language that are embedded in generations of language. All of these play themselves out in adverse ways when they are unleashed in cyberspace.

I move now to consider in legal terms, the antiauthority forms of expression that are causing so much concern among teachers' unions and governmental authorities.

REFERENCES

Adam, A. (2001). Cyberstalking: Gender and computer ethics. In E. Green & A. Adam (Eds.), *Virtual gender: Technology, consumption and identity* (pp. 209–224). New York: Routledge.

Adam, A. (2002). Cyberstalking and internet pornography: Gender and the gaze. *Ethics and Information Technology, 4,* 133–142.

Agence France Presse. (2007, April 18). Foreign students don't fear backlash. *Gazette* (Montreal), p. A4.

Artz, S. (1998). *Sex, power & the violent school girl.* Toronto: Trifolium Books.

Artz, S., & Riecken, T. (1997). What, so what, then what? The gender gap in school-based violence and its implications for child and youth care practice. *Child & Youth Care Forum, 26,* 291–303.

Ashford, M. W. (1996). *Boredom as a neglected issue in violence prevention programs in schools.* Unpublished doctoral dissertation, Simon Fraser University, Burnaby, British Columbia, Canada.

Barak, A. (2005). Sexual harassment on the Internet. *Social Science Computer Review, 23,* 77–92.

Belsey, B. (2005). *Internet usage: Facts and news*. Retrieved July 8, 2005, from http://www.cyberbullying. ca/facts_st.html

Berson, I. R., Berson, M. J., & Ferron, J. M. (2002). Emerging risks of violence in the digital age: Lessons for educators from an online study of adolescent girls in the United States. *Journal of School Violence, 1*(2), 51–71.

Besag, V. E. (1989). *Bullies and victims in schools: A guide to understanding and management*. Milton Keynes, England: Open University Press.

Boulton, M. (1993). A comparison of adults' and children's abilities to distinguish between aggressive and playful fighting in middle school pupils. Implications for playground supervision and behavior management. *Educational Studies, 19*, 193–203.

Boulton, M., & Hawker, D. (1997). Verbal bullying: The myth of "sticks and stones." In D. Tattum & G. Herbert (Eds.), *Bullying: Home, school and community* (pp. 53–63). London: David Fulton.

boyd, d., & Jenkins, H. (2006, May 26). MySpace and Deleting Online Predators Act (DOPA) [Electronic version]. *MIT Tech Talk*. Retrieved August 13, 2007, from http://www.danah.org/papers/MySpaceDOPA.html.

Brail, S. (1996). The price of admission: Harassment and free speech in the wild, wild west. In L. Cherny & E. R. Weise (Eds.), *Wired_women: Gender and new realities in cyberspace*. Toronto: Seal Press.

Campbell, M. (2005). Cyberbullying: An old problem in a new guise? *Australian Journal of Guidance and Counseling, 15*, 68–76.

Chu, J. (2005, August 8). You wanna take this online? Cyberspace is the 21st century bully's playground where girls play rougher than boys. *Time, Canadian Edition*, 42–43.

Crick, N. R., Grotpeter, J. K., & Bigbee, M. A. (2002). Relationally and physically aggressive children's intent attributions and feelings of distress for relational and instrumental peer provocations. *Child Development, 73*, 1134–1142.

Dedman, B. (2000, October 16). Schools may miss mark on preventing violence [Electronic version]. *Chicago Sun-Times*. Retrieved August 12, 2007, from http://www.ustreas.gov/usss/ntac/chicago_sun/shoot16.htm.

Dei, G. S. (1997). Race and the production of identity in the schooling experiences of African-Canadian youth. *Discourse Studies in the Cultural Politics of Education, 18*, 241–257.

Devlin, A. (1997). Offenders at school: Links between school failure and aggressive behaviour. In D. Tattum & H. Graham (Eds.), *Bullying: Home, school and community* (pp. 149–158). London: David Fulton.

Dibbell, J. (1993, December 21). A rape in cyberspace or how an evil clown, a Haitian trickster spirit, two wizards, and a cast of dozens turned a database into a society. *Village Voice, 38*, 36–42.

DiGiulio, R. C. (2001). *Educate, mediate, or litigate? What teachers, parents, and administrators must do about student behavior*. Thousand Oaks, CA: Corwin Press.

Dolmage, W. R. (2000). Lies, damned lies and statistics: The media's treatment of youth violence. *Education & Law Journal, 10*, 1–46.

Finkelhor, D., Mitchell, K., & Wolak, J. (2000). *Online victimization: A report on the nation's youth*. Retrieved August 12, 2007, from http://www.unh.edu/ccrc/pdf/Victimization_Online_Survey.pdf.

Finn, J. (2004). A survey of online harassment at a university campus. *Journal of Interpersonal Violence, 19*, 468–483.

Finn, J., & Banach, M. (2000). Victimization online: The downside of seeking human services for women on the Internet. *Cyberpsychology & Behavior, 3*(5), 785–796.

Gáti, A., Tényi, T., Túry, F., & Wildmann, M. (2002). Anorexia nervosa following sexual harassment on the Internet: A case report. *International Journal of Eating Disorders, 31*, 474–477.

Genta, M. L., Menesini, E., Fonzi, A., Costabile, A., & Smith, P. K. (1996). Bullies and victims in schools in central and southern Italy. *European Journal of Psychology of Education, 11*, 97–110.

Glover, D., Cartwright, N., & Gleeson, D. (1998). *Towards bully-free schools.* Buckingham/Philadelphia: Open University Press.

Hall, M. T. (1999). *Administrative discretion and youth violence in schools: An analysis.* Unpublished doctoral dissertation, Simon Fraser University, Burnaby, Canada.

Handa, S. (1997). *Caught between omissions: Exploring "culture conflict" among second generation South Asian women in Canada.* Unpublished doctoral dissertation, University of Toronto, Canada.

Harmon, A. (2004, August 24). Internet gives teenage bullies weapons to wound from afar [Electronic version]. *New York Times.* Retrieved August 26, 2004, from http://www.nytimes.com./2004/08/26/education.

Harris, M. (2007, June 29). Facebook is for "good" kids – MySpace is for freaks. *Gazette* (Montreal).

Harris, S., & Petrie, G. (2002). A study of bullying in the middle school. *National Association of Secondary School Principals (NASSP) Bulletin, 86*, 42–53.

Haynie, D. L., Nansel, T. R., Eitel, P., Crump, A. D., Saylor, K., Yu, K., et al. (2001). Bullies, victims, and bully/victims: Distinct groups of at-risk youth. *Journal of Early Adolescence, 21*, 29–49.

Henderson, N. R., Hymel, S., Bonanno, R. A., & Davidson, K. (2002). *Bullying as a normal part of school life: Early adolescents' perspectives on bullying & peer harassment.* Paper presented at the Safe Schools Safe Communities Conference (Poster Session), Vancouver, Canada, June, 2002.

Herring, S. C. (2002). Cybervioloence: Recognizing and resisting abuse in online environments. *Asian Women, 14*, 187–212.

Hodges, E. V. E., & Perry, D. G. (1996). Victims of peer abuse: An overview. *Reclaiming Children and Youth: Journal of Emotional and Behavioral Problems, 5*, 23–28.

Hoover, J. H., & Olsen, G. W. (2001). *Teasing and harassment: The frames and scripts approach for teachers and parents.* Bloomington, IN: National Educational Service.

Janoviček, N. (2001). *Reducing crime and victimization: A service provider's report.* Burnaby, BC: Simon Fraser University, prepared for the Feminist Research, Education, Development and Action Centre.

Jiwani, Y. (1997). *Reena Virk: The Erasure of Race? Kinesis.* Vancouver, BC: FREDA Centre for Research on Violence Against Immigrant and Refugee Girls and Women Burnaby, BC: Simon Fraser University.

Jiwani, Y. (2001). *Mapping violence: A work in progress.* Vancouver, Canada: Feminist Research, Education, Development and Action Centre, Simon Fraser University.

Juvonen, J., & Graham, S. (2001). *Peer harassment in school: The plight of the vulnerable and victimized.* New York/ London: Guilford Press.

Katch, J. (2001). *Under deadman's skin: Discovering the meaning of children's violent play.* Boston: Beacon Press.

Kochenderfer-Ladd, B., & Wardrop, J. L. (2001). Chronicity and instability of children's peer victimization experiences as predictors of loneliness and social satisfaction trajectories. *Child Development, 72*, 134–151.

Kumpulainen, K., Rasanen, E., & Henttonen, I. (1999). Children involved in bullying: Psychological disturbances and the persistence of the involvement. *Child Abuse & Neglect: The International Journal, 23*(12), 1253–1262.

Kumpulainen, K., Rasanen, E., Henttonen, I., Almqvist, F., Kresanov, K., Sirkka-Liisa, L., et al. (1998). Bullying and psychiatric symptoms among elementary school-age children. *Child Abuse & Neglect: The International Journal,* 705–717.

Lankshear, C., & Knobel, M. (2006). *New literacies: Everyday practices and classroom learning* (2nd ed.). Maidenhead, England /New York: Open University Press.

Leishman, J. (2002, October 10). Cyber-bullying: The Internet is the latest weapon in a bully's arsenal [Electronic version]. *CBC News. The National.* Retrieved January 27, 2003, from http://cbc.ca/news/national/news/cyberbullying/index.html.

Li, Q. (2005). *Cyber-bullying in schools: The nature and extent of adolescents' experience.* Paper presented at the American Education Research Association (AERA) Conference, Montreal, April, 2005.

Limber, S. P., & Small, M. A. (2003). State laws and policies to address bullying in schools. *School Psychology Review, 32*, 445–455.

Ma, X. (2001). Bullying and being bullied: To what extent are bullies also victims? *American Educational Research Journal, 38*, 351–370.

MacKinnon, R. (2001). Virtual rape. *Journal of Computer Mediated Communication,* 2(4), n.p.

McCarthy, P., Rylance, J., Bennet, R., & Zimmermann, H. (2001). *Bullying from the Backyard to Boardroom* (2nd ed.). Leichhardt, Australia: Federation Press.

McCormick, N., & Leonard, J. (1996). Gender and sexuality in the cyberspace frontier. *Women & Therapy, 19*, 109–119.

McLuhan, M. (1964). *Understanding media: The extensions of man.* New York: Mentor.

Media Awareness Network. (2005). Kids' online activities: Key findings [Electronic version]. *Young Canadians in a wired world: Key findings.* Retrieved January 10, 2006, from http://www.media-awareness.ca/english/resources/special_initiatives/survey_resources/students_survey/key_findings/kids_online_key_findings.cfm.

Mynard, H., Joseph, S., & Alexander, J. (2000). Peer victimisation and post traumatic stress in adolescents. *Personality and Individual Differences, 29*, 815–821.

Nansel, T., Overpeck, M., Pilla, R. S., Simons-Morton, B., & Scheidt, P. (2001). Bullying behaviors among U.S. youth: Prevalence and association with psychosocial adjustment. *Journal of the American Medical Association, 285*, 2094–2100.

National Crime Prevention Council. (1997). *Report on bullying.* Retrieved July 24, 2005, from http://www.crime-prevention.org.

O'Connell, P., Pepler, D., & Craig, W. (1999). Peer involvement in bullying: Insights and challenges for intervention. *Journal of Adolescence, 22*, 437–452.

O'Moore, A. M., & Hillery, B. (1991). What do teachers need to know? In M. Elliott (Ed.), *Bullying* (pp. 56–69). Harlow, England: Longman.

Olweus, D. (1978). *Aggression in the schools: Bullies and whipping boys.* Washington, D.C./New York: Hemisphere, distributed solely by Halsted Press.

Olweus, D. (1991). Bully/victim problems among school children. Basic facts and effects of a school based intervention program. In D. J. Pepler & K. H. Rubin (Eds.), *The development and treatment of childhood aggression.* Hillsdale, NJ: Erlbaum.

Olweus, D. (1993). *Bullying at school: What we know and what we can do.* Oxford, England/Cambridge, MA: Blackwell.

Olweus, D. (2001). Peer harassment: A critical analysis and some important issues (introduction). In J. Juvonen & S. Graham (Eds.), *Peer harassment in school: The plight of the vulnerable and vicitmized* (pp. 3–20). New York: Guildford Press.

Patchin, J., & Hinduja, S. (2006). Bullies move beyond the schoolyard: A preliminary look at cyberbullying. *Youth Violence and Juvenile Justice, 4*(2), 148–169.

Pellegrini, A. D., & Bartini, M. (2000). A longitudinal study of bullying, victimization, and peer affiliation during the transition from primary school to middle school. *American Educational Research Journal, 37,* 699–725.

Pepler, D., & Craig, W. (1997). *Bullying: Research and interventions. Youth update.* Oakville, Canada: Institute for the Study of Antisocial Youth.

Perry, D. G., Williard, J. C., & Perry, L. C. (1990). Peers' perceptions of the consequences that victimized children provide aggressors. *Child Development, 61,* 1310–1325.

Rauste-Von Wright, M. (1992). The function of aggression in the life process of adolescents. In A. Fraczek & H. Zumkley (Eds.), *Socialization and aggression* (pp. 185–199). Berlin: Springer-Verlay.

Razack, S. (1998). *Looking white people in the eye: Gender, race, and culture in courtrooms and classrooms.* Toronto: University of Toronto Press.

Rigby, K. (1997). Reflections on *Tom Brown's schooldays* and the problem of bullying today. *Australian Journal of Social Science, 4,* 85–96.

Rigby, K. (2001). Health consequences of bullying and its prevention in schools. In J. Juvonen & S. Graham (Eds.), *Peer harassment in school: The plight of the vulnerable and victimized* (pp. 310–331). New York/London: Guilford Press.

Rigby, K. (2002). *How successful are anti-bullying programs for schools?* Paper presented at the Australian Institute of Criminology (invited) in conjunction with the Department of Education, Employment and Training, Victoria and Crime Prevention, Victoria, Melbourne.

Roher, E. (1997). *An educator's guide to violence in schools.* Toronto: Canada Law Books.

Roher, E. (2007). *Intimidation.com: Dealing with cyberbullying.* Paper presented at the CAPSLE Conference, Vancouver, BC.

Salmivalli, C. (1999). Participant role approach to school bullying: Implications for intervention. *Journal of Adolescence, 22,* 453–459.

Salmivalli, C. (2001). Group view on victimization: Empirical findings and their implications. In J. Juvonen & S. Graham (Eds.), *Peer harassment in school: The plight of the vulnerable and victimized* (pp. 398–419). New York/London: Guilford Press.

Salmivalli, C., Lagerspetz, K., Björqvist, K., Österman, K., & Kaukiainen, A. (1996). Bullying as a group process: Participant roles and their relations to social status within the group. *Aggressive Behavior, 22,* 1–15.

Sankey, D. (2007, July 18). Beware: Your prospective boss could see you naked on the Net. *Gazette* (Montreal), p. B6.

Schmidt, S. (2006, November 15). Web ensnares teens up to eight hours a day; Instant messages average 40 a day. *Gazette* (Montreal), p. A14.

Schuster, B. (2001). Rejection and victimization by peers: Social perception and social behavior mechanisms. In J. Juvonen & S. Graham (Eds.), *Peer harassment in school: The plight of the vulnerable and victimized.* New York: Guilford Press.

Schwartz, D., Dodge, K., & Coie, J. (1993). The emergence of chronic peer victimization. *Child Development, 64,* 1755–1772.

Schwartz, D., Dodge, K., Pettit, G. S., & Bates, J. E. (1997). The early socialization of aggressive victims of bullying. *Child Development, 68*(4), 665–675.

Sears, J. T. (1993). Responding to the sexual diversity of faculty and students: Sexual praxis and the critically reflective administrator. In C. A. Capper (Ed.), *Educational administration in a pluralistic society* (pp. xiv). Albany: State University of New York Press.

Séguin, R. (2002, November 21). Quebec youth face extortion from peers, survey finds. *Globe and Mail,* p. A8.

Shariff, S. (2003). *A system on trial: Identifying legal standards for educational, ethical and legally defensible approaches to bullying in schools.* Unpublished doctoral dissertation, Simon Fraser University, Burnaby, Canada.

Shariff, S. (2004). Keeping schools out of court: Legally defensible models of leadership to reduce cyber-bullying. Educational forum. *Delta Kappa Pi, 68,* 222–223.

Shariff, S. (2008). *Cyber-bullying: Issues and solutions for the school, the classroom, and the home.* Abington, England: Routledge (Taylor and Francis Group).

Shariff, S., & Strong-Wilson, T. (2005). Bullying and new technologies: What can teachers do to foster socially responsible discourse in the physical and virtual school environments? In J. Kincheloe (Ed.), *Classroom teaching: An introduction* (pp. 219–240). New York: Peter Lang.

Simpson, J. A., & Weiner, E. S. C. (Eds.). (1989). *The Oxford English dictionary* (Vol. 2). Oxford: Clarendon Press/Oxford University Press.

Slee, P. T. (1995). Peer victimization and its relationship to depression among Australian primary school students. *Personality and Individual Differences, 18,* 57–62.

Slee, P. T., & Rigby, K. (1993). Australian school children's self-appraisal of interpersonal relations: The bullying experience. *Child Psychiatry and Human Development, 23,* 272–283.

Smith, D. J. (1995). Youth crime and conduct disorders: Trends, patterns and causal explanations. In M. Rutter & D. J. Smith (Eds.), *Psychosocial disorders in young people: Time trends and their causes* (pp. 389–489). Chichester, England/New York: Published for Academia Europaea by Wiley.

Smith, P. K., & Sharp, S. (1994). *School bullying: Insights and perspectives.* London/New York: Routledge.

Smith, P. K., & Shu, S. (2000). What good schools can do about bullying: Findings from a survey in English schools after a decade of research and action. *Childhood, 7,* 193–212.

Smith, W. J. (2004). Balancing security and human rights: Quebec schools between past and future. *Education & Law Journal, 14,* 99–136.

Snider, M. (2004, May 24). Stalked by a cyberbully. *Maclean's, 117,* 76.

Soloyon, C. (2005, February 2). A gift from the devil: Worry about on-line activities. *Gazette* (Montreal), p. A2.

Spitzberg, B., & Hoobler, G. (2002). Cyberstalking and the technologies of interpersonal terrorism. *New Media & Society, 4,* 71–92.

Stein, N. (1991). It happens here, too: Sexual harassment in the school. *Education Week, 11*(13), 32.

Stein, N. (1995). Sexual harassment in K–12 schools: The public performance of gendered violence. *Harvard Educational Review: Special Issue: Violence and Youth, 65*(2), 145–162.

Stein, N. (1999). *Classrooms and courtrooms: Facing sexual harassment in K–12 schools.* New York: Teachers College Press.

Suler, J. R., & Philips, W. L. (1998). The bad boys of cyberspace: Deviant behavior in a multimedia chat community. *Cyberpsychology & Behavior, 1*, 275–294

Tanner, J. (1996). *Teenage troubles: Youth and deviance in Canada.* Toronto: Nelson Canada.

Tattum, D. P. (1997). Developing a programme to reduce bullying in young offenders' institutions. In D. Tattum & H. Graham (Eds.), *Bullying: Home, school and community* (pp. 159–172). London: David Fulton.

Tattum, D. P., & Herbert, G. (1993). *Countering bullying: Initiatives by schools and local authorities.* Staffordshire, England: Trentham Books.

Tavani, H., & Grodzinsky, F. (2002). Cyberstalking, personal privacy, and moral responsibility. *Ethics and Information Technology, 4*, 123–132.

Tolman, D. L., Spencer, R., Rosen-Reynoso, M., & Porches, M. (2001). *"He's the man!" Gender ideologies and early adolescents' experiences with sexual harassment.* Paper presented at the American Educational Researchers Association (AERA) Conference, Seattle, WA, April.

Tremblay, R. E. (1991). Aggression, pro-social behaviour and gender: Three magic words but no magic wand. In D. L. Pepler & H. K. Rubin (Eds.), *The development and treatment of childhood aggression* (pp. 71–77). Hillsdale, NJ: Erlbaum.

Wason-Ellam, L. (1996). Voices from the shadows. In J. R. Epp & A. M. Watkinson (Eds.), *Systemic violence: How schools hurt children* (pp. 93–104). London: Falmer Press.

Welsh, D. M. (1997–1998). Limiting liability through education: Do school districts have a responsibility to teach students about peer sexual harassment? *Journal of Gender and the Law, 6*, 165–197.

Whitney, I., & Smith, P. K. (1993). A survey of the nature and extent of bullying in junior/middle and secondary schools. *Educational Research, 35*, 3–25.

Wikipedia description of cyber-bullying. (2007). Retrieved May 10, 2007, from http://en.wikipedia.org/wiki/Cyberbullying

Willard, N. (2003). Off-campus, harmful online student speech. *Journal of School Violence, 1*, 65–93.

Willard, N. (2005). *Educator's guide to cyber bullying: Addressing the harm caused by online social cruelty* [Electronic version]. Retrieved December 10, 2005, from http://www.cyberbully.org.

Ybarra, M. L., & Mitchell, K. J. K. (2004a). Online aggressor/targets, aggressors and targets: A comparison of associated youth characteristics. *Journal of Child Psychology and Psychiatry, 45*, 1308–1316.

Ybarra, M. L., & Mitchell, K. J. K. (2004b). Youth engaging in online harassment: Associations with caregiver-child relationships, Internet use, and personal characteristics. *Journal of Adolescence, 27*, 319–336.

Zubrick, S. R., Silburn, S. R., Teoh, H. J., Carlton, J., Shepherd, C., & Lawrence, D. (1997). *Western Australian child health survey: Education, health and competency catalogue 4305.5.* Perth: Australian Bureau of Statistics.

CHAPTER THREE

Cyber Libel or Criminal Harassment: When Do Kids Cross the Line?

Cyberlibel is at such an embryonic stage that conclusions would be both presumptuous and overridden almost immediately by technological advances. Consequently, we feel it is more appropriate to describe [it] . . . as crystal ball gazing.

(Potts & Harris, 2004)

A good reputation is closely related to the innate worthiness and dignity of the individual. It is an attribute that must, just as much as freedom of expression, be protected by society's law. . . . Democracy has always recognized and cherished the fundamental importance of an individual. . . . The reputation tarnished by libel can seldom regain its former lustre. A democratic society therefore, has an interest in ensuring that its members can enjoy and protect their good reputation so long as it is merited.

(*Hill v. Church of Scientology of Toronto*, 1995)

INTRODUCTION

The introductory quotes illustrate the enormous legal dilemmas and concerns that have emerged with the advent of technologies. Teachers, school and government officials, parents, and students who have been victims of demeaning online cyber expression are naturally concerned about their hard-earned reputations. In the case of teachers, student online postings that accuse them of being bad teachers or pedophiles can impact their self-esteem – and even the possibility of finding employment or seeking promotions. Because teachers are in such a position of fiduciary authority vis-à-vis children, school boards may not risk hiring them if there is any doubt about their ability to take on those positions responsibly. Hence, many teachers are asking whether the solutions lie in litigation. If this avenue is adopted, will it in fact make any difference? Moreover, our systems of common law and *stare decisis* (adherence to precedent) have been largely based on traditional responses that worked when the Internet did not exist. Judges who developed many of the legal doctrines at least a century ago would never have dreamed there would come a day when so much expression that might be deemed libelous or defamatory would take place every second, at global levels. These doctrines nonetheless continue to inform legal tests that contemporary judges use to adjudicate defamation and libel decisions. Nor would they have foreseen the permanency and persistence of such expression or the infinite audiences that would gain access to such expression. Although culturally in the West, it may be seen as expeditious to launch lawsuits against cyber offenders, the effectiveness of such an exercise is yet to be determined. Moreover, many judicial systems are already burdened with heavy backlogs and case loads. My doctoral research on the legal obligations of schools disclosed that courts set high thresholds even in cases of egregious physical harm in schools because they want to avoid the floodgates to litigation (Shariff, 2003). As American lawyer David H. Donaldson observes:

We know that as the Internet grows, there will be more and more lawsuits involving libel and defamation.... The only question is if the number of cases will grow steadily or if there will be an explosion of lawsuits all at once.

(Donaldson, as quoted in Potts, 2004a)

Educators and policy makers need to understand how the law of libel and slander might help them, but they also need to realize its enormous complexities and limitations, particularly when applied in the context of the Internet. In this chapter, I address some of the legal considerations that arise by reviewing landmark cases in Canada and the United States. Before doing that, however, I believe it is important to take a look at what is happening in other countries to gain a sense of how countries such as China and India with enormous populations and Japan, which is well known for its technological advances, are coping and responding.

In Chapter 1, I introduced a few international examples of student expression on social networking sites, where teenagers demeaned teachers, school officials, and peers, sometimes in graphically sexual and insulting ways. I begin this chapter by revisiting and adding to those examples, to highlight the cultural influences that inform the online expressions and responses to them. I also bring in statistics from research findings and discuss the legal implications within cultural and social contexts. One common aspect that is disclosed in the research is that no matter what country is involved, student perpetrators insist their "jokes" are taken too seriously and that what they are doing is no different from graffiti on washroom walls. The pattern among offending students is a denial of responsibility by insisting their comments were private and directed toward friends. The difference in legal responses between countries involves a cultural interpretation. It is also dependent on the threshold of people within different cultures to accept such expression as pranks and jokes, or to take them more seriously as actionable torts of defamation, slander, libel, or even criminal charges.

The refusal by young people to take responsibility for the content of their online speech suggests the lack of a moral framework, and perhaps insufficient or inadequate communication or dialogue with adults, about the parameters of ethical speech. Is there really the possibility that young people do not recognize the difference between hurtful and demeaning speech and respectful expression? As I noted in Chapter 2, when such speech crosses over to become bullying, there is a definite shift in power, where the content of the expression is no longer mutually agreed upon as teasing.

This might also have something to do with the difference in mind-sets that children apply toward their conceptions of Internet communications compared with those of adults (Lankshear & Knobel, 2006). I detail this difference in Chapter 5 in the context of school environment and institutional responsibilities. At this point, it is important to be aware that most teenagers and children are growing up in a world that is already immersed in the use of technologies. They seldom distinguish virtual reality from their physical reality – it is all part of their daily lives. This is why they are so much more proficient in its use than adults. Adults, on the other hand, continue to apply traditional frameworks when they conceptualize cyberspace. Hence they view online firewalls as having the same protection as brick walls, when in actual fact they are not the same; young people who are digitally proficient can easily hack through them.

Nonetheless, I want to stress that it is not *technologies* (*mediums*) that are at fault in allowing the spread of offending student expressions. It is the *messages* that are contained in the expression that we ought to be concerned about. Those messages do not originate in cyberspace; they come from our physical and social world, and are embedded within our systemic political structures (Shariff & Johnny, 2007). The tendency is to believe that if we control technologies, negative student comments and attitudes will go away. We cannot snuff out the attitudes that inform the expression. To make cyber-bullying go away, we need to educate young people and engage in dialogue that helps them arrive at their own conclusions about what ethical expression ought to comprise. As the court cases I discuss in this chapter illustrate, there is a responsibility to inform students as to when they cross the line from teasing and horseplay to defamation, cyber libel, and, in some cases, criminal harassment. Young people need to be shown the boundaries of free expression and be informed that those boundaries are not unfettered – they have reasonable limits. However, before we can teach kids what those legal boundaries are, we need to understand them ourselves. This is not an easy task because of the capacity of technologies to evolve at such an incredible rate. As it stands now, however, it is definitely worth an attempt.

To begin, it is important to define "defamation" and "cyber-libel" in the context of antiauthority and peer-to-peer cyber misconduct or bullying. Therefore, the legal discussion that follows the international case studies begins with definitions of defamation and libel, followed by judicial interpretations handed down by North American courts under the law of torts. I bring to light legal doctrines and tests that are used in adjudication of cases on cyber libel that bring into clearer focus existing standards applicable to school cases of cyber libel and inform the policy vacuum for schools. Before embarking on a legal discussion of North American cases, it is worth considering some of the cultural differences and responses to cyber misconduct in Asian countries.

CHINESE CULTURAL INFLUENCES

It is important to put into context the potential impact of technology use in China. The population of cyber citizens has reached 137 million with an average online time of 16.9 hours per week, according to statistics from CNNIC as of January 23, 2007. Of China's cyber citizens, 17.2 percent are under eighteen, and 32.3 percent of them are high school students, which is the highest percentage according to their career (Zhang & Wei, 2007a). The number of mobile phone users reached 487,434 million by the end of April 2007 according to statistics from Chinese Informational Industrial Department. Instant messaging service is frequently used, reaching a height of 304.65 billion across the country, representing an increase of 39.9 percent compared with the previous year. Hence, the influence of the Internet on teenagers has raised concerns in China. People pay more attention to its influence and characteristics. For example, a recent "Survey in Media Demand by teenagers under 18" (cited in Zhang & Wei, 2007b) conducted by the Shanghai Communist Youth League, Shanghai China Young Pioneers Committee, and Shanghai Social Science Young Pioneers Research Bureau indicates that the Internet has played an important role in teenagers' lives. Although they consider newspapers and magazines as primary "information broadcasting tools," the preference is clearly moving to use of the Internet because it provides a freer platform for the sharing of opinions anonymously without worrying about political consequences. This is an especially important consideration given China's human rights record.

Although Chinese government officials have not officially accepted the concept of "cyber-bullying," the Chinese media has begun reporting cases and data concerning cyber-bullying that have occurred in foreign countries. Chinese newspapers are following cyber-bullying research reports from the United States and Great Britain. Chinese educationists, lawyers, media, and Internet experts have paid more attention to teenagers who were cyber-bullied all over the world. According to Zhang Yang (2006, as cited in Zhang & Wei, 2007b), the "Internet can easily raise a teenager's anxiety, as indicated through loss of privacy, internet violence, internet threat, internet fraud, internet sex and internet viruses, which all represent factors for nervousness and anxiety." On the other hand, given the enormous number of Internet users, the justice system might become overwhelmed if too many restrictions are placed on expressions. As a result, there appears to be a higher cultural threshold for pranks and jokes that are expressed as unintentional, compared with stronger and more litigious or zero-tolerance forms of reaction to similar online expressions in Western countries.

Case 1: Modified Photographs of a Teacher

Recall the example I mentioned in Chapter 1 in which a middle school teacher in Foshan Guangdong discovered three photographs of his face with a naked human body, the body of a monkey, and the body of a chicken respectively had been posted online, in the *Foshan Daily Forum*. Xiaorong, the student who modified the photographs, saw no harm in searching pornography and animal pictures online and using the Photoshop software to combine several photographs. He claimed that he did not know he had broken the law, and like some of the North American and British cases that I discuss later, perceived that his actions would be received as a joke. He argued the photographs were not meant to harm his teacher; he simply wanted to make his friends laugh (Zhang & Wei, 2007b).

In Xiaorong's case, although the police believed he should be punished, they took into consideration that he had no motivation to insult others subjectively. Because he was still a high school student, they gave him a warning and fines of 500 yuan. According to Chinese criminal law, those behaviors that harm society but do not belong to criminal activities are penalized by the public security organ based on Regulations of the People's Republic of China on Administrative Penalties for Public Security.[1] This case was judged according to the Article 42.[2] There was no report as to how the school responded to these actions – whether educationally or in any disciplinary forms (Zhang & Wei, 2007b).

This might be because Internet "pranks" or what is called *kuso* are culturally accepted. These online pranks have become popular in China, but they are quite complex, and warrant a dictionary explanation. Wikipedia ("Kuso," 2007) explains that online pranks in China have become a product of entertainment in China, similar to plays or movies. This is the official explanation of Chinese *kuso*:

"Kuso" is the term used in the Chinese world for the internet culture that generally includes all types of camp and parody. Generally speaking, an Internet meme is any faddish popular phenomenon on the Internet. The term may refer to the content itself, the subject of the content, or the phenomenon of its spread. It is discrete, identifiable content as opposed to more general things like a philosophy or a trend. It is spread voluntarily, rather than by trickery, compulsion, predetermined path, or completely automated means. Some people liken Internet memes to a form of art, and digital art on the net to a form of meme. An Internet meme may stay the same over time or it may mutate over time, by chance or by the aggregation of commentary, alternate and parody versions, and news about the meme.

A typical Internet meme is simply a digital file that gets passed from one user to others using whatever formats and transmission means are readily available on the Internet (for example, email, blogs, social networks, instant messaging, and the like). Usually, what is passed is either the content itself or a link (such as a hyperlink) to where the content may be found. The content might be in text, video, image, or other format, and might consist of a joke, a rumor, an amusing picture, a video clip, animation, or graphic, or an offbeat news story.

Often, a person or company becomes infamous by virtue of an embarrassing video, email, or other act. These arise, for example, in the context of dating and relationships, job applications, security cameras and other hidden videos, or collections of bizarre news stories. Many memes are urban rumors, fraud schemes, slander, or false news stories that are either planted deliberately to become a meme, evolve by mistake or rumor, or that jump from an offline source to the Internet. . . . Some web services like snopes.com and the urban dictionary collect lists of such hoaxes, or offer services by which users can fact-check popular claims they find on the Internet in order to determine their source and whether or not they are true. This definition of Kuso was brought into Taiwan in around 2000 by young people who frequent Japanese websites and quickly became an internet phenomenon, spreading to Hong Kong and subsequently the rest of China.

("Kuso," 2007)

There is a popular Chinese sentence online that seems contradictory: "If I like you, I would like to prank you, even though I do not like you but I would still prank you" (Zhang & Wei, 2007a, p. 3). According to Zhang and Wei, the behavior of "prank (*kuso*)" is a form of bullying.

Cases 2 and 3: Piggy and Little Fat Boy

This form of *kuso* was also experienced by a second-year high school student, Qian Zhijun, who became known as "Piggy." He acquired the name when dressed as "Piggy" in a transportation security fair. One of his poses as a pig was captured by someone on camera. The pictures were posted on the marketing for the fair. Photoshop was used to combine Piggy's face with Dingdang Cat, Ali Baba, Shrek, Mona Lisa, the Statue of Liberty, and Jia Baoyu. According to Zhang and Wei's (2007b) report, Qian soon became the first person abused by the Internet in China. Someone even called him "Changeable Piggy." Since then, Piggy has become a popular part of movie posters in China. According to the report, Piggy initially said "he felt bad and terrible at the very beginning. After that, he thought most people were not deliberately trying to hurt him because most of them described Piggy as cute and funny" (Zhang & Wei, 2007b).

Similarly, in another famous Chinese case of *kuso*, the face of a young overweight student described as a "common and normal picture of him" on the Internet (Jaishankar & Shariff, 2008) attracted thousands of people who signed on or hacked into the site to alter and make fun of their target, whom they named "Little Fat Boy."

Case 4: Ning's Sexual Harassment of a Teacher

Ning was a second-year student in high school of Dian Jiang District, Chongqing Province. During the summer of 2004, Ning used his father's cellular phone to send several instant messages containing sexual insults to his Chinese teacher Xiao's phone. Xiao reported this to school principal and warned Ning to stop his improper behavior. Ning admitted he was at fault. Xiao also demanded a personal apology, which Ning refused. Xiao took legal action in December 2004. The court determined that Ning used sexual message insult Xiao deliberately and that his behavior intruded on Xiao's personal rights; however, because Ning was aged under eighteen years, his guardians were deemed responsible. Finally, Ning's guardians wrote an apology letter and paid 500 yuan for mental damages.

This case again is interesting from a range of perspectives. Although the teacher was initially agreeable to an apology and compensation for mental damages, the student maintained that he was simply joking and that he only sent her one message for fun. In China, it appears that the courts consider parents to be responsible for the student's behavior with no reference to whether the school has an obligation to educate against these forms of online expression. The report from my Chinese colleagues (directly from the translation) suggests that the school ought to take an educational responsibility:

What Ning did was just broken the school's rules. The teacher should educate the student but not sue the student. However, after the judgment, both parties did not look for appeals. Concerning about the case and the popularized instant message harassment phenomena, Dian Jiang District Court's judge Huang thought that sending instant messages deliberately could easily cause the violation of rights. However, if those activities want to be defined as violation of rights activities, there must be validated evidences. In this case, Ning admitted the written material about the instant message harassment. The material became the key evidence for the case and determined the judgment.

(Zhang & Wei, 2007b, pp. 5–6)

Another emerging area of cyber-bullying in China is referred to as Internet slander. This involves openly insulting others using force or other methods or fabricating stories to slander others. Under Chinese law they are considered guilty according to Article 246.[3] Zhang and Wei (2007a, July 22, pp. 6) report that there is a lot of slanderous behavior on the Internet. Following are some examples.

Case 5: Internet Slander

Wang Shunhe stole a password from a Web site and used it to send insulting instant messages to another student, Zhou, and Zhou's family. They claimed that this caused psychological damage to the entire family from September 24, 2003, through October 2, 2004. Wang Shunhe also used the Internet to post a thread containing insulting words. He also published the names and phone numbers of members of the family. Family members were inundated with phone calls from across the country and even as far as Singapore. Strangers from Singapore called Mr. Zhou to arrange a one-night stand with his daughter. This action destroyed Ms. Zhou's health and destroyed her reputation. The family filed criminal action and Wang Shunhe was eventually sentenced to two years in prison. The court's opinion in this decision, as we shall see later in this chapter, is not significantly different from North American cases, although in China there appear to be extremes – either imprisonment or simply a fine.

The case examples suggest that the Chinese are not immune from cyber-bullying and that additional studies are needed to understand its real extent in a country with such a large population. I am especially interested in the kinds of responses that will emerge to reduce it.

Case 6: Cyber Vigilantism

Most reports in China relate to adult on adult cyber-bullying. In a well-known case of cyber vigilantism that turned into cyber-bullying, a man posted information about another individual who allegedly had an affair with his wife. He identified his wife's suspected lover by his Web name. This led to a series of postings that revealed the man's name, phone number, and address. Thousands of Web postings denounced the lover, and Internet users telephoned or showed up at his home to shout abuse at him and his family. Lawyers are now calling on the government to protect people from having their personal information made public on the Internet (Bartlett, 2007). Administered in anonymous cyberspace, cyber vigilantism can impinge on many personal and privacy rights.

JAPAN: *NETTO IJIME*

In Chapter 1, I provided some shocking cases of cyber-bullying. They were shocking because Japanese culture has always presented itself as polite and nonconfrontational. Yet the pressures on young people in a highly competitive culture have been emerging as bullying since 1984. *Ijime* (bullying) was first identified as a social problem in Japan in 1984–1985 when sixteen pupils committed suicide under suspected bullying circumstances (Morita et al., 1999, cited in Yoneyama & Naito, 2003). Senoo (2007) explains that since 1985, the number and variety of *ijime* cases have rapidly increased. Among scholars it is widely believed that the nature of *ijime* is related to Japanese cultural and social characteristics such as collectivism and homogeneity (Akiba, 2004; Rios-Ellis, Bellamy, & Shoji, 2000). However, as Hasegawa, Iwasaki, and Nakata (2007) explain, although several severe cases have been reported, there have been no scholarly reports yet on the topic of cyber-bullying.

Japan is considered to be digitally ahead of the rest of the world by at least two generations (Mitchell, 2004), and children are exposed to digital gadgets at a very early age. However, the research on technology use in Japan is surprising, given the number of serious cases of cyber-bullying that have surfaced. Approximately half of eleven-year-old Japanese children use the Internet; however, only about 20 percent were regular users in 2004. Hasegawa, Iwasaki, and Nakata (2006) asked students to answer the question: "I have a computer at home, but I don't use/am not allowed to use the computer." They report that even though many high school students own computers, a large percentage of them do *not* use a computer even if they have one at home. Computer use among elementary schools is even lower.

Two of my graduate research assistants, both of whom have lived and taught in Japan, Julie d'Eon and Yasuko Senoo (2007), began to investigate the prevalence of cyber-bullying in Japan. Initially, their research disclosed little research on the topic, with the exception of Professor Hasegawa's study. However, they stumbled on a police Web site in Japan and found numerous Japanese cases of cyber-bullying – or *netto ijime* (bullying on the Net). Readers will see many similarities in the cases that follow to those reported by Western media on what has been taking place among American and British students.

Cases 1 and 2: Female Perpetrators

d'Eon and Senoo (2007) found that girls, who are generally perceived to be less assertive, undertook what is believed to be first case of cyber-bullying in Japan. A few Grade 9 girls (approximately age thirteen) bullied a Grade 7 student (approximately eleven years old) using a cell phone camera. They took her to a washroom in a shopping mall, removed her clothing, and took pictures of her naked, using two of the group members' cell phones. They then showed the picture to friends and threatened the victim that it would be shown to more people if she reported the incident to teachers. One of them sent the picture to another friend by cell phone. In this case, the school intervened, deleted the picture, and stopped it from being further disseminated (Hasegawa et al., 2007; Senoo, 2007). In February 2007, six other middle school girls in Kobe used their cell phones' digital cameras to photograph another naked (female) victim. They posted the photographs on a bulletin board, inviting online visitors to rank their favorite parts of her body.

The Kobe Prefectural Police filed charges for engaging in obscene acts (Senoo, 2007). The police response in Japan reflects the criminal law approach adopted in China to address issues of cyber-bullying.

Case 3: Flaming

Another criminal case involving Internet flaming involved two Grade 9 male students, who sent around 800 anonymous e-mails to a female student's cell-phone via their home computer in mid-December 2006. These messages said "Die! Feel sick to be with you! Ugly!...Do not come to school!" and so on. The victim's parents found her depressed and asked the police for advice. The boys were arrested for unreasonable nuisance under the prefectured measures. The prefectured measures set down the maximum of six months of imprisonment and the maximum of 500,000 yen (around $5,000 U.S.) in fines for unreasonable nuisance (Senoo, 2007).

There are two Japanese cases of cyber misconduct that were dealt with under libel and slander. Ironically, in North America, anything involving pornography would automatically be dealt with under criminal laws, whereas in Japan, this particular case was treated as libel.

Case 4: Pornographic Novel as Libel

In November 2006, a Grade 9 male student in Akita saw his name used on a pornographic novel Web site. The student was mentally shocked and could not attend the school for a few days. His name was used with the names and depictions of female students in indecent scenes of a novel. The novel was written by anonymous readers using computer and cell phone relay formats. The victim talked to the police, and the matter was under investigation for libel. The Web site administration deleted the novel in December at the request of the police (Senoo, 2007). Similarly, an openly violent case of physical assault that was filmed and uploaded, was dealt with as slander, rather than as assault.

Case 5: Physical Assault as Slander

In November 2006, a first-year high school student in Sapporo posted moving images of himself undergoing physical bullying by several classmates. Two of the offenders, one boy and one girl, were subsequently suspended from the school. In December 2006, eight members of a high school baseball team in Nagano Prefecture were found to have slandered a teammate on a bulletin board. Six offenders were ordered to be restricted to their homes, and the team was banned from competition for three months.

Some of these differences between Japanese responses to various types of online misconduct might be better understood within its highly distinctive cultural context.

Cultural Considerations: *Ijime* and *Netto Ijime*

When Japanese parents use the term *ijime* (bullying), it usually describes extreme psychological and verbal aggression rather than physical aggression (Smorti, Menesini, & Smith, 2003). In that connection, it fits well within verbal and psychological forms of cyber-bullying. Another main characteristic is its collective nature. Because Japanese students spend so much time together in groups, individual leaders single out one member of the group for bullying. The rest of the group follows the leader in isolating the victim (Akiba, 2004; Morita & Kiyonaga, 1994).

Researchers have found that in Japan, 80 percent of the bullying is carried out by a peer group rather than individuals. It happens in close friendships in which the victim is not excluded from the group but harassed for a period before it is someone else's turn. Not unlike patterns found in Western countries, it is students who are perceived to be "good students" that perpetrate and are involved in bullying rather than those who are generally perceived as "problem kids" (Gibson, 2006). *Ijime* has changed its character as traditional Japanese communities collapse and give way to economic and technological development. According to Akiba: "privatization (individualism), along with economic changes in [Japanese] society, have collapsed traditional Japanese communities" (Akiba, 2004, p. 220). He observes the importance of examining the impact of the gap between societal change and the traditional role of schools to foster Japanese cultural values. Senoo (2007) explains that with technological advances, *netto ijime* is becoming more prevalent. McVeigh (2003) suggests that the technology necessitates individual practices that isolate the individual from the social masses. In Japanese culture, this is a new phenomenon.

Because of Japanese homogeneity, victims are generally targeted for personal characteristics or through sexual forms of harassment. Non-Japanese students are rarely mistreated. Rather, they are more likely to be treated as idols because of their racial difference. Akiba has suggested certain invisible characteristics of Japanese victims (2004). From her interviews with middle school students, she found common characteristics of victims, such as "selfish," "persistent," and "noisy," that trigger the feeling of irritation in the *ijime* perpetrators. These types of behavior cannot be easily accepted in Japanese society. Historically, for complex reasons of traditional social organizations, collective power rather than individuality was required for survival. This collectivism exists deep inside Japanese society and is tacitly understood. In this context, being selfish, persistent, or noisy are not understandable behaviors. The person who behaves in these ways is reactively perceived as different from others. Senoo refers to a well-known Japanese proverb: "The nail that sticks out gets hammered down." The victims are chosen "because they are somewhat different from others" (Tanaka, 2001, p. 463) in their behavior. Accordingly, difference can be a point of contention even in homogenous societies and perhaps more so to encourage conformity to the normative culture.

Regarding limited use of computers, despite global perceptions that the Japanese would be avid users of the Internet, Senoo (2007) explains that the Japanese have some strong and unique traditional beliefs in their everyday life that are quite different from those of most religious communities. While Japanese Shintoism is considered a religion, it is largely practiced through tradition, ritual, and myth. These traditional beliefs have a great influence on their behavior and thinking. One of these traditional beliefs is that *hard* work is more valuable than *smart* work. The person who uses a computer or the Internet for his or her homework would be considered as being lazy. Many teachers and schools prefer their students to take their time doing homework using "hardcopy" materials (i.e., books, newspapers, and dictionaries); hence, they do not strongly recommend that students use computers and the Internet unless there is a special need to do so. This cultural preference might be a main cause that formed the resistance to the implementation of computer education in schools.

Gakko Ura Saito: Mobile-Bullying

The findings relating to cellular phones are different from home computer use in Japan. This form of technology is far more popular among Japanese students. These findings are corroborated in Professor Hasegawa's study (Hasegawa et al., 2006), in which he and his colleagues reported a high rate in students' cell phone use (junior high school students, 80.8 percent and senior high school students, 92.9 percent). Hasegawa et al. (2007) also report that 85.7 percent of the junior high school students whom they surveyed and 96.6 percent of the high school students had their own cell phones.

Interestingly, 80.8 percent of the junior high school students and 92.9 percent of the high school students did not have any restriction on their cell phone use. It appears that Japanese parents are less worried about cell phone use because they cannot attract viruses. Apparently, parents do not make the link that cell phone technology and Internet communication are integrally connected and that text messaging and photographs taken on cell phones can easily be posted and dispersed online. Moreover, as Hasegawa et al. observe, parents are more worried about students engaging in blogging and chatting, which could detract from their schoolwork. As the statistics suggest the use of mobile phones is very popular. This is partly because of the expense of landlines in Japan. This has resulted in considerable "mobile-bullying" among students. Pupils have created clandestine school sites (known as *gakko ura saito*) that can only be accessed via mobile phone. These sites have created a new form of group bullying that encourage an entire generation of what Professor Hasegawa calls "anonymous slanderers" (Hasegawa et al., 2007).

As Senoo comments, in the old-style *ijime*, at least the tormentors were known. The electronic version is as vicious, if not more so, because electronic communications afford complete anonymity. As I have noted in the profile of cyber-bullying, among its key features is its anonymity, which makes it far more difficult for school authorities to identify the instigators, intervene, or implement disciplinary and educationally preventative measures. This dichotomy in the cultural orientation toward reduced use of computers to do "work" and the increased incidence of cyber-bullying using both cell phone and Internet technology is specific to Japanese culture for the reasons explained earlier.

Ijime-jisatsu (Suicide Linked to *Ijime*)

Another cultural aspect of *netto ijime* is the increased rate of suicide among young people. *Ijime-jisatsu* is one of the disastrous and culturally incidental consequences of the *ijime* phenomenon in Japan. The number of reported cases of *ijime-jisatsu* had been decreasing for the last two decades before the minister of education received the anonymous suicide note on November 6, 2006. Senoo (2007) cites a BBC newscast that reported five students killing themselves in four days in November 2006. Following these cases, the police force determined that *ijime* was involved in fourteen of the forty cases of student suicides in 1999–2005 after previously reporting that there was no such case in January 2007 (Senoo, 2007). As of February 2, 2007, two suicide cases in 2006 had been officially determined to be *ijime*-related cases by the police. The number increased dramatically by November because of the lack of appropriate intervention.

As Senoo observes, there are some traditional Japanese beliefs and values that make this act an incidental solution of the *ijime* problem in Japan. Unlike other societies, this solution is not strongly tabooed in Japanese society because of their historical warrior culture (*Bushido*), which traditionally regarded suicide "as a responsible way to deal with a problem when faced with no other option" (Hogg, 2006). This view has not yet completely changed even though Japanese lifestyle became modernized a while ago.

Another traditional belief underlying Japanese suicide is its high value on patience related to group harmony. Chinese business management advisor Song Wenzhou comments that Japanese society demands extreme efforts and patience to ensure harmony of its people. Consequently, teachers and parents push victims of bullying to struggle with the problem or make better efforts to integrate into the group, leaving some of them few options other than suicide (Song, 2006). This statement is supported by one actual *ijime-jisatsu* case in Iwaki,

Fukushima. The Fukushima District Court allocated 30 percent of the responsibility for one suicide victim's demise to the victim's parents because they forced him to continue attending school despite the bullying (Ito, 2002, as cited in Senoo, 2007). The forced return to face his perpetrator was built on the notion of *Iwaki-shi ijime-jisatsu jiken hanketsuni tsuite*. This means "Japanese form their identities based on their role and responsibility in a group" (Shiizu & Levine, 2001, as cited in Akiba, 2004, p. 231). This treatment, although seen as reasonable and natural in Japanese society, has negative implications for children in the formative years of identity development. If they are excluded or not given any roles or responsibilities within the classroom group, the psychological damage is enormous.

SOUTH KOREA

Cyber-bullying has also emerged as a concern in South Korea where the government has implemented a law to prevent Internet misuse. South Korea's Ministry of Information has developed a law that will no longer enable cyber perpetrators to hide behind false identities. The new law took effect in July 2007 and will compel Internet service providers (ISPs) to track the originators under the "Internet real-name system" by recording the identification records of users when they post entries. Portal operators will be obliged to disclose personal information such as names and addresses of cyber attackers when their victims want to sue them for libel or infringement upon privacy. Ministry director Lee Ta-Hee observed that "South Korea is an internet powerhouse and it is probably the most wired country in the world. But sadly, the dark side is too dark" (Bartlett, 2007). In South Korea, online mobs distribute victims' home addresses, credit card details, and even their employer's phone numbers. All of Korea's police stations now have a cyber-terror unit to help deal with the problem. The number of cases referred to Korea's Internet Commission tripled last year. The cyber-terror unit recognizes the impact on victims' social status as well as the fear that this generates. According to Chun Seong Lee, liaison officer at the Cyber-Terror Response Centre, cyber-bullying and cyber crime occurs so often in South Korea that it is affecting people's social lives, causing people to drop out of work and school and leading to mental illness.

INDIA

Although there are many Western studies related to cyber-bullying, there is no empirical research in India to unearth this modern phenomenon. Jaishankar and Shariff (2008) cite an unpublished Indian study that found mobile-bullying to be common among the school students. This study investigated the nature and the extent of school students' experience of cyber-bullying using mobile phones. The results showed that 65 percent of the students were victims of cyber-bullying using mobile phones, and 60 percent of the respondents had also been involved in bullying others using mobile phones.

Although bullying is considered to be a serious issue predominantly in Western countries, according to Indian criminologist Jaishankar (Jaishankar and Shariff, 2008), bullying in India is an acceptable part of the culture within and between people from different castes. He notes that bullying in schools or colleges is prevalent. It is sometimes called "ragging," or, when directed at young women, it is known as "Eve teasing" (teasing a virgin). Consequently, few laws or policies to address bullying have been put in place. Given the enormous surge in technology, and the involvement of Indian computer programmers and information technology workers in outsourced U.S. technology firms, the use of modern technologies such as Internet and mobile phones has proliferated, increasing the prevalence of bullying by school and college students. Today, Internet and mobile phones have become part of everybody's lives, and most students carry mobile phones. Although this may seem to be more of a playful prank than a serious offence, it is only the beginning of a trend that can escalate into a serious problem. In this case, the teachers intervened, and the problem was eventually resolved. According to one Indian news report, "In India, where younger and younger kids are discovering the power of the Internet cyber bullying has already started trapping Indian teenagers in its insidious Web" (Kapoor, 2003).

Although few formal studies have been undertaken, a cursory look at Orkut (a social networking Web site; www.orkut.com) shows many similar postings to those on Facebook and MySpace. There is more information available on adult cyber abuse and cyber crime and little so far on cyber-bullying among students. Orkut came to India in February 2006 with a mission statement claiming to help people create a closer, more intimate network of friends and hoping to put them on the path to social bliss, similar to Facebook. It is apparent from the mission statement that the network was established to enable people to interact with each other across the globe by bridging geographic distances. However, according to Rahul (2007), it has since been used for superfluous activities leading to moral degradation and upheaval. A management student from Mumbai was arrested by the police following a girl's complaint about tarnishing her image in the public forum – namely, Orkut. The boy was trying to entice the girl for some time. He threatened her with dire consequences when she resisted his advances. Later, he posted an obscene profile of her on the Orkut portal along with her mobile number. The profile has been sketched in such a way that it draws lewd comments from many who visit her profile. Later, the boy was arrested under section 67 of Information Technology Act of 2000 (India has no separate law for cyber-bullying).

According to Kapoor (2003), legal experts in India do not believe this legislation has a lot of teeth to reduce cyber crime because it was initially designed to promote e-commerce. It is not effective in dealing with cyber-stalking, cyber-bullying, and other forms of online harassment. Kapoor explains that the law does not even define "cyber crime." A brief search in the Orkut profile will reveal "many modified profiles of beautiful girls" (Sengupta, 2006). More recently, India has brought in an Internet censorship policy (Fratina, 2007) allowing it to close down offensive Web sites and blogs. A number of actions have also been brought under cyber-defamation laws.

In another case involving Orkut, a malicious profile of a Delhi schoolgirl was uploaded onto the site. The perpetrators posted obscene photographs and contact details such as her home address and telephone numbers on the profile, using suggestive names such as "sex teacher" to describe her. The matter came to light after the girl's family started receiving vulgar calls; thereafter her father contacted the cyber cell of Delhi Police's Economic Offences Wing. According to the Delhi police sources, the girl is a student in a South Delhi school. The obscene pictures and personal information brought two strangers to the girl's door suggesting that the girl had invited them for sex through Internet. This is the second incident demonstrating Orkut's misuse in New Delhi. Earlier, a flight attendant alleged that someone had opened an account in her name on the Web site, in which she was described as a "sex struck woman."

The majority of cases reported by Jaishankar (Jaishankar & Shariff, in press) relating to Orkut involve sexual harassment of women. The unpublished research report by my law student, Sakina Fratina (2007), includes information on India's first case of cyber-stalking. Ritu Kholi complained to the police that a person had been using her identity to chat over the Internet at the Web site www.mirc.com for four consecutive days. The individual was using obscene language and giving out her telephone number, encouraging them to call her at odd hours. Consequently, she received over forty calls from Kuwait, Mumbai, and Ahmedabad. Finally, the IP (Internet protocol) address was traced, and her perpetrator was arrested under the Indian Penal Code, which among other crimes prohibits the interference with a woman's modesty. There have also been cases in which school principals have been insulted on Orkut.

The foregoing cases of international cyber-bullying and the cultural considerations that are specific to the countries involved provide a general idea of the forms of cyber-bullying that have begun to emerge on the Asian continent and surrounding areas. The responses to such cyber misconduct appear to lean more heavily toward the criminal justice system than toward the law of torts (libel and slander). In many ways, it is not far different from the legal positivist approach that is prevalent in the West, as we shall see later in this book. Notably however, in largely populated countries such as India and China, there appears to be a higher legally accepted threshold for insults and pranks against others. As I mentioned earlier, this may be a way of reducing the floodgates to litigation and keeping perpetrators out of jail.

There is an urgent need for increased and more focused research relating to Internet use, digital literacies, the use of mobile cellular phone systems, and, more particularly, school responses to those forms of cyber communication in Asia. Technological advancement is moving so quickly that it is difficult for researchers, academics, and policy makers to keep up. The educational component to addressing cyber bullying is largely missing from all these countries. As we saw in Japan, India, and South Korea, it is largely the police and not the school that becomes engaged. In China, the parents share responsibility, as they do in Japan.

Is the picture any different in the Western Hemisphere and "down under" in Australia? I turn now to consideration of emerging legal responses in the United Kingdom, United States, Canada, and Australia, as they are applied under the law of torts for cyber libel.

TORT LAW: CYBER LIBEL, DEFAMATION, AND SLANDER

Tort law involves legal remedies that are applied to correct "wrongs" committed intentionally or unintentionally (Linden & Klar, 1994). There are two areas of tort law relevant to cyber-bullying of peers and authority figures: libel and negligence. Given that there is so much concern by school authorities about the antiauthority version of cyber-bullying on social communication networks, I begin this review by taking a look at the issue of libel as a tort – or wrong committed intentionally or unintentionally, and the impact of libelous comments on targets of such expression (teachers and school authorities). Some legal definitions of what we mean by libel and defamation are in order.

An 1840 case continues to provide the classic definition of "libel": "A publication without justification or lawful excuse which is calculated to injure the reputation of another by exposing him to hatred, contempt or ridicule" (B. Parke in *Parmiter v. Coupland*, 1840).

When we consider student online expressions relating to teachers, we can deduce that such comments expose them to "hatred, contempt, and ridicule" and that they are not justified. The question arises when the students insist that their expression was not "calculated to injure the reputation." Such a defence might be more difficult in cases in which photographs are modified to depict sexual poses or when visitors are invited to post derogatory comments. Where the line becomes a little more blurred is in cases that involve student conversations about their teachers on social networking sites such as Facebook. Consider, for example, several North American cases.

KIDS' PERSPECTIVE – THEIR OWN PRIVATE SPACE

As the cleverly selected name for the popular networking tool MySpace.com suggests, young people perceive the online communication spaces as their own – this is "my space" or "our space" and adults should not be privy to what we say. Consider the following case examples of cyber-bullying as reported by news media.[4] The first case is that of Brad Parsons.[5]

Case 1: Brad and His Online Friends

Post meant for friends only, teen says:

Brad Parsons says he never imagined he'd be bounced from his school and see friends arrested when he created a Facebook group for his friends to use to vent about a vice-principal. "We made the group as an inside joke," the sixteen-year-old student at Birchmount Park Collegiate said in a phone interview.

But the teen who "likes hanging out and chilling" with his friends and says he's never caused any trouble, stepped into a grey area when he created the space on Facebook.com, a popular social website, that slagged his school's vice-principal, Mary Burtch and other staff.

Internet experts say Parson's case once more raises interesting questions that don't have clear answers.

"These issues are arising with increasing frequency and I think it's tough to identify how much of this is a legal issue, how much of this is a conduct issue within a school," said Michael Geis, Canada Research Chair of Internet and E-commerce Law at the University of Ottawa. "I think it is hard to identify a right or wrong."

For instance, does a conversation intended to be privately shared among friends, as Parsons says, constitute cyber-bullying, as the school says, if it becomes publicly available?

Parsons argues that while the comments made were mean-spirited and made fun of Burtch, they shouldn't be considered bullying because they were not intended to be seen by her. "It was not online harassment," Parsons said. "We were not in any way trying to get the message to her. We were just talking amongst each other."

Parsons, who plays house-league hockey and is studying to take his G1 driving test, led a protest Friday to decry the school for "suspending people and suspending freedom of speech and opinions on a private chat line."

Four other Birchmount Park students were suspended earlier this week after school administrators discovered the derogatory comments on the website.

What started as a protest with fewer than 100 students tripled in size after someone pulled a fire alarm. Four students were arrested when police were pelted with objects as they tried to direct traffic.

Parsons was told Monday he would be expelled from school but has since heard his punishment might be lighter. He has a meeting tomorrow with the school board that he hopes will clear things up.

His mom, Sylvie, 52, said that as punishment she is taking away Internet access from her son. But she noted that when she went to school, she and her other friends would stand around and say mean things about teachers.

"The technology has changed so it's become a much different thing now," she said.

Parsons said he and his friends have long had problems with Burtch, who Parsons says has singled them out because they hand around in the back of the school where there have been problems caused by students not in his group.

Parsons, whose favorite classes are English and drama, says he was getting good grades and was finishing an essay on *MacBeth* when he was expelled. "I'm losing out on my education because of this and it's going to set me back," he said.

(Chung, 2007)

In Brad's case, it is clear from the support he received that he and his fellow students believed strongly that the comments they made were "private" and not for the eyes of school authorities, least of all Ms. Burtch and her staff. The student protest comprised resistance to the idea that any rules were breached. The students argued that although the comments were mean-spirited, they were not by any means meant to personally harass Ms. Burtch or her staff and hence should not be defined as cyber-bullying.

Brad's case is no exception. There are hundreds of such incidents being reported in the news globally, involving statements by students about school authorities. Consider Bram Koch's situation, for example. Bram took a similar position regarding his freedom of expression rights and focused less on the libelous connotations of his online "joke" that he saw his teacher masturbating in the back of the class.

Case 2: Bram's Bad Joke

Bram Koch, a student at Willowbrook Public School in Ontario, appeared in a radio interview with his father, David Koch, on a Canadian Broadcasting Corporation Radio One talk show, *The Current* (Findlay, 2007). Bram explained to a national radio audience that he did not realize his joke about his teacher would cause so many problems. Bram wrote a joke about his teacher on a friend's Facebook saying that he had seen her masturbating at the back of the classroom. This was brought to the school administration's attention. Bram was subsequently suspended from participating in a field trip to Montreal with his friends that he had been excited about attending.

Neither Bram nor Brad thought twice about the possibility that adults might see what they wrote online, both believing it to be a private space for kids. Moreover, both explained that their expressions were just jokes to be shared with friends. Neither boy realized the ramifications or impact of their very public words. Bram admitted that he never thought of this as cyber-bullying.

Moreover, neither boy gave any thought to the possibility that millions of people access Facebook (Jenkins & boyd, 2006; Roher, 2007). Even with the privacy settings on, the comments on their wall are accessible to friends. What their friends make accessible to others who are not part of the original group is where *Facebook* conversations can move easily from a private domain into a far more public one. Similarly when photographs are tagged by friends, even if they are within a person's privacy settings, those friends may provide access to many other registered communicators. The posting can spread quickly to the computer screens of thousands. Moreover, when comments like this are made about authority figures, rumors among school kids circulate faster, motivating hundreds of kids to log-in within minutes, with the specific purpose of reading the comments. It takes only one whistle-blower to report the posting. Alternately, as more adults, including prospective employers, join Facebook to verify the profiles of applicants, what might have started as a private conversation among friends can become highly public. As both these boys found out, this can lead to a lot of trouble.

Although both boys admitted their jokes were mean-spirited, neither conceded that the school should have the right to intervene. Both insisted that they really believed they were having private conversations. Bram stated that although he no longer uses Facebook, he will continue to look for other spaces (presumably online) where he can communicate privately with his friends.

In both cases, the boys were angrier about the school response than ashamed of their comments. They did not seem to care that when placed in a "public" forum like the Internet, their words might be interpreted as undermining school authority, which in turn could impact the school environment and the learning of all students in the classroom. When asked whether he still attends the teacher's class, Bram said he sits in the back of the classroom and does not look at her. They do not speak at all.

Brad's supporters who carried signs supporting free expression did not believe he did anything wrong. Research suggests that most preteens and adolescence would agree. An Ipsos-Reid poll conducted for Microsoft Canada in 2007 found that 70 percent of respondents aged ten to fourteen said they believe the information they put online is private (Thomas & Canadian Press, 2007). In the United States, there have been similar student protests.

Case 3: Indiana Outrage

Similarly, students in Indianapolis publicly protested suspensions for online postings on MySpace. A Fox News report, in usual sensational fashion, reported the following:

Indiana Students Outraged over Schools' Blog Crackdown.

Increasing crackdowns on what educators deem inappropriate online behavior have outraged students and free-speech advocates who see them as pursuing school rules too far beyond the classroom.

The battleground is online journals, or blogs, and popular Web sites such as MySpace. com where teens post comments about their daily lives – including school.

School officials say such postings can be disruptive to education; critics say schools should not have the power to punish students for comments posted from a home computer.

"The school system has no right to sit there and tell us what we can and cannot do at home. They can control what we do at school, but when it gets home, the only people who can tell us what to do is our parents, not the school," said Kayla Wiggington, a 17-year-old junior at Whiteland High School in suburban Indianapolis who uses MySpace to keep in touch with friends.

The school board in the Whiteland-based Clark-Pleasant school district will vote Octo-ber 17 on a proposed policy that would put students and teachers on notice that they are legally responsible for anything they post online, including material deemed defamatory, obscene, proprietary, or libelous.

(Associated Press, 2006; emphasis added)

The American students, like their Canadian counterparts, also perceived their social networking spaces as their own territory. Cyberspace has become their play space away from adults. They see it as empowering and liberating, and it comes as a shock when they are discovered and punished. They almost feel betrayed, and in many cases are pushing back with lawsuits, a matter that I discuss in Chapter 4. Ironically, Brad and Bram are not much different from the boys on Golding's island in *Lord of the Flies*, who created their own ethical rules in the absence of adult supervision.

As Suler and Phillips (1998) suggest, cyberspace provides a venue for people to express aspects of their personalities that they cannot express in physical spaces. They do this to seek recognition and validation of those spaces. More-over, these researchers suggest that such expressions are a cathartic form of venting for students whose frustrations are not addressed in physical spaces. The same Fox News story also quoted a school official from a separate school that had also expelled students for writing racial comments about their teachers on MySpace. The school official is quoted as saying "Kids look at the Internet as today's restroom wall. . . . They need to learn that some things are not accept-able anywhere" (Associated Press, 2006). What is acceptable? I begin with a look at Canadian tort law for answers, followed by American judicial decisions.

CYBER LIBEL: THE CANADIAN CONTEXT

According to Canadian lawyer David Potts (2004b), Canadian cyber libel law is grounded in a British court decision that goes back almost 100 years (*Vitzelly v. Mudies Select Library Ltd.*, 1900) The case was adopted into Canadian jurispru-dence when it was quoted with approval in *Newton v. Vancouver* (1932), and held that

The defendant in the defence of innocent dissemination will succeed if the defendant shows:
i) that he was innocent of any knowledge of the libel contained in the work dissemi-nated by him;
ii) there was nothing in the work or the circumstances under which it came to him or was disseminated by him that ought to have led him to suppose that it contained a libel; or
iii) that when the work was disseminated by him, it was not by any negligence on his part that he did not know that it contained the libel, then although the dissemination of the work by him was *prima facie* a publication of it, he may nevertheless on proof of the earlier-mentioned facts, be held not to have published it.

This decision might absolve some of the students who claim they "were innocent of any knowledge of the libel . . . disseminated by them" or that "ought to
have led" teachers or peers to suppose that their expression contained libel.
However, a hundred-year-old case is a little difficult to apply given the context
of the Internet and the ability for rapid spread of online postings. When we discussed some of the international cases, I purposely avoided providing definitions
of libel, defamation, and slander because I do not at this time have their exact
legal interpretations. However, in Canada, Bernstein and Hanna explain that
cyber libel can comprise either defamation and/or libellous written comments:

> Simply defined, defamation is the making of a derogatory statement to a third party that
> discredits or impugns the reputation of a person, where the statement is not defensible
> on the grounds that it is true, fair comment or protected on some ground of privilege.
>   (Bernstein & Hanna, 2005)[6]

Bernstein and Hanna confirm that generally libel is defamation in a fixed
medium (written or permanent form), whereas slander is oral defamation (spoken words not recorded or fixed in any medium). In this regard, most defamation on the Internet is properly characterized as libel, whereas verbal comments,
insults, and threats made over cell phones might be considered to be slander
because they are made over electronic airwaves. Text messaging via cell phones
would be constituted as libel. Bernstein and Hanna explain that although cyber
libel is not a new cause of action or an independent tort, it has several distinguishing features and complexities. I suggest that these features are pertinent
to cyber-bullying among adolescent peers.

First, as I have already observed, defamatory comments that are posted on
the Internet can be read by a vast audience. Consider, for example, Ghyslain
Reza. This fourteen-year-old student from Quebec, Canada, videotaped himself
acting out a scene from the movie Star Wars. He forgot his tape in a media room.
The tape was stolen and uploaded on the Internet. Ghyslain rapidly became
known internationally as the Star Wars Kid. The Web site his peers created was
visited by over 15 million people. His video was cloned 106 times, and even
George Lucas, the movie's director, heard about him.

Ghyslain and fellow Canadian David Knight, whose case I have discussed in
Chapters 1 and 2, were both defamed in front of millions of people. This raises
serious legal considerations of whether existing defamation law can sufficiently
remedy or vindicate victims of cyber-bullying. Second, defamed material on the
Internet can be republished quickly and easily and reproduced infinitely. This
makes it difficult to identify the original perpetrator and the extent to which
that person was responsible for the libel. Although the original video was made
by Ghyslain Reza himself, it was stolen and posted on the Internet by known
perpetrators, whom he sued. The extent to which those perpetrators could be
held responsible for the 106 clones of the video that were made from the Internet
version is questionable (Bernstein & Hanna, 2005). Given that there are few
established precedents on distribution of liability in Internet cases, this might

have been a consideration in Reza's out of court settlement for approximately $300,000.

Finally, as Bernstein and Hanna point out, information on the Internet travels through several computer systems between the author and recipients (a variety of intermediaries such as bulletin board messages, social networking sites, blogs, Web pages, e-mails), all of which can be stored on various servers. The information can be easily and repeatedly recalled. This, they note, gives rise to many Internet intermediary liability issues (ibid., p. 7). They quote L. B. Lidsky, who describes the difference between defamation in a physical setting and Internet defamation in the virtual realm:

Although Internet communications may have the ephemeral qualities of gossip with regard to accuracy, they are communicated through a medium more pervasive than print, and for this reason they have tremendous power to harm reputation. Once a message enters cyberspace, millions of people worldwide can gain access to it. Even if the message is posted in a discussion forum frequented by only a handful of people, any one of them can republish the message by printing it or, as is more likely by forwarding it instantly to a different discussion forum. And if the message is sufficiently provocative, it may be republished again and again. The extraordinary capacity of the Internet to replicate endlessly almost any defamatory message lends credence to the notion that 'the truth rarely catches up with a lie.' The problem for libel law, then, is how to protect reputation without squelching the potential of the Internet as a medium of public discourse.

(Lidsky, 2000, as quoted in Bernstein & Hanna, 2005, p. 7)

Bernstein and Hanna (p. 9) explain that for plaintiffs to succeed in a defamation action, they must prove

1. that the statement that the plaintiff is complaining about is "defamatory";
2. that the defamatory statement refers to the plaintiff; and
3. that the impugned statement was published, or made known, to a third person.

Hence David Knight could argue that the statements posted on a Web site next to his photograph labeling him a homosexual and a pedophile are defamatory, that they refer to him as evidenced by his photograph, and that these statements were clearly published and made known to millions of third persons – anyone with Internet access. Similarly, the angry teachers who have been described as pedophiles, or as masturbating in the classroom, could potentially sue the students who posted those comments for cyber libel.

What would their chances of success be in Canada under a defamation suit? According to Bernstein and Hanna, Canadian courts, unlike those in the United States, have been more willing to aggressively vindicate reputation attacks committed over the Internet, with substantial damage awards (ibid., p. 8). The Ontario Court of Appeal has articulated the defamatory test as follows:

A defamatory statement is one which has a tendency to injure the reputation of the person to whom it refers (which tends, that is to say, to lower him [or her] in the estimation of right thinking members of society generally and in particular to cause him [or her] to be regarded with feelings of hatred, contempt, ridicule, fear, dislike or disesteem). The statement is judged by the *standard of an ordinary, right thinking member of society. Hence the test is an objective one.... The standard of what constitutes a reasonable or ordinary member of the public is difficult to articulate. It should not be so low as to stifle free expression unduly nor so high as to imperil the ability to protect the integrity of a person's reputation.* The impressions about the content of any broadcast, or written statement, should be assessed from the perspective of someone reasonable, that is, a person who is reasonably thoughtful and informed, rather than someone who has an overly fragile sensibility. A degree of common sense must be attributed to viewers.

(*Colour Your World Corp. v. C.B.C.*, 1998; emphasis added)

The objective test is whether in the eyes of a reasonably thoughtful person, rather than someone with overly fragile sensibilities, it would lower, discredit, or negatively affect the reputation of the plaintiff and expose him or her to hatred or ridicule. When we consider Bram's case, he wrote about his teacher masturbating in the back of the class, a fact vehemently denied by the teacher.

Although most adults who knew the teacher involved would see the expression for what it is and not take it seriously, a significant concern of late, as explained in Chapter 2, is that prospective employers are now surfing Facebook and other similar social networks to check the backgrounds of prospective applicants. Moreover, postings that discuss a teacher's hygiene or a vice principal's appearance, weight, or accent can create significant embarrassment that might cause some people to withdraw from his or her workplace altogether.

An unsuspecting school principal who may not know about online comments about him or her could in good faith apply for a new employment position and be denied it, because the jokes posted by his students may create a doubt in the minds of his prospective employers that he or she really might be a sexual pedophile. The question that arises is whether even "reasonable" employers, especially in professions such as education, child care, social work, or health care, will take the risk of hiring people into positions of fiduciary authority once their reputations have been marred. If there had been no cases involving teachers and school administrators who have been criminally charged and convicted of engaging in pedophilia and sexual abuse of their charges, then perhaps the matter would be moot because no one would believe the student comments. However, given hundreds of sexual abuse cases in Catholic boarding schools and Native Residential Schools (Stonebanks, in press) as well as teacher misconduct and sexual abuse (Piddocke, Magsino, & Manley-Casimir, 1997), the "ordinary-reasonable person" test may be difficult to apply.

As a number of legal academics have commented (Jafaar, 2002; MacKay & Dickinson, 1998), teachers, like doctors, are held to a higher standard of moral conduct and sometimes pay too heavy a price for the actions they take in their private lives. People work hard to earn a reputation, and losing it because of a frivolous joke online cannot be easy. In many cases, the psychological impact has caused teachers to have nervous breakdowns or go on stress leave. This might explain the immense pressure on teachers' unions internationally to do something to stop antiauthority expression on the Internet.

In peer-to-peer bullying, the impact of this form of cyber-bullying is no less devastating. Consider again the case of David Knight. In David's situation, being labeled as a pedophile internationally might have exposed him to contempt by most reasonable persons. He had career aspirations to become an air cadet and then an airline pilot. His determination and support from family helped him to achieve these career goals. However, the abuse he endured occurred early in the 2000s, before the popularity of Facebook, MySpace, and YouTube. There is no telling whether he would have been accepted into the Canadian air cadets or into pilot training if the military or the airline company he applied were to do a Google search and find online profiles of David described as a sexual predator and pedophile.

Hence, the question at hand is whether most reasonable adults would see the Web site and be sufficiently informed or thoughtful to dismiss the statement, assuming that it was most likely made by kids as a joke. In defining what constitutes a "reasonable, informed, and thoughtful person," we might also consider whether adolescents within the context of peer pressure are sufficiently mature to interpret the statements as true or as defamatory.

Some key Canadian decisions and one Australian ruling relating to cyber libel may shed some light on these questions. Although the cases described here are not in the school context, they contain similarities to the students' online postings. In the first case, *Vaquero Energy Ltd. v. Weir* (2004), Vaquero became aware that anonymous postings on a financial bulletin board operated by Stockhouse Media Corporation contained messages that called the president of Vaquero insane, a moron, and equated him to Adolf Hitler, Saddam Hussein, and Osama bin Laden. The court ruled that these statements would have a significant impact on the reputation of the company and its president and awarded $10,000 CDN for loss of reputation, $40,000 CDN to the president and CEO, and an additional $25,000 CDN as punitive damages to the president.

The courts made similar findings in another case, *Barrick Gold Corp. v. Lopehandia* (2004; cited in Bernstein & Hanna, 2005), which began with a dispute between a large gold-producing company and a mining company as to rights over certain gold reserves in Chile. Lopehandia conducted an Internet campaign over seven months during which he posted false and defamatory material against Barrick to people interested in the gold-mining industry. The accusations included "fraud, tax evasion, money laundering, manipulating world gold prices, misrepresentation, obstruction of justice and crimes against humanity." Barrick was successful in obtaining a motion for default judgment but received only $15,000 CDN in damages because the lower court judge believed that the comments would not be taken seriously by a reasonable reader. The Ontario Court of Appeal overruled this decision and increased the award for general damages to $75,000 plus punitive damages of $50,000. Finally, the court granted a restraining order presenting any further defamatory statements from being made against Barrick or any of its personnel. Relying on an earlier case, *Ross v. Holly* (2004) (as cited in Bernstein & Hanna, 2005),[7] the Court in Barrick observed that Web site postings are far more powerful than e-mail because of their potential to reach a substantially wider audience. Moreover, the court stated:

While it is always important to balance freedom of expression and the interests of individuals and corporations in preserving their reputations, and while it is important not to inhibit the free exchange of information and ideas on the Internet by damages awards that are overly stifling, defendants such as Mr. Lopehandia must know that courts will not countenance the use of the Internet (or any other medium) for purposes of a defamatory campaign of the type engaged in here.

(*Barrick Gold v. Lopehandia*, 2004, as quoted in Bernstein & Hanna, 2005, p. 30)

The Supreme Court of Canada also made clear in *Hill v. Church of Scientology of Toronto* (1995) that a good reputation is as important as freedom of speech, which is not an unfettered right:

A good reputation is closely related to the innate worthiness and dignity of the individual. It is an attribute that must, just as much as freedom of expression, be protected by society's law.... Democracy has always recognized and cherished the fundamental importance of an individual.... The reputation tarnished by libel can seldom regain its former lustre. A democratic society therefore, has an interest in ensuring that its members can enjoy and protect their good reputation so long as it is merited.

(*Hill v. Church of Scientology of Toronto*, 1995)

In a case that is more similar to the situation involving instructors or teachers in positions of authority, the findings in an Australian case, *Cullen v. White* (2003), are relevant. This case involved an educational setting at a university. Cullen was a professor at Divine Word University. One of his former students, William White, created a Web site disputing Cullen's doctoral credentials and posting lewd insinuations that he was a pedophile and inviting others to write defamatory comments. The Australian court stated:

In the present case, I am satisfied that the defamatory publications are likely to have a very harmful effect upon the plaintiff's reputation and his standing as an academic. I also accept that the plaintiff has suffered a great deal of personal distress and anguish as a result of the publications and that they have caused him very considerable annoyance. It is likely that they will make it more difficult for him to obtain appropriate employment in the future. The damages award must compensate him in respect of those matters and be sufficient to signal to the public the vindication of his reputation ... [para. 19]

The plaintiff also seeks exemplary damages. Exemplary damages are awarded where the defendant has been guilty of conscious, high-handed behaviour in contumelious disregard of the plaintiff's rights: *Uren v John Fairfax & Sons* (supra) at 138, 154; *Todd v Swan Television and Radio Broadcasters Pty Ltd* [2001] WASC 334 at [139]. The objects of exemplary damages are to punish the defendant and deter others from similar conduct. They also achieve the appeasement of the victim's sense of grievance: *Cotogno v Lamb* (No 3) (1986) 5 NSWLR 559 at 586 [para. 20].

In my view, this is an appropriate case for an award of exemplary damages. The conduct of the defendant can be attributed only to a conscious desire on his part to cause the plaintiff the maximum amount of damage, hurt and embarrassment by what amounts to a campaign of deliberately offensive vilification [para. 21].

(Cullen v. White, 2003)

The court awarded damages of $75,000 and $25,000 (Australian) in exemplary damages.

Australian and Canadian cyber-libel decisions are promising for victims of cyber-bullying who may want to commence cyber-libel proceedings. However, it is important to emphasize, as Bernstein and Hanna (2005) do, that defamation law, especially in cyberspace, is complex. Therefore, success would largely depend on a range of facts and circumstances specific to each case (see also Lidsky, 2000, for other discussions on cyber libel).

In light of the tendency by Canadian courts to value reputation over freedom of expression (based on the reasonable person test), we might ask what our courts are saying about the responsibility of Internet service providers to monitor and close down bulletin boards, e-mail addresses, and Web sites once they have been notified that cyber-bullying (and as part of it defamation and libel) have occurred. This aspect of defamation law is far more complex and better explained by defamation law experts such as Lidsky (2000) and Bernstein and Hanna (2005). Litigation would entail the launching of a "John" or "Jane Doe" proceeding for defamation. As part of such an action it would be necessary to obtain a court order to compel the ISP or bulletin board operator to disclose the identification information. Furthermore, a determination would need to be made by the courts as to whether the online defamation constituted "broadcasting."

It is worth mentioning a Canadian defamation case, *Newman et al. v. Halstead et al.* (2006), that involved online libel of teachers by an adult, not a student. The case involved numerous plaintiffs (mostly school teachers) who filed a lawsuit for defamation against the adult defendant by the name of Halstead. Halstead was a "community activist" and heavily involved in matters related to the education system through parent organizations and school bodies.

Halstead used e-mail and Web sites to make numerous defamatory statements against the plaintiff teachers, accusing them of violence, bullying, and other inappropriate behavior, both in and out of school. She also implied that some of the plaintiffs were the subject of criminal investigation.

The court found her fully liable for making defamatory statements against the plaintiffs. The court also found that no defenses to defamation were applicable to the case. The court awarded significant damages to the plaintiffs in the amount of $626,000 CDN, including compensatory, aggravated, and punitive damages, in addition to injunctive relief. Halstead was prohibited from making further defamatory comments of the type found in the plaintiff's pleadings, whether by the Internet or otherwise. Moreover, she was required to seek leave from the court before publishing any further statements about the plaintiffs. Although the judgment did not use terms such as cyber-bullying, it did consider Halstead's behavior to be significantly problematic. The intent of the cyber-bullying was to lower the reputations of the teachers involved and to lead to the removal of these teachers from their teaching positions, through pervasive and consistent character assassinations through the use of e-mails, Web site postings, and Internet chat sites, as well as the filing of criminal allegations against certain teachers. Some of the teachers received the brunt of Halstead's attacks more than others. The extent of the harm was varied but severely affected many of the teachers both personally and professionally. It affected their ability to have a rapport with their students as well as parents, some of whom might believe Halstead's stories. Furthermore, the public and widely distributed nature of the comments reduced the possibility of seeking employment elsewhere at other schools.

The American context relating to cyber libel and ISP responsibilities is interesting, and a number of cases are relevant to our discussion.

CYBER LIBEL: THE U.S. CONTEXT

In the United States, according to David A. Myers (2006), one piece of legislation that is relevant to cyber-bullying is the Communications Decency Act (CDA) (U.S. Congress, 1996). This Act grants broad immunity to ISPs. The legislation leaves no one legally accountable for cyber-targeting (which includes cyber-bullying, harassment, stalking, defamation, threats, and so on). Section 230 of this Act provides in part:

(c) Protection for "Good Samaritan" blocking and screening of offensive material.
  (1) Treatment of publisher or speaker. No provider or user of an interactive computer service shall be treated as the publisher or speaker of any information provided by another information content provider.
  (2) Civil Liability. No provider or user of an interactive computer service shall be held liable on account of – (A) Any action voluntarily taken in good faith to restrict access to or availability of material that the provider or user considers to be obscene, lewd, lascivious, filthy, excessively violent, harassing, or otherwise objectionable, whether or not such material is constitutionally protect; or (B) any action taken to enable or make available to information content providers or others the technical means to restrict access to material described in paragraph (1).

(ibid.)

Myers (2006) explains that one landmark case, *Zeran v. AOL* (1997), is the general precedent used by U.S. courts to rule on Internet abuse. This case resulted in leaving no legal accountability for injuries caused by anonymous postings on the Internet. It involved a series of anonymous postings on America Online's (AOL) message board following the Oklahoma City bombings in April 1995. The messages claimed to advertise "naughty Oklahoma T-shirts." The captions on the T-shirts included "Visit Oklahoma . . . It's a Blast!!! " and "Finally a Day Care Center That Keeps Kids Quiet – Oklahoma 1995." The individual who posted the messages identified himself as Ken Z and provided Zeran's phone number as the person to call to order the offensive T-shirts. Zeran received abusive telephone calls and even death threats as a result and notified AOL, which in turn terminated the contract from which the messages originated. However, the perpetrator continued to set up new accounts with false names and credit cards. Zeran finally sued AOL, claiming negligence. The court ruled that Section 230 of the CDA provided absolute immunity to AOL regardless of its awareness of the defamatory material.

The Zeran ruling, Myers notes (2006), maintains the status of Internet providers as "distributors" rather than "publishers." Publishers (e.g., book publishers) are liable for defamation by third parties using their services, especially if they are made aware of them and fail to act to prevent the behavior. The Zeran decision followed a case in which an Internet provider was elevated to the status of "publisher," *Stratton Oakmont v. Prodigy Services Co.* (1995). Prodigy had decided to regulate the content of its bulletin boards (in part, to market itself as a "family-orientated" computer service). By taking on an editorial role, Prodigy opened itself up to greater liability than computer networks that do not edit content. Thus service providers argued that if they agree to monitor and edit online content, they in fact subject themselves to greater liability. This is why most Internet providers ignore reports of abuse. Most are confident that they will not be held liable subsequent to Zeran. The irony of this, as Myers (2006) points out, is that the title of S.230 reads "Protection for 'Good Samaritan' blocking and screening of offensive material." The objective of the CDA was to protect proactive online service providers and preserve competition between ISPs on the Internet.

Myers makes the point that if David Knight were bringing his lawsuit in the United States, S.230 might make it too difficult for him to argue that the Internet provider was aware of and therefore responsible for the Web site with his picture, labeling him as a homosexual pedophile and drug pusher. Nonetheless, he believes "the winds of change are stirring" for S.230 immunity. At the state level, he cites common law case (*Bryson v. News America Publ'ns, Inc.*, 1996). The case involved a fictional story titled "Bryson" written by Lucy Logsdon. Lucy wrote about being bullied at school by Bryson, whom she referred to as a "slut." The real Bryson read the story and remembered living in the same town as Lucy Lodgson. She sued News America for libel and won. The court stated that even though the story was labeled as fictional, it portrayed realistic characters, responding in a realistic manner to realistic events, and that a reasonable reader might logically conclude that the author of the story had drawn on her teenage experiences to write it. Myers suggests that if the courts rely on this case,

David Knight's lawyers might well argue that the Web site with David's picture (labeling him as a pedophile) could reasonably be interpreted as true by those who saw it, resulting in negligence and liability against the Internet provider.

Furthermore, in another case (*Doe v. GTE Corp.*, 2003) involving the secret filming of athletes showering in a change room that was posted and sold on a Web site, the Seventh Circuit Court of Appeals upheld S.230 immunity relying on Zeran, in favor of GTE corporation. However, Judge Easterbrook questioned the reasoning in Zeran, noting that S.230 is supposed to be the "Good Samaritan," blocking and screening offensive material, but, in fact, by eliminating liability for ISPs, it ends up defending abusers and defeating legitimate claims by victims of tortuous abuse on the Internet.

Some American states have created criminal libel statutes. In a 2002 Utah case, *I. M. L. v. State*, a high school student was charged with criminal libel for creating an Internet Web site on which he displayed disparaging comments about his teachers, classmates, and principal. He applied for dismissal of the charges, challenging the criminal libel statute on constitutional grounds. The Utah Supreme Court held that Utah's criminal libel statute was overbroad and unconstitutional. The statute reads as follows:

A person is guilty of libel if he intentionally and with a malicious intent to injure another publishes or procures to be published any libel.

(*I. M. L. v. State*, 2002)

The court held that the statute does not comport with the standard set by the *Times v. Sullivan* (1964), which requires that when the defamatory statements involve public officials, the plaintiff must show that the defendant made the statements with "actual malice" as opposed to "mere malice." Actual malice is defined as making a statement "with knowledge that [the statement] was false or with reckless disregard of whether it was false or not." Common law malice requires only a showing of ill will or spite.

This decision illustrates the support that the courts in the United States give to freedom of expression. The sixteen-year-old student in this case had purported to describe the sexual history of students and teachers at Milford High school. He referred to his principal as a "town drunk" and accused him of sleeping with the secretary of the high school. Another page listed various faculty at the school and made arguably or potentially derogatory comments about most of them, stating that one teacher is a "possible homosexual leading a double life" (para. 2) and that another is "possibly addicted to speed or some other narcotic" (para. 2). He dedicated one page to defending a female student who had apparently been slandered on another Web site. The student had left a piece of paper containing the Internet address of his site in the high school computer lab so that someone would find the site. The judge noted that although the student admitted to creating the site and to hating the principal, the Web site did not appear to be a precursor to school violence. He held that the school had not raised a sufficient claim.

I have managed to locate one U.S. decision that might provide guidance relating to the claim of "privacy" by students who post libelous statement online, claiming they were only meant for certain individuals. The case of *Wagner v. Miskin* (2003) involved a college professor, John Wagner, and his student, Glenda Miskin. In the fall of 1998, Miskin enrolled in a University of North Dakota (UND) physics class and began to harass Wagner through sexually explicit e-mail messages. She also conveyed false statements about him at a UND committee hearing. Wagner filed an action against her alleging libel, slander, intentional infliction of emotional distress, and intentional interference with a business relationship. The District Court, Grand Forks County, entered a judgment on a jury verdict, awarding Wagner $3 million U.S. in damages. The student appealed to the Supreme Court claiming that the District Court had no jurisdiction to hear her claim and that the statements she made at the Committee meeting were not protected by privilege. The court noted that although she disputed his claim for damages of libel at the Committee meeting, he had made no such claim. The court's interpretation might be relevant to claims of "privilege" for statements made on Facebook, for example, based on its description of privileged statements:

A privileged statement... is not privileged for all subsequent publications by virtue of initially being spoken in a privileged proceeding. Miskin seems to assert that once a statement is made in a setting in which it may be privileged, she is free to repeat it at will in other situations. She cites no relevant authority to support her position nor have we found such authority. Even an "absolute" privilege does not permit an individual to categorically republish possibly defamatory statements without consequence *Cf. World Wrestling Fedn. Entm't Inc. v. Bozell*, 142, F. Supp 2 d 514, 534 (S.D. N.Y. 2001 Not in Endnote). (para. 14).

(*Wagner v. Miskin*, 2003)

Although this case does not appear to carry significant clout as Wagner acted for himself, it provides insight into the fact that courts may take this route in holding students accountable for libelous online statements that can be repeated and spread publicly.

NEGLIGENCE, SUPERVISION, AND MALPRACTICE

Moving from whether students can be held responsible for tort law by engaging in cyber libel, there is a second aspect of tort law that applies. This involves the potential for schools to be held liable in an actionable claim for negligence if they do not act quickly to protect student victims of peer-to-peer cyber-bullying. Moreover, it is also worth determining whether teachers, as government agents, can be held legally liable if they fail to educate adolescents to engage in socially responsible discourse.

In "real" space, victims who are injured while at school can bring claims for compensation against teachers and schools for injuries at school or on field trips

(MacKay & Dickinson, 1998). British and North American law historically places on educators a "duty of care *in loco parentis.*" This means that educators have a duty to care for their students as if they were standing in place of their parents. Not only that, an 1893 case, *Williams v. Eady*, established that teachers must act as "careful and prudent parents" when it comes to protecting students.

The key question here is whether this duty of care extends to the responsibility of teachers to *educate* students to be respectful to each other. The "careful parent" legal doctrine does not address teachers' professional responsibilities as *educators*. Although claims for educational malpractice have been made, American courts have categorically denied that schools can be held liable for failing to educate. This implies that teachers cannot be held legally liable when students engage in covert forms of verbal and psychological bullying. The courts maintain that education is a matter of public policy and does not fall into the professional realm as do medical and legal malpractice and that teachers are not considered to be "professionals" in the same sense that lawyers and doctors are. This might be because teachers are generally autonomous in carrying out their teaching duties. As long as they stay within curriculum guidelines, they have the discretion to select educational resources that meet those guidelines.

Jafaar (2002), however, advances a strong argument that public policy is the very aspect of educational malpractice that can work to support victims' claims that are brought against schools. Her arguments are important for victims of bullying. She believes the courts fail to recognize that public education has evolved to develop professional standards of conduct that are no longer confusing and unambiguous. Professional expectations in the public school context are now standardized and easily recognized and therefore should be enforceable at law as a matter of sound public policy.

Jafaar's arguments build on similar positions advanced by Hines (1991) and Parker (1993). She argues that over the past twenty years, as the public school system grew to incorporate the needs of society, the teaching profession has become more standardized. She asserts that even though legislation on schooling might not provide clear standards for teachers as professionals, there are other important sources of public policy that clearly define and establish the professional standards expected from teachers and other education professionals. For example, although the Ontario Education Act provides ambiguous wording with respect to the duty of teachers regarding instruction, "to teach diligently and faithfully the classes or subjects assigned to the teacher by the principal" (s. 264 (1) (a)), in November 1999, the Ontario College of Teachers (OCT) approved and published the Standards of Practice for the Teaching Profession that clarify the scope of this legislated duty. Jafaar (2002) further explains that the fact that the OCT and similar bodies such as the British Columbia College of Teachers have established standards for teacher certification confirms that public school teaching is now a profession, with established standards of professional practice. She argues that the policy directives of teacher certification bodies undermine, if not outright nullify, the argument by courts that no duty of care exists due to the lack of clearly defined standards.

If Jafaar's reasoning is applied to cyber-bullying, a claim might include, for example, a teacher's failure to adhere to British Columbia Performance Standards Guidelines on Social Responsibility (2000). Under these standards, *teachers must monitor the social development of students at different grade levels.* The broader objectives of teaching social responsibility are described as follows:

Human and Social Development is one of the goals of the BC school system. This broad goal further specifies that students are expected *"to develop a sense of social responsibility, and a tolerance and respect for the ideas and beliefs of others."*

(British Columbia Ministry of Education, 1997; emphasis added)

The British Columbia standards provide a framework for monitoring and evaluating a variety of school and classroom programs intended to promote, among other things, student responsibility. Although the standards are discretionary guidelines, they might be useful to courts in determining educational malpractice. However, a better alternative might be to mandate that public school educators receive professional development education regarding bullying in schools as well as knowledge of the relevant legal standards.

In an earlier U.S. case, *Hunter v. Board of Education of Montgomery County* (1982), the dissenting opinion of Judge Davidson provides an anomaly in terms of acknowledging an actionable tort of educational malpractice. In this case, the sixteen-year-old plaintiff claimed that he had negligently been required to repeat first grade and this had social consequences resulting in bullying. It led to embarrassment, learning deficiencies, and "loss of ego strength" (ibid., p. 582). Justice Davidson stated his opinion as follows:

In my view, public educators are professionals. They have special training and state certification is a prerequisite to their employment. They hold themselves out as possessing certain skills and knowledge not shared by non-educators. As a result, people who utilize their services have a right to expect them to use that skill and knowledge with some minimum degree of competence.

(ibid., p. 589)

Judge Davidson argued that he would have articulated the applicable pedagogical standard as one "based upon customary conduct" (Hines, 1991, p. 158), the standard applied in medical malpractice claims, and rejected the commonly held judicial assumption that acceptance of such a claim would result in a flood of litigation:

In recognizing a cause of action for educational malpractice, this Court would do nothing more than what courts have traditionally done from time immemorial – namely provide a remedy to a person harmed by the negligent act of another. Our children deserve no less.

(*Hunter v. Board of Education of Montgomery County*, 1982, p. 590)

It is important to consider that if students are not receiving reciprocal respect from teachers, if they sense that their teachers are not engaged in promoting their well-being and education, if they are tacitly condoning peer-to-peer bullying by turning a blind eye, then all of these might in effect contribute to the antiauthority forms of expression that emerge online. Because most students are not well equipped to raise formal protests regarding a lack of attention to their overall education, the antiauthority forms of cyber-bullying could, in fact, represent expressions of the lack of attention to students' social development.

For example, if particular teachers neglect to provide guidance on civil and social responsibility, if they model forms of bullying themselves and know that the courts will not hold them responsible for educational malpractice in the same way that doctors are held responsible for medical malpractice, they are bound to expend less effort to develop social responsibility in young people. Hence as educational professionals, it seems ironic that teachers who might in fact ignore a central part of their mandate are not held accountable to it, but in turn call loudly for accountability by the very students they have failed to educate in social responsibility. This is where I argue strongly in support of Jafaar (2002) that teachers ought to be held accountable to certain standards to educate for social responsibility in schools. I believe if this were the case, we would witness a lot less of the negative online postings by students about their teachers. It boils down to issues of mutual trust and respect, which my own research suggests are almost absent in many schools.

I believe it is essential to pay more attention to the fact that negligence to educate children for social responsibility can result in egregious psychological harm. A Canadian decision, *Gould v. Regina (East) School Division, No. 77* (1997), left the door slightly ajar to the possibility that teachers might be held liable in cases of egregious (but unspecified) psychological harm to students. In this case, seven-year-old Jacklynne and her parents brought an action against the Board of Education and its employee, teacher Karen Zarowny. Their claim included a claim in negligence and breach of the Education Act, as well as educational malpractice. The plaintiffs alleged that Jacklynne was subjected to "unsatisfactory, inappropriate and objectionable behaviour" (para. 8) by Ms. Zarowny; that she failed to perform the duties of a teacher in accordance with the Education Act; and that she "bullied" the infant plaintiff while she was in her Grade 1 class.

The suit alleged that Ms. Zarowny spoke too loudly in class; bullied, ridiculed, and intimidated her pupils; failed to "fulfill the learning needs of the infant plaintiff;" and modeled intolerance to her students (para. 45). The judge stated that, given the right set of circumstances, conduct that was "sufficiently egregious and offensive to community standards of acceptable fair play" (ibid., p. 18) might support a cause of action for educational malpractice. Although this suggests that egregious forms of bullying and particularly cyber-bullying might indeed qualify, the court did not clarify what circumstances and behaviors might qualify as "sufficiently egregious and offensive." In considering the allegation of bullying by the teacher, Judge Matheson considered how courts should deal with such ambiguity:

> But what standard will the court utilize to judge the appropriateness of the complained of activities? When does speaking in a sufficiently loud enough manner to be heard by all students become unacceptably loud? What one person may perceive as in inappropriately loud and intimidating voice, another person may envision as necessary as an attention getter. And while one student may consider the curriculum as inadequate for his or her needs, the majority of students may reach an opposite conclusion.
>
> It is surely not the function of the courts to establish standards of conduct for teachers in their classrooms, and to supervise the maintenance of such standards. Only if the conduct is *sufficiently egregious and offensive to community standards of acceptable fair play* should the courts even consider entertaining any type of claim in the nature of educational malpractice.
>
> (ibid., p. 18; emphasis added)

Incidentally, this opinion highlights the same difficulties related to recognizing the differences between innocent teasing by peers and bullying. Nonetheless, it would be interesting to determine whether a court would find verbal and cyber-bullying as "sufficiently egregious and offensive" and serious enough to result in psychological harm whether it is instigated by peers against peers, or even if it involves "private" discussions containing libelous comments about teachers. Given the devastating psychological impact on teachers and students, it is plausible that such expression does constitute "egregious psychological harm."

Although peer-to-peer cyber-bullying with its anonymous and nebulous nature ought to be considered offensive to most "community standards of acceptable fair play," it is the antiauthority online postings that have resulted in the most attention from teachers and their unions and from school and government officials. Thus it is in order to conclude that the latter form is deemed to be far more offensive to "community standards of acceptable fair play." The law is slow to change, especially when judges are well aware of the floodgate of litigation that might be unleashed if Internet providers are held liable.

TORT LAW, SUPERVISION, AND RISK

The law of torts and negligence has another area that is applicable to the issue of cyber-bullying. I have dealt with this issue in great detail elsewhere (Shariff, 2003); however, I briefly highlight some of the key legal standards that are applicable to cyber-bullying.

The duty of care obligation on teachers and principals where they are required to act as "careful and prudent parents" was developed more than 100 years ago, when schools were smaller and mainly residential schools. The difficulty of applying it, especially in an era of digital literacies, is less practical.

Nonetheless, failure to supervise students properly can result in an actionable tort of negligence (unintentional tort). The onus is on the student who brings the claim, for example, as a victim of bullying or cyber-bullying, to establish four criteria: (1) that there was a duty of care; (2) that the plaintiff experienced a tangible injury (psychological injury is harder to establish than physical injury); (3) that the injury was foreseeable by the supervisor and could have been prevented; and (4) that the injury was caused by the actions or omissions of the supervisor. Hence, in a case of peer-to-peer cyber-bullying, a victim might report the bullying to the school several times, and the teacher may waive it off as nothing serious or tell the student the problem is a parental responsibility.

If the student attempts to commit suicide and fails and then brings an action for negligence in supervision, it can be argued that there was sufficient tangible psychological harm to cause the student to want to commit suicide; that repeated cyber-bullying was foreseeable; and that it continued because of the failure (omission) by the teacher to prevent it. There are no legal precedents on school negligence in supervision cases relating to cyberspace to date. David Knight's case would have been exemplary had it gone ahead because it would have required the court to consider defamatory Web sites and their role in tort law, both from a supervision and a cyber-libel perspective. However, his claim is now on the way to being settled, so we will not know unless another action is brought before the courts.

Finally, relating to the antiauthority Web sites, it is possible that under tort law a student could be assessed for liability for negligence, even if he claims that he did not intend to harm the teacher with his demeaning words. If the teacher can establish that there was sufficient embarrassment and psychological harm that might cause mental illness or prevent her from finding employment, and if the teacher can establish that the harm from the student expression was "foreseeable" and that the actions or expression of the student "caused" her to become mentally ill, then there is the possibility of liability under tort law. In addition, not realizing that the Internet is public space may not hold out as an excuse.

Although it would be necessary to defer to the expertise of tort law theorists and practitioners, I venture to suggest, that the tort law doctrine of *volenti non fit jura* might come to play. It could be a stretch, but it is worth mentioning. This doctrine works on the principle that if an action carries a certain level of risk and if that risk is known, but if the individual nonetheless undertakes the action, he or she can be held partially liable for any injury resulting from their act. In the case of cyber-bullying, the court might hold that the student knew full well that the Internet is a public space and that he or she ought to be held liable for his or her actions (take for example, cyber libel for defamation of teachers online). It cannot be said for certain whether this doctrine would be applied; hence, at this point it is merely conjecture. Whether the courts continue to rely on century-old principles of tort law to bear in an information age is yet to be seen.

TABLE 3.1. *Tort Law: Cyber Libel and Negligence*

Legal Framework	Standards for Administrators	Standard for Teachers	Standard for Parents	Implied Standard for Students
Tort law (cyber libel)	• Can intervene if nexus to school • Expression must involve "unfair comment" • Expressions that must include an opinion or political statement even if couched in lewd terms can be exempt from libel	• How the libel is interpreted by a person who is *reasonably thoughtful and informed*, rather than *someone who has an overly fragile sensibility* • Can intervene if nexus to school • Expression must involve "unfair comment" • Expressions that include an opinion or political statement even if couched in lewd terms can be exempt from libel	• Need to explain the line at which "joking" in the public realm of cyberspace can cross the line to become libel and result in liability • Need basic understanding of libel laws • International standards – parents responsible for their children's expression online	• Learn that cyberspace is rarely private space • Know limitations on free speech • Learn to make political statements or state opinions in a respectful manner that does not include libel or defamatory statements • Take leadership in encouraging responsible use by peers • Inform others who cross the line • Participate in developing codes of conduct • Help adults to reconceptualize the value of digital literacies
Tort law (supervision)	• Duty of care *in loco parentis* • Obligation to act as "careful and prudent parent"	• Duty of care *in loco parentis* • Obligation to act as "careful and prudent parent"	• Equally responsible for supervising and being aware of their children's online postings and discourse	• Legal doctrine of *volenti non fit jura* says students can be held responsible for their actions if they know the risk involved and still undertake libel – might apply

Table 3.1 summarizes the legal considerations that have been discussed in this chapter. As the cases and Table 3.1 highlighted in this chapter suggest, students are adamant regarding their rights to free online expression, taking the position that their statements are not meant to be libelous. How successful have they been in their claims for constitutional protection of free expression? Chapter 4 highlights a range of constitutional cases that clarify standards at established and emerging law as to the limits of on- and off-campus speech and the extent of school responsibilities to reduce it.

REFERENCES

Akiba, M. (2004). Nature and correlates of ijime – bullying in Japanese middle school. *International Journal of Educational Research, 41*, 216–236.

Associated Press. (2006, October 2). Indiana students outraged over schools' blog crackdowns [Electronic version]. *foxnews.com*. Retrieved October 5, 2006, from http://www.foxnews. com/story/02933217121,00.html.

Bartlett, L. (2007, March 29). Cyber bully concern grows [Electronic version]. *cooltech iafrica.com*. Retrieved March 29, 2007, from http://cooltech.iafrica.com/features/729468.htm.

Bernstein, A., & Hanna, B. W. (2005). *Cyberlibel: Defamation proofing your online world*. Paper presented at the Ninth Annual Canadian IT Law Association Conference, Montreal.

British Columbia Ministry of Education. (1997). Policy circular number 97–04 (pp. 9–10).

Chung, M. (2007, March 25). Online comments were "inside joke." Posts meant for friends only, teen says [Electronic version]. *TheStar.com*. Retrieved August 15, 2007, from http://www.thestar. com/article/195823.

d'Eon, J., & Senoo, Y. (2007, February 10). *Cyber bullies in Japan: A cultural perspective. Study Material*. Paper presented at the initial team meeting of the International Cyberbullying Research Project, McGill University, Montreal, funded by the Social Science and Humanities Research Council of Canada (SSHRC). Shaheen Shariff, Principal Investigator.

Findlay, G. (2007, May 2). Facebook: Student and parent [Electronic version]. *The Current*. Retrieved May 2, 2007, from http://www.cbc.ca/thecurrent/2007/200705/20070502.html.

Fratina, S. (2007). India's Internet censorship policy. Unpublished report produced as part of the International Cyberbullying Research Project, McGill University, Montreal, funded by the Social Science and Humanities Research Council of Canada (SSHRC). Shaheen Shariff, Principal Investigator.

Gibson, C. (2006, August). Standing up to cyber bullies [Electronic version]. *Adelaidean: News from the University of Adelaide*. Retrieved November 28, 2006, from http://www.adelaide.edu.au/adelaidean/issues/13601/news13683.html.

Hasegawa, M., Iwasaki, K., & Nakata, H. (2006). Junior high and high school students' real knowledge and the assessment of risk in using the Internet. *Bulletin of Liberal Arts and Social Science Studies in Kinjo Gakuin University*, 1–12.

Hasegawa, M., Iwasaki, K., & Nakata, H. (2007). *Junior high and high school students' actual knowledge and the assessment of risk in using Internet (Interim Report)*. Paper presented at the initial team meeting of the International Cyberbullying Research Project, McGill University, Montreal, funded by the Social Science and Humanities Research Council of Canada (SSHRC). Shaheen Shariff, Principal Investigator. Translation by Yasuko Senoo.

Hines, M. A. (1991). Malpractice in education. In W. F. Foster & F. Peters (Eds.), *Education & law: Strengthening the partnership* (pp. 154–162). Georgetown, Canada: Canadian Association for the Practical Study of Law in Education (CAPSLE).

Hogg, C. (2006, December 6). Japan's deadly bullying problem [Electronic version]. *BBC News Online*. Retrieved August 14, 2007, from http://news.bbc. co.uk/2/hi/asia-pacific/6213716.stm.

Jafaar, S. B. (2002). Fertile ground: Instructional negligence and the tort of educational malpractice. *Education & Law Journal, 12*(1), at 131–132.

Jaishankar, K., & Shariff, S. (2008). Cyber bullying: A transnational perspective. In F. Schmallager & M. Pittaro (Eds.), *Crimes of the Internet*. (pp. 66–83.) Upper Saddle River, NJ: Prentice Hall.

Jenkins, H., & boyd, d. (2006, May 30). Discussion: MySpace and Deleting Online Predators Act (DOPA) [Electronic version]. *Digital Divide Network*. Retrieved June 12, 2006, from http://www.digitaldivide.net/articles/view.php?ArticleID=592.

Kapoor, G. (2003, May 26). School spats: Fights, squabbles and school rivalries take a nasty turn online [Electronic version]. *Rediff India Abroad*. Retrieved August 12, 2007, from http://www.rediff.com/netguide/2003/may/26bully.htm.

Kuso. (2007). *Wikipedia*. Retrieved August 14, 2007, from http://en.wikipedia.org/wiki/Kuso.

Lankshear, C., & Knobel, M. (2006). *New literacies: Everyday practices and classroom learning* (2nd ed.). Maidenhead, England/New York: Open University Press.

Lidsky, L. B. (2000). Silencing John Doe: Defamation and discourse in cyberspace. *Duke Law Journal, 49*, 862–865.

Linden, A. M., & Klar, L. N. (Eds.). (1994). *Canadian tort law: Cases, notes & materials* (10th ed.). Markam and Vancouver, Canada: Butterworths Canada.

MacKay, A. W., & Dickinson, G. M. (1998). *Beyond the "careful parent": Tort liability in education*. Toronto: Emond Montgomery.

McVeigh, B. J. (2003). Individualization, individuality, inferiority, and the Internet: Japanese university students and e-mail. In N. Gottlieb & M. McLelland (Eds.), *Japanese Cybercultures*. London: Routledge.

Mitchell, A. (2004, January 24). Bullied by the click of a mouse [Electronic version]. *Globe and Mail*. Retrieved August 10, 2007, from http://www.theglobeandmail. com/servlet/story/RTGAM.20040124.wbully0124/BNStory/Front/?query=bullying.

Morita, Y., & Kiyonaga, K. (1994). Ijime: *Kyôshitsu no yamai* [Bullying: Pathology in classrooms] (2nd ed.). Tokyo: Kanedo-shobô.

Myers, D. A. (2006). Defamation and the quiescent anarchy of the Internet: A case study of cyber-targeting. *Penn State Law Review, 110*, 667–686.

Parker, J. C. (1993). Educational malpractice: A tort is born. *Education & Law Journal, 4*, 163–187.

Piddocke, S., Magsino, R., & Manley-Casimir, M. (1997). *Teachers in trouble: An exploration of the normative character of teaching*. Toronto: University of Toronto Press.

Potts, D. (2004a). Defamation on the Internet. Retrieved September 11, 2007, from http://www.cyberlibel.com/introduc.html.

Potts, D. (2004b). *Liability for libel on the Internet*. Retrieved September 9, 2007, from http://www.cyberlibel.com/liabilit.html.

Potts, D., & Harris, S. (2004). *Crystal ball gazing (What is libel and other questions)*. Retrieved September 6, 2007, from http://www.cyberlibel.com/crystal.html.

Rahul. (2007, March 21). Orkut: The sex hub! [Electronic version]. *Merinews*. Retrieved August 12, 2007, from http://www.merinews.com/catFull.jsp?articleID=124543.

Rios-Ellis, B., Bellamy, L., & Shoji, J. (2000). An examination of specific types of ijime within Japanese schools. *School Psychology International, 21*(3), 227–241.

Roher, E. (2007). *Intimidation.com: Dealing with cyberbullying*. Paper presented at the CAPSLE Conference, Vancouver.

Sengupta, S. (2006, November 16). Orkut: The new danger [Electronic version]. *Merinews*. Retrieved August 12, 2007, from http://www.merinews.com/catFull.jsp?articleID=123746&category=Technology&catID=4.

Senoo, Y. (2007). Netto-ijime (cyber-bullying): Bullying moves to cyberspace. Unpublished term paper for EDEM 609 Issues in Education Masters course, Prof. Shaheen Shariff, Department of Integrated Studies in Education, Faculty of Education, McGill University.

Shariff, S. (2003). *A system on trial: Identifying legal standards for educational, ethical and legally defensible approaches to bullying in schools*. Unpublished doctoral dissertation, Simon Fraser University, Burnaby, Canada.

Shariff, S., & Johnny, L. (2007). *Censorship!...or...Selection?: Confronting a curriculum of orthodoxy through pluralistic models*. Rotterdam, The Netherlands: Sense.

Smorti, A., Menesini, E., & Smith, P. K. (2003). Parents' definitions of children's bullying in a five-country comparison. *Journal of Cross-Cultural Psychology, 34*, 417–432.

Song, W. (November 2, 2006). Ijime ga jisatsu ni tsunagaru nihon no 'kuuki' [Electronic version]. *Nikkei Business Online*. Retrieved March 18, 2007, from http://business.nikkeibp.co.jp/article/manage/20061031/112784/.

Stonebanks, C. (in press). *The James Bay Cree*. Rotterdam, The Netherlands: Sense.

Suler, J. R., & Phillips, W. L. (1998). The bad boys of cyberspace: Deviant behavior in a multimedia chat community. *Cyberpsychology & Behavior, 1*, 275–294

Takach, G. S. (1999). Internet law: Dynamics, themes and skill sets. *Canadian Business Law Journal, 32*, 1–83.

Tanaka, T. (2001). The identity and formation of the victim of "shunning." *School Psychology International, 22*, 463–476.

Thomas, C., & Canadian Press. (2007, May 1). Discipline over student postings on Facebook highlight need for education: Ont [Electronic version]. *Redorbit breaking news*. Retrieved August 15, 2007, from http://www.redorbit.com/news/education/919877/discipline_over_student_postings_on_facebook_highlight_need_for_education/index.html.

Yoneyama, S., & Naito, A. (2003). Problems with the paradigm: The school as a factor in understanding bullying (with special reference to Japan). *British Journal of Sociology of Education, 24*, 315–330.

Zhang, W., & Wei, J.-Y. (2007a). *Internet use in China*. Paper presented at the initial team meeting of the International Cyberbullying Research Project, McGill University, Montreal, funded by the Social Science and Humanities Research Council of Canada (SSHRC). Shaheen Shariff, Principal Investigator.

Zhang, W., & Wei, J.-Y. (2007b, July 22). *The cyber-bullying research (China II)*. Hangzhou, China: Zhejiang University, funded by the Social Science and Humanities Research Council of Canada (SSHRC). Shaheen Shariff, Principal Investigator, McGill University, Montreal.

CHAPTER FOUR

Student Free Expression: Do the Schoolhouse Gates Extend To Cyberspace?

[W]hile children assuredly do not shed their constitutional rights at the school-house gate, the nature of those rights is what is appropriate for children in school.

Morse v. Frederick (2007), p. 15

Disliking or being upset by the content of a student's speech is not an acceptable justification for limiting student speech.... Speech within the school that substantially interferes with school discipline may be limited. Individual student speech which is unpopular but does not substantially interfere with school discipline is entitled to protection.

Beussink v. Woodland R-IV School District (1988)

INTRODUCTION

Chapter 3 engaged in a discussion about cultural differences in the way Asian countries are beginning to address students' cyber misconduct compared with countries in the West. I provided legal definitions for defamation and cyber libel and discussed North American and Australian jurisprudence on cyber libel in the context of a number of controversial case examples. Throughout I noted that despite the very public exposure such expressions receive, students maintain that schools have no right to intervene and argue that when they do, school authorities are intervening in private conversations among friends. Moreover, when students have been suspended for their online comments about teachers, some have protested and challenged their schools in court for infringing rights to freedom of expression.

In this chapter, I examine some of those challenges, to highlight what the courts have said about students' rights to free speech, limits on that speech, and limits on the rights and responsibilities of schools to intervene. The court rulings relating to student speech on- and off-campus clarify reasonable guidelines on its limits and the extent of school responsibilities to intervene. However, judicial decisions have been fairly mixed as they relate to the online *content* of such speech, particularly when it comes to assessing the impact on the targets of that speech. Moreover, it will be more useful to engage in an analysis of court approaches to the free expression claims in this chapter if we have some grounding and appreciation of the contemporary contexts in which such speech takes place. For example, one of the key points of contention is supervision. Students already feel they are oversupervised. As with the boys on Golding's island in *Lord of the Flies*, they have finally found an infinite space that is not constantly inhabited by adults. They do not want "Big Brother" watching them at all times while they communicate with friends online. Many parents and civil libertarians agree. They do not believe it is the school's right or responsibility to punish children for engaging in cyber misconduct on home computers. For example, as Bram Koch's father stated on the CBC Radio interview on *The Current*, he was offended when the school basically "walked into his home and told his son what he couldn't do at home" (Findlay, 2007).

Accordingly, I begin this chapter by addressing the issue of adult supervision of kids' spaces and how this causes them to respond or react. Second, to understand both sides of the dispute (free expression versus control of speech), we need to examine more closely the mind-sets that adults bring to their understanding of digital literacies and online communication, compared with students' mind-sets. Therefore, I present theoretical approaches that help to put the current debate into perspective. Third, before engaging in discussion and analysis of the freedom of expression cases, I briefly highlight judicial decisions that consider the impact of online expression. Not all of those decisions were made within a constitutional framework; nonetheless, they provide some indication of what courts have said about how seriously cyber expression that appears libelous or threatening ought to be taken. This is particularly important in relation to its potential impact in the "physical" or offline" world.

SUPERVISION: DOES SCHOOL AUTHORITY APPLY IN CYBERSPACE?

Human beings, like animals, have always been territorial, and as Darwin (2003) informed us, it is all about survival of the fittest. When it comes to the debate involving online student expression that threatens the survival of teacher and school authority as we have known it, this debate becomes very much about survival of the fittest. What makes us different from other animal species is that most animals nurture, protect, and teach their young survival skills for short periods of time and then let them roam independently to learn and fend for themselves. Although in the animal world many dangers lurk in unknown spaces, there is almost an instinctive element of trust by the adults that they have done their best to prepare their young for these dangers. How their offspring use learned survival skills to navigate the dangers is left up to them – unsupervised.

On the other hand, humans teach children how to eat, clean themselves, and communicate; we protect and nurture them until they are old enough to go to school. Once they are at school, we suddenly place more emphasis on supervision, discipline, authority, subordination, punishment, and consequences, with less attention to social survival skills they will need in the contemporary world. High schools rarely teach students how to sustain long-term partnerships with a spouse, nor how to parent, manage finances, budget, food shop, or run a home, although most home economics classes make a superficial effort to do so. Few social studies classes teach students how to network with people who could mentor them in their careers, or even how to use a credit card, avoid getting in debt, or stay healthy (although admittedly schools are increasingly focusing on improved wellness). Nonetheless, we have generally shifted the focus away from preparing our young for life to controlling their behavior, making them conform to rules and laws designed for the benefit of adults, such as zero-tolerance policies and legislation. If those rules do not work, we bring in the police and criminal justice system to keep them in their proper place (Apple, 1990; DiGiulio, 2001; Giroux, 2003; Kincheloe, 2005; McLaren, 1991).

As one of my graduate students, Andrew Churchill, aptly observes, we supervise children's play spaces from a young age. Andrew cites soccer and baseball leagues as examples that are set up to formalize young people's games from the age of four and five. How often have we heard about overzealous and competitive coaches and parents pressuring children to perform at soccer or hockey games, to the point of abuse and breakdown from stress? Moreover, in the last two decades or so, fear of pedophiles and murderers kidnapping children while they play outside has resulted in around-the-clock supervision, even though most adult baby boomers remember roaming free to play for hours without adult supervision.

Exploring the Cyber Forest

Cyberspace to kids is like a forest that awaits discovery for a formerly caged animal. There is much to explore, learn, navigate – an infinite world of wonders but also many dangers. I use this exaggerated metaphor intentionally to argue that technologies have provided youngsters with the spaces they need to explore and learn about issues that are relevant and have meaning to them. Cyberspace provides an arena that gives the impression of being largely unsupervised by adults. In cyberspace, young people can roam free and socialize with peers in a world where parents and teachers are not welcome. So valued has this space become for young people that even those who are victims of cyber-bullying are reluctant to report it for fear that the technology (cell phones or computers) will be withdrawn or that the adults will not understand what is taking place because some of them "do not even own a cell phone" (Campbell, 2005).[1]

Yet as danah boyd (Jenkins & boyd, 2006) reminds us, because of mobile phones, college students report greater ongoing communication with their parents than in previous generations. She cites Misa Matsuda as arguing that networked technologies allow youth to maintain "full-time intimate communities." Hence new media are allowing young people to become more deeply connected to their peers and also to their family members. This provides powerful open channels for communication. These are positive factors that are rarely communicated in news headlines or referred to when we hear how the "Web ensnares" teens (Schmidt, 2006).

Jenkins (Jenkins & boyd, 2006) suggests that most parents and supervisors understand their children's experiences in the context of their memories of their own early years. For the baby-boom generation, those defining experiences involved playing in backyards and vacant lots within suburban neighborhoods, socializing with their friends at the local teen hangout, and participating within a social realm that was constrained by the people who went to one's local school. All of that, he says, is changing. His colleague, danah boyd (ibid.), agrees. She notes that social networking tools such as MySpace and Facebook play a key role in youth lives because they service as "digital publics." This is best explained in her own words:

These sites play a key role in youth culture because they give youth a space to hang out amongst friends and peers, share cultural artifacts (like links to funny websites, comments about TV shows) and work out an image of how they see themselves. They also serve as digital publics, substituting for the types of publics that most adults took for granted growing up, but are now inaccessible for many young people – neighborhood basketball courts, malls, parks, etc. Youth are trying to map out a public youth territory for themselves, removed from adult culture. They are doing so online because their mobility and control over physical space is heavily curtailed and monitored.

(ibid.)

In support of these comments, Jenkins explains that much of the activity that our generation enjoyed as kids is today occurring online:

What teens are doing online is no better and no worse than what previous generations of teens did when their parents weren't looking. The difference is that as these activities are being digitized, they are also being brought into public view. Video games bring the fantasy lives of young boys into the family room and parents are shocked by what they are seeing. Social networks give adults a way to access their teens' social and romantic lives and they are startled by their desire to break free from restraints or act older than their age. Parents [and teachers] are experiencing this as a loss of control but in fact, adults have greater control over these aspects of their children's live than ever before.

(ibid.)

Jenkins goes on to observe that digital technologies simply bring to the surface teenage behaviors that have always been present. These are recorded more permanently online:

Indeed, one of the biggest risks of these digital technologies is not the ways that they allow teens to escape adult control, but rather the permanent traces left behind of their transgressive conduct. Teens used to worry about what teachers or administrators might put in their permanent records since this would impact how they were treated in the future. Yet, we are increasingly discovering that everything we do online becomes part of our public and permanent record, easily recoverable by anyone who knows how to Google, and that there is no longer any statute of limitations on our youthful indiscretions.

(ibid.)

To be more open to the ways in which students are using the Internet and engaging in digital literacies, it is also important to be aware of the mind-sets through which adults tend to approach those tools, compared with the mind-sets that young people adopt. Consider what some of the other experts who study technologies and digital literacies have to say on the issue.

Although most adults use e-mail, Internet, and cell phones, they do not rely on them as tools of social communication to the extent that young people do. Such tools are an integral aspect of virtual (and physical) social networks that have emerged among adolescents and youth with the advent of new technologies. Mediums such as Facebook, MySpace, MSN, SMS, blogs, text messaging, and bulletin boards have become essentials within the lived realities of young people – much more so than those of adults. Many adults continue to perceive technology as a *means to an end* – a *medium*, whereas for young people, the *medium is an integral aspect of the message* – a phenomenon that Marshall McLuhan (1964) introduced some years ago. This is why, as *Time* magazine (Chu, 2005) reported recently, teenagers use computers, Blackberries, and cell phones to communicate, even when their peers or siblings are in the same or neighboring rooms.

Technology has become another normative framework and tool on which young people rely to communicate with one another. However, virtual spaces are extremely different from physical ones, and as such they generate a new set of social conventions among youth. Yet from preadolescents to university students, young people seem to master the technological tools at their disposal with little or no trouble, whereas adults are generally more technologically challenged and frequently turn to young people for guidance. Moreover, cyberspace allows for participation by an infinite audience (on public Web sites, for instance). The world has opened up to children and youth in vastly different ways than it did for their parents and teachers.

ADULT MIND-SETS AND THE DIGITAL DISCONNECT

Although more adults are venturing to join social networking groups, I believe their motivations are to understand the tools better rather than to enjoy their benefits. Parents and teachers, in general, rarely use MSN, MySpace, or Face-book. This increases the disconnectedness of adults and allows them a superficial understanding of the realm of possibilities. It also limits their appreciation of the potential for knowledge transfer in cyberspace.

TABLE 4.1. *Some Dimensions of Variation between the Mind-Sets*

MIND-SET 1	MIND-SET 2
The world is much the same as before, only now it is more technologized or technologized in more sophisticated ways:	The world is very different from before, largely as a result of the emergence and uptake of digital electronic internetworked technologies:
• The world is appropriately interpreted, understood, and responded to in broadly physical-industrial terms. • Value is a function of scarcity. • Tools are for producing. • The focus is on individual intelligence. • Expertise and authority are "located" in individuals and institutions. • Space is seen as enclosed and purpose-specific. • Social relations are viewed in the context of "bookspace" – a stable "textual order."	• The world cannot adequately be interpreted, understood, and responded to in physical-industrial terms. • Value is a function of dispersion. • Tools are for mediating and relating. • The focus is on collective intelligence. • Expertise and authority are distributed and collective (hybrid experts). • Space is seen as open, continuous, and fluid. • Social relations are viewed in the context of emerging "digital media space" – texts in change.

Lankshear and Knobel (2006) have developed a "mind-set" paradigm that illustrates the differences in the mind-sets of most adults and children as they *conceptualize*, use, and approach technology. Table 4.1 features examples from their comparison of the two paradigms (p. 38).

The mind-set paradigm describes the differences in the way that adults (with some exceptions) compared with most young people have adapted to new technologies depending on their worldview and mind-set. Most adults have mastered e-mail and computer technologies, but only superficially. They tend to conceptualize them from Mind-set 1 and attempt to accommodate "it" – what they perceive as "the" new technology and "digital literacy" – to their physical world.

Lankshear and Knobel (2006) argue that it is important to understand and approach new technologies and digital literacies as emerging digital media spaces, texts in change (as opposed to the textual order of book space), and a world that focuses on collective intelligences rather than individual intelligence. Cyberspace opens up a world that provides the media and tools to mediate and relate knowledge rather than tools that simply produce knowledge that can be submerged in orthodoxy and conformity.

Young people have adapted quickly to the cyberworld – a world that cannot be interpreted or responded to in "physical-industrial" (Lankshear & Knobel, 2006) terms but one that enables and accepts collaborative and interactive participation. We have always talked in education about giving students a voice, engaging them in their learning. Yet now that we have the capabilities (that indeed *students* are opting to use), the adults in their lives – parents, teachers, school administrators, and researchers – feel excluded. We are often held back because of the mind-set we adopt. This in turn contributes to sense of disempowerment, and for teachers who value their status and authority over that of students, it becomes a crisis.

Richard Lanham (1995) suggests that under contemporary conditions the notion of "literacy" has extended its semantic meaning from that of being able to read and write to the ability to understand information however presented (as cited in Lankshear & Knobel, 2006, p. 2). This means that digitally literate people must be capable of moving from one medium to another – from text to image to sound and back with fluidity. Lankshear and Knobel explain that the value of digital litera*cies* lies in their ability to help us adapt the message to a range of mediums that can be used for different audiences.

In the context of schools, it becomes clear that the tendency of school boards is to adopt Mind-set 1. The immediate reaction is to keep children safe by installing firewalls and block filters as though they were in the physical world (similar to the kinds of roadblocks, fences, and restraints that would work in real space) or ban the use of cell phones, iPods, and social communications networks in the school and sometimes in the home as punishment. The following comments by the school superintendent in the Birchmount School case evidences the mind-set toward "technology" as something that can be controlled as one entity: "[B]ullying using *a new information technology*...gives kids way more power than they've had" (school superintendent Anne Kerr as quoted in Girard & Nguyen, 2007).

The Limitations of Mind-Set 1

Young people adopt Mind-set 2 and understand the value of digital litera*cies* as *enabling tools – for mediating and relating*. Ultimately, students can easily hack through firewalls – and may seek out the content that schools and parents attempt to censor because of efforts to prevent access. Consider this Australian example. The *Herald Sun* in Melbourne (Higginbottom & Packham, 2007) reports that sixteen-year-old Tom Wood, a Melbourne schoolboy, broke through the federal government's new $84 million Internet porn filter within 30 minutes. Apparently, it took him just over half an hour to bypass the government's filter. Tom also showed reporters from the *Herald Sun* how to deactivate the filter with a few clicks of his mouse. The report says that the teenager ensured that the software's toolbar icon was not deleted. This left his parents under the impression the filter was still working. Tom is a former victim of cyber-bullying and feared that other computer-proficient children would bypass the government filter and put it on the Internet for their friends to use. According to the report, the boy had already spoken to Australian Communications Minister Helen Coonan about cyber safety during a forum in May 2007, saying it was a "horrible waste of money." He had suggested the federal government could have developed a better Australian-made filter that would be cheaper than the overseas blocking device that cost so much.

In response to the *Herald Sun*'s inquiries, the Australian government added an Australian-designed filter, Integard, to the Web site the following Friday. Tom promptly proceeded to break through the new Australian filter within 40 minutes. The government's response to that feat was that they had anticipated children would find ways to get around the NetAlert filters. To prevent that from happening too often, they had contracted suppliers to provide continuing updates. After spending so much taxpayers' money on these filters, the minister noted: "Unfortunately, no single measure can protect children from online harm and . . . traditional parenting skills have never been more important." The filters are designed to stop access to sites on a national blacklist, bar use of chat rooms, and can be tailored by parents to stop access to sites.

Tom stressed that the filters were missing the mark by a long way regardless of how easy they were to break. His words illustrate how little credit we give to youngsters who can see beyond the immediate need to control online expression to the larger and deeper issues that ought to be addressed.

Filters aren't addressing the bigger issues anyway. . . . Cyber bullying, *educating children on how to protect themselves and their privacy are the first problems I'd fix.* . . . They really need to develop *a youth-involved forum* to discuss some of these problems and ideas for fixing them.

(Higginbottom & Packham, 2007; emphasis added)

No expert on cyber-bullying or technology could have put this more succinctly and so insightfully. It is essential that we involve and educate children, but it appears that there is a need to educate ourselves first.

It turns out that the NetAlert scheme cost AU $189 million, which includes $84.4 million for the National Filter Scheme, plus funding for online policing, a help line, and education programs. The Australian government will also offer the option of filtering by Internet service providers. The report states that under its filter program, households can download the filter from or have it sent out to them. Tom's words and activism in showing the lack of thought and futility that goes into many government policy responses that are grounded in Mind-set 1 is crucial to an improved understanding and response to cyber-bullying and misconduct. As we move forward in this text, I present support for Tom's position to explain why it is essential to engage young people in developing collaborative and educational responses to cyber-bullying that absolutely cannot be resolved simply through the purchase of expensive blocks and filters. Nor will they be resolved through the censorship of technologies that are too far advanced to be controlled in traditional ways.

When Mind-set 2 informs the use of digital literacies, as Lankshear and Knobel observe, expertise and authority are no longer top down but involve "collective, hybrid experts" (2006, p. 38). Thus, as they explain, literacy (the ability to read and write), have taken on completely new meanings, such as "the ability to understand information however presented" (ibid., p. 2). These authors are concerned, however, that once people in positions of authority think they understand digital literacy and apply the "it" perspective to institutional contexts of learning, they attempt to control, standardize, and manipulate the tools, technology, and content, as they have done with conventional literacy and the promotion of conformity and orthodoxy:

> Like conventional literacy, digital literacy is being "schooled" to conform to the logic of manipulative institutions (compulsory consumption of services), and to be made into something manageable at the level of totalizing systems. Given space we would run a full argument for cultural practices of computing that parallels [Ivan] Illich's [(1971)] argument for how learning as a cultural practice has been schooled under the logic of manipulative institutions. Indeed, with official constructions of "digital literacy" cultural practices of computing are actually turned into compulsory, consumption of curricularized and certificated learning.
>
> (ibid., p. 7)

These experts on new technologies argue in favor of adopting a sociocultural approach to digital literacies instead of an autonomous model. They explain that according to an autonomous model, literacy consists of skills, tools, and techniques, with more of a focus on cognitive competencies and user abilities. The mind-set adopted remains the same as that applied for Western alphabetical literacy – which consists in mastery of letters and phenomena that are coded and printed. They explain further that unfortunately when this model is applied to digital literacies, it is too simplistic:

> "Digital literacy" consists in so many lists of what the abstracted skills and techniques are that a proficient person can "do." Once they "have" them they can then put them to useful purposes in work, at home, at school, etc., and function "competently." Courses that set about "teaching" learners these tools and techniques, and certify them when they are finished. (The process is almost precisely the opposite from what, for example, young people do when they set about learning how to play online games and to become part of an online gaming community) . . .

> Critique of the autonomous model of literacy from the standpoint of socio-cultural theory does not deny that elements of skill and technique are involved in practices of reading and writing. Obviously, they are necessarily present. The point is, however, that these "skills" and "techniques" actually differ in important ways when they are embedded in different practices which involve different purposes and where there are different kinds of meaning at stake (compare, for example, "searching"). Moreover, the skills and techniques of decoding and encoding do not actually take us very far at all on their own. This is because reading and writing is always "reading and writing with meaning" and this meaning is not primarily, or even substantially, a function of some "skill" or "technique" that might be called "comprehension." It is predominantly a function of social practice, social context, and of Discourse (Gee, 1996) in a sense that is very close to Wittenstein's (1953) concept of "forms of life."
>
> (ibid., p. 8)

I find it ironic that, once again, it is *sociocultural context, value of discourse,* and *meaning making* that are overlooked as institutions grapple with adapting to new technologies. This is no different from what we have seen in the controversies surrounding the banning of traditional textbooks (Shariff & Johnny, 2007). It is no wonder, then, that when students engage in forms of online discourse defined as "cyber-bullying," school officials and teachers tend to place the full responsibility on the shoulders of parents or on behavior "problems" with the students.

In adopting the autonomous approach, schools have tended to overlook their obligation as *educators* to encourage socially responsible and critically informed dialogue and discourse among students. As we have seen, adults feel lost in cyberspace because their mind-set still overwhelmingly resides in the physical world. Hence, when addressing some of the serious emerging issues that concern online harassment, homophobia, death threats, and racial, sexist, and homophobic slurs perpetrated by some students against others (which fall under the umbrella of bullying and cyber-bullying), some educators and researchers look for oversimplified and manageable responses. They search for standardized assessment and intervention tools, as well as evaluation models grounded in their physical world, which they organize into manageable "buckets" as they search for strategies and national "blueprints" to control the emerging problems related to cyber-bullying.

For example, at recent advisory meetings on cyber-bullying (PREVNet, 2006), one group of Canadian experts, comprising academics, researchers, school administrators and officials, students, and nongovernmental organizations, was brought together to discuss cyber-bullying. The objectives were to gain a better understanding of the problem, to develop policy, and to plan interventions and programs to address the issue in schools. Participants were presented with statements such as "bullying hurts" and "bullying is a relationship problem" and asked to consider the cyber-bullying and technology issues within the message of these statements. These "buckets" or statements not only ignored the *sociocultural context* and *diversity* in which bullying occurs but also overlooked the *complexities and range of digital literacies in cyberspace* and their *enabling abilities for mediating and relating.* The approach also ignored the political and systemic hierarchies of power that can develop over time in many schools and greatly affect administrative efforts to foster inclusive, cohesive, and collaborative school environments. Ironically, it was primarily the youth seated around the table at the PREVNet meeting who reminded adult experts – the researchers, psychologists, educators, and sociologists – that it was important to *reconceptualize* their notions of relationships in cyberspace. The young participants spoke about the possibilities of mediation in cyberspace and most insisted that digital literacies have opened up a world with the potential for positive and interesting social relations. The meeting culminated with the decision to create an online advisory committee, where the youth helped adult scholars and educators navigate through cyberspace. The success of such a committee will largely depend on the commitment and recognition of a sociocultural dimension by the network leaders.

As Lankshear and Knobel (2006) explain, the "it" approach seeks to nor-malize, manipulate, and fit the use of new technologies into a nicely packaged and manageable product that can then be marketed across the country and internationally as a "blueprint" that will help to manage the problem. This is the same conceptual approach that underpinned the overwhelming failure of antibullying programs in the physical school context. Since the mid-1990s, schools have been inundated with antibullying programs that were marketed as the "solution" to all bullying problems. Few were successful because they oversimplified the environmental and biological influences, including systemic forms of racism, sexism, homophobia, and ableism (see Anand, 1999; Shariff, 2004; Shariff & LaRocque, 2001). I argue that such an approach yet again represents a form of "selection" as censorship – where the underlying socio-cultural influences and institutional barriers that we have addressed earlier in this book are overlooked as legitimate concerns – whether they occur in the physical school setting or in virtual space.

For the reasons stated here, few adults know how to access or "supervise" what their students and children are doing on home computers, Blackberries, and personal cell phones that have text-messaging and photographic capabil-ities. Therefore, as young people venture easily into the vast and borderless realm of cyberspace, few adult guidelines exist to help users develop ethical responsibilities.

This loss of "control" and media framing of the Internet as fraught with dangers invites the desire to regain control through the only means familiar to adults – through punishment and discipline, or legalized and "forceful" means if necessary. Because "technology" is understood within an adult mind-set to put too much power into the hands of young people, a movement among edu-cators internationally for governments, school boards, and teachers' unions has arisen to develop stronger laws and codes of conduct, clamp down on the "bullies," and avoid the type of anarchy that took hold of the boys on Golding's island. Moreover, because "technology" provides the tools for these forms of bullying, the thrust is to ban or manage "it" to the greatest extent possible by disallowing cell phone, iPod, and laptop use in classrooms and "banning" access to Facebook and similar networks by withdrawing computer privileges as punishment. Before moving on to look at the policy approaches that have emerged as a result of the adult mind-set and reaction to student online expressions, it is important to consider what the courts have said about such expression. This will give us a better idea of how compatible govern-ment and school policy responses are, with the substantive legal responsibil-ities that are laid out under established and emerging law relating to student expression.

FREEDOM OF EXPRESSION VERSUS SAFETY AND PRIVACY

There have been mixed court rulings on the extent of school responsibilities or expectations to interfere when students engage in forms of cyber-bullying from personal computers. In one case, the "Phlashlyte" underground newspaper was critical of school policy. Given that this expression might not have been as offensive as some of the sexual and demeaning commentaries posted online, the court noted:

School officials may not judge a student's behavior while he is in his home with his family nor does it seem . . . they should have jurisdiction over his acts on a public street corner.

(*Sullivan v. Houston Indep. Sch. Dist.*, 1969)

When cyber misconduct first began to emerge in lawsuits, some U.S. judges refused to acknowledge that online harassment contains a violent message. Consider some of the initial court rulings on cyber harassment. In one instance, a student set up a Web site denouncing the administrators and teachers at a university. This Missouri case involved a seventeen-year-old student who was suspended for ten days for creating a Web site from home. The site included vulgar language and made critical comments about the school's homepage. He was ordered to take down the page, an injunction was granted, and the suspension was cancelled on the following basis:

Disliking or being upset by the content of a student's speech is not an acceptable justification for limiting student speech. . . . Speech within the school that substantially interferes with school discipline may be limited. Individual student speech which is unpopular but does not substantially interfere with school discipline is entitled to protection.

(*Beussink v. Woodland RIV School District*, 1988)

The court went on to say that fear of disruption to the school environment must be a *reasonable fear* – not an "undifferentiated fear." The court had a point regarding the "undifferentiated" and "reasonable" fear. As I have discussed elsewhere in a recently published book directed towards parents and classroom teachers (Shariff, 2008), and in the preceding chapters, the fear created by media reports, harsh school policies, and concern about reputation could result in a "chilled environment." In some schools, the reaction to student expression might be the result of an already "poisoned" environment, causing irrational fears in the minds of teachers that the Internet is helping students get out of control. Similarly, in *United States of America, Plaintiff v. Jake Baker* (1995) (as cited in Wallace, 1999), Jake Baker posted a story to the newsgroup alt.sex.stories. His story graphically described the rape and torture of a university classmate. He also communicated (via e-mail to a friend) his plans to actually carry out the rape. Students who read the story were outraged and charged him with criminal harassment. The district court threw out the claim holding that because there was no possibility of physical rape on the Internet, there could be no claim for harassment. Moreover, the court was reluctant to infringe on Baker's freedom of expression rights. The precedents set by these courts were followed in *The People v. B. F. Jones* (1886).

The case involved sexual harassment of a female participant in a MUD (multiuser domain) group by Jones, a male participant. The court explained that

It is not the policy of the law to punish those unsuccessful threats which it is not presumed would terrify ordinary persons excessively; and there is so much opportunity for magnifying undefined menaces that probably as much mischief would be caused by letting them be prosecuted as by refraining from it.

(as cited in Wallace, 1999, 288)

This reluctance by the courts to avoid involvement in the quagmire of cyberspace is not surprising. The courts have also typically adopted a hands-off approach in matters of educational policy. In the realm of physical violence in schools, for example, U.S. courts have set a high threshold for plaintiffs to bring claims for negligence against schools, in some cases even when students have been shot or knifed (Shariff & Strong-Wilson, 2005).

As the court said in the 1969 case, *Tinker v. Des Moines Independent Community School District*, "students do not leave their rights to free expression at the school house gates." Consequently, it is important to make an informed assessment that where online comments posted about teachers are honest and close to the truth, they ought not to be reacted to with such force. Where the comments are clearly libelous or threatening, it is worth talking to the students to determine the source of their anger. Is the anger rooted in a poisoned school environment? Are the resulting cyber comments the only outlet of expression for students? The following case is an example of a school's overreaction to student online discourse.

In a Washington State case, a tongue-in-cheek Web site, the "Unofficial Kentlake High Home Page," was created by Emmett, a high school senior, cocaptain of the basketball team, with a 3.95 grade point average. (In North America, a 3.95 grade point average out of 4.0 means that Emmett was a straight "A" student.) The Web site included positive and negative disclaimers and joke obituaries. The purpose of the joke obituaries was to release some of the tension of exams and assignments, where students wrote their own obituaries for a laugh. On the basis of the joke obituaries, an online voting system began on the Web site about "who should die next" and become the subject of the mock obituaries. Someone reported the Web site to the media, who reported the site as including a "hit list" of people Emmett was planning to kill. The Web site was immediately taken down, and Emmett was expelled for "intimidation, harassment, disruption to the educational process, and violation of Kent School District copyright." A restraining order was also granted. Emmett sued the school, and the court stated the following:

The School District argues, persuasively, that school administrators are in an acutely difficult position after recent school shootings.... Web sites can be an early indication of a student's violent inclinations.... The defendant, however, has presented no evidence that the mock obituaries and voting were intended to threaten anyone, did actually threaten anyone, or manifested any violent tendencies whatsoever.

(*Emmett v. Kent School District No 413*, 2000)

The court drew attention to the overreaction by the school, which was out of context to the online joke about people being killed. In this case, the court ruled that the fact that the Web page was created outside of school grounds without school supervision was relevant to the school's ability to discipline, even if the intended audience was school-based.

This case is important for students such as Brad and Bram, discussed in Chapter 3, who were suspended for their online expressions. These boys believed that their comments were outside of school jurisdiction, as well as some of their parents, would support the *Emmett* decision as being fair. However, other judicial decisions have made it clear that if there is a nexus (or connection) to the school (peers, teacher, school property), then there is an absolute right to intervene.

For example, the court handed down a different ruling in a Pennsylvania case. J. S. was a student in the eighth grade at Nitschmann Middle School during 1997–1998. Kathleen Fulmer had taught there for twenty-six years as a math teacher. J. S. informed a fellow student that he had created a "Teacher Sux" Web site that included on it:

> Why Fulmer should be fired
> She shows off her fat f____ legs
> She's a bitch
> Why should she die?
> Give me $20 to help pay for the hitman
> Diagram of Mrs. Fulmer with her head cut off
> (*J. S., a Minor, v. Bethlehem Area School District* (2000)

After viewing the Fulmer site, the principal informed Mrs. Fulmer because he took the threats seriously. Mrs. Fulmer was frightened, fearing someone would try to kill her. Mrs. Fulmer had lasting effects, including stress, anxiety, and loss of appetite, sleep, weight, and sense of well-being. The court stated that schools must teach by example the shared values of a civilized society. It is not socially acceptable to threaten or harass those that are charged with educating our youth. The student's Web site materially disrupted the learning environment. The principal was embarrassed by the student's allegations, and Mrs. Fulmer felt threatened. Teachers and students were aware of the student's disdain for school officials and discussed the Web site at school. This behavior presented a substantial interference with the educational process.

The school board voted to expel the student permanently from its schools. The student appealed, and the decision went to trial. The trial judge supported the decision. On appeal to the Commonwealth Court of Pennsylvania, the court upheld the expulsion because the contents of the Web site constituted threats that were criminal in nature and not constitutionally protected (ibid.).

This decision was similar to a Canadian case of telephone bullying, where fourteen-year-old Dawn Marie Wesley hanged herself after one of her classmates uttered the words "You're f....g dead!" over the phone after ten days of intense bullying (*R. v. D. W. and K. P. D.*, 2002). Dawn Marie's perpetrator was charged with criminal harassment because the "perceived intent to harm" was taken seriously by the victim as actual intent to harm, resulting in her suicide. Although this was a lower court ruling, it may have opened the door to future claims, including those involving cyber-bullying, in which perceived intent of harm is real. Biber et al. (2002, as cited in Glaser & Kahn, 2005) found that unwanted sexual comments and harassment online were found to be most threatening. They suggest that the online medium may be more frightening than face-to-face harassment, especially because the perpetrator can take refuge in his or her virtual identity.

Fourteen-year-old D. W. H., the teenager who said the words, was held criminally liable but maintained throughout that she had no intention of killing Dawn-Marie. D. W. H. was invited on various American television talk-shows including that of celebrity Oprah Winfrey, and in some cases made to apologize publicly for Dawn-Marie's death – something that I felt was too harsh a punishment for a teenager who uttered words that young people often use in uncontrolled anger but rarely mean literally.

To make matters worse, D. W. H. was an aboriginal Canadian. The Caucasian girls who had joined her in bullying Dawn-Marie were let off with no criminal liability or court sentence. What was even more unfair in my opinion was a lecture delivered to D. W. H.'s aboriginal community on bullying by U.S. "bullying" expert Barbara Coloroso ("It's a girl's world: A documentary about social bullying," 2004 [video]).[2] It seems ironic that an aboriginal community that had sustained generations of bullying and abuse from North American settlers, a community that had its children torn away from its families and placed in Catholic residential schools to be beaten and sexually abused by priests, a community that bears the scars of generations of displaced families and cultural traditions because of colonization, was also subjected to a lecture on why bullying is not acceptable. The First Nations people in Canada were subjected to terrible abuses by European colonists who wanted to "civilize" them. Hence, I would argue that we are never justified as a society to take "bullying" at face value. There is always a larger context that requires attention. This is why I seriously caution against being too quick to lay blame on children and the Internet, without critically questioning our own institutional systems and power hierarchies.

Landmark school cases from both Canada and the United States, however, do provide some direction as to where the courts stand under existing law and how they might rule in cases of cyber-bullying that require censorship of student expression by schools. In each of these cases involving free speech in schools, one of the key considerations is *space* – or where the expression occurs. Questions of where the speech originated (on- or off-campus), who instigated it, how it affected others, and how it was addressed by officials inform the deliberations of this issue by the courts. As we attempt to apply these deliberations to the contemporary context, we must remind ourselves that even though cyber-bullying takes place in the electronic airwaves, it creates unwelcome physical school environments where equal opportunities to learn are greatly reduced

(Shariff, 2003). Cyber-bullying, regardless of where it originates, is an *educational* issue. However, as I have stressed earlier in this chapter, responses to it cannot be addressed and accommodated to fit a convenient package of interventions to be blueprinted. The legal considerations discussed now support my view that a conceptual understanding of the freedom versus authority issues that emerge as a result of cyber-bullying are far more complex.

Constitutional Considerations

In most democratic nations, freedom of expression is guaranteed to its citizens. In the Canadian context, Section 2 of the Charter (Canadian *Charter of Rights and Freedoms*, Schedule B, *Constitution Act*, 1982, *Canada Act*, c. 11 [UK]) provides that everyone is entitled to freedom of "thought, belief, opinion and expression." These freedoms are only limited by Section 1 of the Charter, which helps the courts weigh and balance individual rights with the collective rights of the greater good in a democracy. Accordingly, Section 1 of the Charter states that the rights set out in it are subject "only to such reasonable limits prescribed by law as can be demonstrably justified in a free and democratic society." Any school policy that infringes on individual rights must therefore be justified by the policy maker as having *a pressing and substantial objective* to protect the greater good of society. The onus also rests with policy makers to establish that the rights in question will be infringed *as minimally as possible* (see *R. v. Oaks*, 1996).

According to MacKay and Burt-Gerrans (2005), the Section 1 analysis has generally been applied to justify protecting the widest possible definition of freedom of expression. These scholars explain that expression is constitutionally protected as long as it is not violent (*Irwin Toy Ltd. v. Québec (Attorney General)*, 1989). This means that *any expression that intends to convey nonviolent meaning* is normally safeguarded by the courts. This wording is critical when we consider the student postings online. Depending on the exact content of the expression, if students are simply joking about their teachers and *intend to convey nonviolent meaning*, it should be safeguarded by the courts.

This interpretation has been extended to the school setting. For instance, one of the best-known Canadian cases of protected freedom of expression in schools is *Lutes v. Board of Education of Prairie View School Division No. 74* (1992). The case involved a rap song that contained a message to students to reduce promiscuity. Chris Lutes sang a song by Salt 'N' Pepa titled "Let's Talk about Sex" in school even though the song had been banned by the school district. He was suspended and sought judicial review. The court found that his freedom of expression rights under Section 2(b) of the Canadian *Charter of Rights and Freedoms* had been violated and that the policy banning the song did not reasonably justify the infringement of those rights. In fact, the court stated that this was an overreaction to an educational song about sexual abstinence because an assistant superintendent was visiting the school at the time when Lutes, knowing who he was, continued to sing it in his presence.

A U.S. court took a similar position involving a student's political speech on MySpace. The main issue in the case, *A.B. v. State of Indiana* (2002), was whether a high school student's messages on a MySpace page constituted protected political speech under Indiana State constitutional protections regarding freedom of expression. Article 1, Section 9, of the Indiana Constitution reads:

No law shall be passed, restraining the free interchange of thought and opinion or restricting the right to speak, write, or print, freely, on any subject whatever, but for the abuse of that right, every person shall be responsible.

The student, A. B., was prosecuted on six counts of harassment in juvenile court for posting messages on two MySpace pages (one created by a friend and another by herself) with respect to her principal, which the state alleged constituted harassment. Her message on her friend R. B.'s MySpace page read as follows:

Hey you piece of greencastle shit
What the fuck do you think of me [now] that you can['t] control me? Huh?
Ha ha ha guess what I'll wear my fucking piercings all day long and to
School and you can['t] do shit about it! Ha ha fucking ha! Stupid Bastard!
Oh and kudos to whomever made this [I'm] pretty sure I know who).
Get a background.

(appellant's application p. 69)

The next day she posted: "die . . . gobert . . . die" (ibid., p. 70). Separate from the Web page created by her friend R. B., A. B. created a publicly accessible group on MySpace under the group name: "Fuck Mr. Gobert and GC School" (ibid., p. 71). Mr. Gobert testified that he never received these postings directly but only viewed them on the respective Web sites after gaining access to them. The juvenile court stated the following when it handed down a nine-month probation sentence with various conditions attached:

As the well known U.S. Supreme Court decision "One knows Pornography when one sees it," this court finds that such language is obscene in the context used by [A. B.] [A. B.] was not exercising her constituted rights of free speech in such a tirade – but to use the most vulgar language she could. Moreover she was not expressing her opinion in her writing.

(para. 1, n.p., Court of Appeal reasons for Judgment)

A. B. appealed the decision on the grounds that her freedom of expression rights had been infringed. The appeal court reviewed Article 1 and noted that to be protected, the form of speech should constitute "the free interchange of thought and opinion." The appeal court found that A. B. was strongly protesting the school policy against ear piercing and that although she conveyed this message using foul language, she was still making a political statement. The second prong of the test was whether the principal, Mr. Gobert, had established that the harm he received was analogous to "tortuous injury." The court found that he had failed to do this and concluded that, indeed, A. B.'s right to freedom of expression had been infringed. The court overturned the juvenile court probation for harassment, ruling as follows:

> [W]e are mindful that political expression is not shielded from all criminal liability. *Price*, 622. N. E.2 d at 954. As we stated before, "when the expressions of one person cause harm to another in a way consistent with common law tort, an abuse under Section 9 had occurred." *Id*. At 964: see also *Shoultz*, 735 N. E. 2 d at 825–26. Here, the State failed to produce any evidence that A.B.'s expression inflicted particularized harm analogous to tortuous injury on readily identifiable private interests as required to rebut A.B.'s claim of political speech. Based on the evidence before us, we find that there is insufficient evidence to support that A.B.'s adjudication of harassment based on her posted message of February 15, 2006, is consistent with her right to free speech contained in Article 1, Section 9 of the Indiana Constitution. Therefore, we hold that A.B.'s conviction for harassment contravened her right to speak, as guaranteed by the Indiana Constitution. Accordingly, we remand to the trial court with instructions to vacate her adjudication.
>
> (ibid., p. 10)

This decision, like Lutes, has significant implications for policy as it relates to student expression on social communications networks and Web sites. Both cases provide support for the protection of *substantive* expression – which has clear objectives, no matter how it is conveyed, even if foul language is used. Forms of expression that simply demean the reputations of teachers and peers without any underlying political message or stating of an opinion might more readily be considered to be harassment or, as discussed in Chapter 3, libel.

Most U.S. cases continue to use a triumvirate of cases that took place more than forty years ago as standard guiding precedents. These cases, and subsequent decisions that rely on the standards set out by the U.S. Supreme Court, bring to clearer focus the limits on student free expression in the school context. While the triumvirate of cases do not apply to cyberspace, subsequent cases involving student expression off-campus have continued to rely on them.

Expression as "Material and Substantive Disruption"

The decisions rendered in Lutes and A. B. support a standard for free speech in schools established in U.S. cases: unless student expression *materially and substantially* disturbs the learning process, it cannot be censored or suppressed. For instance, in a landmark 1969 case, *Tinker v. Des Moines Independent Community School District* (1969), John and Mary Tinker and Christopher Eckhardt were suspended because they wore black armbands to school as a silent form of political protest against the Vietnam War. They had ignored school administrators' warnings not to wear them. They sued the school district under the freedom of expression provisions of the First Amendment. The court ruled in favor of the students, stating the famous dictum that "[i]t can hardly be argued that either students or teachers shed their constitutional rights to freedom of speech or expression at the schoolhouse gate" (*Tinker v. Des Moines Independent Community School District*, 1969, p. 506).

Servance (2003) explains that the key to the *Tinker* holding is that unless schools can show a valid reason for restricting it, students should be allowed to express their right to free speech. The court acknowledged, however, that this is not an unfettered right. Students have a right to regular speech unless that speech either materially disrupts a school's ability to carry out its mission in an orderly fashion or infringes on the rights of others to be free from harassment. It is the *material and substantial* standard created in *Tinker* that courts continue to apply in contemporary cases. As noted by Justice Fortas:

> The principle of these cases is not confined to the supervised and ordained discussion which takes place in the classroom. The principal use to which the schools are dedicated is to accommodate students during prescribed hours for the purpose of certain types of activities. Among those activities is personal intercommunication among the students. . . . This is not only an inevitable part of the process of attending school; it is also an important part of the educational process. A student's rights, therefore, do not embrace merely the classroom hours. When he is in the cafeteria, or on the playing field, or on the campus during the authorized hours, he may express his opinions, even on controversial subjects like the conflict in Vietnam, if he does so without "materially and substantially interfere[ing] with the requirements of appropriate discipline in the operation of the school" and without colliding with the rights of others . . . *but conduct by the student, in class or out of it, which for any reason – whether it stems from time to time, place, or type of behavior – materially disrupts classwork or involves substantial disorder or invasion of the rights of others is, of course, not immunized by the constitutional guarantee of freedom of speech.*
>
> (ibid.; emphasis added)

There is no question that Justice Fortas was referring to the school environment as it was then, but if this standard continues to apply in contemporary cases of free expression and supervision, it is arguable that the prescribed hours of schoolwork have changed as students are increasingly expected to work on computers and access the Internet for their school-based assignments outside of school hours. Furthermore, a key point in this statement is that personal communication among students "is not only an inevitable part of the process of attending school; it is also an important part of the educational process" (ibid.). It can be argued that if intercommunication among students is an integral aspect of the educational process, and if such communication "materially or substantially" disrupts the learning of others (thereby affecting their rights of equal access and opportunities to learn without harassment or discrimination), schools have the authority to censor it. The learning environment in schools is no longer restricted to the campus. It is fluid. Interaction in the physical school setting continues in cyberspace. Students (and teachers) through e-mail continue their intercommunication in cyberspace. Thus the on-campus/off-campus distinction is not easily defined. It is much more realistic to consider the educational environment in terms of physical and virtual contexts in which learning and student communication takes place.

When the nature of student intercommunication crosses the invisible but very real line from regular horseplay and teasing to bullying, there exists a responsibility for an educational response from schools, especially when there is a nexus to the school (Mitchell & Kendall, 2007; Roher, 2007). When the bullying moves into the virtual school environment without any supervision or attention from educators, it can have devastating consequences not only on student learning but also on student health (Shariff, 2004).

Cyber-bullying against peers, teachers, or school officials has a profound impact on the learning of all students, both on and off school property. Justice Fortas's comments regarding student conduct in class or out of it are applicable in this regard: "[w]hether it stems from time to time, place, or type of behavior – materially disrupts class work or involves substantial disorder or invasion of the rights of others is, of course, not immunized by the constitutional guarantee of freedom of speech" (*Tinker v. Des Moines Independent Community School District*, 1969, p. 513). Accordingly, it makes sense that if the courts are to continue relying on *Tinker*, that it is this aspect of the case that applies to restrictions on freedom of speech in the cyber-bullying context. This is not to say that I disagree with the decision in the context of the silent political protest that was made by the students concerned in the case. I wholeheartedly agree that students do not leave their rights to free speech at the schoolhouse gate. I stress, however, that when such speech comprises harassment and abuse of other students and embarrassment of teachers and school officials without being addressed through some form of dialogue and communication with the students involved, it creates a hostile and unwelcome environment for students (both on campus and in cyberspace) because it disrupts the educational objectives of schools.

Chapter 5 addresses the issue of school environment in greater detail to illustrate that it is not just the students who can poison the learning environment but also the teachers and school officials, depending on how they develop and implement educational and disciplinary policies and practices.

Expression as "Disruption of Basic Educational Mission"
In the U.S. context, a new standard on student speech was set in 1986. The Supreme Court held in *Bethel School District No. 403 et al. v. Fraser, a minor, et al.* (1986) that schools may prohibit speech that undermines their "basic educational mission" (p. 504). The case involved a campaign speech made by student Matthew Fraser that contained insinuations to sexual and political prowess:

I know a man who is firm – he's firm in his pants.... [He] takes his pants and pounds it in.... He doesn't attack things in spurts – he drives hard, pushing and pushing until finally – he succeeds.... [He] is a man who will go to the very end – even the climax for each and every one of you.

(ibid.)

The school suspended Fraser, noting that his speech distressed some students at assembly. He was not allowed to speak at graduation and sued the school under his First Amendment rights to free speech. Responding to the dissenting opinions in *Tinker*, the court voiced its concerns about the need for schools to retain control over student behavior and noted that schools are not the type of arena for the type of vulgar expression in Fraser's speech. The court noted that schools should not have to tolerate speech that is inconsistent with school values. While the court acknowledged that it is crucial to allow unpopular speech, it emphasized that schools have a vital role in preparing students to participate in democratic society, by teaching students the "appropriate form of civil discourse" necessary in civil society (ibid., p. 511).

Of significant relevance to censorship of online student expression today, this ruling also stated that schools must teach students the boundaries of socially acceptable behavior (Servance, 2003). The court stated that threatening or offensive speech has little value in a school setting and cannot be ignored by schools. Moreover, the court noted that the speech infringed the rights of others (although it did not specifically state it, on the rights of females in the audience). The sexual insinuations to rape were clearly offensive and threatening to students.

The *Fraser* decision extends *Tinker* and is also, in my view, applicable to censorship of student freedom of expression in the cyber-bullying context. As I have explained in Chapters 2 through 4, a substantial amount of the emerging research on Internet communications discloses sexual harassment, sexual solicitation, and threats against women or female students. Not only does this form of cyber-bullying materially disrupt learning and impede educational objectives, it creates power imbalances within the school environment and distracts female students from equal opportunities to learn. Consistent with the *Fraser* ruling, expression of this infringes their constitutional rights in an educational context and creates a hostile and negative school environment (physical and virtual).

The triumvirate of cases was also relied on recently in a landmark U.S. Supreme Court decision, *Morse v. Frederick* (2007). This well-publicized case, more commonly known as the "Bong Hits for Jesus" case, involved the off-campus expression by Frederick, a senior student at an Alaska high school. Although this case has no connection to the Internet, some of the issues it dealt with might well be applied by a court on the limits of student expression outside school grounds and even in cyberspace. The facts of the case are as follows. On January 24, 2002, the Olympic Torch relay was scheduled to pass by the school, so the principal, Morse, allowed students and staff to watch the relay as an approved school event or field trip. Students were allowed to line up on both sides of the street, and some stood across the street from the school. Frederick and his friends unraveled a fourteen-foot banner bearing the phrase "BONG HITS FOR JESUS" as the torch bearers and camera crews passed by. (A "bong" is a device for smoking marijuana.) Morse approached the group and demanded that the banner be taken down. All the students except Frederick complied. Morse took the banner and told Frederick to go to the office, after which she suspended him for ten days. Morse informed the court that her reasons for suspending him were due to his advocacy of drug use during a school-sanctioned event.

Frederick sued Morse and the school board, claiming violation of his First Amendment free expression rights. At first instance, the court granted Morse and the board summary dismissal of the claim, holding that Morse had not violated Frederick's rights. The Ninth Circuit Court of Appeals, however, reversed the lower court ruling, finding a violation of Frederick's First Amendment rights.

At the Supreme Court level, a 5–4 majority, in a controversial decision, reversed the Ninth Circuit decision. The court found that because the banner advocated the use of illegal drugs, a school principal could restrict, at a school event (whether on campus or outside of it), student speech where such speech can reasonably be regarded as promoting illegal drug use. The case is important for our purposes because it marks some recognition by the top U.S. court of the ability of the principal to exercise control over student behavior and expression outside the strict boundaries of the school and is somewhat of a departure from the usual emphasis of free speech over governmental authority control that usually marks U.S. decisions on student speech. The landmark precedent could plausibly influence further judicial decisions regarding control of communications on the Internet. However, given that the subject matter in this case was the well-recognized danger of drug use, it may be a stretch to say that because school principals can control expression related to that issue, they can also control expression that affects the school but emanates from home computers or personal cell phones. On the other hand, the court relied strongly on the *Tinker* and *Fraser* cases, bringing into the framework of analysis the standards of "material and substantial disruption to learning" and disruption of the "educational mission." Some of the quotations from the case are interesting and include the following:

1. On page 2 of the reasons for judgment, the court quoted *Fraser*, which quoted from *Tinker*: "[T]he rights of students must be applied in light of the special characteristics of the school environment."
2. On page 10 of the reasons for judgment, again quoting *Fraser*, the court stated that "the constitutional rights of students in public school are not automatically co-extensive with the rights of adults in other setting."
3. On page 11, the court noted: "*Kuhlmeier* acknowledged that schools may regulate some speech even though the government could not censor similar speech outside of school" and the famous *Tinker* quote: "[W]hile children assuredly do not shed their constitutional rights at the schoolhouse gate, the nature of those rights is what is appropriate for children in school."
4. Finally, on page 15 of the reasons for judgment, the court said this: "School principals have a difficult job, and a vitally important one. When Frederick suddenly and unexpectedly unfurled his banner, Morse had to decide to act – or not act – on the spot."

(*Morse v. Frederick*, 2007, p. 15)

All of these statements by the Supreme Court suggest that student free speech in a school *context* (not necessarily within school grounds) can legitimately be controlled by school authorities, if such expression is perceived to have a negative influence on other students or disrupt learning. The last point that refers to the principal's need to make an on-the-spot decision under pressure is very relevant to recent controversies in which students have been immediately suspended for their online expression. The decision also suggests that students cannot expect the same amount of freedom off school grounds as adults can to say what they want. In the context of cyber-bullying, the quote "while children assuredly do not shed their constitutional rights at the schoolhouse gate, the nature of those rights is what is appropriate for children in school" could apply to both sides of the schoolhouse gate if there is a nexus to the school. There are a number of decisions that support school intervention if there is a nexus to the school.

Nexus: Computers as School Property

Under Section 8 of the Canadian Charter of Rights and Freedoms, everyone has the right to be free from unreasonable search and seizure. Hence protection of privacy is guaranteed within reasonable limits in a free and democratic society. Furthermore, Section 7 of the Charter states that "everyone one has the right to life, liberty and security of the person." In the cyber-bullying context, both these sections are relevant. The boundaries with respect to the obligations on schools to override search and seizure rights to protect others must be balanced with the right to life, liberty, and security of the person. Furthermore, victims might argue that their rights to life, liberty, and security of the person are infringed under Section 7 when schools fail to intervene and protect them from cyber-bullying.

Based on Section 1 considerations, the courts generally give priority to the safety of the greater number of stakeholders as justification for overriding privacy rights. For example, the Supreme Court of Canada, in *R. v. M. R. M.* (1998), ruled that as long as a school principal is not acting as an agent of the police, he or she can search student lockers if there is a suspicion of hidden weapons or drugs. The high court held that school lockers are the property of schools. When there is a danger to safety and learning of the students, the infringement on student privacy rights can be reasonably justified under Section 1 of the Charter. Given the devastating psychological consequences of cyber-bullying on victims and the entire school environment, it is possible that in a Charter interpretation that requires a balancing of the victim's right to safety under Section 7 and the perpetrators' right to computer privacy under Section 8 and free expression under Section 2(b), the court might rule in favor of the victim.

For example, MacKay and Burt-Gerrans (2005) explain that the rationale used by the Supreme Court in *R. v. M. R. M.* was that students should already have a lowered expectation of privacy because they know that their school principals or administrators may need to conduct searches in schools and that safety ought to be the overriding concern to protect students. This perspective strongly resembles the *Morse v. Frederick* decision in terms of the lowered expectation of privacy. The high court explained its interpretation of a safe and ordered school environment:

Teachers and principals are placed in a position of trust that carries with it onerous responsibilities. When children attend school or school functions, it is they who must care for the children's safety and well-being. It is they who must carry out the fundamentally important task of teaching children so that they can function in our society and fulfill their potential. In order to teach, school officials must provide an atmosphere that encourages learning. During the school day, they must protect and teach our children.

R. v. M. R. M., 1998)

This statement by the court is also highly significant to indirect or unintentional cyber-bullying of teachers. The statement places a high responsibility on teachers and the protectors of children and disseminators of education.

The court's rationale is along the line of U.S. cases that have also confirmed school lockers as the property of schools. Therefore, it is not an infringement of constitutional rights to search and seize the contents if they breach school policies (*Singleton v. Board of Education*, 1995). For example, the courts noted in *People v. Carlos Overton* (1967) that schools can issue policies regarding what may be stored in school lockers. Correspondingly, educators are entitled to conduct spot checks or involuntary searches of lockers to ensure that students comply with these regulations. In fact, the courts regard the inspection of student lockers not only as a right but also as a *duty* of schools when it is believed that a student is using school property to harbor illegal materials. This logic could certainly be applied to the cyber-bulling context if schools have a censorship policy regulating the type of content that may be sent or received from school computers. For instance, it could be argued that, similar to lockers, e-mails are owned by the school because they are transmitted using school property. Therefore, if a student is suspected of sending harassing comments via e-mail or has found such comments while browsing on school computers, the school officials should consider it their responsibility to monitor and discipline this activity.

This point might be further justified by other cases (including *Garrity v. John Hancock Mut. Life Ins. Co.*, 2002), which found that employers have a right to inspect employee e-mail accounts when employees are notified that messages are accessible to a third party. With regard to school searches, we can also consider cases such as *New Jersey v. T. L. O.* (1985). In this ruling, it was held that although students have a legitimate expectation of privacy within the school setting, schools also have a right to search student property, without a warrant, if there are reasonable grounds for suspecting that the student is violating either the law or the regulations of a school. If this is expanded to cyberspace and the virtual school environment, it could be argued that the nexus to school is no longer limited to physical space. Therefore, although students have a legitimate expectation of privacy for their online conversations, if there is some connection to the school, especially to teachers as authority figures, it follows that something needs to be done about it. Again, it would seem reasonable for schools to apply this rationale if there is reason to believe that students are using school computers or school Web sites to conduct illegal activity such as the harassment of others.

TABLE 4.2. *Freedom of Expression Standards*

Legal Framework	Standards for Administrators	Standard for Teachers	Standard for Parents	Standard for Students
Constitutional Principles – Freedom of Expression Canadian Charter	• Must justify infringement of rights to protect greater good and minimally impair stakeholder rights	• Must justify infringement of rights to protect greater good and minimally impair stakeholder rights	• Teach children that freedom of speech is a right but not an "unfettered right"; it is not unlimited, and there are boundaries	• Know their rights to free expression • Know the limits on those rights • Can be held accountable for overstepping limits
American First Amendment	• Can intervene if expression *materially and substantially disrupts learning* • Can intervene if expression *disrupts educational mission* • Expression that contains opinion or protest is protected regardless of how obscene or lewd unless administrator can prove harm to reputation or psychological harm • Can intervene if expression is on school computers or Web sites	• Can intervene if expression *materially and substantially disrupts learning* • Can intervene if expression *disrupts educational mission* • Expression that contains opinion or protest is protected regardless of how obscene or lewd unless an administrator can prove harm to reputation or psychological harm		• Expression can be opinion or political statement and can be lewd or obscene but cannot be defamatory or libelous (unfair comment) and cannot *materially or substantially disrupt learning or the educational mission* • Cannot express from school computers or Web sites

CONCLUSION

So far I have identified standards that relate to tort law (cyber libel and negligence in supervision) and to constitutional rights (freedom of expression vs.
privacy). These legal frameworks and case law were presented within the context of why students might continue to believe that they have more rights to
privacy and protected speech in cyberspace than in the real world. I discussed
the adult tendency to oversupervise children compared with the childhoods of
previous generations. I highlighted differences in the mind-sets of adults and
children as they conceptualize and approach the Internet and digital literacies.
I illustrated a range of cases to identify and clarify a set of reasonable expectations for schools on the extent of their responsibilities to act, as set out in
Table 4.2. Having learned about reasonable expectations of schools in navigating the completing rights and responsibilities, we can now look at emerging
policy responses that are being applied through new laws, statutes, proposed
bills, and informational Web sites that provide guidelines for schools. We can
determine whether these legal and policy responses meet the judicial standards
expected of schools or whether they fall short in some way.

One area of law that we have not yet brought into the picture – human
and civil rights jurisprudence – is instructive in helping us make such a determination. In Chapter 5, I draw on tribunal and judicial decisions involving
harassment and bullying that adjudicated institutional responsibilities to provide school environments conducive to learning. The chapter considers whether
jurisprudence applies to the cyber context and whether the policy responses
meet the mark.

REFERENCES

Anand, S. S. (1999). Preventing youth crime: What works, what doesn't and what it all
    means for Canadian juvenile justice. *Queen's Law Journal, 25,* 177–249.
Apple, M. W. (1990). *Ideology and curriculum* (2nd ed.). New York: Routledge.
Campbell, M. (2005). Cyberbullying: An old problem in a new guise? *Australian Journal
    of Guidance and Counseling, 15,* 68–76.
Canadian Charter of Rights and Freedoms, Schedule B, Constitution Act, 1982, Canada
    Act, c. 11 (UK).
Chu, J. (2005, August 8). You wanna take this online? Cyberspace is the 21st century
    bully's playground where girls play rougher than boys. *Time, Canadian Edition,* 42–
    43.
Darwin, C. (2003). *The origin of species.* New York: Signet Classics.
DiGiulio, R. C. (2001). *Educate, mediate, or litigate? What teachers, parents, and admin-
    istrators must do about student behavior.* Thousand Oaks, CA: Corwin Press.
Findlay, G. (2007, May 2). Facebook: Student and parent [Electronic version]. *The
    Current.* Retrieved May 2, 2007, from http://www.cbc.ca/thecurrent/2007/200705/
    20070502.html.
Girard, D., & Nguyen, L. (2007, March 24). Students, police clash [Electronic version].
    TheStar.com. Retrieved April 1, 2007, from http://www.thestar.com/article/195604.

Giroux, H. (2003). *The abandoned generation: Democracy beyond the culture of fear.* New York: Palgrave Macmillan.

Glaser, J., & Kahn, K. B. (2005). Prejudice, discrimination, and the Internet. In Y. Amichai-Hamburger (Ed.), *The social psychology of the Internet.* Oxford, England: Oxford University Press.

Higginbottom, N., & Packham, B. (2007, August 26). Student cracks government's 85M porn filter [Electronic version]. *Herald Sun.* Retrieved August 26, 2007, from http://www.news.com.au/story/02359922304224-421,00.html.

It's a girl's world: A documentary about social bullying. (2004). [Video.] Montreal: National Film Board of Canada.

Jenkins, H., & boyd, d. (2006, May 30). Discussion: MySpace and Deleting Online Predators Act (DOPA) [Electronic version]. *Digital divide network.* Retrieved June 12, 2006, from http://www.digitaldivide.net/articles/view.php?ArticleID=592.

Kincheloe, J. L. (2005). *Classroom teaching: An introduction.* New York: Peter Lang.

Lankshear, C., & Knobel, M. (2006). *New literacies: Everyday practices and classroom learning* (2nd ed.). Maidenhead, England /New York: Open University Press.

MacKay, A. W., & Burt-Gerrans, J. (2005). Student freedom of expression: Violent content and safe school balance. *McGill Journal of Education, 40,* 423–443.

McLaren, P. (1991). Schooling the postmodern body: Critical pedagogy and the politics of enfleshment. In H. A. Giroux (Ed.), *Postmodernism, feminism, and cultural politics: Redrawing educational boundaries* (pp. 144–173). Albany: State University of New York Press.

McLuhan, M. (1964). *Understanding media: The extensions of man.* New York: Mentor.

Mitchell, K. E. W., & Kendall, P. E. (2007, April). *YouTube, MySpace and Facebook: Emerging issues for educators.* Paper presented at the Canadian Association for the Practical Study of Law in Education (CAPSLE), Conference, Vancouver, Canada.

PREVNet. (2006, December 15). Cyber-bullying Meeting. PREVNet, Promoting relationships and eliminating violence, a national network funded by Canadian Centres for Excellence, Toronto.

Roher, E. (2007, April). *Intimidation.com: Dealing with cyberbullying.* Paper presented at the Canadian Association for the Practical Study of Law in Education (CAPSLE) Conference, Vancouver, Canada.

Schmidt, S. (2006, November 15). Web ensnares teens up to eight hours a day; instant messages average 40 a day. *Gazette,* p. A14.

Servance, R. L. (2003). Cyber-bullying, cyber-harassment and the conflict between schools and the First Amendment. *Wisconsin Law Review, 6,* 1213 at 1215.

Shariff, S. (2003). *A system on trial: Identifying legal standards for educational, ethical and legally defensible approaches to bullying in schools.* Unpublished doctoral dissertation, Simon Fraser University, Burnaby, Canada.

Shariff, S. (2004). Keeping schools out of court: Legally defensible models of leadership to reduce cyber-bullying. Educational Forum. *Delta Kappa Pi, 68,* 222–223.

Shariff, S. (2008). *Cyber-bullying: Issues and solutions for the school, the classroom, and the home.* Abington, England: Routledge.

Shariff, S., & Johnny, L. (2007). *Censorship!...or...Selection?: Confronting a curriculum of orthodoxy through pluralistic models.* Rotterdam, The Netherlands: Sense Publishers.

Shariff, S., & LaRocque, L. (2001). *Unpublished report on violence in schools and school anti-violence policies for British Columbia Ministry of Education.* Simon Fraser University, Vancouver, Canada.

Shariff, S., & Strong-Wilson, T. (2005). Bullying and new technologies: What can teachers do to foster socially responsible discourse in the physical and virtual school environments? In J. Kincheloe (Ed.), *Classroom teaching: An introduction* (pp. 219–240). New York: Peter Lang.

Wallace, P. (1999). *The psychology of the Internet*. Cambridge, England: Cambridge University Press.

CHAPTER FIVE

Fostering Positive School Environments: Physical and Virtual

You don't know me . . .
　But I know you . . .
　I've been watching you at school . . .
And if you don't want to die . . . I'd sleep with one eye open
　Down on your knees, bitch!
　　Raveger, Raveger

(Shariff, 2001)

INTRODUCTION

My first experience with cyber-bullying began with an e-mail from "Raveger, Raveger." The e-mail was sent to our daughter Shelina (pseudonym), when she was about fifteen years old, in Grade 11 at a high school in British Columbia, Canada. We came home one afternoon and found her pale and frightened, which was unusual for this normally feisty teenager. She handed us a printout of the e-mail that is quoted above. As a parent, I was concerned about Shelina's safety. Was this a pedophile? Was it an adult at school? If a student was involved, did he know her walking route home from school? The reference to watching her at school brought the threat into the realm of the physical school environment, despite the fact that it was sent over the weekend from a home computer. School police liaison officers were unsuccessful in tracing the e-mail, and our efforts to trace the source of the e-mail through the Internet service provider (ISP) met a brick wall. First there was no response to our calls and e-mails. When eventually contacted, an ISP manager explained that he could not shut down the e-mail source to protect the client's free expression rights.

A male classmate eventually confessed that he and three others had sent the e-mail from his home computer. Once the boy learned police were involved, he owned up to being coerced by the primary instigator, Mike (pseudonym). Apparently Mike had wanted to date Shelina, who had refused his advances and sought revenge through e-mail. Although school administrators were provided with the perpetrators' names, the boys were not disciplined because the e-mail was not sent from school. Consequently, the harassment continued at school, where Shelina was stalked and verbally bullied by the boys, who continued to go by the name of "Raveger." During one classroom project, the boys insisted on having Shelina join their group. The teacher saw no problem with that, becoming impatient at Shelina's reluctance to join them. Shelina burst into tears. Once the problem was explained, the teacher confessed to having no prior knowledge of the incident, despite the principal's commitment to us that he would inform all Shelina's teachers about the threats the four boys had perpetrated.

This very personal example of cyber-bullying raised a number of important issues for me as a parent and educator. There were concerns, of course, about the e-mail being sent from a home computer, on a weekend, and received on a weekend. Hence it raised all the on-campus/off-campus issues relating to who is responsible that I have discussed in previous chapters. I have also addressed the issue of the responsibility of the ISP to close the Web site down, based on the *Zeran v. America Online, Inc.* (1997) precedent in Chapter 3; hence it is not surprising that the ISP provider did not bother to return our calls for at least a week. There are a number of concerns that this e-mail raises that I have not addressed, however, which I deal with in this chapter. The first concern is the issues of sexual and homophobic harassment and their prevalence in cyber-bullying. I also mentioned this issue in Chapter 2 but would like to provide some background in here on the biological and socializing influences that shape young people's identities, their attitudes, and, ultimately, their behavior toward others, whether face to face or online.

That aspect of the discussion then leads into a review of relevant human and civil rights jurisprudence on sexual and homophobic harassment and the role of that jurisprudence in determining institutional responsibilities to provide positive school environments that are nondiscriminatory and inclusive. As the discussion in this book so far has disclosed, what takes place in the virtual environment has significant impact on the experiences of students and teachers in the physical school setting. Accordingly, if cyber expression and conduct is useful, empowering, and positive, this will be reflected in the school environment. If it is defamatory, libelous, discriminatory, and tacitly condoned, it will result in a chilled or poisoned environment in which the problems will simply perpetuate themselves. Protection of children as provided by United Nations International Convention of the Rights of the Child and state and provincial child protection laws might also contribute to the fostering of such an environment.

Accordingly, I have organized this chapter to inform readers about the biological and social influences that contribute to the development of male and female identities within their homes and cultural contexts, followed by socializing influences that shape their sense of location or identity within those contexts and greater society, including cyberspace as a social environment. I incorporate research findings on the extent of sexually charged online bullying from several articles I have written on gendered cyber-bullying as part of a consultation for the United Nations secretary general (Shariff, 2006; Shariff & Gouin, 2006). This is followed by a look at what the human and civil rights jurisprudence suggests as appropriate standards of institutional responsibility to ensure harassment-free environments, responsibilities to protect under international human rights provisions, and state and provincial obligations under child protection laws. The chapter culminates in a table that highlights institutional legal responsibilities.

GENDERED INFLUENCE ON CYBER-BULLYING

Previous chapters suggest a number of gender differences in the way males and females engage in cyber-bullying and communicate with friends through online social networks. As we have seen, many perpetrators are male teenagers. Is aggression really bred in the bones of young men, or is it simply the way in which their biological conditions at prepuberty and during puberty combine with the social messages they receive from their caregivers and educators? The statistics presented in Chapter 2 suggest that females are more often targets of sexual harassment, cyber threats, cyber-stalking, and unsolicited pornographic materials. However, more fascinating are the studies suggesting that cyberspace has, in many countries and cultures, had a liberating effect on girls. I highlight studies in this chapter that report how communication technologies have helped girls and young women become more social and confident and to develop a new sense of identity and agency that helps them break free from cultural and social nonfeminist expectations and stereotypes.

The role of the home, especially parents and caregivers in supporting and enhancing gender roles, is especially important. Gender roles that are allocated from a young age play out in cyberspace. Those roles also influence the ways in which adults approach technology use by girls and boys. They further play a significant role in informing the perspectives of government and school policy makers, teachers, the media, and other members of the community, each of whom have a stake in what children learn and express.

Socialization

As soon as children come out of the womb, while still at the hospital, they are learning. When they come home with their parents, they begin to incorporate through sense, smell, sound, movement, language, and their parental responses various cues about communication and the fact that they are social beings in their new world. Before we move on to consideration of the social factors that so often define gender roles in our society, we might ask whether biology has anything to do with whether children will eventually engage in bullying in any of its forms as they get older. The debate about whether the tendency for violence is rooted in biology or the environment has not been entirely resolved.

The Biology of Bullying

Some suggest that nature and nurture both affect bullying. Biology and the social, family, and educational environments that students experience are the primary forces involved in bullying. Genes, hormones, personality traits, or physiological impairments occurring during pregnancy or early infancy can significantly affect later development. As Boyd observes, "What's bred in the bone will come out in the flesh" (2000, p. 95). Writing in 2007, we can now add: "What's bred in the bone will come out in physical and virtual flesh" as kids take on new personalities in cyberspace. Environmental influences can be considered the "nutritional elements" that interplay to result in positive or negative behaviors. It is important to look at the biological and environmental factors in schools, in the home, and in cyberspace that affect student identifies, attitudes about themselves, and behaviors toward others. Understanding how these factors affect students helps us gain insight into how and why bullying of any kind occurs.

Relevant scholarship in the past two decades has largely defined bullying as a "developmental" problem – focusing on aggressive tendencies or behavior of individual "bullies" and suggesting that those individuals need "intervention" or "treatment." In other words, the matter has been, and continues to be, studied from a paradigmatic psychological perspective – as a *health* issue. This is slowly changing as developmental psychologists and other researchers globally have begun to realize the importance of *context*. It is important nonetheless to highlight briefly some of the biological influences that might make a difference in whether a student engages in bullying, becomes constantly targeted as a victim, or stands by as an observer.

Biological factors, including genetics, hormones, allergies, overactive thyroids, attention-deficit disorders, and other physiological influences can influence young children's propensity to bully. Children who exhibit chronic behavior problems from biological sources comprise approximately 6 percent of the school population (National Crime Prevention Council [NCPC], 1997; Shariff, 2000). Two major sources of concern here are nutrition and medication. Research tells us, for example, that substance abuse and lack of nutrition during pregnancy or the preschool years impair the growth of brain cells and that fetal alcohol syndrome (FAS) affects one-third of young offenders (NCPC, 1997). A number of researchers found that violent offenders have distinct personality traits that originate in early childhood, such as hyperactivity, impulsivity, poor concentration, inability to defer gratification, and low empathy. Others have found that these traits remain constant through to adulthood (Reiss, Roth, & National Research Council [U.S.], 1993).[1]

Olweus's (2001) international study on bullying corroborates these studies. He found that bullying behavior starts early and persists into adulthood.[2] However, according to the NCPC (1997), the neurological effects of FAS, including hyperactivity, disruptive behavior, and attention-deficit disorder (ADD), can be offset by good nutrition and emotional support from adults. Furthermore, studies reported by the NCPC found that reading to children at an early age stimulates nerve and cell growth. Children who are malnourished at home can be hospitalized and nurtured back to health (although the damage may not be completely reversed). What is not known is whether children with these kinds of physical challenges engage in or perpetrate cyber-bullying. This would be an interesting study to undertake, given the numbers of youth from India and China, some of whom experience malnutrition from poverty.

Another significant factor is genetics with a special focus on gender differences, which is the primary reason I have introduced biological considerations in this chapter on home and gender. Given that, in general, boys tend to engage in more aggressive forms of bullying and girls in more psychological and covert forms, it is plausible that the differences might be due to genetics. It is noteworthy that psychological forms of bullying can equally aggressive, as seen in studies reported later in this book. Some studies show that human aggression is biologically determined but that its influence on human behavior is minimal.[3] Boyd (2000), however, argues strongly that genetic factors in male aggression cannot be discounted. He points to empirical evidence that the criminality of biological parents is more strongly correlated with crime in children who were put up for adoption than with the criminality of parents who adopted them.[4]

There is considerable research evidence that hormones play a role in influencing behavior.[5] Boyd (2000) makes a case for testosterone as a critical factor in male aggression. He traces the research on this all the way back to Aristotle, who, 2,500 years ago, noted the physiological effects of castration on men. While castration can have a social impact on men's behavior, approximately 100 years ago scientists determined that the internal secretions of the testes also have a physiological effect on male aggression. D. H. Starling coined the word "hormone" (which means "to set in motion") for the "chemical messages" that cause certain behaviors (ibid., p. 119).

Boyd refers to what criminologists call the "age-crime curve" (ibid., p. 121) to support his claim that hormones are critical contributors to male aggression. He observes that in the United States, Canada, and Britain, violent crime by young men increases markedly around age fifteen, reaches a peak before age twenty, and then declines by age of thirty. By age forty, it becomes a rarity. Significantly, this pattern of male violence can be found in every nation for which reliable evidence is available. According to Boyd (2000), the age-crime curve for homicide in the United States, for example, is shaped like Mount Everest. Significantly, although the curve in the United Kingdom is about one-tenth the height of the U.S. curve, it is identical in shape. This might confirm the prevalence of cyber-bullying and, in particular, sexual and homophobic harassment online, at adolescence, a topic to which I return later.

A number of studies (Artz, 1998; Boyd, 2000; DiGiulio, 2001; Lanctot, 2001) indicate that both genders increase their violent behavior between Grades 5 and 10 or 11 (ages nine to fifteen or sixteen) around the first onset of puberty and through to the midteens. Tolman, Spencer, Rosen-Reynoso, and Porches (2001) report an increase in, for example, homophobic bullying and sexual harassment among adolescent boys. They surveyed eighth-grade students (148 girls and 133 boys) in a suburban middle school serving working- and middle-class white and Latino students. Students were asked to report the types and levels of sexual harassment they had experienced at the school. The researchers were struck by how the teenagers' emerging sexuality and exploration of early romantic relationships pervaded the school environment. They heard how people "hooked up" and "broke up" and how the boys watched each other "kicking g's" (kicking gays). They noticed that boys experienced tremendous pressure to publicly demonstrate their heterosexuality to their male peers. This translated into making sexual comments about girls and their bodies, or acting in an overtly sexual way in relation to girls. The researchers observed that

Participating in this form of sexual harassment, whether by making the comments or colluding with boys who do, was not only *normalized* by the boys as simply part of being a boy, but an integral aspect of *proving that they are not gay and therefore not subject to harassment themselves.* Further, through listening to boys' and girls' descriptions of their experiences with harassment, alongside their experiences with early romantic relationships, sexual harassment in early adolescence began to sound like a "dress rehearsal" of sorts for heterosexual relationships.

(Tolman et al., 2001, pp. 1–2; emphasis added)

They explained that sexual harassment is so normalized that both genders often fail to report it. As I mentioned in my discussion of the statistics on cyber-bullying in Chapter 2, this is an important observation that researchers could miss. This is why narrow definitions of "bullying" or "cyber-bullying" might miss important statistics on sexual, homophobic, or racial harassment, or combinations of those forms, because the children being surveyed may not consider them to fit within their understanding of bullying. An increase in the prevalence of sexual bullying just before and during adolescence is definitely corroborated in the research findings on cyber-bullying presented earlier. The Tolman study has important implications for the safety of both genders. The more intense the pressure is on boys to prove they are not gay, the more girls are subjected to sexual harassment. Boys perceived to be gay are also targets for severe and persistent homophobic bullying.

Suicide and homicide rates are other indicators of the influence of testosterone. Before puberty, girls and boys have approximately equal rates of homicide and suicide (Boyd, 2000; DiGiulio, 2001). However, by age thirteen, male rates of homicide and suicide are twice as high as female rates; by age sixteen, male rates are four times as high, supporting Boyd's argument that genetics play an important role:

Testosterone is inextricably tied to male sexuality, and the intensely sexual period of adolescence is when we all begin developing relationships. We are competing with our peers, advertently or inadvertently, for the attraction of potential sexual partners; we learn of betrayal, of unrequited love, and of love lost . . .

At any age problems with intimate relationships can produce conflict, hostility, and violence. But in adolescence, when testosterone is rushing about the testes, and young men are still on a learning curve, the potential for aggression and violence is at its apex. What happens when, in these circumstances, young men experience confusion, misunderstanding, and disappointment? In the absence of corrective influences, it is not surprising that young men express anger, irritability, aggression and violence.

(Boyd, 2000, p. 137)

The rush of hormones in adolescence means the potential for aggression and violence is at its apex. What happens when, in these circumstances, young men experience confusion, misunderstanding, and disappointment? In the absence of corrective influences, it is not surprising that young men express anger, irritability, aggression, and violence. Puberty and hormones might also have this effect on girls, although less dramatically compared with the effects of testosterone on boys.[6] Most serious cases of female bullying[7] involve disputes about relationships with boys that might also be influenced by hormones, as the girls reach puberty and experience sexual arousal. It appears that biological influences might explain at least part of the equation. Consider now the environmental influences on bullying, which I believe have a significantly larger impact on the persistence and extent of bullying and cyber-bullying.

Society at large, the home, and the school are the principal environmental influences on bullying. General attitudes toward violence in society may influence children to engage in bullying. For example, when adults model high levels of tolerance for violence, children may decide that it is an acceptable form of behavior, regardless of whether adults tell them it is wrong. Moreover, children and adolescents internalize the violence they see in movies, on TV, and in music videos and may regard it as socially acceptable.

Gender Socialization Begins at Home

Gender socialization also begins at home. Depending on whether young people are supported through dialogue and communication with parents, invested in trusting relationships, and are happy and comfortable at home, the way in which they are socialized also affects how young people might participate in cyber-bullying or adopt leadership roles in trying to prevent their peers from engaging in it.

Environmental influences in the home, especially during early childhood and adolescence, might account significantly for children's motivations to bully (NCPC, 1997). When parents do not bond with their infants in a trusting relationship, children cannot develop confidence to explore their social environment or develop autonomy and are motivated to seek power and validation through aggression and bullying.[8] A large body of literature establishes a correlation between early negative familial experiences and aggressive behavior in children.[9] The research confirms that child abuse in the home contributes significantly to a range of negative consequences such as poor self-concept, aggressive tendencies, alcohol and drug abuse, sexual promiscuity, and depression. Studies have also found, however, that a strong parent-child bond reduces aggression in later life (Farrington et al., 1992, as cited in Hall, 1999; Nelson & Lewak, 1988). In the context of cyberspace, this could make the difference between engaging in cyber-bullying, accessing pornographic and hate sites, or making the decision to avoid those sites and stay away from peers who engage in online harassment and insults.

Female Gender Roles

These findings are consistent with research on bullying showing that it begins at an early age and that perpetrators and victims experience low self-esteem, lack of confidence, and suicidal feelings. This does not, however, explain the behavior of girls who also engage in aggressive physical bullying or persistent and vicious cyber-bullying. Some studies suggest that this tendency might have something to do with the fathers. Artz (1998) reports interesting findings in a study of physically aggressive girls from middle-class homes. She discovered that girls with aggressive fathers tended to exhibit the level of aggression expected of males. The girls also engaged in more typical female bullying techniques, such as stalking or tricking others into meeting them in isolated places so that they could beat them up.

In her interviews, Artz found that each girl who engaged in aggressive physical and covert psychological bullying had been sexually abused by either her father or a male family member or male family friend. The girls were neglected and received little support from their mothers, who were also dominated by their spouses. To regain their sense of power, the girls blamed victims for breaking unwritten rules (e.g., calling them a "bitch" or "whore") or accused them of stealing a boyfriend. In their minds, this justified the violence. Artz believes that the girls engaged in physical bullying to seek attention and admiration from boys and to fill the void from lack of attention from their fathers. They were also more sexually active than most girls their age.

Imagine the power that the anonymity of the Internet might provide to such girls. Rumors and gossip in the physical or virtual school environment have been identified as reasons for increased violence in a number of high-profile bullying cases.[10] In each case, the perpetrators spread rumors about the victim's attempts to steal her boyfriend or spread the word that the victim had called a popular girl a "bitch." Also in each case, the social group began to gossip and churn up resentment against the victim. This method of bullying is covert because victims do not have the opportunity to defend themselves but suffer the effects of the lies and whispering about them. It results in isolation and ostracism, creating the power imbalance that helps the perpetrators convince themselves that their actions are justified.

One plausible explanation might be that girls, who may be more submissive in face-to-face communications, may not feel so constrained by online communications. Their assertive online communication skills may lead to online harassment. Ybarra and Mitchell (2004) found that youth who are victims in offline environments are significantly more likely to harass others in online environments (51 percent). This issue is further complicated by caregiver-child relationships, delinquency, psychosocial challenges, and Internet use. Similarly, Wolack, Mitchell, and Finkelhor (2003) found children who had high levels of conflict with parents and those who were highly troubled (with higher levels of depression and victimization or troubling life events) were more likely to engage in close online relationships, increasing their vulnerability to online exploitation.

Boyd (2000) has drawn our attention to environmental conditions that influence male biology toward aggression. One could reasonably assume, then, that the way girls are socialized can promote psychological and covert forms of bullying. The social norm regarding girls is that they are more delicate than boys and should express themselves verbally, rather than physically. It is regrettable, but not surprising, then, that girls would use their verbal and social skills to manipulate and isolate those they bully. An incidental finding of the Artz (1998) study was that when asked what they would most like to do in the future, all subjects answered that they wanted to be married and have children.

It is ironic that the traditional female role of home, marriage, and children is so ingrained in the psyches of children, regardless of whether they are from unhappy homes, that they have nonetheless been socialized to view marriage and family as desirable goals. These findings are also interesting when juxtaposed with the online experiences of girls in North America, India, and Japan. According to McMillin (2005) and Gregson (2005) online social networking among girls in India and Japan in particular have helped them develop identities that are both independent of their traditional domestic roles in the home but, in many ways, also integral to those roles. The social networking sites have provided these girls and women with the ability to interact with peers with similar lived experiences and yet not come into conflict with family members who do not like them to socialize outside of the home before they are married (or even after they are married). The Internet has allowed them the freedom to construct online identities that are significantly more confident. In a number of cases, these identities have led to job opportunities outside the home that would not have been available to them without those social networking sites. Consequently, it is important to appreciate the liberating role of social networking sites, which researchers in India and Japan have found are used predominantly by girls and women.

McMillin (2005) reports a study of computer use by teenage girls in Bangalore, India. Only 30 percent of those surveyed responded (most likely because many girls in India still do not have access to technology despite the burgeoning IT industry in India). The author notes that e-mail and websurfing for the teenage girls in India, although it was disclosed to be only a small part of their leisure activities, was "an integral component of a matrix of rituals of identity expression" (ibid., p. 175). McMillin observes that computer use actually facilitated a continuation of their gender roles:

As a new media technology, the computer, with television, facilitated a continuation of their gendered roles as residents of the private, domestic sphere. Yet, through their Internet and email connections and their consumption of limited global products despite the dangers associated with them, they could cautiously explore new boundaries in virtual space. While the nation around them lumbered along according to a postcolonial clock that measured only the nation's backwardness and developmental lag as compared to industrialized metropolis, the teen girls in this study were right alongside their Western counterparts, communicating through email, surfing the Internet, and watching current news, fashions, music albums, and comedies in concurrent time. . . . With the increase in multinational corporations in Bangalore and more specifically, call centres, which are hungry for young, English-speaking, urban females fresh out of private, English-language high schools and colleges, the Indian teen may indeed be on the brink of discovering the Internet as a medium that transports her from private restrictions to public freedom. . . . Of course, IT-based call centers are themselves hierarchical and may replicate exploitative colonial regimes, yet it is evident that the Internet, coupled with television, will present a formidable influence in how the Indian teenage girl visualizes her urban, gendered and national identities and articulates her freedom and consuming agency.

(ibid.)

To avoid online harassment, girls in India use cyber cafes in groups because have gained a reputation for being able to "safely" (ibid., p. 174) connect the girls to public spaces. Although some of the girls admitted to using chat rooms to keep in touch with friends, one of the girls, Swetha, a seventeen-year-old, said she stayed away from these spaces:

I am not regular in chat rooms. I used to be when I was younger but now I know there's a lot of bullshit, lots of porn and cyber sex. You should be careful – many girls go in (to chat rooms), then cyber sex things happen, then they get really depressed.

(ibid., p. 170)

In Japan, girls become particularly engaged in *shoujo anime*, where they fall in love with animated online characters and participate in fan clubs in the *shoujo* series. Gregson (2005) notes that girl fans of *shoujo* do not necessarily identify with the female lead characters. She notes that they do not engage with the characters because they want to see talented or sweet, kind girls become heroines in the story. These girls use Web sites to talk about the boys they like from their favorite anime stories and to put up pictures of those boys on their Web site. Gregson suggests that the girls of *shoujo anime* have "moved their bedroom discussion to the Web" (ibid., p. 137). As with the teens from India, the Internet has become a safe haven within which they can try out their independence online from the safety of their homes but engage in very public discussions about topics they would never share in public offline. Hence the anonymity of the Internet in some cultures provides a cocoon that allows young women to engage more actively in a public sphere without giving up their cultural ties and commitments to their families.

Male Gender Roles

It is also important to consider how men and boys are socially constructed as perpetrators, and women as victims. Although there seem to be hundreds of studies on female behavior online, there is a dearth of articles relating to males, with one or two exceptions. There is a need to understand the gendered nature of the phenomenon. Adam (2002) contends that the ways in which virtual and nonvirtual violations of the body enforce authority and reinforce the submission of the victim cannot be discounted. I agree, especially as there is also sufficient evidence in the research to suggest that homophobia directed at male victims is prevalent on the Internet (Chu, 2005; Harmon, 2004; Leishman, 2002). However, to ignore the larger gender pattern associated with violence is to miss a basic insight into the social reality of violence as a means of control and intimidation. In other words, it tends to be perpetrated downward along a power hierarchy, reinforcing societal gender inequalities (Herring, 2002).

An interesting article by Suler and Phillips (1998) investigated the ways in which social hierarchies develop online communities such as the "Palace" (created by The Palace Incorporated [TPI] client and server programs), "Mansion," and "Welcome" (related chat rooms). Suler and Phillips observed that two factors shape the universal and specific forms of what they refer to as "deviant" behavior within these communities. One is technical, and one is social. The technical aspects play an important role because every chat community is built on a unique software infrastructure that offers specific technical features for how people experience the environment and interact with each other. They suggest that no matter what technical features are offered, someone will find a way to abuse them. Suler and Phillips explain that "if you build it, some will exploit it" (ibid., p. 276). For example, "snerts" can use sounds and visual images to harass others when these features are technically available in the chat room.

They also note that social factors may be partially or completely independent of the technical aspects of the environment, and this is because every culture or subculture develops standards of acceptable or unacceptable behavior. They reference theories of "cultural relativity" to explain that what is normative behavior in one culture is not necessarily considered "normal" in others. Take note that what may be considered normal or deviant within one chat-room culture may not be perceived as deviant in another. Here are excerpts from their description of the ways in which the anonymity of the chat rooms where "avatars" (or different personas) are adopted reflect some of the participants' deeper problems that emerge as a result of their earlier socialization:

Much has been said about how anonymity on the internet disinhibits people. Feeling relatively safe with their real-world identity hidden, people say and do the things they otherwise would not normally say or do in the face-to-face world. Parks and Floyd explained this phenomenon in terms of the social context cues, theory and social presence theory. The absence of relational cues (visual, tactile, auditory) as well as physical proximity to another person may result in behavior that is nonconforming according to usual social norms. In some cases, that has a positive effect. People may be more honest, open, generous, and helpful. In other cases, however, the nasty side of a person gets unleashed, accompanied by a tendency to de-personalize others. Hence the snert. It is possible that the positive effects may outweigh the negative. In their research of Usenet newsgroups, Parks and Floyd were rather surprised that the deviant behavior was not as widespread as believed.

(ibid., p. 277)

As Suler and Phillips observe, not everyone wants to be totally invisible, with no name, identity, presence, or interpersonal impact. They argue that everyone wants and *needs* to express some aspect of who they are and to have those aspects acknowledged and reacted to. They suggest that anonymity on the Internet allows people to set aside some aspects of their identity to express other aspects safely:

Snerts need someone to react to and affirm their offensive behavior. This need is a bit different than simply catharting their frustrated drives, as the "Eros-ridden" idea suggests. Snerts are trying to express some unresolved and warded-off feature of their troubled identity in an attempt to have it acknowledged. Unfortunately, they do it in a way that abuses other people. Under ideal conditions, they may be able to accept and work through those inner feelings and self-concepts that torture them. If not, they will continue to venture that ooze through their on-line snert identities, while safely dissociating it from their "real world" identity.

(ibid.)

They explain that instead of the anonymity releasing individuals' nasty side, they may experience the lack of an identity as toxic. Consequently, they may feel frustrated about not being identified or having a place in the group. This may cause some "newbies" to act out their frustration in an antisocial manner online. They need to feel that they have some kind of impact on others regardless of whether it is negative or positive. This is similar to the child who acts out when he or she wants attention and is being ignored, even if they know full well that the attention might be in the form of scolding and punishment. They note that humans predictably prefer to connect with others if the alternative is no connection at all. Some snerts who join chat rooms may unconsciously justify their misbehavior and blame the online community for taking away their identity. In other words, they reject people because they feel rejected themselves.

If we consider this assessment of the reasons some teens may act out online in chat rooms and even on social networking sites such as Facebook and MySpace, it allows us to appreciate a need to address the *reasons underlying* that behavior and *not* the behavior itself. This certainly puts into perspective that some of the students who post negative comments about their teachers may realize it will be detected and may in fact be calling for attention from those particular teachers.

Suler and Phillips also explain that although some studies suggest that girls engage in more discriminatory exclusive forms of psychological violence than boys, they seem to be outnumbered by males, who tend to engage in more sexual and violent forms of bullying. They argue that when online, males – especially teenage males – may "have a more difficult time restraining or constructively expressing their Eros-ridden nature – i.e. they are not as mature" (ibid., p. 275). However, there are also other early socialization factors that may be significant here. In his book *Real Boys*, Pollack (1998) describes what he has learned after many years of working with boys who have severe emotional and behavioral problems. He explains that at birth, and for several months after, male infants are more emotionally expressive than female infants, but by the time, they reach elementary school, they tend to internalize most of their feelings – a pattern that continues throughout their lives.

Pollack cites two reasons for this general trend. The first is the use of shame in the "toughening-up" process as it applies to boys. Pollack notes:

Boys are made to feel shame over and over, in the midst of growing up, through what I call society's shame-hardening process. The idea is that a boy needs to be disciplined, toughened up, made to act like a "real man," be independent, keep the emotions in check. A boy is told that "big boys don't cry;" that he shouldn't be a "mama's boy." If these things aren't said directly, these messages dominate in subtle ways in how boys are treated – and therefore how boys come to think of themselves. Shame is at the heart of how others behave toward boys on our playing fields, in schoolrooms, summer camps and in our homes.

(ibid., pp. 11–12)

The second reason, argues Pollack, is the separation of a boy from his mother at an early age and then again in adolescence (coming out from "behind his mother's skirt"). Pollack suggests that these separations are responsible for boys' suppressing feelings, which surface as physical aggression when they reach puberty. Pollack found that boys deal with their shame by suffering silently and retreating behind the mask of masculinity – and by failing to report bullying if it happens to them. Consequently, it can be difficult for parents and teachers to gauge what is really going on in young men's heads – and whether they might be either the victims of bullies or bullies themselves.

Another psychologist supports many of Pollack's observations. In a heart-rending book titled *Lost Boys*, Garbarino (1999) reports on the early life experiences of several young American men, most of whom are on death row for murder. He explains that neglect and abuse of boys, combined with socialization that requires them to hide their emotions and maintain a tough exterior, can have explosive results. He provides four reasons for male aggression: Boys become hypersensitive to negative social cues. They may interpret non-threatening glances or looks as threatening: "This one looked at me funny yesterday . . . That one is bothering me . . . See that guy there? I think he's got a blade hidden" (p. 81). They also become oblivious to positive social cues. This means that even when people are kind to them, they cannot remember; they remember only negative social cues. They develop a repertory of aggressive behaviors that are readily available and easily invoked to protect themselves and prove that they are strong. Finally, they conclude that aggression is a successful way of getting what they want, and in the Internet likely provides the tools through which to obtain the power they need and the validation they crave in their lives.

Given these research findings and the context behind sexual harassment, whether online or offline, and the potential for gaining equality that cyberspace provides for girls in some cultures, it is important to consider what the law says about institutional responsibilities to provide discrimination-free environments. Because we know that what takes place in the virtual world of children has significant impact on their physical environment, it may be possible to extend some of the human rights principles that have emerged in the jurisprudence to cyberspace as a "virtual school environment."

HUMAN AND CIVIL RIGHTS JURISPRUDENCE: SCHOOL ENVIRONMENT

It may be some time before the Supreme Court of Canada rules on the censorship issues involved in cyber-bullying because such cases are generally brought under tort law for negligence and under human rights law. This does not suggest, however, that human rights considerations are not implied or expected. A number of Canadian human rights cases on sexual harassment (e.g., *Robichaud v. Canada (Treasury Board)*, 1987) have ruled that institutions are responsible for providing safe environments for their employees even if the sexual harassment by a coworker occurs outside the workplace. The fact that the victims must face their tormentors in the workplace imposes an obligation on the employer to address the problem effectively. This case is relevant to censorship of online student expression because school officials often maintain that they are not responsible for harassment by schoolmates that occurs virtually and outside school hours. Yet as the high court confirmed in *Robichaud v. Canada (Treasury Board)* (1987), if the victim has to face the perpetrator within the institution, the institution is responsible for correcting the problem no matter where the harassment actually takes place. The high court reiterated that to meet the broader objectives of human rights law (namely, to eradicate antisocial conditions in society), human rights law must be consistent with Charter principles. Therefore, institutions must ensure that individuals have equal opportunities to learn and work without fear of harassment. In this case, equal opportunity to work or learn was at issue. Section 15 (1) of the Charter reads as follows:

Every individual is equal before and under the law and has the right to the equal protection and equal benefit of the law without discrimination and, in particular, without discrimination based on race, national or ethnic origin, colour, religion, sex, age or mental or physical disability.

(Canadian *Charter of Rights and Freedoms*, Schedule B,
Constitution Act, 1982, Canada Act, c. 11 [UK])

The high court also established in *Ross v. New Brunswick School District No. 15* (1996) that schools must provide conditions that are conducive to learning. Although the *Ross* case involved the free speech of a teacher who distributed anti-Semitic publications outside of school, the following statement from the ruling has been quoted in almost every Charter argument for a positive school environment:

[S]chools are an arena for the exchange of ideas and must, therefore, be premised upon principles of tolerance and impartiality so that all persons within the school environment feel equally free to participate. As the board of inquiry stated, a school board has a duty to maintain a positive school environment for all persons served by it.

(para. 42)

Even though Ross's anti-Semitic publications were distributed outside the school context, the court noted that he poisoned the school and classroom environment for his Jewish students within the classroom. They knew about his publications and felt threatened, fearful, and uncomfortable. Hence, if we are to draw on the rationale used in the *Ross* case, it would seem that the on-campus/off-campus (physical vs. virtual space) distinction is moot. It is the *effect* of the harassment, bullying, and threats – despite the fact that they are made outside of the physical school setting – that is important. If they prevent students from learning in the physical school setting, if they create a poisoned environment for any student, then it is the school's responsibility to step in and censor it.

In the case of Azmi Jubran (*Jubran v. North Vancouver School District et al.*, 2002; mentioned in Chapter 2), even though he was not gay, his appearance caused the majority of students in his class to tease him as being gay for the duration of his four years at Handsworth Secondary School in North Vancouver. The British Columbia Human Rights Tribunal ruled that the school had created a negative school environment by failing to protect Jubran or discipline the perpetrators. The tribunal ruled that they did an inadequate job of educating the students to be inclusive and socially responsible. Upon appeal by the school board and the high school, the British Columbia Supreme Court adopted a narrow construction of the case. The judge ruled that because the claim was brought under Section 8 of the *Human Rights Code* (which protects homosexuals from harassment), and because Jubran claimed that he was *not* homosexual, he had no claim. Fortunately, the British Columbia Court of Appeal rendered a more thoughtful and practical ruling, overturning the Supreme Court decision and reinstating the tribunal decision. The court reiterated that Jubran had every right to a claim against the school and school board because they fostered and sustained a negative school environment in which he was prevented from equal opportunities to an education free of discrimination and harassment (see Shariff & Strong-Wilson, 2005).

A "deliberately dangerous" school environment was also the subject of a controversial landmark decision in 1998. The U.S. Supreme Court broke tradition with avoiding the floodgates in the case of *Davis v. Munroe* (1998). The case involved persistent sexual harassment of a Grade 5 female student, Lashonda Davis, whose parents informed the teachers and the school principal numerous times, but nothing was done to protect her. Lashonda's grades dropped, and her health was negatively affected. In a majority 5–4 decision, the Supreme Court ruled that in failing to act to protect Lashonda, the school had created a "deliberately dangerous environment" that prevented "equal opportunities for learning" (*Davis v. Munroe*, 1998). It could plausibly be argued that cyber-bullying (peer-to-peer and antiauthority) creates a similarly dangerous environment for victims in the physical school setting.

With all the attention paid to students' antiauthority cyber expression, the foregoing court cases remind us that we should not overlook the fact that many students experience cyber-bullying on a daily basis. More important, educators ought to be aware that it is their responsibility to ensure their lack of attention to it does not result in tacit condoning or the creation of a deliberately dangerous school environment for their students. I now report two recent North American studies on the gendered nature and extent of cyber-bullying in high schools and also students' recognition that they would be happier if their teachers and school administrators were kinder to them.

PEW INTERNET STUDY

The Pew Internet & American Life Project disclosed some interesting findings (Lenhart, 2007). The study involved a nationally representative phone survey of 935 teenagers and found that one in three teens using the Internet experienced online harassment. Not surprisingly, as with other studies, girls are more likely to be the victims. What is different in this study is that most of the teens surveyed said they are more likely to be bullied *offline* than online. This is an important finding given the legal institutional obligation to ensure a school environment that is free of discrimination and bullying.

Lenhart also reports that about one-third (32 percent) of all American teenagers who use the Internet say they have been targets of a range of annoying and potentially menacing online activities – such as receiving threatening messages; having their private e-mails or text messages forwarded without consent; having an embarrassing picture posted without permission; or having rumors about them spread online. Older teens (aged fifteen to seventeen) said they were more likely to have had someone forward or publicly post private messages – 18 percent of older teens have experienced this, compared with 11 percent of younger teens.

Two-thirds of all teens (67 percent) said that bullying and harassment happened more *offline* than online. Fewer than one in three teens (29 percent) said that they thought that bullying was more likely to happen online, and 3 percent said they thought it happened both online and offline equally. Girls were a bit more likely than boys to say that bullying happens more online (33 percent of girls vs. 25 percent of boys), although overall, both boys and girls say that kids their age are more likely to be harassed offline. In focus groups conducted by the project, one sixteen-year-old girl casually described how she and her classmates bullied a fellow student:

There's this boy in my anatomy class who everybody hates. He's like the smart kid in class. Everybody's jealous. They all want to be smart. He always wants to work in our group and I hate it. And we started this thing, some girl in my class started this I Hate [Name] MySpace thing. So everybody in school goes on it to comment bad things about this boy.

(Lenhart, 2007, p. 2)

This corroborates the earlier British studies I reported in Chapter 2 in which students are often bullied because they are "smart" or perceived as too intelligent (Boulton & Hawker, 1997).

Gender Differences
The Pew Internet & American Life Project also found that girls are more likely than boys to say that they have ever experienced cyber-bullying. Thirty-eight percent of online girls reported being bullied, compared with 26 percent of online boys. The study found that older girls are more likely to report being bullied than any other age and gender group, with 41 percent of online girls aged fifteen to seventeen reporting these experiences. Teens who use social network sites such as MySpace and Facebook and who use the Internet daily are also more likely to say that they have been cyber-bullied. Nearly four in ten social network users (39 percent) have been cyber-bullied in some way, compared with 22 percent of online teens who do not use social networks.

The Online Rumor Mill
The studies on gendered differences mentioned earlier in this chapter are corroborated by the Pew findings with respect to the online spreading of rumors. This study found that at least 13 percent reported that someone had spread rumors about them online. Girls are more likely to report someone spreading rumors about them than boys, with 16 percent of girls reporting rumor-spreading compared with 9 percent of boys. Social network users are more likely than those who do not use social networks to report that someone had spread a rumor about them (16 percent vs. 8 percent). The report quotes one middle school girl as saying:

I know a lot of times online someone will say something about one person and it'll spread and then the next day in school, I know there's like one of my friends, something happened online and people started saying she said something that she never said, and the next day we came into school and no one would talk to her and everyone's ignoring her. And she had no idea what was going on. Then someone sent her the whole conversation between these two people.

(Lenhart, 2007, p. 3)

Threats against Older Girls

As with the studies reported by Ybarra and Mitchell (2004) and Ybarra, Mitchell, Finkelhor, and Wolak (2007), the Pew survey also found that at least 13 percent of the older girls had received threatening e-mails. The comments of one fifteen-year-old boy are also pertinent to my earlier discussion of adolescents who are unaware of the line at which their pranks and jokes can be perceived as real threats, causing their targets to become extremely frightened.

I played a prank on someone but it wasn't serious. . . . I told them I was going to come take them from their house and kill them and throw them in the woods. It's the best prank because it's like "oh my god, I'm calling the police" and I was like "I'm just kidding, I was just messing with you." She got so scared though.

(Lenhart, 2007, p. 3)

Why Teens Engage in Cyber-Bullying

As part of their focus groups, the Pew researchers asked teens about online experiences they had with bullying and harassment. The students informed them that adolescent cruelty had simply moved from the schoolyard, the locker room, the bathroom wall, and the telephone onto the Internet. As I have reminded readers throughout this book, cyber-bullying is not much different from the adolescent cruelty that has always taken place – including the graffiti on bathroom walls about disliked peers and teachers. What changed is not the kids but the medium. Therefore, we must be careful where we place the blame. As Lenhart observes, the simplicity of being able to replicate and quickly transmit digital content makes bullying quite easy. As one of the research subjects commented: "Just copy and paste whatever somebody says." Her middle school peer warns:

You have to watch what you say. . . . If that person's at their house and if you say something about them and you don't know they're there or if you think that person's your friend and you trust them and you're like, "Oh, well, she's really being annoying," she could copy and paste and send it to [anyone].

(Lenhart, 2007, p. 5)

Another middle school girl describes how the manipulation of digital materials can be used to hurt someone. "Like I was in a fight with a girl and she printed out our conversation, changed some things that I said, and brought it into school, so I looked like a terrible person" (ibid.).

Interestingly, some of the teenagers felt that the mediated nature of the communication insulated teens from the consequences of their actions. One high school boy responded to the question whether he had heard of cyber-bullying:

"I've heard of it and experienced it. People think they are a million times stronger because they can hide behind their computer monitor. Also known as 'e-thugs.' Basically I just ignored the person and went along with my own civilized business." A middle school girl described "stuff starting online for no reason."

(ibid., p. 5)

Homophobia

Some of the students in the focus group spoke about homophobia and intolerance as fueling cyber-bullying. One middle school girl related witnessing the following harassment: "I have this one friend and he's gay and his account got hacked and someone put all these really homophobic stuff on there and posted like a mass bulletin of like some guy with his head smashed open like run over by a car. It was really gruesome and disgusting" (ibid., p. 5).

As Lenhart observes, bullying has entered the Digital Age; however, the "impulses" behind it are the same. It is those impulses that we need to address so that teens become more thoughtful about their actions.

MONTREAL RESEARCH

My own recent research in elementary and high schools in Montreal, Quebec, Canada, where we surveyed students in Grades 6 through 9 (aged eleven to fifteen years), corroborates many of the Lenhart findings, although the sample of students was smaller. We administered surveys to more than 500 students at four high schools and two elementary schools in the English Montreal School Board. Of these, 54 percent were male, and 46 percent were female.

Of the students surveyed, 95 percent had Internet service in their homes, and 5 percent did not. Surprisingly, only 37 percent owned a cellular phone, and 63 percent did not. Table 5.1 shows the response of students to questions regarding their experience of being cyber-bullied or engaging with others on cyber-bullying. At first glance, these statistics do not seem disturbing given individual questions – for example, the highest response was for "have you ever been called a negative name or been harassed because of your physical appearance?" However, 70 percent said "often" or "occasionally" to at least one question; 35 percent said "often" or "occasionally" to at least four questions; 16 percent said "often" to at least one question; and 16 percent said "often" to at least three questions. Because all the questions related to some form of racial, sexual, homophobic, or other threat, harassment, or insult, it can be concluded that the percentages of students in this sampling experienced fairly high rates of cyber-bullying and, more significantly, that their school environments were therefore more conducive to these forms of cyber-bullying.

We also asked about their "alternative" online behaviors, such as taking on different ages of personalities. We found that 43 percent admitted to having pretended to be a different age online, and 22 percent have tried a different personality. Again, what was most telling was that 58 percent of the students

TABLE 5.1. *Experience Being Cyber-Bullied (Shariff, 2007b)*

	Often	Occasionally	Never
Called negative name or harassed because of physical appearance	6%	28%	66%
Called a negative name or harassed because of ability	5%	27%	68%
Called negative name or harassed because of clothing or dress	4%	16%	81%
Been labeled as gay/lesbian even if not	4%	23%	73%
Been cyber-bullied by a student who attends your school	3%	12%	80%
Called a negative name or harassed because of disability	3%	9%	87%
Continued to receive even when asked person to stop	3%	9%	89%
Called a negative name or harassed because of ethnicity	3%	9%	89%
Received a threatening message that made you afraid	3%	8%	89%
Received angry, rude, or vulgar e-mail	3%	26%	72%
Discovered someone else had pretended to be you online	2%	21%	77%
Received a threatening message from someone you do not know	2%	12%	86%
Been deliberately excluded by others online	2%	10%	89%
Been put down harassed or targeted on a Web site	2%	7%	91%
Called negative name or harassed because of religion	2%	5%	93%
Had someone send or post personal information about you	2%	11%	88%
Received a threatening message from someone at school	2%	11%	87%
Been subjected to unwanted sexual suggestions	2%	5%	94%
Had anyone's sexually explicit pictures sent to you	1%	8%	90%
Called a negative name or harassed because of gender	1%	6%	93%
Called a negative name or harassed because of sexual orientation	1%	2%	87%
Were afraid to open e-mail or read cell phone messages for fear	1%	5%	95%
Received angry, rude, or vulgar message via cell phone text messaging	1%	3%	96%

said "yes" to at least one question and 14 percent said "yes" to at least four questions. Other questions included the following:

- Have you tried to be older so that you can get into adult Web sites? (15 percent said "yes")

- Do wild and crazy things you could never do in real life? (14 percent said "yes")
- Have a different physical appearance? (13 percent said "yes")
- Act meanly as you never would face to face? (12 percent said "yes")
- Say hurtful things you would never say face to face? (10 percent said "yes")
- Take someone's name and pretend to be him or her? (9 percent said "yes")

(Shariff, 2007b)

The lower percentage rates for "act meanly as you never would face to face" or "say hurtful things you would never say face to face" might be because popular discourse among adolescents in physical settings already contains expletives and words such as "you're a hoe [whore]" and "I'll bust a cap in your ass" (I'll shoot you) as part of the regular conversation when they are speaking among themselves. As observed in Chapter 2, at the Jubran human rights tribunal, students testified that they often speak to friends this way. Therefore, when asked a question about whether they might say mean things online, the responses are lower because kids have a higher threshold for what they define as "mean" things – that is, it would have to be a really nasty remark to be meant hurtfully and hence the lower numbers of responses. This corroborates some of the case examples I presented earlier from India, China, and Japan and later in this book where I explain that young people do not realize when they are being "mean" and find it hard to recognize the line at which their expression can be hurtful.

I was particularly interested in analyzing the results of our survey because the Lester B. Pearson School Board where we conducted our research has been doing a considerable amount of work related to understanding cyber-bullying. I wanted to see whether the board's initiatives had made a difference. Accordingly, we simultaneously conducted twenty-seven adult interviews with teachers ($n = 18$) and school administrators ($n = 9$) and juxtaposed some of their answers with the results from the student surveys. Some of the students had given examples of the kinds of cyber-bullying that were taking place:

- An eighth-grade boy randomly sent e-mails from the school computer lab quoting a threatening line from a movie.
- Students told an elementary teacher that a student was writing bad things about her online.
- A mother responded to inappropriate comments coming to her son online by telling them they were behaving inappropriately. The students responded rudely and inappropriately to her.
- A student repeatedly sent harassing audio messages to another student's e-mail account.
- Two girls had a falling out, and one of them threatened to post some compromising pictures of the other on a Web site.
- A girl or a group of girls were insulting another girl on her own Web site.

Adult Perceptions

When asked whether they were aware of any children in the school receiving threats or being harassed through electronic mediums, all nine school administrators said yes, but when the teachers were asked how informed they were about the issue of cyber-bullying, here are some of their responses (Shariff, 2007a):

- I can realize and conceptualize how easily it's done but no, I don't have a lot of experience with it.
- It's hard for me to say if it goes on often, if they don't tell me.
- I don't think that they communicate that well to adults. Maybe out of fear.

When asked where it starts, 63 percent of the students said it starts at school. This is what the educators said:

- The monitoring of our computer labs is very strict; no one is allowed to use the labs without supervision.
- A lot of those sites are blocked, so a lot of that stuff doesn't happen in the school.

Opinions about Cyber-Bullying

When asked their opinions about cyber-bullying, the surveys revealed important information. For example, 32 percent agreed or strongly agreed with the statement that online bullying can't hurt someone, "it is just words in cyberspace." Moreover, 34 percent agreed or strongly agreed that it is a normal part of the online world and no one can do anything to stop it. Paradoxically, 88 percent agreed or strongly agreed with the statement that "People can be really hurt, and I know some of them." These are high statistics that suggest students do realize people can be hurt. When we see the examples of cyber-bullying and the typical forms of denial by students that they did not mean to hurt others and were just "joking," there appears to be a dichotomy. This dichotomy is complex and indicates the importance of educator awareness of the problem and their increased attention to fostering a school environment that engages students in the rule making. It also draws attention to the need for adults to overcome their mind-set toward the use of technologies and discover the educational potential of the Internet. I explain these and a range of other issues in Chapter 7.

Further, 48 percent of respondents agreed or strongly agreed with the statement that it is the school's responsibility to stop online bullying. However, in response to the statement, "If students bully each other at home, it is only the parents' responsibility," 24 percent strongly agreed and 36 percent agreed (60 percent).

Consider Figure 5.1. There is a clear difference of opinion between what the students consider to be a matter of privacy to be dealt with by parents

What is the school's role?

Student Perspectives:

	Sagree	Agree	Disagree	Sdisagree
If students bully each other at home, the school has a responsibility to stop it.	7%	21%	46%	26%
It is the school's responsibility to stop on-line bullying.	15%	33%	40%	11%
If students bully each other at home, it is only the parents' responsbility.	24%	36%	34%	7%
If someone is being hurt on-line using the school network, the school should be told.	53%	35%	9%	3%

Sagree = strongly agree; Sdisagree = strongly disagree

Adult Perspectives:

•It's our responsibility 100%.
•We do get involved. Even though parents say that's none of your business that didn't start here. As soon as the school environment changes as soon as the child does not feel safe in the environment and that their ability to learn is impeded. Our mandate is 100% for the safety and security of the people in this building.
•This is such a new area and it's so fast and convenient and so blurry that I don't know that there's only one right answer (…).

Teachers
☐ Yes
■ No
☐ I don't know

Administrators
☐ Yes
■ No
☐ I don't know

'blurry'   'complicated'   'grey area'   'boundaries'

FIGURE 5.1. What is the school's role? (Shariff, 2007c)

and what the school sees as its responsibility. Notably, 46 percent disagree and 26 percent strongly disagree (70 percent) with the statement that if students bully each other at home, the school has a responsibility to stop it. Put simply, students do not believe schools have a right to intervene when the expression takes place on home computers. Paradoxically, 100 percent of the educators interviewed stated they had a responsibility to intervene, even if it takes place at home. As I have already discussed, these are the differences of opinion that have fueled the controversies among students, schools, and parents on the privacy issues – and boundaries of responsibility. The schools see it as a 100 percent mandate to keep students safe.

These questions were designed to obtain some idea of students' and educators' understanding of civil rights on- and off-campus, in school, outside of school, and in cyberspace. Although the students we interviewed did not seem to think their rights were being infringed by school interference (which appears to contradict the case examples involving student protests), the educators were clearly upset with the general parental stance that schools have no right to interfere when the expression occurs at home.

Significantly, in response to the statement "The solution to cyber bullying lies with students because they know the online Web," 42 percent agreed, and 23 percent strongly agreed (65 percent).

Another important finding is students' response to the following statements: "If adults treated young people more kindly students would treat each other

What about rights?

Student Perspectives:

	Sagree	Agree	Disagree	Sdisagree
I have the right to say anything I want on-line because of freedom of expression.	10%	16%	37%	38%
Adults created the Internet, now they should live with the consequences.	15%	19%	49%	18%
Adult's should stay out of young people's communication.	15%	20%	45%	19%

Sagree = strongly agree; Sdisagree = strongly disagree

Adult Perspectives: Relevancy of the charters

☐ Yes
■ No
☐ I don't know

Teachers & Administrators

•*They thought that I was invading their children's privacy and actually rather than appreciating my efforts I got an earful of you know, 'what's it your business, or what are you doing?'*

Administrator

FIGURE 5.2. What about rights? (Shariff, 2007c)

the same way" (62 percent agreed or strongly agreed). Seventy-one percent said they were less likely to bully if they were happy at school; 83 percent said, "I would like to create a more kind and respectful world." Moreover, 81 percent agreed or strongly agreed with the statement that cyber-bullying is a worse problem than it was the previous year; 72 percent would report it if they could do so anonymously.

What did the school think about all this? One administrator chalked it up simply to acknowledging that there is a "problem."

Well we tell, we educate them, we tell them what it is, but after that we have tell them . . . you can come and speak to us, we do have a program if you do, we do have a plan, if we do. But it's a matter . . . first of all acknowledging there is a problem, educating the kids as to what it is, and then making sure those kids feel comfortable telling staff and admin[istration] about what is going on. But [the problem] is so new to them and so new to us.

(Shariff, 2007c)

This response demonstrates the lack of confidence in many school administrators – the uncertainty with which they approach the issues, which might sensitize the students to the fact that their administrators and teachers simply don't know what to do. However, the students have made it clear that if they were in a school environment where the adults were kinder to them, where they could be kinder to others, and where they were happy, there might be less

TABLE 5.2. *Would I Report It? (Shariff, 2007c)*

	Yes	No	Blank	
If you were a victim would you:				
Tell your parents or guardian about it	66%	25%	8%	
Tell your friends about it	65%	26%	9%	
Report it to your teacher, principal, or school counselor	51%	41%	9%	
Report it to the police	23%	62%	9%	
Keep it to myself and not tell anyone	12%	76%	12%	
If you witnessed cyber-bullying taking place and a student was being hurt, would you:				
Report it to your teacher, principal, or school counselor	58%	30%	13%	
Tell your parents or guardian about it	44%	41%	14%	
Tell your friends about it	58%	27%	15%	
Report it to the police	21%	79%	20%	
Keep it to yourself and not tell anyone	11%	71%	18%	
	Strongly Agree	Agree	Disagree	Strongly Disagree
I would report cyber-bullying if I could do it anonymously	32%	40%	21%	7%

bullying. There is certainly a will on the part of young people not to engage in bullying, and as we will see in the next chapter, this largely depends on the environment that the school creates through policy responses – whether welcoming or autocratic.

I now highlight one more finding from the Quebec research. An important part of a welcoming school environment is the confidence with which students feel they can report bullying or cyber-bullying. Table 5.2 reports the findings.

Even though 66 percent would report bullying or cyber-bullying to their parents, and 58 percent would report it to their teacher, principal, or school counselor if someone was being hurt, it is disturbing to see that 30 percent said they would not report it to school officials even if someone was being hurt. Moreover, 40 percent would only report it if they could do it anonymously.

Administrators always talk about dependence on a plan or program. What they lose sight of is that sometimes it is not necessary to have a plan. It is simply important, as this administrator said, to acknowledge that there might be a problem. In doing so, it is critical to realize that communication with students is a two-way endeavor. Teachers and school officials must begin to recognize that they may be contributing to the problem. If this is the case, no program will fix it until adults acknowledge their contribution to the problem and work to change it.

Consider once again the example of Bram, who made sexual jokes online about his teacher. On a CBC Radio talk show, Bram confessed to the radio interviewer that he still attends the teacher's class, but neither of them speak to each other or look at each other. This likely results in tensions that other students feel strongly. Unspoken anger can fester and poison the classroom environment. Leaving things suspended in an uncomfortable climate after an incident has been reported and publicized without talking about it and acknowledging at in class does not get to the root of the attention-seeking behavior. Even though students claim that they consider Facebook to be private, the demeaning comments are in and of themselves attention seeking. Pupils might be interested in having only their peers read their concerns (as expressed jokingly), but in cases in which they are sufficiently angry at their teachers, they may subconsciously want that message to reach the teachers in an indirect way, just as the unruly child behaves badly to get any kind of attention, even if it involves punishment (Suler & Phillips, 1998). This cathartic expression empowers students, making up for inadequate feelings they might experience in their relationships with certain teachers. One extreme example is that of Kimveer Gill. Kimveer Gill had been posting photographs of himself with enormous firearms on a grunge Web site only days before September 13, 2006, when he walked into Dawson College in the heart of Montreal in broad daylight and started shooting randomly at students. It was later determined that Gill had been bullied as a student. Regrettably, those who saw the photographs did not take them seriously or realize that this was a desperate call for help. Gill killed one girl and seriously injured several students before shooting himself and then being shot to death by police in the school cafeteria.

ARE CHILD PROTECTION LAWS RELEVANT TO CYBER-BULLYING?

As I mentioned in earlier chapters, teachers and school officials have generally been reluctant to intervene when peer bullying or cyber-bullying is involved for various reasons, yet they do not hesitate to call for legal action when they themselves become the targets. When it comes to fostering a positive school environment where all children feel welcome, a number of scholars have argued that the human rights obligation, as well as tort law, duty of care goes hand in hand with an obligation to protect children from child abuse. In this regard, Professor William Foster (1991) of Canada and Jean Healey (2005) of Australia have both suggested that child protection legislation ought to be applied to bullying in schools. Both scholars argue that if schools are not doing an adequate job of protecting victims of bullying from abuse by their peers, they might be more responsive and diligent if they are required to report it as they are required to report suspected cases of adult against child abuse under child protection laws. Healey reports close correlations in the research on the detrimental psychological impact of child abuse and bullying, such a long-term depression, lowered grades, physical illness, loss of confidence, and so on. Healey describes a serious case of physical bullying that went to litigation, which she believes might have been handled differently had there been applicable child abuse legislation specifically related to bullying. The claimant in this case had been severely abused by peers on numerous occasions, often resulting in physical harm. He was systematically and psychologically abused throughout his high school education. He was thrown against a wall, causing a concussion, and had garbage forced into his mouth. He was pushed to the ground on three separate occasions, resulting in hospitalization during some of these incidents. He had a seizure at school following one such incident; however, school officials continuously described his involvement as "fighting" despite consistent reports that he was a quiet and compliant student with a minor speech impediment who was picked on. Teachers continuously failed to identify the incidents as abusive, seeing each incident as a separate fight rather than a chain of persistent and deliberate assaults.

The case was settled out of court; however, Healey observes that had the 1998 child protection legislative provisions been in place, the school could have been required to report every incident of abuse, triggering a range of protective responses. She reports that child abuse issues were afforded a high profile in New South Wales schools in the wake of the Wood Royal Commission of 1996 that resulted in a 1997 report implicating a number of educators in child abuse matters. This resulted in prosecution and incarceration for some educators on the basis of failure to notify suspected cases of abuse of children and young people in their care. In 1998, the New South Wales Department of Education instituted a review of procedures for reporting child abuse. This extended regulations that previously applied only to sexual abuse notifications to require that all suspected or reported forms of abuse involving young people be appropriately notified. This was in response to a review of the Children (Care and Protection) Act, 1987.

In Canada, similar concerns arose in the early 1990s that linked the failure of schools to report suspected child abuse. Foster (1991), like Healey, suggested that child abuse legislation across Canada should be extended to cover bullying, subsequent to the murder of Reena Virk in British Columbia and the suicide deaths of Hamed Nastoh and Dawn Marie Wesley from being bullied. Foster, however, observed that child abuse legislation across Canadian provinces was inconsistent. The age of protection varied from province to province: reporting requirements, procedures for investigation and follow-up, and training of teachers were largely dependent on the province in which an event occurred. This made it difficult to confirm consistent standards for child protection across Canada.

Although suggestions to apply child abuse legislation in severe and persistent cases of bullying have not been taken up, at least in Canada, they are important considerations in the cyber-bullying context. As I have explained, cyber-bullying spills over into the physical school environment and vice versa; and the abuse can be magnified because the extension into cyberspace allows the perpetrators to abuse the victim twenty-four hours a day – he or she can never escape it. Given that schools not only have an institutional responsibility under the human rights jurisprudence highlighted in this chapter to foster and sustain positive learning environments, they are also required to do so under the provisions of the International Convention of the Rights of the Child to protect, provide for, and engage (allow participation) all children in their learning. Dismissing extreme forms of peer-bullying, whether it is cyber-bullying, physical bullying, psychological bullying, or all of these as simply "fighting" or "part of growing up" should no longer be an option for teachers or school officials. We know too much about the detrimental effects of bullying in any of its forms. As Healey suggests, although there may be various objections raised to the reporting bullying as a form of child abuse, there is a professional obligation to do so:

A range of ethical and professional issues can be identified as discouraging the use of the legislation for the purpose of reporting peer abuse, yet it must be noted that reticence to offer this form of protection to children who are abused by peers is professionally questionable. A case can be made for the inclusion of peer abuse under the scope of child protection legislation in order to provide appropriate and immediate intervention for victims and professional protections for teachers, but further professional preparation is necessary to ensure implementation as well as a genuine commitment to the reduction of peer abuse in school settings. Specific and community-endorsed provisions already exist for the protection of children and young people from abuse, so the proposal that this should be applied in the case of peer abuse should not be too challenging, given the impact of peer abuse. The protection and safety of students in relation to their peers must be paramount and legally supported.

(Healey, 2005, p. 66)

However, Healey also acknowledges a downside that could result in continued underreporting. This involves teachers' perception that their professional autonomy is being censored:

Fundamental to the concept of "professionalism" are notions of specialized knowledge, ethical standards and practice and autonomy. In acquiring professional qualifications and recognition practitioners across all fields have the expectation that the judgments and decisions they make under these auspices have been pre-validated. The ethics and standards proclamation of a variety of professions involved in child protection delineate strict expectations for the maintenance of privacy, and adherence to protective organizational procedure. These have been devised to ensure that within this framework the decisions taken will be legitimate, have positive outcomes for clients, and not be unnecessarily restrictive. For some individuals however, mandatory notification poses a significant challenge to their professional self-regard and indeed evidence is emerging that the removal of discretionary reporting has resulted in under-reporting.

(pp. 66–67)

The fact that scholars see the extension of child abuse legislation to bullying in schools is important and worth consideration as one possible way to increase teachers' appropriate attention to and focus on the problem. Regardless of the fact that some teachers may underreport, it is likely that at least some of the

TABLE 5.3. *Legal Standards*

Legal Framework	Standards for Administrators	Standards for Teachers	Standards for Parents	Standards for Students
Human or civil rights laws (institutional responsibility)	Duty to avoid "deliberately dangerous environment" or "poisoned environment" International Convention of the Rights of the Child – entitled to Protection, Provision & Participation	Duty to avoid "deliberately dangerous environment" or "poisoned environment"; encourage children's participation rights	Must be aware of their children's rights to learn in an environment free of discrimination that is conducive to learning	Know that when they harass or cyber-bully, they create a poisoned school environment (virtual and physical) that affects learning
Child and youth protection laws	If extended to peer abuse, this would require reporting of bullying and cyber-bullying, investigation, monitoring, follow-up, and staff training with legal consequences for failure to report or follow up	If extended to peer abuse, this would require reporting of bullying and cyber-bullying each time it occurred with legal consequences for failure to report	If extended, parents of victims could expect schools to act on their reports to protect their children	Could expect improved protection from the schools and know that their reports of bullying or cyber-bullying would be taken more seriously because there would be a consequence to the teachers and school officials if they ignored or tacitly condoned the bullying

serious cases of peer bullying and cyber-bullying may receive the attention they need sooner than later, saving lives and reducing negative impact on the children and the school environment.

The legal standards relating to the responsibility to provide a school environment that is free of discrimination and conducive to learning are summarized in Table 5.3.

To engage usefully the legal standards regarding the legal responsibilities of educators as they extend to a virtual school environment, we also need a frame of reference that informs us about how the rules of the game are and ought to be defined in *real* space. It is in our physical space that power relations among stakeholders are established. Once we understand the levels of power stakeholders wield in physical settings that shape the rules of conduct, discourse, and learning, it will be easier to appreciate why certain stakeholders such as teachers and their unions are most vocally opposed to the emerging rules of knowledge in cyberspace. The power struggles are not limited to federal and local imbalances; they are further complicated by the power agendas and *desire for agency* in shaping learning. This is because learning ultimately affects the normative societal hegemonies that have in the past successfully sustained curricula of orthodoxy in schools.

In the next chapter, I present examples of new and proposed international legislation that demonstrates how new technologies bring enormous challenges to stakeholders who are comfortable with controlling and limiting children's ideas, spaces, and learning opportunities. Ultimately, banning resources that limit what students hear, learn, explore, express, and absorb is what results in negative, antiauthority, and discriminatory forms of expression that are the objects of control in the first place.

REFERENCES

Adam, A. (2002). Cyberstalking and Internet pornography: Gender and the gaze. *Ethics and Information Technology, 4*, 133–142.

Artz, S. (1998). Where have all the school girls gone? Violent girls in the school yard. *Child & Youth Care Forum, 27*(2), n.p.

Boulton, M., & Hawker, D. (1997). Verbal bullying: The myth of "sticks and stones." In D. Tattum & G. Herbert (Eds.), *Bullying: Home, school and community* (pp. 53–63). London: David Fulton.

Boyd, N. (2000). *The beast within: Why men are violent.* Vancouver, Canada: Greystone Books.

Canadian *Charter of Rights and Freedoms*, Schedule B, Constitution Act, 1982, Canada Act, c. 11 (UK).

Chu, J. (2005, August 8). You wanna take this online? Cyberspace is the 21st century bully's playground where girls play rougher than boys. *Time, Canadian Edition*, 42–43.

DiGiulio, R. C. (2001). *Educate, mediate, or litigate? What teachers, parents, and administrators must do about student behavior.* Thousand Oaks, CA: Corwin Press.

Foster, W. F. (1991). Child abuse in schools: The statutory and common law obligations of educators. *Education & Law Journal, 4*, 1–59.

Garbarino, J. (1999). *Lost boys: Why our sons turn violent and how we can save them.* New York: Free Press.

Gregson, K. S. (2005). What if the lead character looks like me? Girl fans of *Shoujo* anime and their Web sites. In S. R. Mazzarella (Ed.), *Girl wide web: Girls, the Internet and the negotiation of identity.* New York: Peter Lang.

Hall, M. T. (1999). *Administrative discretion and youth violence in schools: An analysis.* Unpublished doctoral dissertation, Simon Fraser University, Burnaby, Canada.

Harmon, A. (2004, August 24). Internet gives teenage bullies weapons to wound from afar [Electronic version]. *New York Times.* Retrieved August 26, 2004, from http://www.nytimes.com/2004/08/26/education.

Healey, J. B. (2005). Peer abuse as a legislated child protection issue for schools. *Australia & New Zealand Journal of Law & Education, 10,* 59–71.

Herring, S. C. (2002). Cyberviolence: Recognizing and resisting abuse in online environments. *Asian Women, 14,* 187–212.

Lanctot, N. (2001). *Violence among females from adolescence to adulthood: Results from a longitudinal study.* Paper presented at the Vancouver Conference on Aggressive and Violent Girls. Simon Fraser University, Vancouver, Canada.

Leishman, J. (2002, October 10). Cyber-bullying: The Internet is the latest weapon in a bully's arsenal [Electronic version]. *CBC News. The National.* Retrieved January 27, 2003, from http://cbc.ca/news/national/news/cyberbullying/index.html.

Lenhart, A. (2007, June 27). Data memo [Electronic version]. *Pew Internet & American Life Project.* Retrieved August 14, 2007, from http://www.pewinternet.org/pdfs/PIP%20Cyberbullying%20Memo.pdf.

McMillin, D. C. (2005). Teen crossings: Emerging cyberpublics in India. In S. R. Mazzarella (Ed.), *Girl wide web: Girls, the Internet, and the negotiation of identity* (pp. 161–178). New York: Peter Lang.

National Crime Prevention Council. (1997). *Report on bullying.* Retrieved July 24, 2005, from http://www.crime-prevention.org.

Nelson, G. E., & Lewak, R. W. (1988). Delinquency and attachment. In R. L. Jenkins & W. K. Brown (Eds.), *The abandonment of delinquent behaviour: Promoting the turnaround* (pp. 85–98). New York: Praeger.

Olweus, D. (2001). Peer harassment: A critical analysis and some important issues (Introduction). In J. Juvonen & S. Graham (Eds.), *Peer harassment in school: The plight of the vulnerable and victimized* (pp. 3–20). New York: Guildford Press.

Pollack, W. (1998). *Real boys.* Markham, Canada: Fitzhenry & Whiteside.

Reiss, A. J., Roth, J. A., & the National Research Council (U.S.) Panel on the Understanding and Control of Violent Behavior. (1993). *Understanding and preventing violence.* Washington, DC: National Academy Press.

Shariff, S. (2000). *Identifying successful school and community programs for youth: An evaluation rubric and compendium of sources.* A research project of Youth Justice Education Partnerships supported by Justice Canada [Electronic version]. Retrieved July 23, 2005, from http://www.acjnet.ca.

Shariff, S. (2001). E-mail from "Raveger, Raveger." In *Legal Context of Education, EDUC 445. Course Study Guide.* Burnaby, BC: Centre for Distance Education, Simon Fraser University.

Shariff, S. (2006). Cyber-Hierarchies: A new arsenal of weapons for gendered violence in schools. In C. Mitchell & F. Leech (Eds.), *Combating gender violence in and around schools* (pp. 33–41). London: Trentham Books.

Shariff, S. (2007a). Adult perceptions of cyber-bullying. Compiled by research assistant Julie d'Eon. Unpublished research conducted as part of a three-year research project on cyber-bullying, funded by Social Science and Humanities Research Council of Canada (SSHRC). Shaheen Shariff, McGill University, Principal Investigator.

Shariff, S. (2007b). Unpublished research conducted as part of a three-year research project on cyber-bullying, funded by Social Science and Humanities Research Council of Canada (SSHRC). Shaheen Shariff, McGill University, Principal Investigator.

Shariff, S. (2007c). What's the school's role? What about rights? and would you report it? Data compiled by research assistants Andrew Churchill, Julie d'Eon, and Tomoya Tsutsumi. Tables and figures prepared by Andrew Churchill. Unpublished research conducted as part of a three-year research project on cyber-bullying, funded by Social Science and Humanities Research Council of Canada (SSHRC). Shaheen Shariff, McGill University, Principal Investigator.

Shariff, S., & Gouin, R. (2006). Cyber-dilemmas: Gendered hierarchies, new technologies and cyber-safety in schools. *Atlantis – A Women's Studies Journal, 31*, 26–36.

Shariff, S., & Strong-Wilson, T. (2005). Bullying and new technologies: What can teachers do to foster socially responsible discourse in the physical and virtual school environments? In J. Kincheloe (Ed.), *Classroom teaching: An introduction* (pp. 219–240), New York: Peter Lang.

Suler, J. R., & Phillips, W. L. (1998). The bad boys of cyberspace: Deviant behavior in a multimedia chat community. *Cyberpsychology & Behavior, 1*, 275–294.

Tolman, D. L., Spencer, R., Rosen-Reynoso, M., & Porches, M. (2001). *"He's the man!" Gender ideologies and early adolescents' experiences with sexual harassment.* Paper presented at the American Educational Researchers Association (AERA) Conference, Seattle WA.

Wolak, J., Mitchell, K. J., & Finkelhor, D. (2003). Escaping or connecting? Characteristics of youth who form close online relationships. *Journal of Adolescence, 26*, 105–119.

Ybarra, M. L., & Mitchell, K. J. K. (2004). Online aggressor/targets, aggressors and targets: A comparison of associated youth characteristics. *Journal of Child Psychology and Psychiatry, 45*, 1308–1316.

Ybarra, M. L., Mitchell, K. J. K., Finkelhor, D., & Wolak, J. (2007). Internet prevention messages: Targeting the right online behaviors. *Archives of Pediatric and Adolescent Medicine, 161*(2), 138–145.

CHAPTER SIX

Censoring Cyberspace: Can Kids Be Controlled?

Bullying using a new information technology . . . gives kids way more power than
they've had.
　　　(School superintendent Anne Kerr, as quoted in Girard & Nguyen, 2007)

INTRODUCTION

School authorities look for ways to control online expression that defames or
insults peers and teachers, believing it has become completely out of control. Is
this really the case? Why is there such a fear among school officials that information technologies give students too much power? This chapter looks at ways
in which school stakeholders influence the development and implementation
of censorship laws that are designed to control not only what students express
but also what they learn on a regular basis. The concern among school officials
that information technology gives students too much power is grounded in the
fear that technology can also change *knowledge production* and *control* of that
knowledge production. As a result, the normative role of schools is challenged
and compromised. Consequently, educators look for legal options grounded
in positivistic responses, such as criminal law, legislation that forces schools
and libraries to filter certain programs (Deleting Online Predators Act, 2006),
and zero-tolerance policies rooted in military models of discipline (Skiba &
Peterson, 1999). Yet as we have seen in earlier chapters, students are raising
substantive legal defenses, grounded in fundamental principles of justice.

In my book with Leanne Johnny (Shariff & Johnny, 2007), I highlighted
ways in which various stakeholders from school communities, such as school
officials, teachers, parents, and special interest groups, have always engaged in
positivist forms of censorship to shape and sustain a curriculum of orthodoxy
that conforms to normative standards and expectations (see also Shariff &
Manley-Casimir, 1999). Any changes to the status quo that threaten to shake
the foundations of power in schools and place it in the hands of less powerful
stakeholders are generally seen as a threat that must be quelled.

The quote at the beginning of this chapter, from a school superintendent (Girard & Nguyen, 2007), confirms the kind of adult mind-set that Lankshear and Knobel (2006) explain, which limits adult understandings of digital literacies and their enormous potential for *education*. The concern about too much power in the hands of children reflects the reality that we have rarely empowered children in educational contexts. Many countries have treaty agreements under the United Nations International Convention of the Rights of the Child (United Nations, 1989) in which commitments have been made to ensure the "three Ps" – protection, provision, and participation of children. Under the treaty, a report must be filed with the United Nations every four years. The last report filed by Canada received good grades for protection and provision but did not do as well in the participation category, especially as reported by schools (Howe & Covell, 2000).

Allowing students to participate or engage in their learning requires a conscious effort on the part of teachers and school administrators to give them responsibility, hold them accountable for their actions, and use technologies to engage in learning through making positive social contributions. As I show in Chapter 8, this is not difficult to implement once educators put their minds to it.

In Chapters 3 and 4, I discussed cases of cyber libel that suggest there is a definite line – fine though it is – between unfettered free expression and the point at which it moves to become criminal harassment, defamation, or libel. The onus is on the plaintiff to establish that his or her professional reputation was so negatively affected by the speech, that remedies or some form of compensation is due to them. This establishes that the perpetrators ought to be disciplined for their misconduct in some way. An alternate approach on the part of educators might be to teach young people what that line is and help them to understand through dialogue and engagement with technologies why certain forms of expression can be so damaging to an individual's reputation.

As we saw in Chapter 4, lewd or obscene expression can be allowed if it is making a political statement or stating a legitimate opinion about an issue. This raises interesting questions about how student online statements about a teacher's hygiene or didactic and autocratic teaching style might be handled. In a couple of Canadian cases, students were suspended for basically stating the truth. The teachers they mentioned did have autocratic teaching styles; one teacher did need to take a shower, and another who was described as a lesbian was indeed an "out" lesbian. In Canada, a claim for infringement of freedom of expression by suspended students in this situation might go two ways. Canadian courts, as noted in Chapter 3, have stated that a teacher's reputation is just as important, if not more so, than free speech. On the other hand, based on *Lutes* (*Lutes v. Board of Education of Prairie View School Division No. 74*, 1992), free speech, as in the U.S. case involving A. B. (*A. B. v. State of Indiana*, 2007) is acceptable even if lewd and obscene as long as it is stating opinion or making a point. The onus would then be on the teachers to show damage to their reputations. However, if the speech is simply made for the purpose of harassing someone and ruining his or her reputation or if it materially and substantively affects learning, or if it goes against the educational mission of the school, then schools are justified when they intervene.

The right to intervene is less of an issue than *how* they choose to intervene. As we saw in Chapter 5, the onus rests on schools to ensure that the illegitimate forms of harassment grounded in sexual and homophobic discrimination or racial prejudices do not contaminate or poison the school environment. Again, this connotes responsibilities on the part of educators to do what they are professionally supposedly trained to do, to educate students to engage in socially responsible discourse. However, as I argue in this chapter, professional development programs for teachers and school administrators do not prepare them to address these issues. Few teachers or school administrators know what the limits of free speech are without reading and analyzing some of the judicial decisions we have reviewed in this book – to recognize the fine line at which such expressions contravene the law. To understand these concepts, it is necessary to have some exposure and experience with a reasoning process. Learning about one's rights and responsibilities takes time. Often, educators complain that there is no time; accordingly, they are forced to make arbitrary and reactive decisions. In Chapter 8 I suggest ways that teacher education and professional development can be improved to address these gaps toward ultimately developing nonarbitrary and thoughtful policies regarding cyber-bullying.

In the meantime, the knee-jerk response of teachers' unions, school, and governmental offices involves calls for action reminiscent of military calls to arms to forge into battle against young upstarts who wage a war using lewd and obscene language on the Internet. Moreover, as the headlines I cited in Chapter 1 disclose, the news media has pounced on this response to sensationalize reactions by labeling them "battles" and "wars." What is more, news headlines and stories are framed in such a way as to convince the public that kids are out of control and that technologies are to be blamed (Edwards, 2005). A misconception among some stakeholders is that it is possible to "ban" and filter these technologies to control them. We saw earlier that a sixteen-year-old cracked the Australian government's $84 million computer program, in minutes. The filter had been designed to control social networking sites and chat rooms.

TEACHERS SHAPE LAW AND SOMETIMES IMPEDE LEARNING

Under this controversial heading, I look at the role of teachers as influential stakeholders. I am disturbed by the strong reaction to antiauthority forms of expression teachers have taken up globally, compared with their relative lack of attention to peer-to-peer bullying and cyber-bullying. The latter forms of bullying have taken place for many years, as described in Chapter 2. The general response of teachers to peer cyber-bullying is that it is not their place to get involved in online expression that takes place from home computers, off school grounds. Research shows (S. Shariff, 2003) that teachers believe parents

TABLE 6.1. *Teachers on the Experience of Cyber-Bullying*

	Definitely Experienced				Definitely Not	
Yourself personally	4.7	84	3	3	2	5	4
Other teachers or administrators in your school	3.7	41	16	11	9	12	11
Your students	3.3	33	11	14	12	18	11
Students in your school	2.7	16	13	19	17	25	10

Reproduced with permission of the Ontario College of Teachers (2007).

ought to be responsible for their children's conduct at home. Again, this might have something to do with the lack of professional development and teacher education programs to address these emerging issues. Nonetheless, the current reaction to online antiauthority forms of cyber expression (described as cyber-bullying by teachers and the media) reflect the double standards in the form and speed of responses when the tables are turned and teachers become targets. This makes one wonder about how teachers are implementing their common-law duty of care, *in loco parentis*, to protect and educate their students about civil responsibility. One recent study, however, disclosed that teachers might have cause for concern about antiauthority cyber-bullying. Despite the high statistics found, I maintain that double standards exist.

Teachers as Targets

The Ontario College of Teachers (OCT, 2007) recently publicized a study reporting shocking results from a teacher's perspective. The study revealed that 84 percent of respondent teachers report have experienced antiauthority forms of cyber-bullying in the form of obscene or defamatory student online statements; 41 percent know about this happening to other teachers; 33 percent report knowing about it happening to their own students, and 16 percent know about it happening to students at their school. Here are some excerpts from the study:

Question: As you know, there's been some talk in the media about cyberbullying, where students publish obscene or defamatory pictures or statements online for the purpose of hurting others. To what extent has each of the following experienced cyberbullying?

Table 6.1 provides responses to this question.

Forty-five percent said this happened by e-mail, and 44 percent said this happens on chat rooms, social networking sites, and "bashboards." Thirty-two percent found defamatory content on personal Web sites and blogs, 31 percent via text messaging, 19 percent through the use of photographs and video clips, and 15 percent on personal voting-booth Web sites.

Question: In what form have those incidents of cyber-bullying typically occurred?

A. e-mail
B. chat room or
   bashboard content
C. content on
   personal Web sites
   or blogs
D. text messaging
E. photographs or
   video clips
F. personal voting-
   booth Web sites

DNK (do not know/no
opinion)

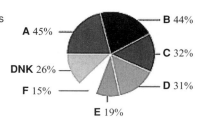

FIGURE 6.1. Typical forms of cyber-bullying. Reproduced with permission from the Ontario College of Teachers (2007).

See Figure 6.1. The teachers considered criticism of their clothing, appearance, and mannerisms, as well as of their grading practices, as the most serious forms of antiauthority online expression. When asked whether they believed such activities contribute to teachers leaving the profession prematurely, 19 percent of those surveyed believed it did. Twenty-one percent of the teachers thought this also contributed to students dropping out of school, whereas 24 percent believed cyber-bullying affected student dropout rates. Twenty-four percent felt it decreased classroom quality (because of the spill-over effect into physical spaces).

Question: Which of the following best describes your school's position on cyberbullying?

A. There are
   formal, well
   understood rules
   with potential
   consequences.
B. There may be
   formal rules but
   they are not
   widely
   understood.
C. There are
   informal rules.
D. There are no
   rules.

DNK (do not know/no
opinion)

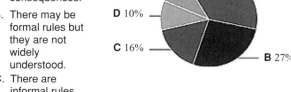

FIGURE 6.2. School's position on cyber-bullying. Reproduced with permission from the Ontario College of Teachers (2007).

Question: Which of the following opinions on students harassing students with cyber-bullying is closest to your own?

A. Schools or boards should sanction students involved in harassing other students online.
B. Most or all incidents of cyber-bullying should be reported to the police.
C. There's not much that schools or boards can do to protect students from other students harassing them online.

DNK (do not know/no opinion)

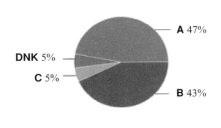

FIGURE 6.3. Students harassing students. Reproduced with permission from the Ontario College of Teachers (2007).

Also perturbing were findings that whereas 46 percent of teachers believed that their school or school boards ought to sanction students for these online forms of expression, 41 percent of English-speaking teachers believed that most or all incidents of cyber-bullying should be reported to the police. French-speaking teachers allocated more responsibility to the schools and school boards (59 percent), and 30 percent believed police should be involved.

See Figure 6.2. Forty-three percent of teachers also felt that peer-to-peer cyber-bullying should be reported to the police, although 47 percent believed their board should sanction students.

See Figure 6.3. This study might provide some indications as to why teachers' unions have come under so much pressure. If 84 percent of teachers believe they have been cyber-bullied through online postings, it is important to determine what is going on. Teachers are increasingly filing grievances with their unions, adding a "quasi-legal" dimension to already litigious issues. Moreover, many of them (20 percent) believe that cyber-bullying contributes to teachers leaving the profession.

My research on censorship in schools (Shariff & Johnny, 2007; Shariff & Manley-Casimir, 1999) might provide answers. This research disclosed that teachers' unions are often pressured by their membership into galvanizing the implementation of laws and policies that help teachers retain positions of power. Antiauthority cyber expression has the effect of making teachers powerless. Hence it is not surprising that some of them might want to leave the profession as a result. The OTC, which commissioned the survey, has done a good job of putting a well-rounded perspective on the issue. In the same issue that released the survey results, Schriever (2007) interviewed a number of experts on the subject of cyber-bullying, including myself, and obtained a consensus that banning technologies and suspending students are not the best options.

Lawyer Eric Roher and Dr. Faye Mishna, an associate professor at the University of Toronto, concurred with my advice that there is an obvious need to engage with students to address why such a high number of teachers (84%) report being demeaned online by students. The OCT reiterates my position that rather than looking for "how-to" lists, teachers should engage with their students and attempt to learn more about technology use. They also need to find out whether their pupils are engaged in learning and whether their school experiences are positive or frustrating. To that end, the Canadian Teachers' Federation (CTF) has also taken positive steps.

After several incidents in which high school teenagers were caught making derogatory postings about their teachers across Canada, CTF, an organization representing approximately 220,000 teachers, came under significant pressure to do something about it. Of course, the media reported this as a battle with the headline, "Teachers Declare War on Cyber-Bullying" (Brown, 2007). They reported the unanimous passing of a resolution to form "an emergency work-group to hammer out a national policy this fall on the use of cell phones in class and school penalties for using blogs, email and any form of technology to hurt other people's feelings" (ibid.). In actual fact, the resolution was designed less to "wage a war" than to bring together a task force comprising experts on the subject to understand Internet use among students, the nature of cyber-bullying, and the boundaries of intervention in cyberspace.

One objective of this initiative is to establish ethical standards relating to technology use, identify the legal responsibilities and expectations of Canadian teachers, and develop materials that support these standards toward implementation of consistent national policies and guidelines. I believe the CTF has taken an important step in understanding the issues and that rather than "hammering out" a national policy, as the media describes it, the federation's policy makers have undertaken in-depth research and are approaching the matter thoughtfully in partnership with national scholars and technology experts. The wording of the resolution is given in Figure 6.4.[1]

The one concern I have with the wording of this resolution lies in paragraph c, which states "the need to deal with it forcefully" followed by "advice on ways to deal with it." As a partner in the process, I advise the task force to eliminate the word "forcefully," especially given that they have yet to obtain informed advice from national experts. Many words could be substituted for "forcefully," such as "collaboratively" or "the need to deal with it by drawing on pedagogically sound approaches." In light of the fact that the primary mandate of teachers is to educate, I believe the word "educate" could also appear more prominently in the resolution.

JULY 12, 2007

BE IT RESOLVED THAT the Canadian Teachers' Federation take urgent action on issues arising from the use of electronic communications in ways that harm students and/or teachers and in ways that are harmful to the education process. Such action should include but not be limited to:

a)   development and dissemination of policy with respect to the appropriate use by students, teachers, parents and the general public of new communications technologies including, but not limited to, e-mail, Web 2, blogs, social networking Internet sites (e.g. Facebook, YouTube, etc.), text messaging, and cell phones within the context of schools, students, and the professional lives of teachers and administrators. Further, this policy should examine the ethical standards associated with the use of these technologies.

b)   development of partnerships for action to educate students, teachers, parents and the general public of the consequences of inappropriate use of communications technologies in activities that constitute cyber-bullying.

c)   development of materials for distribution by CTF alone or in partnership with Member organizations and others about the seriousness of cyber-bullying, the need to deal with it forcefully, and advice on ways to deal with it.

d)   conduct of research, analysis and dissemination of information gathered by CTF alone or in partnership with Member organizations and others.

e)   formation of a national work group of CTF Member organization staff who will consult with such others as necessary before developing and recommending to the CTF Board of Directors a national action plan on matters arising from communications technology use, including cyber-bullying.

FIGURE 6.4. Canadian Teachers' Federation communications technology concern resolution.

What Drives the Urgency?

What I find most ironic about this "urgent" need to address cyber-bullying as expressed by teachers is that for decades, bullying between schoolchildren was generally accepted as a part of growing up, especially in schools. Even the OTC Survey (2007) shows that whereas 84 percent of respondents reported having been cyber-bullied and 41 percent knew about their colleagues being cyber-bullied, only 33 percent definitely knew about their students experiences with this, and 25 percent said that they definitely did not know about their students being cyber-bullied. These results suggest that teachers may be less attuned to their students' experiences as victims of cyber-bullying. Some of my doctoral research findings, as highlighted below, support this proposition.

It was not until Dan Olweus (1978) published his work on the serious consequences of bullying in the late 1970s that interest in the subject really took hold. Before that, children who were victimized and complained were perceived to be "tattletales" and of weak character. It was not until as recently as early 2006, when Facebook, MySpace, LinkdIn, Ratemyteacher.com, and other online social networks really began to surface as popular venues to discuss authority figures that a larger number of teachers began to pay serious attention to cyber-bullying. It has now become a priority for teachers in many countries. Peer-to-peer bullying and cyber-bullying appears to have been less of a problem. Consider some of the findings from my doctoral research regarding teachers' responses to traditional bullying.

A Wall of Defense

Evidence in the research on traditional bullying suggests that until recently (the beginning of the this century) teachers and school officials involved in well-publicized cases of bullying and emerging litigation[2] are alleged to display a pattern of denial, culminating in a "wall of defense" that emerges through complaints filed in court or conveyed in personal communications[3] by at least nineteen Canadian victims of bullying. David Knight, mentioned in earlier chapters, and his mother, Nancy, supported these claims in a lawsuit they filed against their school in Ontario, Canada, but that is now in settlement negotiations. Several Canadian cases serve as examples in which teachers, with the support of school officials, refused to take bullying seriously despite repeated reports from students who were being targeted. From this small number, few cases went to court because most were settled before trial. However, the parents of these children formed advocacy groups to publicize their experiences and frustration with the way their schools handled their situations.

Teenagers Azmi Jubran, Hamed Nastoh, Jamie Dufour, Andrew Forin, and Dawn-Marie Wesley were all victims of bullying. In every case (with the exception of Wesley), the parents reported the incidents to the school, and in each case, the parents publicly claimed that little action was taken by the school to protect their children. Azmi Jubran, as I have noted, eventually brought a human rights challenge against his school and principal; Hamed Nastoh ended his life by jumping off a bridge; Jamie Dufour's parents commenced a civil action for gross negligence but abandoned it before the trial; Andrew Forin was suspended from school for filming a school fight made public by the media, and Dawn-Marie Wesley hanged herself after receiving a threat from one of her perpetrators, despite having visited a school counselor for help.[4]

Most of the parental accusations were not adjudicated by a court or tribunal and therefore remain accusations rather than proven facts, because most were settled out of court or abandoned. Nonetheless, the pattern of complaints is so consistent across all the cases that the schools' actions (or lack thereof) cannot be ignored or discounted. All the bullying cases contain the following pattern of complaints against schools:

- Teachers and administrators often assumed the victim invited the bullying and often denied that bullying was a problem at the school.

- All the schools noted that they had zero-tolerance policies and antibullying programs. They referred to mission statements, school policies, and student codes of conduct, apparently assuming that *stated intent* absolved them of responsibility to implement them appropriately.
- Teachers and school officials accused parents of overreacting and apparently viewed them as troublemakers and harassers.
- If the victim retaliated against the perpetrators, the *victim* was suspended more often than the perpetrator.[5]
- The bullying continued well after teachers and school officials were made aware of the situation.
- Victims had to leave the school while the perpetrators remained, without being held accountable for their actions (until, in some cases, public outcry resulted in criminal charges being made against the perpetrators). Little or no action was taken to suspend or otherwise discipline the perpetrators, despite the existence of zero-tolerance policies.
- Teachers and school officials refused to acknowledge the problem and therefore did not make a concerted effort to investigate the bullying or provide consistent protection of the victim.

Tacit Condoning of Peer-to-Peer Bullying

One may well wonder why educators would tolerate bullying among peers and why students have so little faith in gaining support from school officials. One possible reason for this is the lack of knowledge or awareness that certain forms of behavior do, in fact, constitute bullying. Time might also be a factor. Boulton and Hawker (1997) suggest that some teachers might not address psychological bullying (unless it is directed at them) simply because they have little time to deal with the problem. They note that physical injuries take precedence over verbal bullying because they can be established with more certainty in court.

Thus the various demands on teachers, including classroom instruction, student supervision, and the unlimited possibilities for perpetrators to cyber-bully their peers might cause them to become overwhelmed and ignore the problem unless it involves authority figures. Moreover, MacKay and Flood (2001) observe that budget restrictions and staff shortages may make it difficult for teachers to follow through adequately on policy directives. Teachers today must deal with large class sizes, ethnic diversity, and students with a range of abilities and disabilities who come from varying backgrounds and social classes. This level of diversity presents many opportunities for discriminatory forms of bullying and less time for teachers and administrators to address them. Consequently, the school climate can become less tolerant of individual students' differences and more reliant on harsher zero-tolerance policies[6] that are randomly applied to all students, irrespective of each student's situation.

Smith and Sharpe's (1994) study involving 7,000 British students in Sheffield revealed that some teachers showed little concern for bullying victims. In some schools, teachers even instigated bullying through name-calling. Although these teachers represent only a small percentage of those in Sheffield schools, it is troubling that such attitudes exist. Today, teachers are better educated on how to communicate positively with students, and one would hope that the situation would have improved during this time. Regardless, given the proliferation of information and programs that have emerged since the 1990s, the sudden concern among teachers to deal urgently with cyber-bullying because they are now its targets suggests that most are realizing for the first time its psychological impact and its effect on their *working* environments, yet many overlooked the impact of peer-to-peer bullying on students' *learning* environments in the past.

As I noted earlier, perpetrators are often leaders who can be well liked by teachers and peers (DiGiulio, 2001; Juvonen & Graham, 2001; Katch, 2001; Olweus, 1978). This may explain why some teachers do not take victim complaints seriously. If teachers witness only the good behavior of certain perpetrators, they may not believe victims' claims. Moreover, as the National Crime Prevention Council (1997) reports, victims are often unpopular with peers or teachers. Research by Petersen and Rigby (1999, as cited in Campbell, 2005) also found that many young people do not report bullying or cyber-bullying because they think their report will not be believed or that the incident will be trivialized by adults. They found that less than 25 percent ever report bullying because they "do not have much faith that adults can solve the problem and fear that adults might make it worse" (Peterson, 1999, as quoted in Campbell, 2005). Both my own research (Shariff, 2007) and Campbell's (2005) confirm that students are reluctant to report cyber-bullying to teachers because they believe nothing will be done about it.

Some theorists (Jiwani, 2001; Larson, 1997; Perkins, 1997; Razack, 1998; Sefa-Dei, 1997; Wason-Ellam, 1996) suggest that teachers might be particularly insensitive to the needs of children who are already marginalized on the basis of race, sexual orientation, poverty, or disability (or ability), unwittingly creating a discriminatory school environment. Glover, Cartwright, and Gleeson (1998) report that those teachers who had never experienced bullying or racial or other forms of discrimination may not recognize teasing as bullying.

Now that they are on the receiving end of the cyber-bullying, teachers may stand up and taking notice. Scholars have also made the important observation that although the student population in North American, British, and European countries is ethnically and culturally diverse, and increasingly so, a parallel diversity is not reflected in school staff or administration. Razack (1998), Dei (1997), and others (Epp, 1996; Handa, 1997; Jiwani, 2001; Perkins, 1997) note that the majority of teachers and school administrators in Western schools are predominantly white, whereas the student population includes many students of Asian, African, Hispanic, East Indian, and Middle Eastern descent. They point out that despite being aware of discrimination, some educators continue to view conflict through Eurocentric, androcentric, and middle-class lenses. Teachers apply their own frame of reference to others' reality, and if the behavior does not fit their experiences, they may not consider the possibility of harm. This makes it difficult for many bullied students to identify closely with their teachers – and vice-versa.

PARENT VERSUS TEEN CYBER-BULLYING

Recently, a highly disturbing and controversial case has drawn significant attention from media and the justice system in the United States. The case involves a forty-seven-year-old Missouri woman, Lori Drew, who took on the identity of a sixteen-year-old boy named Josh to lure her daughter's thirteen-year-old friend Megan into an online relationship. Posing as Josh, Mrs. Drew's messages, initially friendly, suddenly turned nasty on October 15, 2006, culminating in a statement that read "The world would be a better place without you" (Maag, C., 2007, http://www.nytimes.com/2007/11/28/us/28hoax.html, accessed January 13, 2008). Megan Meier had trusted in "Josh" as her online boyfriend. Devastated, she took this message literally and committed suicide. While the teen was already on anti-depressants, this email is assumed to have pushed her over the edge. Her mother discovered her in a closet, hanging from a belt (ibid.)

Controversy has arisen over the fact that local and federal authorities in Missouri investigated the case but did not press charges against Mrs. Drew because her online behaviour "might've been rude, it might've been immature, but it wasn't illegal" (ibid.). However, the U.S. Attorney's office in Los Angeles is reported to be looking into the case with a view to charge Mrs. Drew with federal wire fraud, as well as cyber fraud against MySpace, as its head office New Corp., is based in Beverly Hills, California. Although the possibility for successful prosecution of MySpace is minimal because of established legal precedents that categorize ISP providers as "distributors" and not "publishers," absolving them of the obligation to monitor discourses on their networking sites (see discussion of cyber libel in Chapter 3), this case is worth watching for its own precedent-setting value if Mrs. Drew is successfully prosecuted for wire fraud. Regardless of the legal issues it raises, it supports my argument from an ethical perspective, that adults are sometimes the worst abusers of cyberspace. Similarly, it is often adults that frame reality to fit their own agendas, most often at children's expense.

School Officials, School Reputations, and the "Official" Story

Many schools continue to rely on the traditional authoritarian approaches toward school and student management that have been around for decades, since the time when schools were much more ethnically homogeneous. Unfortunately, those models are less effective in a pluralistic school population, especially when new technologies and cyber-bullying are involved.

As we have seen, the Internet has created new dilemmas for educators, and many of them state they are unprepared for and quite uncertain how to handle these issues; yet they are very vocal when the bullying is directed at them.

Moreover, reports from Britain, the United States, and many other parts of the world suggest that educators' policy and practice responses continue to be reactive and more heavily focused on control of behavior than on prevention through education options. Some of those responses are featured later in this chapter. First, however, consider these comments in 2006 by a school standards government official, as reported in the *Guardian*:

A culture of disrespect and failure to take responsibility will not be tolerated.... It's easy to lose sight of the fact that pupil behaviour in the majority of schools is good for most of the time.... But it takes only a handful of poorly behaved pupils to make life difficult for teachers and disrupt the education of other pupils.

(Press Association, 2006)

When we consider the legal responsibility of schools to ensure that they do not create a "deliberately dangerous" or "poisoned" environment, as discussed in Chapter 5, this school official's comments illustrate that although he attempts to meet his obligations to foster a culture of respect, the means that he suggests (suspensions) are in and of themselves largely intolerant. What school officials do not realize when they implement zero-tolerance approaches is that they might be modeling the very forms of intolerance that students are protesting online. As with the case of A. B. (*A. B. v. State of Indiana*, 2007) in Chapter 4, quite often students are protesting autocratic approaches that already create a negative school culture.

Another factor that often plagues school administrators are poor relationships between administration and their staff, and among the staff members themselves. This makes for a potent recipe. For example, the administrators at one school that experienced antiauthority forms of student expression explained that they were frightened of returning to school after the summer because the teachers were seeking "blood." The teachers' anger toward some of the students was surprising given that even the administration admitted most student comments were innocuous and close to the truth. There appeared to be few libelous comments with one or two exceptions.

In attempting to understand the rage of the teachers who demanded that at least four of the students be removed from the school, I asked the school administrators about the culture at the school.[7] Our conversation disclosed that the school had a history of fractured political relationships. The school was taken over by several school boards throughout its history and had experienced changes with many new administrators who came and left, while many of the staff remained at the school. Because of its prestigious academic reputation, the school is popular with teachers and parents. The teachers and student body are largely homogeneous (mainly from European backgrounds) with few students from other ethnic groups. Many of the teachers are set in their ways, endorsing a disciplinary and didactic approach rather than the more interactive and open approach advocated by the Quebec Ministry's educational reform package. Relationships between the teachers themselves within departments have not been friendly, and relationships between faculty and administration have also been hostile.

It became apparent during my conversation with school administrators that the teachers at this school might be using the Facebook incidents as a way to get back at school authorities. The effect of frustrations that have festered for many years appear to have exploded to the surface. Unfortunately, the students became scapegoats of the power struggle between faculty and school authorities.

In this political struggle, the fact that the students are immature, make mistakes, and do not necessarily realize the impact of their comments is lost. Moreover, the realization that teachers are responsible for educating students to engage in inclusive and socially responsible discourse is also overlooked as teachers take entrenched positions. These situations create chilled and poisoned school environments that support violence and discrimination, making it difficult to learn. It is not surprising, then, that the discontent of the school climate was reflected in student online comments about their teachers. Although the entire focus has been on the students and their bad behavior, teachers and schools are missing the crucial signs that indicate something is wrong at their schools that this needs to be addressed immediately. This could require an entire restructuring of the school culture when negative feelings are so embedded and endemic. Suspending and removing students who have the courage to comment (albeit in immature ways) on a poisoned school culture will by no means fix the problem. The students are not always the problem. The Internet and Facebook and YouTube are not always the problem. The problem resides within the school culture – with the long-time teachers and their negative feelings about the way things are done and with every new administrator who attempts to second guess what exactly the teachers want and who are in some ways afraid of teachers' protests and their pressure to give in to their decisions. These are the hierarchies of stakeholder power that can play themselves out in schools. School officials often fail to realize that in leaving issues unresolved, they are in fact creating a deliberately dangerous environment for both students and teachers and thus failing to meet their legal responsibilities to foster positive school environments.

Extension of power to teachers under legislation, combined with a zero-tolerance environment, may also create unequal opportunities for students from traditionally excluded groups or students who are biologically predisposed to behavioral problems. Ross-Epp (1996) suggests that when schools emphasize complicity and competition, they perpetuate systemic violence against marginalized students:

Systemic violence is found in any institutionalized practice which adversely impacts on students. To be damaging, *practices do not have to have a negative impact on all students. They may be beneficial to some and damaging to others.*

(p. 3, emphasis added)

Thus many practices that are assumed to be beneficial may, in fact, be the very processes that marginalize some students. The following are some examples.

The Official Story

Consider Andrew Forin's case. Andrew, a teenager and an avid videographer, had heard about a prospective fight on the school grounds and decided to videotape two boys who were beating up a smaller child while a large number of supporters looked on, cheering. After taping the fight, he went to his weekly job at a television station where he showed his tape to one of his supervisors. She offered him $300 for it without explaining the ramifications to him. The tape was immediately distributed to media networks, which aired the tape that evening. School officials were angry that Andrew had sold the tape to the media and suspended him the next day but did little to discipline or even interview the students who conducted the beating, even though its brutality drew questions from the public about the problem of bullying at the school. As we know, the media are known to sensationalize events (see also Dolmage, 2000). Andrew found himself in a catch-22 situation: The school suspended him, claiming that his video gave the school a "black mark," and at the same time, he became a victim of media sensationalism. The furor over his video diverted attention from the most important issue: the actual bullying and beating of a smaller boy that had occurred at the school. The perpetrators were not disciplined until the public called for charges of criminal assault, which were filed twelve months after the beating took place. It appeared that teachers and administrators were less concerned about the bullying than the school's reputation and public image.

Larson (1997) found a similar pattern in her investigation of a racial conflict in a U.S. school and offers an explanation for this pattern of denial among teachers and school administrators. She notes that administrators have traditionally been more concerned with good housekeeping and school reputation than with examining what drives the conflicts in the first place. When bullying or violence is publicized, it reflects poorly on a school's reputation. Therefore, the initial tendency can be to downplay the situation or deny that a problem exists. Moreover, instead of investigating the root causes of a situation, schools sometimes redefine the problem, blaming the victim, or implying that he or she is a danger to others.

Larson examines an American case in which black students who were bussed to an all-white school attempted to draw attention to a racial problem by burning a flag at a talent competition. The black students were immediately suspended for being dangerous, even though one of them was an honor-role student and had no record of violence. Larson concludes that by magnifying the perceived danger of the black students' actions, school administrators failed to address the root problem of racism at the school.

Teachers' and school officials' responses in these cases have similarities to a number of the recent cyber-bullying cases involving students' online postings about teachers and school personnel. At a Roman Catholic school in Ontario, nineteen students were suspended for "bullying" their school principal on a Web site. Student postings included calling the school principal "The Grinch of School Spirit," directing sexually explicit remarks at him and displaying pictures of Osama bin Laden and Adolf Hitler. Consider the observations of one school official:

[W]hile the school board has dealt with students cyber-bullying each other, he is not aware of any previous attack on a staff member, which is a transgression of the board's code of conduct. . . . This is very dangerous ground these kids are treading on. It's not conducive to the moral tone of the school, and it undermines authority. It is damaging to the reputation of this school.

(Rusk, 2007)

The reporter interviewed a student who said that suspended students included the president and other members of the student council who had been added as officers of the chat room without their permission. Although she agreed that the online postings were slanderous, in her opinion the punishment was too harsh because it would go on the students' record and prevent them from being accepted at universities of their choice. Although the undermining of authority is definitely a serious issue, it is not clear why victimization of children who might commit suicide as a result of cyber-bullying is less important. The school official in this case did say that if it had involved peer-to-peer bullying, the students would have received even longer suspensions. Yet this leaves open the question as to what schools believe will be accomplished by harsh punishment. Whether students receive a ten- or twenty-day suspension makes little difference in the context of alleviating the issue, other than getting the perpetrators out of school administrators' hair for a few days and calming the teachers.

SELECTION OR CENSORSHIP?

Although I have already dealt extensively with the role of teachers in addressing bullying and cyber-bullying, it is important to highlight their power in shaping what children learn and access through a censorship perspective. Teachers and principals are the most accessible school personnel, and therefore the majority of challenges that relate to what children learn and how they are expected to communicate are first directed to them (as opposed to school counselors, school commissioners, and school trustees). Increasingly, we see that what teachers discuss in the classroom is under the lens of public scrutiny. Therefore educational specialists often need to engage in a great deal of self-censorship, especially when examining political issues in the classroom. These education officials, in an attempt to avoid conflict or potential legal suits, may acquiesce to the demands of protesters. Consequently certain topics or resources may not appear in the classroom. Moreover, educators have been found to engage in self-censorship on a regular basis (Arons, 1986; Dick & Canadian Library Association, 1982; Shariff & Johnny, 2007; Shariff & Manley-Casimir, 1999). These authors all explain that censorship controversies among parents, students, and teachers can cause a chilling effect in the school environment, and thus their educational decisions on the types of resources to include and the content of dialogue and classroom discussions may be motivated by a need to protect themselves. A controversial book banning case in Surrey, British Columbia, Canada, is a clear example, as parents threatened to sue any teacher within the Surrey School District who ventured into discussions of homosexuality in the classroom. This resulted in a chilled silence by teachers in the district who did not speak up against the banning of the children's books from kindergarten classrooms, even though many found the books innocuous and helpful in addressing homophobia, bullying, and cyber-bullying (see Shariff, Case, & Manley-Casimir, 2000 for details on this case).

Noll (1994) confirms that highly publicized educational resource challenges have a ripple effect in the classroom because they dissuade teachers from discussing certain topics with students. This concludes in a type of self-censorship in which education officials fail to include materials that are approved by the ministry for fear of invoking anger or dissent in their school communities. As noted earlier, the tendency among many teachers and school officials is to avoid controversy by banning or attempting to sweep sensitive issues under the rug in the hope they will go away and school reputations may be preserved. As I have argued elsewhere (Shariff & Johnny, 2007; Shariff & Manley-Casimir, 1999), this tactic almost always backfires in heated controversy. Whether it is in books or in online communication, the minute there is any disagreement about whether such content should be censored or banned, people run to buy the book before it is taken off the shelves or immediately log on to the offending Web sites to read the offensive content and make a determination of their own. The recent controversies relating to material posted on Facebook, YouTube, and other sites have had exactly that effect. Although technology providers are less reluctant to remove the content, there is often a delay of a day or two before some postings can be removed. As Roher (2007) explains, the complainant has to establish that the content is sufficiently offensive to be removed from a site. As I discuss in the next chapter, the jury is still out on what forms of online content can be considered sufficiently serious to be removed.

Parents as Censors

Parents are among school stakeholders influenced by the way in which the media frames certain situations. Parents elect school board trustees, who in turn bow to pressure from government officials to restrict and control what sources of knowledge are presented to children in schools. School principals and teachers, in turn, bow under pressure from parents, schools boards, politicians, and the media, concerned about their public image and reputation in the educating of "moral" citizens. In turn, they self-censor or restrict access to or expression of certain forms of student communication. What they all fail to realize is that instead of creating a positive, empowering, and engaging learning environment, these intersecting and interlocking systems of oppression (Razack, 1998) stifle creativity, growth, and intellectual inquiry and innovation. They instead provide a breeding ground for prejudice and bigotry, autocratic hierarchies of power, and marginalization of students from underrepresented or underprivileged groups who do not meet the norm. Parents often assert their "parental prerogative" to intervene in what their children are exposed to or learn at school. In the literature on school censorship, there are numerous examples of parents who pressure school boards, administrators, and teachers into banning educational resources containing sexual content, information on witchcraft, references to homosexuality, and so on to which they do not want their children exposed (Arons, 1986; Dick & Canadian Library Association., 1982; Shariff & Johnny, 2007; Shariff & Manley-Casimir, 1999).

It is important to consider not only the positions that parents are taking with respect to the issue of cyber-bullying but also the history of parental prerogative in school censorship controversies. The role of parents in shaping what forms of knowledge and information children are exposed to in schools cannot be discounted. Parents can wield great power when they organize to pressure school boards and administrators into censoring perspectives they do not want to reach their children.

Parental Prerogative on Educational Resources

My research to date on parental prerogative to challenge schools on educational resources discloses that the majority of protests come from parents who feel that certain topics, books, or films are ill suited for children. What is clear is the power parents have over school boards, schools, and government to shape what is selected for inclusion or censored from school classrooms (and now online learning).

The American Library Association (2006) estimates that in the United States, more than 70 percent of book challenges come from parents alone. Increasingly parents have also begun to assert their parental prerogative and their right to have a say in what their children are taught in the curriculum, as well as in the way they are socialized in public schools. The following examples of school censorship cases in which parents have challenged what their children are exposed to may not be directly related to cyber-bullying, but they show the extent of control that parents can exercise on schools to ban certain kinds of information.

Since the introduction of the Johannes Gutenberg printing press in 1455, the issue of banned books has escalated. Foerstel (1994) explains that once speech could be printed, it became a commodity to be controlled and manipulated on the basis of religion, politics, or profit. On the Internet, these opportunities are multiplied infinite times, which in turn limits the amount of control that can be exerted. Until now, books have been challenged and banned worldwide for a variety of reasons. Where young children are involved, overprotective parents have pulled no stops to prevent their children from being exposed to harmful books and resources – from the trivial depiction of a bottle of wine being brought to a sick mother in a picnic basket in the fairytale "Little Red Riding Hood" by the Grimm brothers (Foerstel, 1994), to witchcraft and wizardry in David Booth's famous fourth-grade readers, the Impressions series. Booth's series contains a story titled "In My Feet" in which a pair of giant boots kidnaps a child's parents and takes them away. Parents in Alberta, influenced by Jerry Falwell's right-wing religious group in the United States, were so upset by the witchcraft in the story, they held the principal of a school in Mayo, Alberta, hostage. These powerful stakeholders threatened not to release him unless he removed the books (Shariff & Manley-Casimir, 1999).

A review by Jalongo and Creany (1991) found that children's books are usually censored for three reasons:

1. mature or realistic content inappropriate for a young and captive audience,
2. profane or obscene language, and
3. inappropriate sexual content.

Herzog's (1995) study on school censorship in the rural hills of Appalachia in the United States supported these findings. Herzog categorized school censorship by looking at the nature of censorship events, the objects of censorship, the initiators of censorship, and the motivation of the protestors. Her research confirmed what I have already noted – that the nature of school censorship centers around community values, school location, cultural influences, religious beliefs, and public controversies – what Steven Arons (1986) refers to as "corrosive, irreconcilable and proliferating conflict between government and family" (p. 8). Herzog also observed that the objects of censorship include curriculum materials, school texts, school library books involving cultural literacy, scary stories, fantasy, folktales, violence, the occult, witchcraft, taboo words, secular humanism, sexuality, creationism versus evolution, and political correctness. She observed that the initiators of censorship primarily consist of those who seek to maintain a curriculum of orthodoxy and conformity. This generally involves the far-right censorship network. At the other end of the spectrum, censorship is increasingly initiated by those farther to the left.

Censors have also targeted young adult literature. Sacco (1994) notes that literature directed toward this age group emerged in the 1930s, but it was only in 1967 that a new type of young adult novel came into play – the "problem" novel. Problem novels deal with issues that youth encounter in their journey toward adulthood. Topics covered by these books often include taboo topics such as abortion, sex, homosexuality, racism, violence, abuse, and so on. Over the years, the quality of young adult novels has improved significantly, to the point that teachers are increasingly using problem novels as classroom texts, replacing classic novels that students no longer find interesting or relevant. However, with the introduction of such novels in classrooms came problematic censorship controversies. Parents often challenge books that contain numerous swear words and obscenities. Bringelson (2005) explains that for a young adult to be able to imagine a scene, the author must use the slang and vulgar expressions that youth use today. At this point, it is important for the teacher to step in and explain that they do not condone such language. The books are mainly used to help youngsters appreciate that in some contexts in the real world, offensive language is used.

Sexuality in young adult novels also invites censorship. This can include a teenager's first sexual experience, masturbation, sexual desires, abortions, menstruation, and homosexuality. It is well known that adolescents are curious about sexuality and thus important that they are exposed to information within a supportive environment. Such books allow students to learn about the realities of life without being embarrassed. Nonetheless, books such as Alice Munro's novel, *Lives of Girls and Women*, in which the main character sees male genitalia for the first time, was petitioned to be banned from a Toronto high school in 1982 (Wallechinsky, Wallace, Basen, & Farrow, 2005). Similarly, Mrs. Serup, a parent in Prince George, British Columbia, removed the books *Boys and Sex* and *Girls and Sex* from the Prince George High School library. When asked to return them, she filed a lawsuit, claiming that her free expression rights under Section 2(b) of the Canadian Charter of Rights and Freedoms had been infringed by the school administration. The British Columbia Court ruled that her behavior was disruptive to student learning and that having the books in the school library did not offend her expression rights. She was concerned that she did not want her teenage son to learn about sex at school.

British Columbia in Canada seems to attract censorship controversies. In 1993, in Abbotsford, a right-wing Christian community, teenager Katherine Lanteigne wrote a play titled *If Men Had Periods* and submitted to a competition for $1,000 scholarship. The play was banned from the competition. This drew so much media attention that the local newspaper, the *Vancouver Sun*, held a debate to assess people's views on whether it ought to have been banned. Katherine was given $1,000 to air the play on the Canadian Broadcasting Corporation airwaves – the country's national broadcasting system. Katherine's teacher commented that the play in and of itself was not good enough to win the competition but the board should have allowed her to enter it. Instead, a mediocre play received more attention than the winning play. This supports my position that when educators attempt to sweep sensitive matters under the rug, they in fact emerge with twice the prominence and generally embarrass the censors. Books that are banned often sell more copies than they would have because people rush out to buy them to see what the controversy is about. Other young adult books that have sparked controversy include Judy Blume's novel *Are You There God? It's Me, Margaret*, which deals with masturbation, menstruation, and intercourse.

Violence is another topic that some parents want their children to avoid. Anthony Burgess's *A Clockwork Orange*, which depicts rape and violence, has invited many protests when it has been a required high school text. Moreover, the Captain Underpants series by Dave Pilkey was reported by the American Library Association (2006) as the most challenged book of 2005 because its antifamily content was perceived as unsuited to the age group and violence. Steven Arons defines the motivation of the protestors as "a general struggle for meaning...one between the forces of private dissent and the agents of public orthodoxy" (as quoted in Shariff & Manley-Casimir, 1999, p. 161). Those who challenge school curriculum are often motivated by one or more of the following:

• Religious and moral differences
• Fundamentalist parental overprotection or modern liberal values
• Politics, authoritarianism, and a desire to protect administrative jobs
• Fear of psychological manipulation
• Different interpretations of the purpose of education
• Fear of change
• Words and meanings taken out of context

The popular Harry Potter children's books have appeared on many library and school challenged book lists (Wyman, 2000b). Parents question the appropriateness of Harry Potter books for use in the classroom because they depict wizardry and witchcraft and apparently "carry a serious tone of death, hate, lack of respect and sheer evil" (Shariff, Case, & LaRocque, 2001). J. K. Rowling's response is generally one of resignation. She states that if we attempt to ban all books that mention witches, we would have to remove most classical children's stories. Through her characters, Rowling introduces young readers to the endless conflict between good and evil. She explains that Harry represents a child with a deep moral conscience who has a "human underbelly" (as quoted in Wyman, 2000a). Moreover, Rowling stresses the difference between choosing the right path as opposed to finding an easy way out of a difficult moral situation. Child psychologist Bruno Bettelheim (1989) concurred with this perspective many years ago. Bettelheim explained that when stories force children to confront good and evil through witchcraft, magic, and other forms of imagination, it actually helps them develop a moral framework for understanding the differences between right and wrong. The deepest conflicts between stakeholders are related to values. In the following case, the disputes were over religious and secular values.

As already noted, religious parents have had significant impact in having books depicting same-sex families removed from the curriculum in some school districts, while at the same time, same-sex parents assert their rights to have their children's family backgrounds validated in the curriculum. Parents also assert their rights in the realm of special education, from requesting full integration of children with special needs into regular classrooms to the streaming of gifted students in separate classes or specialized programmes where they can learn with peers at their own intellectual levels. With an increasing public distrust of the school system, parents have also expressed their rights to review student records and question teachers' evaluation of their children's progress. At times, parents can get carried away in their zeal to protect their children.

It is no surprise, then, that the complexities of new technologies have parents and schools feeling helpless and out of control. Fear of change and fear of what their children will learn or access in cyberspace is a legitimate concern for parents – especially those who were formally able to influence the schools to address their parental prerogative.

Government Influence

Although governments such as the European Union play a vital role in developing responses to cyber-bullying, British Web sites, proposed U.S. legislation (e.g., the Deleting Online Predators Act [DOPA] of 2006), and similar legislation in Singapore, South Korea, and India, they also have a large influence on the initial selection of learning resources. Governments have significant power in shaping the types of student expressions that are allowed in schools, informing and molding young people's attitudes and values within the school itself. Most schools are agents of the state. Their primary responsibility is to develop young people's values and dispositions toward civil and social responsibility, so that they can contribute constructively to the democracies in which most of them live. Nonetheless, the political and systemic thrust toward control of information often makes this antithetical to the spirit of education and democracy.

The legislative initiatives that a number of governments have introduced are largely in reaction to demands by the public and educators to do something about cyber-bullying. The proposed DOPA bill referred to in Chapter 7 is one example, as is the amended Ontario Education Act and the legislation introduced by the South Korean government that criminalizes certain forms of online expression (see Chapter 3).

Censorship of expression, whether it is in the form of what students say or what they read and learn, is not a new phenomenon in schools. Governments have always promoted political agendas through the types of learning materials they approve. However, until the advent of information technologies, those materials were generally tactile – in the form of textbooks, library books, videotapes, photographs, tape recordings, and so on. They were not a moving target as expression and information now are, in cyberspace.

Apple and Christian-Smith (1991) remind us that educational resources are not simply "delivery systems" that convey a set of objective "facts." Instead, they are creations designed and selected by people with a particular set of interests. The recent panic to amend existing legislation and bring in new laws to "control" bullying and cybers bullying indicates that many politicians are nervous about online student expression because they cannot control information that is accessed online and therefore cannot ban it. In other words, they cannot ban specific online content because it takes different forms, in blogs, chat rooms, e-mail, MSN, cell phone texts, online videos, and social networks such as Facebook.

When government officials approve learning materials that favor one world-view over another, it is arguable that they engage in shaping knowledge by failing to represent multiple perspectives. This point is exemplified in a number of conservative states in the United States and some Canadian provinces where official textbooks omit any discussion of homosexuality as a legitimate lifestyle. This in turn might play a significant role in the level of homophobic cyber-bullying that takes place. The United States, of course, is not the only nation where the education system is vulnerable to the interests of politicians. In many countries, the government is one of the primary institutions through which education is offered to the public, and therefore the selection of educational materials and policies has close links to the ideological interests of those who govern the nation.

School Boards

Along with ministries of education, school boards also have significant discretionary powers. For example, in British Columbia, Canada, Section 85 of the School Act states that school boards have the power both to "determine local policy for the effective and efficient operation of schools" and to "approve educational resource materials and other supplies and services." Moreover, Section 76(3) suggests that "the highest morality will be inculcated but schools will be run on a strictly secular and non-sectarian basis." On one hand, this provides board members with the autonomy needed to select resources and policies suited to the needs of their school community. However, when it advocates the "inculcation" of the "highest morality," it raises important questions about whose values can be considered to be of the "highest morality?"

On the other hand, it is arguable that even the decisions of board members are susceptible to political pressures and outside influences. For instance, as elected officials, school trustees are accountable to their voters and vulnerable to the demands of special interest groups. One of the ramifications of this structure is that educational decisions are sometimes propelled by the need to appease powerful voices rather than a genuine concern for the diverse perspectives and values of the school community. With the emerging concerns relating to insults that have been posted on social communications tools such as Facebook and YouTube, school boards, like the governments in various parts of Canada, the United States, Ireland, and England, have had to bow under considerable pressure from teachers' federations and teachers' unions.

With the emergence of cyber technologies, school board officials worldwide are undoubtedly concerned about how to manage access to information that was previously much easier to control. As the diversity within school populations becomes more multicultural, multiethnic, multireligious (and more interesting), the challenges for school boards increase as they attempt to navigate competing rights and interests. As the OCT survey shows (See Figure 6.5 above) teachers believe that school boards have a significant responsibility to formulate and explain rules and state the potential for consequences. However,

Question: Which of the following statements best describes any policy that your school or board may have on how students may communicate on the Internet and web sites or in e-mail and chat room?

A. There are formal, well understood rules with potential consequences.

B. There may be formal rules but they are not widely understood.

C. There are informal rules.

D. There are no rules.

DNK (do not know/no opinion)

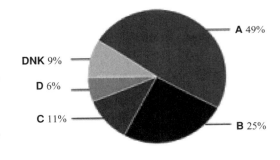

FIGURE 6.5. School policy. Reproduced with permission of the Ontario College of Teachers (2007).

the expectations of school boards by teachers need to be reconceptualized to stress that they concentrate on improving the school culture rather than engaging in punitive codes of conduct. As the OCT survey question that follows evidences, most school boards implement formal rules with potential consequences. Although the questions did not allow for expansion to determine whether such formal rules might be supplemented or supported by initiatives that engage students in a discussion about why they should not engage in cyber-bullying, in and of itself the response of 49 percent of the participants suggests that this may not be the case.

Media Influence on Censorship and Positivist Laws

Given that issues involving antiauthority cyber-bullying have begun to emerge only recently (2006–2007), few scholarly studies have yet qualitatively surveyed its incidence and school responses. Therefore, throughout this book, I have had little choice but to rely to some extent on media reports and on personal communications from school administrators and teachers to discuss case studies. I reiterate that I am all the while conscious that there may be aspects of those cases that are not disclosed in the media reports or personal communications. Nonetheless, I contend that no matter how the media frames the issues, there are definitely clear patterns that emerge in most reports. These reflect the fact that students and technologies have become scapegoats for deeper systemic hierarchies of power within schools and among stakeholders that ought not to be overlooked in our attempts to address the policy vacuum.

I support Edwards (2005) and Mazzarella (2005) when they caution that the news media can control reality to a certain extent by framing stories to fit certain agendas and control the message to place the spotlight on certain issues over others. When media reporters and editors select information and wording to formulate a new story, they in effect become powerful "censors" of information that ought to reach the public but is often left out of the picture or given less focus. Engaging in critical media literacy is not a simple task, but it is an essential one. An entire body of scholarship has emerged in the last decade to convince us about the utility and necessity of engaging in critical media literacy (Chomsky, 2007; Macedo & Steinberg, 2007; Shaheen, 2000, 2003).

Although I did not systematically go through more than 100 new report articles on the topic of cyber-bullying to identify specific patterns, as I write this book, I have quickly become aware of clear patterns. I am at present surrounded by at least forty or fifty print media reports, many of which were reported in the last year (2006–2007), as they relate to antiauthority forms of online social networking postings by high school students.

Good Students Get Caught

One of the patterns that emerged in many of the news media articles about kids who were suspended from school for their online postings is that they were all generally good students. Each one ran astray and paid too heavy a price for his or her teenage horseplay. For example, Brad Parsons is described as a "teen who 'likes hanging out and chilling' with his friends"; it is noted that "he and his friends have long had problems with [a vice-principal]" and that their group was singled out because they hung around in the back of the school where "other students created problems." He is then by implication described as a model student:

[Parsons,] whose favourite classes are English and drama, says he was getting good grades and was finishing an essay on *Macbeth* when he was expelled.... "I'm losing out on my education because of this and it's going to set me back," he said.

(Chung, 2007)

As Edwards would argue, all this emphasis on the fact that Brad is a good student who likes English and drama, who had ongoing problems with the assistant principal, and who will now likely lose out on his education (together with his mother's comments to the effect that all students say mean things about teachers) have the combined effect of trivializing the content of the online expression that got him into trouble in the first place. Nor do we hear the side of the assistant principal as to the nature of the ongoing "trouble" this particular group of kids who hung out in the back of the school had with her (or she had with them). Moreover, the article states conflicting facts as to whether he was expelled or not. Earlier on, the article says that Brad had been told he was going to be expelled but wasn't, and the same article later states as a fact that he was expelled. The school superintendent is reported to confirm in a different, later, and better balanced report that Brad was not in fact expelled, although he claimed to reporters that he had been (Girard & Nguyen, 2007).

Even though I am strongly against suspensions for this form of cyber-bullying, and although I do believe these youngsters when they say that they did not realize the seriousness of the demeaning words they use online, it does bother me that in presenting Brad as a squeaky-clean student who wouldn't think of doing wrong, the media trivializes the fact that his expression was potentially libelous. It is important that students are shown that some of their comments could render them liable for a legal offence such as cyber-libel. Moreover, even though many students maintain their belief that their online banter constitutes private conversations, as Edwards (2005) would argue, the media angle taken in this case shifted the focus away from the need to be engage with the teens to discuss the issues they were having with their assistant principal. Clearly there were conflicts. The article also precluded an explanation from her perspective. It is highly likely that the assistant principal was having as much trouble with the teens as they were with her when they "hung out" in the back of the school.

Hence, although I do not believe these tensions should be conceptualized as a battle, nor do I necessarily agree with the formal and rather harsh initiatives that are emerging internationally to address this form of cyber-bullying, I certainly do not absolve the students of responsibility. What I would like to see are increased efforts to guide them to take responsibility for their actions. We ought to help them understand the impact their expression has on the overall climate and learning within the school and also find out whether their comments are the result of a poisoned environment that exists within the school.

Another media account presents the experiences of teenager Julia Wilson in a similar way ("California Grade 9 Girl Questioned," 2006). Julia is described as a teenager from a well-to-do suburb. The article implies that someone who has hearts on her knapsack could do nothing wrong. Julia wrote on her MySpace page the words "Kill Bush" with a dagger through them to express her opinion against the Iraq War. On the basis of the decision relating to A. B.'s (*A. B. v. State of Indiana*, 2007) described in Chapter 4, her right to free expression might have been upheld in a court of law. The impact of Julia's online threat was minimized because of her racial background and the economic status of her parents. Had a Muslim student done the same thing in her place, it is plausible that he or she might not have gotten off so easily, even if his parents lived in a wealthy neighborhood like Julia's. The following excerpts make Julia appear completely innocent, which takes the focus off the fact that she *did* write the words "Kill Bush" and regardless of how much she did not agree with the Iraq War, this was not the way to express her views:

"I wasn't dangerous. I mean, look at what's (stenciled) on my backpack – it's a heart.... I'm a very peace-loving person," said Wilson, an honor student who describes herself as politically passionate. "I'm against the war in Iraq. I'm not going to kill the president."

Moreover, presenting her as a clueless teenager is equally effective at presenting her as a sweet and innocent teenager,

"Are you serious!?!? Omg. Am I in a lot of trouble?" her daughter wrote back, using code for "Oh, my God."

(ibid.)

Quite clearly, given her decision to organize a protest against the war in Iraq and the fact that she is an honors student, she is bright enough to realize that when she posted the expression, it would definitely draw a reaction. My point in discussing this article is to show that although the teen clearly made a mistake and did not immediately realize the implications of her actions, teens ought to take some responsibility. In Julia's case, her parents took the positive steps of guiding her toward constructive activism on an issue about which she felt strongly. Organizing a protest against the Iraq War gave her the agency she had sought online and a feeling that she could contribute to solving the problem. In other cases in which students have made negative comments about their teachers, they, too, are using the Internet as a tool for agency – a place where they feel empowered to do something about a poisoned environment at their school or trouble with a teacher. Regrettably, they quickly find out that this form of agency is not as effective, and this is where a nonreactive but educational approach would provide them with alternate avenues to express their feelings and contribute to changing their learning environment.

Cyber-Criminals: Police as Heroes

In contrast to the report of Brad Parsons as a model student, two other media reports on the same story focused on the student protest and the "clash" between students and police. One of them in the *Toronto Star* (Girard & Nguyen, 2007) read as follows:

Four teenagers have been arrested after a protest over the punishment of a fellow high school student turned violent when police, trying to divert traffic, were pelted by objects including a bottle and a skateboard.

The ugly incident outside Birchmount Park Collegiate Institute in the Danforth Avenue and Birchmount Road area yesterday followed the suspension earlier this week of five students after school administrators discovered derogatory comments about Birchmount Park staff. . . .

"Everyone was on the road and then things started flying and the cops started flipping out," said Ryan Duffy, 16, a Grade 11 student who saw the melee in which angry protesters yelled at police and chased officers as the young men were arrested, handcuffed and pinned on the ground, then thrown into cruisers.

The use of words such as "ugly," "pelted," and "pinned on the ground, then thrown into cruisers" highlights the power of the state in winning the battle. In the same article are comments by the superintendent noting that "bullying using a new information technology . . . gives kids way more power than they've had" (ibid.).

The message that the battle is about power between schools and students comes through clearly in many similar media reports – and if the students are getting too much power using new "technology," then the police will heed the call to order and put them back in their place, using force if necessary.

Although the students in this case are also reported as having provoked police officers (apparently throwing bottles and skateboards), it is the way that this media report presents the sequence of events that is suggestive of who is wins the battle when the heroes are brought in. Moreover, note the superintendent's use of the word "technology" rather than "technologies." This is an example of the adult mind-set toward technologies that Lankshear and Knobel (2006) have drawn to our attention. It implies that technology is a singular entity – just like "digital literacy" can be controlled and managed – suggesting a lack of appreciation of its plurality and fluidity.

I want to emphasize again that I do not believe the students involved are absolved of responsibility for their words and actions. I have already illustrated this, using examples of the media reports that make the perpetrators look like victims. This is the elusive fine line that always comes up between free expression and authority.

RECONCEPTUALIZING LAW IN CYBERSPACE

I have already discussed how the courts have significant impact on shaping public policy within the context of my introduction to Chapter 1. Suffice it to say that no matter how much the courts attempt to block the floodgates to litigation relating to cyber-bullying and various forms of cyber misconduct, they can ultimately expect to rule on many such cases. I believe we are at the point in lawmaking when century-old legal precedents, although they have some value as shown in earlier discussions of cyber libel in Chapter 3, must be distinguished from cases involving cyberspace. I believe that the multiplicity, permanence, fluidity, and sheer breadth of cyberspace lends itself much more effectively to a plurality of legal frameworks as I explained in Chapter 1. Unfortunately, the initial response to cyberspace has been quite the opposite.

In Chapter 7, I look at some of the positivist legal responses that have emerged in response to cyber-bullying and consider them in the context of the legal standards identified in earlier chapters to highlight the benefits of a legally pluralist approach in addressing cyber-bullying. That legally pluralist framework is then incorporated into educational models, which are explained in Chapter 8 with recommendations on how they would be more compatible with the legal standards identified here.

REFERENCES

American Library Association. (2006). *Challenged or banned books* [Electronic version]. Retrieved December 1, 2006, from http://www.ala.org/ala/oif/bannedbooksweek/challengedbanned/challengedbanned.htm.

Apple, M. W., & Christian-Smith, L. K. (1991). The politics of the textbook. In M. W. Apple & L. K. Christian-Smith (Eds.), *The politics of the textbook* (pp. 1–21). New York: Routledge.

Arons, S. (1986). *Compelling belief*. Amherst: University of Massachusetts Press.

Bettelheim, B. (1989). *The uses of enchantment: The meaning and importance of fairy tales*. New York: Vintage Books.

Boulton, M., & Hawker, D. (1997). Verbal bullying: The myth of "sticks and stones." In D. Tattum & G. Herbert (Eds.), *Bullying: Home, school and community* (pp. 53–63). London: David Fulton.

Bringelson, C. (2005). On intellectual freedom [Electronic version]. *Intellectual Freedom & Social Responsibility, 24*. Retrieved November 22, 2006, from http://www.scholibraries.ca/articles/154.aspx.

Brown, L. (2007, July 13). Teachers declare war on cyber-bullying [Electronic version]. *TheStar.com*. Retrieved August 13, 2007, from http://www.thestar.com/article/235675.

California Grade 9 girl questioned about threats to Bush on MySpace [Electronic version]. (2006, October 13). *Yahoo! News Canada*. Retrieved October 16, 2006, from http://ca.news.yahoo.com/s/capress/061013/ztechnology/myspace_bush_threat.

Campbell, M. (2005). Cyberbullying: An old problem in a new guise? *Australian Journal of Guidance and Counseling, 15*, 68–76.

Chomsky, N. (2007). Preface to *The myth of the liberal media*. In D. Macedo & S. R. Steinberg (Eds.), *Media literacy: A reader* (pp. 24–26). New York: Peter Lang.

Chung, M. (2007, March 25). Online comments were "inside joke." Posts meant for friends only, teen says [Electronic version]. *TheStar.com*. Retrieved August 15, 2007, from http://www.thestar.com/article/195823.

Dei, G. S. (1997). Race and the production of identity in the schooling experiences of African-Canadian youth. *Discourse studies in the cultural politics of education, 18*, 241–257.

Deleting Online Predators Act. H.R. 5319. (2006).

Dick, J., & Canadian Library Association. (1982). *Not in our schools?!!!: School book censorship in Canada: A discussion guide*. Ottawa: Canadian Library Association.

DiGiulio, R. C. (2001). *Educate, mediate, or litigate? What teachers, parents, and administrators must do about student behavior*. Thousand Oaks, CA: Corwin Press.

Dolmage, W. R. (2000). Lies, damned lies and statistics: The media's treatment of youth violence. *Education & Law Journal, 10*, 1–46.

Edwards, L. Y. (2005). Victims, villains, and vixens. In S. R. Mazzarella (Ed.), *Girl wide web* (pp. 13–30). New York: Peter Lang.

Foerstel, H. N. (1994). *Banned in the U.S.A.: A reference guide to book censorship in schools and public libraries*. Westport, CT: Greenwood Press.

Girard, D., & Nguyen, L. (2007, March 24). Students, police clash [Electronic version]. *TheStar.com*. Retrieved April 1, 2007, from http://www.thestar.com/article/195604.

Glover, D., Cartwright, N., & Gleeson, D. (1998). *Towards bully-free schools*. Buckingham/Philadelphia: Open University Press.

Handa, S. (1997). *Caught between omissions: Exploring "culture conflict" among second generation South Asian women in Canada*. Unpublished doctoral dissertation, University of Toronto, Toronto.

Herzog, M. J. R. (1995). School censorship experiences of teachers in southern Appalachia. *International Journal of Qualitative Studies in Education, 8*, 137–148.

Howe, R. B., & Covell, K. (2000). Schools and the participation rights of the child. *Education and Law Journal, 10*, 107–123.

Jalongo, M. R., & Creany, A. D. (1991). Censorship in children's literature: What every educator should know. *Childhood Education, 67*, 143–148.

Jiwani, Y. (2001). *Mapping violence: A work in progress.* Vancouver, BC: Feminist Research, Education, Development and Action Centre, Simon Fraser University.

Juvonen, J., & Graham, S. (2001). *Peer harassment in school: The plight of the vulnerable and victimized.* New York/London: Guilford Press.

Katch, J. (2001). *Under deadman's skin: Discovering the meaning of children's violent play.* Boston: Beacon Press.

Lankshear, C., & Knobel, M. (2006). *New literacies: Everyday practices and classroom learning* (2nd ed.). Maidenhead, England/New York: Open University Press.

Larson, C. L. (1997). Is the Land of Oz an alien nation? A sociopolitical study of school community conflict. *Educational Administration Quarterly, 33*, 312–350.

Maag, C., (28 November, 2007). A hoax turned fatal draws anger but no charges. The New York Times. http://www.nytimes.com/2007/11/28/us/28hoax.html., accessed January 13, 2008.

Macedo, D., & Steinberg, S. R. (2007). *Media literacy: A reader.* New York: Peter Lang.

MacKay, A. W., & Flood, S. (2001). Negligence principles in the school context: New challenges for the "careful parent." *Education & Law Journal, 10,* 371–392.

Mazzarella, S. R. (Ed.). (2005). *Girl wide web. Girls, the Internet, and the negotiation of identity.* New York: Peter Lang.

National Crime Prevention Council. (1997). *Report on bullying.* Retrieved July 24, 2005, from http://www.crime-prevention.org.

Noll, E. (1994). The ripple effect of censorship: Silencing in the classroom. *English Journal, 83*, 59–64.

Olweus, D. (1978). *Aggression in the schools: Bullies and whipping boys.* Washington, DC/New York: Hemisphere.

Ontario College of Teachers. (2007). COMPAS state of the teaching profession [Electronic version]. *Professionally Speaking, the Magazine of the Ontario College of Teachers.* Retrieved August 28, 2007, from http://www.oct.ca/publications/PDF/survey07_e.pdf.

Perkins, C. (1997). Any more colorful we'd have to censor it. In S. deCastell & M. Bryson (Eds.), *Radical in-ter-ventions: Identity, politics and differences in educational praxis* (pp. 247–268). Albany, NY: SUNY Press.

Press Association. (2006, February 8). Teachers to be given powers outside school [Electronic version]. *Guardian Unlimited.* Retrieved July 22, 2007, from http://education.guardian.co.uk/pupilbehaviour/story/0,,1705138,00.html.

Razack, S. (1998). *Looking white people in the eye: Gender, race, and culture in courtrooms and classrooms.* Toronto: University of Toronto Press.

Roher, E. (2007, April). *Intimidation.com: Dealing with cyberbullying.* Paper presented at the Canadian Association for the Practical Study of Law in Education (CAPSLE) Conference, Vancouver, BC.

Ross-Epp, J. (1996). Schools, complicity, and sources of violence. In J. Ross-Epp & A. M. Watkinson (Eds.), *Systemic violence: How schools hurt children* (pp. 1–25). London: Falmer Press.

Rusk, J. (2007, February 13). High school suspends 19 for bullying principal on Web site [Electronic version]. *Globe and Mail.* Retrieved February 13, 2007, from http://www.theglobeandmail.com/servlet/story/RTGAM.20070213.wxfacebook13/BNStory/.

Sacco, M. (1994). The censorship of young adult literature. In J. E. Brown (Ed.), *Preserving intellectual freedom: Fighting censorship in our schools* (pp. 63–72). Urbana, IL: National Council of Teachers of English.

Sefa-Dei, G. (1997). Race and production of identity in the schooling experiences of African-Canadian youth. *Discourse: Studies in the Cultural Politics of Education, 18*, 241–256.

Shaheen, J. G. (2000). Hollywood's Muslim Arabs. *Muslim World, 90*, 22–42.

Shaheen, J. (2003). Reel bad Arabs: How Hollywood vilifies a people. *Annals of the American Academy of Political Social Science, 588*, 171–193.

Shariff, S. (2003). *A system on trial: Identifying legal standards for educational, ethical and legally defensible approaches to bullying in schools.* Unpublished doctoral dissertation, Simon Fraser University, Burnaby, BC.

Shariff, S. (2007). Unpublished research conducted as part of a three-year research project on cyber-bullying, funded by Social Science and Humanities Research Council of Canada (SSHRC). Shaheen Shariff, McGill University, Principal Investigator.

Shariff, S., Case, R., & LaRocque, L. (2001). Begging the questions: The court of appeal decision in the Surrey school board controversy. *Education & Law Journal, 11*, 85–111.

Shariff, S., Case, R., & Manley-Casimir, M. (2000). Balancing competing rights in education: Surrey School Board's book ban. *Education & Law Journal, 10*, 47–105.

Shariff, S., & Johnny, L. (2007). *Censorship!...or...Selection?: Confronting a curriculum of orthodoxy through pluralistic models.* Rotterdam, the Netherlands: Sense.

Shariff, S., & Manley-Casimir, M. E. (1999). Censorship in schools: Orthodoxy, diversity & cultural coherence. In K. Petersen & A. C. Hutchinson (Eds.), *Interpreting censorship in Canada* (pp. 157–181). Toronto: University of Toronto Press.

Schriever, B. (2007). Cyberbullying: Students have always gossiped and complained about their teachers. But in cyberspace such behaviour can take a life of its own [Electronic version]. *Professionally Speaking, the Magazine of the Ontario College of Teachers.* Retrieved August 28, 2007, from http://www.oct.ca/publications/professionally_speaking/September_2007/cyberbullying.asp.

Skiba, R., & Peterson, R. (1999). The dark side of zero tolerance: Can punishment lead to safe schools? *Phi Delta Kappan, 80*, 372–376, 381–383.

Smith, P. K., & Sharp, S. (1994). *School bullying: Insights and perspectives.* London/New York: Routledge.

United Nations. (1989). *Convention on the rights of the child.* New York: United Nations.

Wallechinsky, D., Wallace, A., Basen, I., & Farrow, J. (2005). *The book of lists.* Toronto: Alfred A. Knopf Canada.

Wason-Ellam, L. (1996). Voices from the shadows. In J. R. Epp & A. M. Watkinson (Eds.), *Systemic violence: How schools hurt children* (pp. 93–104). London: Falmer Press.

Wyman, M. (2000a, October 21). Rowling thunder. *Vancouver Sun*, pp. B1, B5.

Wyman, M. (2000b, October 26). You can lead a fool to a book but you can't make them think. *Vancouver Sun*, pp. A1, A4.

CHAPTER SEVEN

The Tragedy of the Commons: Lessons for Cyberspace?

Ruin is the destination toward which all men rush, each pursuing his own best interest in a society that believes in the freedom of the commons. Freedom in a commons brings ruin to all.

(Harden, 1968)

INTRODUCTION

According to Thomas McMorrow (2007), cyberspace, in some ways, works much like a commons. Fulfillment of its potential presupposes maximum public access. In England, a commons is a place where cattle are herded to graze together. Like the commons, cyberspace remains empty and frustrated without *collective* human involvement. McMorrow explains that much in the same way that herdsman bring their cattle to graze together on the commons, "mouse-wielding drivers" (p. 2) of the Internet need to be brought together in an unconfined space. The unconfined aspect of that space is important. He observes that the tragedy, or irony, of the commons resides in the fact the very principle of freedom of access on which it is based also inevitably leads to its destruction:

[A] space that all can enter is a space that all can abuse. Each herdsman in seeking to maximize her gain adds one more head of cattle, since the benefit of having one more of her cows grazing in the commons accrues to her alone, whereas the negative consequences of overgrazing must be borne equally by everyone. In the end, though, with each person trapped in this logic, the number of cattle grazing goes beyond what the commons can sustain, and the land becomes worthless to everyone. The problem is that while the herdsman feels compelled to increase her herd without limit, she wishes to do it in a world that is limited. No technical solution serves as an exit from this trap. Bigger commons or more resilient strains of grass only forestall the problem. The answer is not to be found in technology alone.

The only way the tragedy can be avoided is for people to change their behavior. Destruction of the commons is inevitable only so long as people only prize their short-term self-interest. The key is temperance but self-restraint within this context is not only

190

difficult but ultimately ineffectual when it consists in a solitary act alone. *What is needed is collective recognition of the mutual benefit of the commons, a genuine willingness on behalf of everyone to make the necessary sacrifice to secure the common good, and a general programme of action for everyone to follow. In other words, there need to be guidelines; for the promise of the commons to be fulfilled, there have to be laws.*

(McMorrow, 2007, emphasis added)

McMorrow notes that, accordingly, if we imagine cyber-bullying as a consequence of the licentious abuse of cyberspace, like overgrazing is an abuse of the commons, and are looking to reduce, prevent, or altogether root it out, we must acknowledge three important factors:

1. Any change in the *status quo* will ultimately rest on the decision of individual students to behave differently.
2. In order for any coordinated effort to be made (and only a coordinated effort makes sense if the aim is to eradicate widespread abuse of cyber space) the legitimate purpose behind cyberspace must be identified.
3. The purpose identified must be acceptable to the people who actually use cyberspace. It does not make sense to elaborate a set of guidelines on the use of cyberspace that presupposes a purpose that students themselves reject. In other words, we cannot assume that students are going to engage in cyberspace for educational purposes alone. While certainly we can help them to appreciate cyberspace as an educational resource, in addition to a social space where they can develop positive social relationships, education is about cultivating this attitude, which needs to be drawn out, and not imposed.

This analogy is helpful to appreciate why we need mutually beneficial guidelines for the use of cyberspace. How is it useful to students? How is it useful to adults? Within those categories are an enormous diversity of reasons. Hence, although the purpose of the commons is singular – namely, providing a place where cattle can be brought to graze – the purposes of cyberspace are numerous, evolving, and ambiguous. This adds to the complexity of the role of educators as the "herders" and educators. Their role is at once educative and normative. While the cattle have one purpose, to feed themselves, the nurturing motivations of students can be pluralistic.

Kids have established without a doubt that cyberspace can nurture their social relationships, confidence, and sense of identity (especially as we saw with girls in Japan and India). Moreover, their insistence on the fact that certain forms of online communication are beyond the realm of adult supervision suggests that they perceive these spaces as providing them with autonomy, and agency to change their lives. These are crucial considerations when setting guidelines on appropriate uses of cyberspace. Students play an essential role in determining their own learning and behavior. This was also evidenced in the cyber libel and freedom of expression cases presented in earlier chapters, in which Lutes

(*Lutes v. Board of Education of Prairie View School Division No. 74*, 1992), A. B. (*A. B. v. State of* Indiana, 2007), and even Brad Parsons and Brad Koch asserted their right to express what they felt, using the genre of language that they felt best conveyed their opinions.

From a policy perspective, then, this suggests that to protect students from cyber-bullying or from encouraging sexual predators while affirming their autonomy requires striking a fine balance. Van Praagh (2005) notes that "individual autonomy for children is elusive if premised on the notion of being left alone" (p. 1348). Yet of course, we cannot be with our children all the time. As they grow older, the time they spend by themselves will only increase. Constant surveillance of their actions, whether in cyberspace or in the classroom, is not only impractical, it is also harmful to their growth as human beings.[1] Golding (1954) demonstrated in *Lord of the Flies* that the disastrous consequences of subjugating children to constant external control are glaringly clear the instant they manage to slip out of our watch. The novel, as I have observed in earlier chapters, evidences how aware children are of the power hierarchies that adults construct both with them and among themselves.

LAW: A QUESTION OF INDIVIDUAL (STUDENT) DECISION MAKING

In calling for legally positivist (or punitive) responses to cyber-bullying, stake-holders often forget that the classroom is not the only environment in which children learn. Moreover, as teachers themselves acknowledge, they are not the unique source of all learning, although, as the previous chapter highlighted, teachers often attempt to control and construct knowledge through censorship. Similarly, it is equally absurd to presume that the state legal order made up of statutory provisions and court judgments is the only legal normative order to which children are subject, and yet, as I have argued throughout this book, the response to bullying and cyber-bullying over the last decade or more has been to clamp down, control, and stamp out the bullying through suspensions, expulsions, and legislation that adds bullying to the list of criminal offences that can result in fines and jail sentences (see Chapters 3 and 6).

As Lankshear and Knobel (2006), Jenkins and boyd (2006), and McMorrow (2007) all observe, learning takes place at recess playing with friends, after school watching TV, at the table having dinner with the family, in baseball parks and on hockey rinks, in the evening surfing the Internet or social networking spaces such as MySpace and Facebook, or at the library reading a book (not to mention countless other spaces, interpersonal interactions, and points in time). There are legal decisions being made throughout all these forms of learning. Every time an individual human being makes a decision that can be symbolized as being governed by rules (such as in a game of cards), they are making legal decisions. McMorrow cites as an example a driver's choice to stop at a red light rather than barrel through the intersection. His action may be symbolized as the decision to follow a general rule that drivers are to stop at intersections when the traffic light is red. Likewise, a student's choice to get up in the morning and go to school rather than sleep in may be symbolized as the decision to follow a general (normative) rule that students are to attend school. Of course, a specific driver's decision to stop at a red light may in point of fact have much less to do with any rule requiring him to do so and much more to do with the steady stream of Mack trucks blocking the intersection. Similarly, the reason a student makes sure to get up and out in the morning to school may have much less to do with any law against truancy and much more to do with the fact she wants to avoid seeing her abusive father before he returns from his night shift at work. McMorrow observes that to say that in either of these latter two instances, the driver or the student is following official state law is a hollow statement. Although their behavior may converge with that prescribed by certain statutory provisions, those same statutory provisions do not provide the normative basis for their actions.

Although stiff penalties might be in place to ensure that the driver continues to stop at red lights even when the coast seems clear (for the protection of everyone who uses the roads) and that the student keeps attending school even when her dad is not around (because schooling is accepted as a normative requirement for children in society), it is more likely that the driver followed the rules because he saw the Mack trucks lining up and recognized he risked his life if he failed to stop at the light. Many of us are guilty of slowing down at stop signs but failing to stop in certain instances when there is no other traffic around. Yet in rush-hour traffic we automatically stop at all traffic signs because we recognize the higher potential of danger if we do not follow the rules.

I use this example to argue that adolescents such as Brad and Bram discussed earlier in the book will not stop cyber-bullying or engaging in negative uses of cyberspace because they know that they might be suspended by law. In fact, as we saw, Brad's suspension did nothing to prevent him from gathering up his friends to launch a protest. Similarly, Bram's suspension only made him feel he was treated unfairly, leaving little room for remorse or consideration of why he was suspended. Further, as we saw with A. B. (*A. B. v. State of Indiana*, 2007), she was not afraid to challenge her school principal online and to chide him for not being able to do anything to her in cyberspace.

Even the most institutional legal positivist of the twentieth century, Hart (1997) seriously criticizes this "order backed by threats" concept of law. He believes that what makes law distinctive from other forms of social control is its normative character. For law to be normative (indeed, for law to be law), it must give rise to an obligation on behalf of the legal subject. The obligation to comply with the law or rule must come from the individual. In this way, Hart explains, when we speak of law, we necessarily speak of obligation. In this sense, obligation involves recognition from a legal subject that he or she ought to act in compliance with a particular rule. Hart's conclusion, therefore, is that law functions as an affair of rules, not as a set of orders backed by threats (Hart, 1992, as cited in McMorrow, 2007).

Nonetheless, Hart, within the positivist tradition, also contends that it is not a rule's normative content alone that makes it law but its satisfaction of formal conditions (Rule of Recognition). This means that for a norm to become legitimate, it must be recognized by those officially charged with the task of making laws, such as school or government policy makers, legislators, and the judiciary. However, as society becomes more complex, this perspective becomes too simplistic. As McMorrow (2007) asks, if all law sprang from one identifiable source and its prescriptions anticipated every human dilemma that was known and understood by every individual, then Hart's interpretation might be accurate. However, he observes that when we make prescriptive laws with the threat of harsh punishment, we forget that "as much as people live in systems, systems live in people" (McMorrow, 2007, p. 8). Prescriptive laws cannot anticipate every human dilemma. The interpretation of laws and rules, especially as we have seen in previous chapters, are subject to contextual situations, power hierarchies, and individual agency. In fact, this is specifically why constitutional and human rights provisions and school law in various states and provinces in various countries are purposely broad in wording. Consider again, for example, Section 76(3) of the British Columbia School Act (Canadian province), which says that "the highest morality will be inculcated but school will be conducted on a strictly secular and sectarian basis."

This section of the act has invited significant controversy over polemic interpretations of what constitutes the "highest morality." For religious stakeholders, it constitutes a religious morality and as noted in the Surrey School Board book banning controversy (*Chamberlain* v. *Surrey School District No. 36*, 2002), this law was interpreted as supporting the morality that informs homosexual partnerships.

As Lon Fuller (1964) explains, the problem with a managerial conception of law, such as the approach that school boards prefer, is that it assumes law functions merely as the one-way projection of state authority onto its citizens. Fuller argues that law is in fact much more interactive than the managerial model assumes. In a managerial context, the subordinate follows the directives he or she has been given to serve a purpose set by his superior, but the reasons for following such orders are not always based on serving the sole purposes of the manager. They have to be relevant and beneficial in many ways to the subordinate. Fuller explains:

The law-abiding citizen, [on the other hand], does not apply legal rules to serve specific ends set by the lawgiver, but rather follows them in the conduct of his own affairs, the interests he is presumed to serve in following legal rules being those of society generally. The directives of a managerial system regulate primarily the relations between the subordinate and his superior and only collaterally the relations of the subordinate with third persons. The rules of a legal system, on the other hand, normally serve the primary purpose of setting the citizen's relations with other citizens and only in a collateral manner his relations with the seat of authority from which the rules proceed (pp. 207–208).[2]

These are important observations as they relate to the legalistic responses to "manage" and "control" cyber-bullying. Consider the following legislative and policy responses, all of which place too much emphasis on positivistic approaches that threaten punitive consequences for noncompliance rather than responses in keeping with an open and inclusive school climate (physical or virtual). Such school management approaches fail to take into consideration contextual influences, or the individual agency of students, educators, librarians, and parents, toward whom such legislation is directed.

LEGAL AND POLICY RESPONSES: A FEW EXAMPLES

As noted earlier, Britain's largest teachers' union, the Professional Association of Teachers, called for the government to legislate the closing of YouTube because it has attracted many negative postings by students against their teachers (Asthana & Smith, 2007). Until the teachers' union works out that censorship battle with British politicians, it is noteworthy that Britain already has a comprehensive and informative Web site that specifically informs parents, teachers, and other public stakeholders about cyber-bullying, which I detail shortly. In the meantime, readers will recall that the response to cyber-bullying in most of the international countries highlighted in Chapters 1 and 3 was generally of a legal positivist nature. These include implementing laws and policies that seek criminal recourse including imprisonment or fines or civil recourse with compensation under the common law of torts, such as cyber libel and defamation. I have briefly mentioned legislation and policies implemented or proposed by various countries such as Japan, Thailand, India, and Australia in those chapters. The following legal and policy responses have emerged in Western democracies.

Deleting Online Predators Act (DOPA; H.R. 5319, 2006)

In May 2006, a Republican Pennsylvania representative, Mike Fitzpatrick, introduced the DOPA bill to the U.S. House of Representatives, with the intent to protect children who use the Internet from online predators. However, there are serious concerns that, if enacted, the bill would censor the autonomy of school teachers and librarians to determine which Web sites are safe and place it in the hands of a government-appointed commission. The bill's broad definition of "social networking Web sites" can include Facebook, MySpace, YouTube, and even Wikipedia, Yahoo, Amazon, and other informative Web sites, as well as offending ones. The proposed bill amends the Communications Act of 1934.[3] Wikipedia reports that similar bills to ban or restrict access to social networking sites have been introduced in Georgia and North Carolina. These bills would impose criminal penalties on any social communications network that allows children to join the chat room or communications network without parental consent. When consent is granted, the Web site would also be required to give parents full access to it. Oklahoma's House Bill 1715 (2007)[4] would require schools and libraries to block access to the Internet in its entirety for minors who do not have consent. Similarly the Illinois Social Networking Prohibition Act[5] (State of Illinois, SB1682, 2007) would require all public libraries and schools to block access to any social networking site for users of all ages. These proposed state bills are consistent with the recent demands made by teachers' unions in Britain and, to a lesser extent, in Canada. According to Wikipedia, the original legislation, the "Commercial Social Networking Web sites," was much less restrictive and defined these sites as follows:

Sec. 2(c) (J) A commercially operated Internet Web site that:
(i) that allows users to create web pages or profiles that provide information about themselves and are available to other users; and
(ii) offers a mechanism for communication with other users, such as a forum, chat room, email, or instant messenger. "Chat rooms" were defined as:

Sec. 2(c) (K) Internet websites through which a number of users can communicate in real time via test and that allow messages to be almost immediately visible to all other users or to a designated segment of all other users.

(Wikipedia, 2007c)

Popular Web sites that fit this definition include MySpace, Friendster, Live-Journal, and Facebook. According to Wikipedia, however, this definition could also include a range of other informative and commercial Web sites, such as Amazon and Yahoo.[6] The proposed DOPA bill has been amended to read as follows:

(J) COMMERCIAL SOCIAL NETWORKING WEBSITES; CHAT ROOMS

Within 120 days after the date of enactment of the Deleting Online Predators Act of 2006, the Commission shall by rule define the terms 'social networking website' and 'chat room' for purposes of this subsection. In determining the definition of a social networking website, the Commission shall take into consideration the extent to which a website is:
(i) is offered by a commercial entity;
(ii) permits registered users to create an online profile that includes detailed personal information;
(iii) permits registered users to create an online journal and share such a journal with other users;
(iv) elicits highly-personalized information from user; and
(v) enables communication among users.

(Wikipedia, 2007c)

This new language allows a federal communications commission to define the terms, and this might mean that it could even restrict Web sites such as Wikipedia.

Wikipedia reports that although people on both sides of the debate are in favor of blocking online predators, the larger controversy relates to the effectiveness and drawbacks of the measures being taken by the legislation. The greatest concern involves censorship of the professional autonomy of teachers and librarians.

Wikipedia lists the arguments presented by both sides of the debate. The Republican representative Michael Fitzpatrick and his supporters argue that the Internet is taking over at a "dizzying pace" and that he as a parent has serious concerns about dangerous predators. The bill's proponents argue that the Internet makes children comfortable talking to strangers, which is dangerous, hence the need to restrict chat rooms and online social networks.

Opponents of the bill have focused on efforts to revise it to address directly the problem of online predators and prevent blocking of harmless or educational Web sites. As Representative Bart Stupak summarized: "Unfortunately, child predators are not the target of today's bill. This will not delete online predators. Rather, it will delete legitimate web content from schools and libraries" (Wikipedia, 2007c).

In an interview in May 2006, Internet experts Henry Jenkins and danah boyd were asked to provide their opinions on DOPA (Wright, 2006). According to boyd, the proposed law would extend current regulations that require all federally funded schools and libraries to deploy Internet filters. She expressed the concern that the law is so broadly defined, it would limit access to any commercial site that allows users to create a profile and communicate with strangers. Although the partial intent of the legislation is to target MySpace, it would also block numerous other sites, including blogging tools, mailing lists, video and podcast sites, photo-sharing sites, and educational sites such as NeoPets.

Professor Jenkins agreed with boyd and explained that, in theory, the bill would allow schools to disable these filters for use in educationally specified contexts. Jenkins noted that, in practice, most schools would not bother to implement the filters and instead would simply lock down their computers and walk away because of the fear of being charged or fined under this legislation. He believes that teachers who want to take advantage of the educational benefits of these tools would face increased scrutiny and pressure to discontinue their educational practices. Likewise, students would lack the ability to explore these resources through independent research or social activities. Moreover, he explained that economic status reduces access to technologies because of a lack of affordability in the home. Students who were already deprived of technologies at home because of insufficient financial resources would be further affected in their learning. As it is, such students are generally left far behind in their learning and ability to function in a world that thrives on technology use. Because of its restrictions on library and school use, this legislation would cut off any possibility for teens without access to computers at home, thereby reducing their extended sphere of social contacts outside the school and home. This supports Fuller's explanation as to the reasons people might obey the law. If teachers and librarians are afraid of being fined, they will not be serving the law to protect the protective interests of their students because they will know that, in fact, DOPA would restrict access to programs and networks that will benefit young people. They will lock down their computers because to leave them turned on and not use the filters would not serve their individual or professional purpose.

Moreover, as boyd observed, most major technology companies are moving in the direction of social software, using social features to help users find information, get recommendations, and share ideas. All of this would be restricted. She argued that the assumptions underlying the proposed legislation are flawed because proponents assume that nothing good can be achieved through participation in social networking cites. She observed that it would not be surprising to find that none of DOPA's proponents have ever signed up to the sites and really examined the potential that can be achieved. The underpinnings of the legislation are therefore clearly rooted in the adult mind-sets as presented in the paradigmatic approaches to technologies presented by Lankshear and Knobel (2006). As an example of the restrictions that would occur even if the legislation was limited to MySpace, boyd noted that many high school students currently contact college students through MySpace to learn about their colleges and universities and decide whether to apply for admission. They develop mentorship relationships that would be prohibited by DOPA. Professor Jenkins put this into further perspective:

Suppose, for the sake of argument, that MySpace critics are correct and that MySpace is, in fact, exposing large numbers of teens to high-risk situations, then shouldn't the role of educational institutions be to help those teens understand those risks and develop strategies for dealing with them? Wouldn't we be better off having teens engage with MySpace in the context of supervision from knowledgeable and informed adults? Historically, we taught children what to do when a stranger telephoned them when their parents were away; surely, we should be able to teach them how to manage the presentation of their selves in digital spaces. The proposed federal legislation does nothing to help kids confront the challenges of interacting with online social communities; rather, *it allows teachers and librarians to abdicate their responsibility to educate young people about what is becoming a significant aspect of their everyday lives. Our responsibilities as educators should be to bring reason to bear on situations which are wrought with ignorance and fear, not to hide our eyes from troubling aspects of teen culture.*

(Wright, 2006, emphasis added)

In its descriptions of various Web sites, Wikipedia explains that many Web sites allow public user profiles and provide forums. Examples include Yahoo, Amazon, Slashdot, RedState, CNET Networks, and thousands of others. This potentially qualifies them as social networking Web sites regardless of the content within the Web sites. Consider further some of the educational uses and benefit of such sites.

Educational Use of Technologies

According to Wikipedia, most U.S. school libraries already have filters on incoming Internet access because of the Children's Internet Protection Act (CIPA; Wikipedia, 2007a). Opponents of the bill argue that the language of the bill would simply extend such filtering to include Web sites on the basis of specific technologies rather than specific content, including Web sites based on those technologies that are used for educational purposes. Some educators have incorporated blogs and wikis (online information sites and communication tools such as Wikipedia, an online encyclopedia that welcomes contributions by a range of online users with expertise on specific topics), into classroom lessons for students. These online resources are considered useful as critiquing and editing tool for students' work and as a forum for comments and suggestions by teachers and other students. These educators also favor such technologies because they enable discussion outside of the classroom that can involve students and teachers as well as parents. Here are some examples provided on Wikipedia relating to the educational benefits of such technologies:

Will Richardson, a teacher in New Jersey, set up a blog for student discussion of *The Secret Life of Bees* and invited author Sue Monk Kidd to join the chat. She was able to answer the students' questions about the book and give more insight than the teacher alone would have been capable [of]. A separate blog was set up to allow parents to discuss the book in parallel with the students.

Some school administrators are using blogs to communicate news and information about events to parents and students. The homepage for the Meriwether Lewis Elementary School in Oregon is updated with notes from the PTA. The principal and teachers are using blogging software to allow parents and students to view up-to-date information from the school.

The Pawtucket Public Library in Pawtucket, Rhode Island is one of a number of public libraries that have created their own MySpace profile webpage. These libraries are attempting to communicate with young adult patrons more effectively through the use of online methods to which young adults are becoming accustomed.

The Bering Strait School District relies heavily on a MediaWiki-driven curriculum content system. The district's Open Source student information system, DART, links its teachers and students directly to wiki content, as well as many RSS-fed district resources, podcasts, and vodcasts. Students have contributed many of the Wiki's 4,800 or so pages for academic credit during school hours. DART tells them what their key weaknesses are and [provides] links to the resources they need to help master those curriculum standards.

The bill would allow minors strictly limited access to those sites. For schools, access would be allowed only with adult supervision *and* if the site is being used for an educational purpose. For libraries, access would be allowed only if parental authorization is given and the parents are informed that "sexual predators can use these websites and chat rooms to prey on children."

(Wikipedia, 2007c)

Library Support for Online Education

The American Library Association, generally a strong opponent of censorship involving books and literature, is also against introduction of the DOPA legislation. The association has asked its members to oppose the bill. The association's former president, Michael Gorman, explains: "We know that the best way to protect children is to teach them to guard their privacy and make wise choices."

To this end, libraries across the country offer instruction on safe Internet use" (Wikipedia, 2007c). On July 11, 2006, the executive director of the Young Adult Library Services Association (YALSA), Beth Yoke, testified before the Subcommittee on Telecommunications and the Internet under the Committee on Energy and Commerce. She defined the ALA and YALSA combined stance on the issue by saying:

> Youth librarians believe, and more importantly know from experience, that education about safe Internet practices – for both youth *and* parents – is the best way to protect young people. We believe that the overly broad technological controls that would be required under DOPA are often ineffective given the fast-moving nature of modern technology. Further, such technological controls often inadvertently obstruct access to beneficial sites. In essence, we believe that this legislation will lead to the blocking of essential and beneficial Interactive Web applications and will further widen the digital divide.
>
> (Wikipedia, 2007c)

As with the teachers, DOPA would censor librarians' professional autonomy and local support from library trustees, elected school boards, and community members and place it in the hands of federal commissioners who would have no background or knowledge about the communities in which the libraries were situated. Moreover, on the basis of our knowledge that the Australian government spent $84 million on a similar filtering system that was quickly shown to fail, it is likely that the costs to U.S. taxpayers of implementing DOPA in the United States would be significantly higher.

It is important to emphasize again the lack of attention to *context* by this U.S. bill. Opponents of DOPA argue that this federal action could degrade the authority of those responsible for safe use of the libraries, whereas up to 80 percent of the funding for the library or school is locally derived (Wikipedia, 2007c).

Opponents of the bill have argued that the research presented by Representative Fitzpatrick in support of the bill had found only two cases of rape or sexual assault through Internet solicitations in two surveys covering 3,001 children aged ten to seventeen. According to Wikipedia (Wikipedia, 2007c), a Youth Internet Safety Survey suggested that, overall, the number of children being sexually solicited online in 2005 compared with 1999 has declined. This suggests that Internet users are becoming more savvy in avoiding such solicitations. Children aged ten to seventeen, however, are being harassed and cyber-bullied more by their peers – not by strangers.

The European Union (EU) has taken a similar but more flexible approach to the problem.

European Union

In Europe, although cyber safety of children appears to be an important topic, action seems to be currently confined to research. Interestingly enough, the

EU encourages legal action by nation-states. This is most likely because of issues of sovereignty and respecting cultural differences as Europe deals with an increasing influx of immigrants and refugees from its previous colonies. In France, an existing bill on juvenile delinquency has been amended specifically to deal with the problem of "happy slapping," which involves a physical attack on an unsuspecting victim, which an accomplice tapes the act, usually with a video phone, and then disseminates it by mobile phone or on the Internet. This is discussed later in the chapter.

Council of Europe

The Council of Europe Media Division (Human Rights: Protecting Media Freedoms) has sponsored the production of an Internet Literacy Handbook. This handbook contains a fact sheet on bullying and harassment that addresses how cyber-bullying and harassment are to be dealt with at school and at home. Under the heading "Safety and Ethical Issues," the fact sheet proposes an approach that includes conflict resolution as part of school curriculum, training staff and students to deal with instances of bullying, provision of positive support to both the students who are targeted and the students who are exhibiting such abusive behavior, and the implementation of acceptable use policies to monitor how the Internet is used in schools. It also suggests classroom activities such as role-playing activities and discussion groups to deal with cyber-bullying issues and provides best practice instructions for students. The fact sheet on mobile technology also mentions the growing concern about mobile-bullying, specifically happy slapping.

Council of Europe Draft Convention on Cyber Crime (2001, June 29)

There is a lot of commentary on the flaws of this document that could be used to predict the possible difficulties encountered in trying to deal with cyber-bullying at an international level. Criticisms largely center on the fact that it focuses solely on law enforcement and is seen as detrimental to civil liberties and industry interests. Also, the goal to attain consistency in legislation on cyber crime among signatory states has lead to vague and ambiguous wording in the convention. It is also notable that although "cyber crime" is not explicitly defined in the convention, it does not seem in this context, to include cyber harassment, cyber-stalking, or cyber-bullying, addressing only computer-related forgery and fraud. The only article that addresses the well-being of children is Article 9, "Offences Related to Child Pornography."

Europe's Information Society: Public Consultation – Safer Internet and Online Technologies for Children

The European Commission is investigating the harm mobile phones do to young children, including exposure to inappropriate content, expense, bullying, and sexual predation. The commission mentions bullying "through the distribution of abusive or compromising messages and photos amongst children as a particular concern." It was found in May 2007 that 70 percent of European children aged twelve to thirteen had mobile phones, as did 23 percent of eight to nine year olds ("Europe investigates," 2006). The commission has launched a public consultation with the aim of identifying the most effective way of making the Internet and other communication technologies safer for children. The return date for questionnaires was June 7, 2007, and these are most likely being analyzed at the time of this writing. The introductory information to the questionnaire mentions that children may be exposed to harmful content and conduct, such as bullying and harassment, on the Internet. Interestingly, it also mentions that, because the Internet is the primary channel for the distribution of evidence of sexual abuse of children, children themselves may face serious legal consequences for the distribution of such material. It is acknowledged that means of addressing the risks involved with online technology use can involve many actors, at many levels, including public administration in member states, child-care organizations, the technology industry, financial institutions, schools, parents, and the European Commission. The European Commission has already implemented a succession of Safer Internet programs, the most recent of which, Safer Internet Plus, will end in 2008.

Safer Internet Plus Program

The current European Commission program (2005–2008) established by Decision No 854/2005/EC of the European Parliament has four main aims: fighting against illegal content, tackling unwanted and harmful content, promoting a safer environment, and awareness-raising. The fact sheet (European Commission, 2007c) defines harmful content as "any content that teachers, parents, or other adults responsible for children, think is harmful to them." This leaves little room to consider the agency of children, developing autonomy in children to decipher, weigh, and decide what harmful content might constitute and making informed decisions against reviewing it online. The report also notes that definitions vary from one culture – and one person – to the next. This highlights one of the major difficulties attached to international action against cyber-bullying – respecting cultural differences – and yet this, I would argue, is the most important aspect of the response. It is at least encouraging that the EU is taking into account the personal and cultural differences in conceptualizing its policy approaches.

The fact sheet also states that although the EU has set standards and clarified many legal issues, Internet concerns cannot be tackled by law alone and are generally far greater than parents realize. Concerted action is needed as greater access to broadband Internet and third-generation (Internet) mobile phones are becoming common.

Emphasis is placed on education of parents and children, with action at member-state level essential but stimulated and encouraged by the EU. This approach is commonly taken by the EU toward controversial topics (subsidiarity). To respect sovereignty and cultural differences, the EU puts vague guidelines in place and allows the individual member states to implement the suggestions as they see fit. Ironically, in the case of the Internet and cyber-bullying, this approach runs into immediate problems because the Internet does not respect sovereign borders. An important aspect of this program is that is has a wide scope covering diverse technologies such as third-generation phones, online games, chat rooms, instant messaging, and peer-to-peer file transfer, as well as also diverse content, including racism and violence. The drafters of the program name networks of civilian hotlines as essential to combating cyber-bullying because many people are wary of contacting the police. The Safer Internet Plus program currently funds a Project called EU Kids Online (European Commission, 2007a). The project, slated to run from 2006 to 2009, will examine research carried out in eighteen member states on how children use the Internet and new media. It aims to evaluate the social cultural and regulatory influences affecting both risks and parents' and children's responses to them. One of its main aims is to examine methodological issues relating to cross-cultural analysis to establish best practice guidelines for research on children's Internet use. The Web site has a data repository of empirical research projects concerning children and the Internet in Europe and encourages contact from other researchers working in the same area. A biannual newsletter is also published.[7]

Legislation in France

In March 2007, the French government signed into law a bill amending previous delinquency laws, with the purpose of criminalizing "happy slapping" (Wikipedia, 2007d). Article 44 of the Bill[8] equates the filming or photographing of certain violent crimes with being an accomplice to that crime and creates a new felony for the broadcasting of such crimes. Civil rights groups have criticized this law as inhibiting people from recording incidents of police brutality or engaging in civilian journalism. This approach, unlike that in England (described subsequently), addresses the harm caused by the filming and dissemination of such videos and not simply the harm caused the assault in question.

Canadian Responses

In the previous chapter, I discussed at some length a resolution that has been drafted by the Canadian Teachers' Federation to develop policy responses to cyber-bullying (especially the antiauthority forms emerging on social networking sites). As far as existing legislation is concerned, education in Canada comes under provincial jurisdiction, and some provinces have reacted in a similar vein to American and European approaches. Ontario has been the most active province in bringing in legislation to address bullying when it created the controversial Safe Schools Act in 2000. The Act gave teachers discretionary power to suspend students indefinitely until a board of trustees could meet and decide on whether they should be expelled. This raised concerns among parents as to how the Act would affect students' education in the meantime. The Act was then embedded into the Ontario Education Act, which has recently been amended yet again to address the outcry by teachers and school administrators about the antiauthority forms of cyber-bullying on social networking sites. Bill

212 of the Education Amendment Act dated April 16, 2007, at a first reading, stated:

> A principal shall consider whether to suspend if he or she believes that the pupil has engaged in any of the following activities while at school, at a school-related activity *or in other circumstances where engaging in the activity will have an impact on the school climate.*
>
> (Roher, 2007, emphasis added)

This section is sufficiently broad as to cover the expressions about teachers on Facebook and similar networking tools. Interestingly, although the amended Act also adds "bullying" as allowing for suspension (and not expulsion), there is no specific reference to "cyber-bullying." Legal experts (R. Flynn, personal communication, July 27, 2007) suggest this might be due to the controversial issues raised by the student protests against infringement of their freedom of expression when schools suspend them for what they perceive as "private" conversations among friends.

When introducing the bill to the Ontario legislature, there was considerable debate as to whether the Act's definition of "bullying" includes "cyber-bullying." The minister of education stated as follows on April 25, 2007:

> One of the issues that came up most often after I introduced this legislation in the House was cyber-bullying, and that changes to the legislation would include the possibility for schools to respond to behaviors that may not technically take place in school but that would have an adverse effect on the school climate. This is a reality our students are dealing with.
>
> As I said, bullying is not currently listed as an infraction, and I believe it's about time we recognize the seriousness of these behaviors. I know there will be questions about definitions of bullying. We're going to work with the definition that was hammered out by the action team, and that will be finalized in policy guidelines.... During our consultation on bullying [with the Safe Schools Action Team], we were told that in many schools bullying was not taken seriously. We also learned that many students are affected by bullying in its various forms: physical, verbal, social or, as is becoming increasingly common, internet bullying.
>
> The action team provided a definition that covers all forms of bullying. Our reports define bullying as a form of repeated aggression used from a position of power, which can be physical, verbal or social. It is a dynamic of unhealthy interaction, and includes repeated aggression as opposed to just a singular incident.
>
> (quoted in Khoday, 2007)

Although earlier chapters have talked about which forms of bullying are taken more seriously than others, when the minister of education says it is time to take bullying "seriously," she speaks within the context of legislating bullying in the positivist sense that legitimizes suspensions for students who engage in the forms of bullying she defines. I find it interesting that although this amendment was expedited as a result of the antiauthority forms of cyber-bullying against teachers in Canada, neither the minister nor the amendment make reference to this form, even within the definition. The focus appears to be on peer-to-peer bullying. The minister's assumption is that the only way to take bullying "seriously" is by legislating the response to it. She also contradicted her earlier statements to the media which expressed her desire to move away from a zero-tolerance approach, and yet the actions taken by the ministry are more legalistic than supportive of educational programs to learn more about how to address the issues. In this respect, the British government appears to have been significantly more proactive.

British Responses

Considerable work has been conducted in Britain to address bullying and cyber-bullying from a contextual and pluralistic perspective; however, these are com-plemented by positivist legislation that continues along the lines of the countries mentioned earlier. Hence Great Britain, like Canada, is sending confusing mes-sages about what approach it considers best.

The government has published comprehensive guidelines for schools deal-ing with cyber-bullying accessible at a Web site called Don't Suffer in Silence (Department for Children, Schools and Families, 2007), which offers exten-sive information for children, parents, and school staff about cyber-bullying. However, the names of the legislation that it cites to help in addressing cyber-bullying would suggest they are grounded in positivist law. Under the heading, "What can you do about it?" it states, "The law is on your side" and that the Protection from Harassment Act, the Malicious Communications Act 1988, and Section 43 of the Telecommunications Act may be used to combat cyber-bullying. A link is provided to a Web site called WiredSafety, one page of which provides information on British law relating to cyber-stalking and harassment (WiredSafety, n.d.).

Under Section 1 of the Malicious Communications Act 1998, it is an offence to send indecent, offensive, or threatening letters, electronic communication, or other articles to another person; under Section 43 of the Telecommunications Act 1984, it is a similar offence to send a telephone message that is indecent, offensive, or threatening. In both cases, the offense is punishable with up to six months of imprisonment or a fine of up to £5000. Because the malicious communications offence is wider ranging than the telecommunications offence, it is more likely to be used by the police than the Telecommunications Act offence.

In most cases involving malicious communications or cyber-stalking, how-ever, there will be more than one offensive or threatening letter or telephone call, and therefore the police will often choose to charge the offender with an offense contrary to Section 2 of the Protection from Harassment Act 1997, also punishable with up to six months of imprisonment. Part of the reason for using this charge is that when someone is convicted of an offense under the Protection from Harassment Act 1997, the court can grant a restraining order preventing him or her from contacting their victim again. Breach of a restraining order is punishable with up to five years of imprisonment. A restraining order cannot be imposed for a conviction under the Malicious Communications or Telecommunications Acts.

If the e-mails, cyber-stalking, and other forms of harassment that come under cyber-bullying cause victims to fear that violence will be used against them, the police can choose to charge the offender with an offense contrary to Section 4 of the Protection from Harassment Act 1997, which is punishable with up to five years of imprisonment and also allows the court to grant a restraining order.

If the e-mails, cyber-stalking, and other forms of cyber-bullying are racist in nature or motivated by religious hostility, charges of "racially or religiously aggravated harassment" contrary to Sections 32(1)(a) or 32(1)(b) of the Crime and Disorder Act 1998 can be brought against the perpetrators. If convicted, offenders could face up to seven years imprisonment.

In many situations the recipient of malicious messages knows who the sender is. It may be a former partner or a relative, which may mean that the victim is reluctant to involve the police. In such circumstances, the victim could consider taking out an Injunction under Section 3 of the Protection from Harassment Act 1997. However, the Web site advises readers to always inform the police, especially if the messages are in any way threatening. Even if the police decide not to prosecute, they may give the offender a formal warning, which could be used in evidence if perpetrators repeated their behavior in future.

In addition to pursuing criminal prosecution against offenders, victims of harassment can sue the offender under Section 3 of the Protection from Harassment Act 1997 for damages arising out of the anxiety caused by the harassment and any financial loss it caused.

The British Web site does not mention any cases that have been filed under these forms of legislation in the context of cyber-bullying. The focus of the various applicable legislative frames referred to on the British Web site is largely punitive. Nonetheless, the Web site contains some important educational information for parents, teachers, students, and other stakeholders. For example, it urges parents and young people to work together to prevent and "tackle" it whenever it occurs. Some of the advice for various stakeholders contained on the site provides that school governors and head teachers have a duty to ensure that they include bullying via mobile phone and Internet in their mandatory antibullying policies, that these policies are regularly updated, and that teachers have sufficient knowledge to deal with cyber-bullying in schools. Significantly, the policy guidelines recommend that

- All e-communications used on the school site or as part of school activities off-site are monitored
- Clear policies are set about the use of mobile phones at school and at other times when young people are under the school's authority
- Internet blocking technologies are continually updated and harmful sites blocked

- They work with pupils and parents to make sure new communications technologies are used safely, taking account of local and national guidance and good practice
- Security systems are in place to prevent images and information about pupils and staff being accessed improperly from outside school
- They work with police and other partners on managing cyber-bullying
- They provide accessible information, advice, and support for students who need it

The site also recommends the British Educational Communications and Technology Agency (Becta) schools e-safety site (Becta, 2007), which has excellent suggestions for the development of acceptable use policies in schools.

What I like best about Becta's suggestions is that creating a safe Internet communications technology (ICT) learning environment must include "an infrastructure of whole-school awareness, designated responsibilities, policies and procedures; an effective range of technological tools; and a comprehensive internet safety education program for the whole school community" (Becta, 2007). The Becta policy guideline suggests three basic components:

1. Raising awareness of the issues and how they impact the particular school environment and the pupils within particular schools. They suggest that awareness can be raised, in part, by a comprehensive Internet safety program for the entire school community. Importantly, the guidelines suggest that the program should be continuous. Although it should respond to specific incidents and issues, it should also provide information about emerging technologies, as well as those already embedded within the culture of the school.
2. The second priority is to establish a clear understanding of the responsibilities of all stakeholders involved in the education of children and young people with regard to Internet safety. This includes head teachers and school principals, governing bodies (e.g., school boards), administrators, classroom teachers, school counselors, librarians, parents, and, of course, the pupils themselves.
3. The third priority involves an "infrastructure of effective policies and procedures" described as the "backbone to effective practice." Acceptable use policies should detail the ways in which the ICT facilities can and cannot be used in school by both pupils and staff. These documents should contain a list of consistent sanctions, procedures, and support strategies for dealing with misuse. Although these strategies would include management documents, staff use agreements, student and parent use agreements, policies for educating staff and students on Internet safety issues, and specific procedures for misuse, an important consideration is that the policies "need to balance the desirability of fully exploiting the vast educational potential of new technologies with providing safeguards against risks and unacceptable material and activities."

In this regard, although it advocates some controls and filtering, it also suggests the need to balance this with an awareness of the potential and benefits of new technologies.

Although the policy guidelines recommend wide-ranging coverage of fixed and mobile Internet technologies, those provided by the school (such as PCs, laptops, webcams, and digital video equipment), as well as technologies owned by students and staff that are brought onto school property such as mobile phones, camera phones, personal digital assistants (PDAs), and media players, they should also recognize the important educational benefits of such tools. Most important, the Becta guidelines recommend attention to the following:

Remember, also, that an effective internet safety policy needs to be tailored to the individual needs of your school. . . . Your policy must consider the particular circumstances of your school, such as race, gender, ethnicity and religious beliefs of pupils and staff, and factors such as the digital divide and access to ICT outside school, which may all have an impact upon the ways in which children and young people use the internet, and the types of potentially risky behaviors they engage in. It is not sufficient to merely take a template and insert your school name – the policy will lack ownership and authority, and may leave your school open to risk. . . . To be truly effective, all school internet safety policies need to be regularly reviewed with all stakeholders and updated to take account of new and emerging technologies and changes in local circumstances.

Ideally, school internet safety policies should be embedded within a cycle of establishment, maintenance, ongoing review, modification, reporting and annual review, supported by technological solutions wherever possible. By following this process, schools can ensure that they have a rigorous and effective internet safety program in place.

(Becta, 2007)

These are important recommendations because research on the poor success of traditional antibullying programs and policies was due to the lack of attention to individual differences within schools. Blanket antibullying programs and policies were implemented without attention to cultural contexts, demographics, economic influences, and so on, with the result that they did little to address the concerns or motivations of the students who perpetrated bullying (Anand, 1999; DiGiulio, 2001).

Although it is not within the scope of this book to go through everything on the British government Web site for parents, teachers, and other stakeholders, the site is well worth a visit and, I would argue, quite advanced compared with EU and North American responses as far as comprehensive information and policy guidelines are concerned. Yet Britain's teachers' unions are loudly calling for the banning of YouTube. Although I have not attempted to determine whether many teachers in Great Britain access the government Web site, it would be worth exploring the extent to which this site has been marketed to educators and parents – how many know about it and use its resources and the extent to which schools are actually using it to develop their policies to address cyber-bullying in Britain. It is important to find out whether the tax payers' dollars spent by the government on this Web site are successful in creating the awareness and providing comprehensive education to British schools and parents. How many and how often are parents and students accessing this Web site? In the following incident involving happy slapping, it is apparent that the British government's Web site has made little difference.

Happy slapping is believed to have originated in London as part of the garage music scene. Although there is no legislation specifically dealing with it as there is in France, assault charges have been made in certain cases. In one case, a sixteen-year-old girl was seriously assaulted on her way home from school, and the incident was filmed and posted online. Despite the fact that a significant amount of the distress the victim suffered was due to the video being shown to her peers at school, a school spokesman was quoted as saying simply that "this is a police matter which happened outside school" ("Mother rages," 2005) When dealing with the Internet and third-generation mobile phone technology, which is accessible by students both inside and outside of school, such an approach does not begin to deal with the problem.

BACK TO THE DRAWING BOARD

In this chapter, I have attempted to show that a legal positivist approach is prevalent among educators and government policy makers and that this comes through predominantly in official legislative and policy responses to cyber-bullying. As explained in Chapter 6, this is a reflection of the deeply embed-ded normative structures and hegemonic perspectives that control and con-struct knowledge in schools (Shariff & Johnny, 2007). I have also argued using McMorrow's (2007) analogy of the cyberspace as the "commons" that the chal-lenges of educating children and supervising their social interactions demands reconceptualization of what we mean by law and policy to control young peo-ple's actions. As Chapters 4 through 6 demonstrated, young people do not make decisions about their expression or behavior in a vacuum. Their actions are informed by biological and socializing influences and the varying contexts in which they develop or adapt their identities. Children employ agency and autonomy to make decisions about what they deem is acceptable online behav-ior. Moreover, when we bring issues of reputation, the right to state an opinion or make legitimate comments about school policies or personnel, and the insti-tutional obligation to provide positive school environments that are free of discrimination (virtual and physical), it becomes clear that current approaches, well intentioned and seemingly sensible to educators and politicians, are on the wrong track. The objections to the DOPA legislation and the Australian example of the teenager who cracked two government-mandated Internet fil-ters within thirty and forty minutes, respectively (Higginbottom & Packham, 2007) make it clear that new or adjusted lenses are essential to inform the development to policy and practice guidelines.

I now turn to my concluding chapter, in which I present alternate models and perspectives rooted in a combination of critical educational, substantive, and legally pluralistic perspectives that show greater promise of educating students and school personnel about the complexities of cyber-bullying by modeling and supporting autonomous student decisions that will help them abide by the law through their own agency and responsibility.

REFERENCES

Anand, S. S. (1999). Preventing youth crime: What works, what doesn't and what it all means for Canadian juvenile justice. *Queen's Law Journal, 25*, 177–249.

Asthana, A., & Smith, D. (2007, July 29). Teachers call for YouTube ban over "cyber-bullying" [Electronic version]. *Guardian Unlimited*. Retrieved August 22, 2007, from http://observer.guardian.co.uk/uk_news/story/0,,2137177,00.html.

Becta. (2007). *What is an acceptable use policy?* Retrieved August 23, 2007, from http://schools.becta.org.uk/index.php?section=is&catcode=ss_to_es_pp_ aup_03 &rid=11087.

Department for Children, Schools and Families. (2007). *Don't suffer in silence.* Retrieved August 23, 2007, from http://www.dfes.gov.uk/bullying/.

DiGiulio, R. C. (2001). *Educate, mediate, or litigate? What teachers, parents, and administrators must do about student behavior.* Thousand Oaks, CA: Corwin Press.

Europe investigates dangers of mobiles to children [Electronic version]. (2006, July 27). *Out-Law News.* Retrieved August 22, 2007, from http://www.out-law.com/page-7141.

European Commission. (2007a, June 7). *EU Kids Online.* Retrieved August 23, 2007, from http://www.eukidsonline.net/.

European Commission. (2007b, February 2). *Making the Internet a safer place: The safer Internet fact sheet* [Electronic version]. Retrieved August 22, 2007, from http://ec.europa.eu/information_society/doc/factsheets/018-saferinternetplus.pdf.

European Commission. (2007c, July 31). *Safer Internet plus programme.* Retrieved August 22, 2007, from http://ec.europa.eu/information_society/activities/sip/programme/index_en.htm.

European Committee on Crime Problems. (2001, June 29). *Draft convention on cyber-crime* [Electronic version]. Retrieved June 29 from http://www.privacyinternational.org/issues/cybercrime/coe/cybercrime-final.html.

Flynn, R. (2007, July 27). Private communication: Interpretation of changes to Bill 212. In S. Shariff (Ed.). Toronto.

Fuller, L. (1964). *The morality of law: A reply to critics.* New Haven, CT: Yale University Press.

Golding, W. (1954). *Lord of the flies.* New York: Penguin Putnam.

Harden, G. (1968). The tragedy of the commons. *Science, 162*, 1243–1248.

Hart, H. L. A. (1997). *The concept of law* (2nd ed.). Oxford, England: Oxford University Press.

Higginbottom, N., & Packham, B. (2007, August 26). Student cracks government's 85M porn filter [Electronic version]. *Herald Sun.* Retrieved August 26, 2007, from http://www.news.com.au/story/02359922304224-421,00.html.

House Bill No. 1715, State of Oklahoma (2007).

Jenkins, H., & boyd, d. (2006, May 30). Discussion: MySpace and Deleting Online Predators Act (DOPA) [Electronic version]. *Digital Divide Network.* Retrieved June 12, 2006, from http://www.digitaldivide.net/articles/view.php?ArticleID=592.

Khoday, A. (2007). *Bullying*. Unpublished report produced as part of the International Cyberbullying Research Project, McGill University, Montreal, funded by the Social Science and Humanities Research Council of Canada (SSHRC). Shaheen Shariff, Principal Investigator.

Lankshear, C., & Knobel, M. (2006). *New literacies: Everyday practices and classroom learning* (2nd ed.). Maidenhead, England/New York: Open University Press.

McMorrow, T. (2007). *Lord of the bullies: Advocating a student-centred approach to legal research into cyber-bullying*. Unpublished paper submitted for graduate course at McGill University.

"Mother rages at 'slap attackers'" [Electronic version]. (2005, May 19). *BBC News Online*. Retrieved August 14, 2007, from http://news.bbc.co.uk/2/hi/uk_news/england/manchester/4563419.stm.

Roher, E. (2007, April). *Intimidation.com: Dealing with cyberbullying*. Paper presented at the Canadian Association for the Study of Law in Education (CAPSLE), Conference, Vancouver, Canada.

Shariff, S., & Johnny, L. (2007). *Censorship! . . . or . . . Selection?: Confronting a curriculum of orthodoxy through pluralistic models*. Rotterdam, the Netherlands: Sense.

Van Praagh, S. (2005). Adolescence, autonomy and Harry Potter: The child as decision-maker. *International Journal of Law in Context, 1*, 335–373.

Wikipedia. (2007a). *Description of the Children's Internet Protection Act*. Retrieved August 23, 2007, from http://en.wikipedia.org/wiki/Children%27s_Internet_Protection_Act.

Wikipedia. (2007b). *Description of the Communications Act of 1934*. Retrieved August 23, 2007, from http://en.wikipedia.org/wiki/Communications_Act_of_1934.

Wikipedia. (2007c). *Description of the Deleting Online Predators Act of 2006*. Retrieved August 23, 2007, from http://en.wikipedia.org/wiki/Deleting_Online_Predators_Act_of_2006#_note-thomas#_note-thomas.

Wikipedia. (2007d). *Description of happy slapping*. Retrieved August 23, 2007, from http://en.wikipedia.org/wiki/Happy_slapping#_note-9.

WiredSafety. (n.d.). *Cyberstalking and harassment*. Retrieved August 23, 2007, from http://wiredsafety.org/gb/stalking/index.html.

Wright, S. (2006 (May 26)). MySpace and Deleting Online Predators Act (DOPA) [Electronic version]. *MIT Tech Talk*. Retrieved August 13, 2007, from http://www.danah.org/papers/MySpaceDOPA.pdf.

CHAPTER EIGHT

Cyber Collaboration: Models for Critical Legal Pluralism in Teacher Education Programs

A legal rule is legitimate only to the extent that it can capture people's imaginations and make them believe it is worth engaging with and participating in the normative framework proposed. Moreover, the legitimacy of a legal rule depends on a minimum functionality common to all rules: its capacity to effectively capture, shape, and refract parties' perceptions of problems. In brief, a legal rule ceases to be a command and instead becomes a hypothesis of action and interaction.

(Macdonald & Kong, 2006, p. 22)

INTRODUCTION

In Chapter 7, I explained that according to Hart's (1997) legal positivism perspective, the task of the legal subject is simply to follow the list of instructions that have been stamped and certified as the law in accordance with the principles of legality. Consequently, legal subjects are presented as being similar to employees in a company who carry out the tasks they have been assigned by their manager not out of fear of punishment but, quite simply, because the boss says so. In the educational context, this is doubly problematic because as important as it is for there to be a certain level of order in the way students communicate online or in class, if that level of order comes at the expense of students being able to develop a healthy ability to question formal authority, then they will miss an important lesson in their development, both as thinkers and citizens.

In other words, the "do as I say because I said so" approach defeats the purpose of educating students about why certain forms of expression, even when they are stating an opinion, might be less hurtful and demeaning if they are not couched in sexual and homophobic language. As I illustrated in Chapter 7, the zero-tolerance response to bullying and cyber-bullying is rooted in a positivist paradigm, originating in a military model that leaves no room for dialogue or discussion. The newspaper headlines, framed to sensationalize the issues, reflect the clear intent of educators and policy makers to "clamp down," "win the war," and ban student expression. This does not make students feel valued as intelligent or thinking citizens of society.

As the strong opening quote in this book illustrates, it is adults who model and sustain the very forms of violence and discrimination, the barriers of intersecting and interlocking forms of racism, sexism, homophobia, and ableism, that are reflected in the attitudes and expressions conveyed by their pupils online. Cyber-bullying, especially in its antiauthority form, is nothing new. It strongly mirrors the symptoms of an adult society that has been infected by systemic and hegemonic hierarchies of power that often play themselves out as violence, whether verbal or physical. Simply because these forms of violence are regularly depicted in adult movie productions and in video games does not negate that adults create such productions based on actual adult behaviors. This reinforces the fact that our society accepts and thrives on violence and enjoys the corporate and financial benefits it reaps from its popularity.

It is therefore ironic that when young people reflect the behaviors and attitudes modeled and reinforced by adults, those very adults clamp down on such behavior and snuff it out – or at least, sweep it under the carpet lest the education system is perceived to be failing its mandate.

As I asked in Chapter 1, what is the mandate of educators in a world that is rapidly changing as a result of evolving technologies and digital literacies? If I say that our mandate is to develop socially responsible, confident, civic-minded, and contributing citizens in society, my words may sound as hollow as the school policies and mission statements that talk about "fostering inclusive school environments" or using acronyms such as the three "Rs" for "respect," "responsibility," and "rights. These lofty goals are easier said than done, as I have attempted to illustrate in highlighting the complexities. It is difficult to achieve a balance when navigating between stakeholder rights and interests in physical and virtual space. Yet at no time has it been more important to reconceptualize the way we understand and deliver knowledge, administer schools, or apply certain rules and laws to manage the "commons" of physical and cyberspace all at once. As Golding's (1954) island demonstrates, when anarchy already exists in society, it is not difficult to understand why future generations behave the same way. In other words, the boys' relationships on that island without adults broke down because these young people were simply the products of the society that raised them. Hence, if we are to make a difference in addressing the issues of laws and rules in cyberspace, we need to come at the issues from a different perspective. Little progress can be expected, unless competing stakeholder rights and interests are addressed through critical and pedagogically informed programs and policies. Teachers and school administrators need to be better equipped not only to address contemporary dilemmas but also to dig deeper to reach the heart of a societal problem. Teacher education and professional development programs have, to date, done a poor job of equipping educators to navigate stakeholder claims. The Internet and digital literacies have complicated matters even further.

A TYPOLOGY OF LAWS: COMPREHENSIVE LEGAL FRAMEWORKS

Elsewhere (Shariff, 2008), I have noted that to develop a cohesive and collaborative stakeholder approach to addressing the dilemmas of cyber-bullying, a pragmatic shift is necessary. Such a shift ought to inform the way we conceptualize issues of censorship and cyber-bullying. Key gaps that are evident in the cyber-bullying controversies include the following:

1. The need for informed and improved teacher education and professional development of school officials and policy makers.
2. The need to level the power hierarchies among stakeholders to reconceptualize schooling through collaborative and nonrestrictive learning approaches. It is important that these are grounded in a comprehensive foundation of digital literacies, critical pedagogies, leadership, and substantive law, such that we learn together with children and take advantage of the enormous fluidity, capacity, and communicative and learning potential that contemporary technologies provide.
3. The need to canvass a typology of laws instead of rooting all our responses in positivist and reactionary policies, to instead identify and clarify a range of standards that can reasonably be expected of educators and students, as I have done in Chapters 3 to 5.
   As McMorrow (2007) explains:

Such a conception of law [a typology of laws], one that eschews formal state recognition of a norm as a precondition for its "legality," allows for a much more pluralistic approach to legal inquiry. Even if the primary goal of one's research is to figure out how a statutory provision ought to be changed to better address cyber bullying, it is necessary to understand the implicit and inferential norms to which students advert in deciding how to behave. A typology of legal norms, orders, processes, methodologies and institutions sensitizes us to the inherent plurality of legal normativity and underscores just how arbitrary a single formal criterion for legality necessarily is.[1] This typology may be graphed along two axes, one representing law's sites and the other law's modes. First, the site of law (its manner of elaboration) may be explicit or implicit; this depends on whether the norm came into being as a result of a deliberate creative process or not. The mode of law (the way meaning may be extracted from norms) comprises the second axis of this normative typology; this relates to how a given norm is articulated.

On the one hand, there are formal norms that are presented canonically and typically reflected in words like those of a statute. However, a formal norm may not necessarily be explicit in terms of the fact they may never have been consciously elaborated. Thus, norms derived from commercial practice are at once formal and implicit. In contrast to canonically formulated norms, there are inferential norms. Unlike formal norms, these do not possess a fixed textual or practical formulation. Thus, judicial decisions constitute examples of explicit yet inferential norms. While the courts are conscious of the fact they are elaborating legal norms, the *ratio decidendi* of a court judgment cannot be reduced to a precise rule through the simple application of a succinct formula; it must be inferred from the entire text of the judgment. Inferential norms may also be implicit. For example, the general principles at the foundation of a normative system like justice or equity are fluid concepts that are nowhere either written out or summed up in canonical form.

(pp. 10–11)

Put in layperson's terms, this description supports my position for a pluralistic and contextual understanding of how the law is developed, formalized through statute or common law (judicial interpretation), interpreted by judges within a range of legal frameworks and normative constructs, interpreted by policy makers, and implemented as policy decisions. Hence my review and analysis of case law and statutory measures as presented in Chapters 3 to 5 was purposely designed to illustrate that the law is not singular; that it is developed, interpreted, applied, and rooted in a range of normative and legal doctrines and frameworks; and that it must be interpreted and applied within the sociological contexts that it governs. Just as Lankshear and Knobel (2006) argue for a pluralistic and sociologically grounded approach to understanding and implementing digital literacies, so, too, it is essential, in my view, that legal and policy responses to cyber-bullying be understood and implemented within a comprehensive, contextual, and pluralistic framework if such responses are to be useful at all. At the risk of oversimplification, I have tabled some of the legal standards extrapolated under various legal frameworks in Chapters 3 to 5, and combine them here (see Table 8.1). However, simply laying out a set of legal standards for educators and policy makers, many of whom have minimal background in law, is not sufficient.

I propose a formula for teacher education and professional development that incorporates these standards into a model that combines critical legal literacy grounded in substantive and legally pluralistic modes of law, as well as educational theories grounded in critical pedagogy and leadership. Together, it is plausible that these will better prepare educational professionals to develop informed, thoughtful, nonarbitrary, ethical, and legally responsible solutions and policy responses to cyber-bullying, without having to engage in legally positivist models and zero-tolerance battle with kids or technologies.

A CRITICAL LEGAL LITERACY

Although initiatives promoting law-related education over the last two decades have provided schools with a significant amount of information in the form of pamphlets and "how-to" manuals, school administrators rarely refer to them, or they wait to do so until they have a crisis (Shariff & Strong-Wilson, 2005). I propose that what is needed instead is critical legal literacy – a way of educating teachers and school administrators about substantive and pluralistic legal principles that make sense in their everyday professional practices. I propose a Critical Legal Literacy Model (Shariff 2007) for teacher education and professional development of school administrators that combines knowledge of legal principles that are relevant to educational policy decisions.

TABLE 8.1. *A Plurality of Legal Standards Relevant to Cyber-Bullying*

Legal Framework	Standards for Administrators	Standards for Teachers	Standards for Parents	Implied Standards for Students
Tort law (cyber libel)	• Can intervene if nexus to school • Expression must involve "unfair comment" • Expressions that include an opinion or political statement, even if couched in lewd terms, can be exempt from libel	• Understand how the libel is interpreted by a person who is *reasonably thoughtful and informed*, rather than *someone who has an overly fragile sensibility* • Can intervene if nexus to school • Expression must involve "unfair comment" • Expressions that include an opinion or political statement, even if couched in lewd terms, can be exempt from libel	• Need to explain the line at which "joking" in the public realm of cyberspace can cross the line to become libel and result in liability • Need basic understanding of libel laws • International standards – parents are partially responsible for their children's online expression	• Learn that cyberspace is rarely private space • Know limitations on free speech • Learn to make political statements or state opinions in a respectful manner that does not include libel or defamatory statements • Take leadership in encouraging responsible use of technologies by peers • Inform others who cross the line • Participate in developing codes of conduct • Help adults to reconceptualize the value of digital literacies
Tort law (supervision)	• Duty of care in loco parentis • Obligation to act as "careful and prudent parent"	• Duty of care in loco parentis • Obligation to act as "careful and prudent parent"	Equally responsible for supervising and being aware of their children's online postings and discourse	Legal doctrine of *volenti non fit jura* says minors can be held responsible for their actions if they know the risk involved and still undertake libel

Constitutional principles – freedom of expression (Canadian Charter, U.S. First Amendment to the Constitution)	• Must justify infringement of rights to protect greater good and minimally impair stakeholder rights • Can intervene if expression *materially and substantially disrupts learning* • Can intervene if expression *disrupts educational mission* • Expression that contains opinion or protest is protected regardless of how obscene or lewd unless administrator can prove harm to reputation or psychological harm • Can intervene if expression was made using school computers or Web sites	• Must justify infringement of rights to protect greater good and minimally impair stakeholder rights • Can intervene if expression *materially and substantially disrupts learning* • Can intervene if expression *disrupts educational mission* • Expression that contains opinion or protest is protected regardless of how obscene or lewd unless administrator can prove harm to reputation or psychological harm	• Teach children that freedom of speech is a right but not an "unfettered right"; it is not unlimited and there are boundaries	• Know their rights to free expression • Know the limits on those rights • Can be held accountable for overstepping limits • Expression can be opinion or political statement and can be lewd or obscene but cannot be defamatory or libelous (unfair comment) and cannot *materially or substantially disrupt learning or the educational mission* • Can't express opinions from school computers or Web sites using foul language
Criminal law	• Perceived intent is equal to real threat • Wire fraud might be a successful option for false identification or identity theft online causing perceived intent to harm (e.g. Lori Drew case)	• Need awareness of where cyber-bullying crosses the line to become criminal threat (e.g., pornographic, racist, homophobic)	Need awareness of where cyber expression crosses the line to become perceived as criminal "threats" and teach their children	• Know that unintended threats can be perceived as real threats, resulting in criminal liability
Child and youth protection laws	If extended to peer abuse, this would require reporting of bullying and cyber-bullying, investigation, monitoring, follow-up, and staff training with legal consequences for failure to report or follow-up	If extended to peer abuse, this would require reporting of bullying and cyber-bullying each time it occurred, with legal consequences for failure to report	If extended, parents of victims could expect schools to act on their reports to better protect their children	Could expect improved protection from schools and know that their reports of bullying or cyber-bullying would be taken more seriously because there would be a consequence to the teachers and school officials if they ignored or tacitly condoned bullying

Moreover, all legal research presupposes a certain conception of law. Although it is possible to base legal research related to cyber-bullying on the theoretical foundations of institutional legal positivism, such an inquiry is confined to statutes passed by legislatures and decisions handed down by courts in certain state jurisdictions. It ignores the substantial scholarship illustrating the deficiencies of such an approach to understanding law that I have presented throughout this book, particularly in Chapters 6 and 7. Of course, it is one thing to show that as far as legal theories go, a critical legal pluralism is preferable to institutional legal positivism. However, my research projects on cyber-bullying are expressly directed toward elaborating a set of policies that address an audience of educators, not legal theorists. If educators ordinarily understand law in the institutional legal positivist sense of the word, then why go to the trouble of justifying an alternative such as my critical legal pluralist approach to understanding law as enumerated in Table 8.1 and Figure 8.2? The reason is that the prevalence of institutional legal positivist thinking among educators is precisely what stands in the way of any effective implementation of policy objectives, no matter how well informed and articulated those objectives may be.

My Critical Legal Literacy Model illustrates why positivist legal background on its own is not enough. Multidisciplinary pedagogical elements and an understanding of substantive legal principles model are also essential for the success of this approach. Accordingly, I suggest educational perspectives that teachers and policy makers can easily identify as congruent or compatible with the legal principles identified in Table 8.1. In the last eight years of research and teaching about the intersection of law and education, I have developed the Critical Legal Literacy at preservice and graduate levels that serves my students well. Although qualitative studies on the effectiveness of this model are yet to be conducted, practicing teachers and administrators who currently work in the field, as well as prospective teachers and school administrators who attend my courses, comment on its practicality and utility. Moreover, this approach helps educators gain an improved conceptual understanding of their legal obligations to students and critically assess the role of their own agency and assumptions in decision making. The Critical Legal Literacy approach is illustrated in Figure 8.1.

I also introduce two models and a concept map that were developed as part of my preservice teacher education and professional development at McGill University over the past four years. I believe these models contribute significantly to meeting not only the legal responsibilities outlined in Table 8.1 but also inform the development of proactive and collaborative policies on cyber-bullying at international levels.

A CRITICAL LEGAL LITERACY MODEL FOR TEACHER EDUCATION

My Critical Legal Literacy Model is grounded in a conceptual understanding of substantive legal principles and legal pluralism. These are not the same as the positivist or punitive aspects of law that on which educators tend to rely.

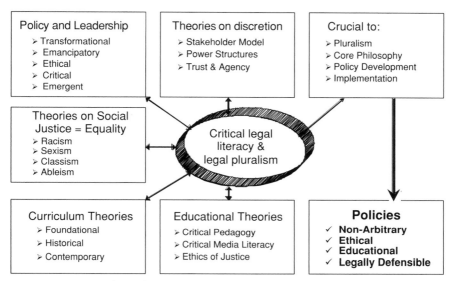

FIGURE 8.1. Critical Legal Literacy Model (Shariff, 2006).

Such reliance leads to assumptions among teachers and school administrators that the law has no place in pedagogy or educational policy. Let me elaborate on the model:

Legal Literacy

Legal literacy for educators prepares them to apply substantive legal principles that inform the fundamental ideals of democracy and civil behavior toward others. Through discussion and analysis of case law that provides various educational, programmatic, and policy challenges, the model includes competing rights and stakeholder conflicts such as the free expression and privacy debate in cyberspace. Teachers learn to apply practical exercises and knowledge to an improved understanding of the legal standards included in Table 8.1. More specifically, teachers gain a hands-on understanding of what we mean when we talk about equality; freedom of expression; freedom of religion on conscience; the right to life, liberty, and security; the right to be free from unreasonable search and seizure; and so on, in a constitutional sense, by working through case studies and legal analysis. They learn the extent of their responsibilities of supervision under tort law as in loco parentis and their obligations as "careful and prudent parents." My approach gives teachers an opportunity to learn how courts balance and weigh competing rights and how this balancing of rights and responsibilities is an integral aspect of running a democratic school system.

I find it disturbing that so few teachers and school officials have a minimal grounding in substantive law. This limits their understanding of law as an instrument of control – which requires them to handle every situation through adversarial, punitive, and positivist solutions. As I explained in earlier chapters, censorship and didactic control of what children learn in schools contributes to the discriminatory and demeaning attitudes that rear their ugly heads in the content of student expression (cyber-bullying) against peers and teachers. Elsewhere (Shariff & Johnny, 2007), I have written that many of the comprehensive perspectives and forms of knowledge omitted from our school system are censored either behind closed doors or in such a skillful way that it is not always obvious. For example Apple and Christian-Smith (1991), in their discussion of learning materials, remind us that textbooks are the product of a selective tradition – "someone's selection, someone's visions of legitimate knowledge and culture, one that in the process of enfranchising one group's cultural capital disenfranchises another's" (p. 4). Although these scholars concede that some modern texts have aimed to incorporate multicultural perspectives, they argue many of these perspectives are only mentioned in passing rather than discussed in any great depth. Moreover, Taylor argues that when the reality of another is not adequately represented it can lead to a sort of social oppression. He states:

Equal recognition is not just the appropriate mode for a healthy democratic society. Its refusal can inflict damage on those who are denied it. The projection of an inferior or demeaning image on another can actually distort and oppress, to the extent that the image is internalized. . . . Race relations and discussions of multiculturalism are undergirded by the premise that the withholding of recognition can be a form of oppression.
(Taylor, as cited in McDougall & Philips Valentine, 1999, p. 335)

The manner in which knowledge is constructed for our school system is undoubtedly an important consideration for how we understand and define student expression and acceptable forms of communication. Take, for instance, the work of scholars such as Montgomery (2005). He found in his exploration of racism in schools that although Canadian history textbooks seem to acknowledge examples of racism, it is presented as isolated occurrences that take place only among exceptionally flawed individuals. He argues that "this depiction of Canada as a space of vanquished and managed racism . . . perpetuates mythologies of white settler benevolence while it at once obscures the banal racisms upon and through which the nation state is built and rebuilt" (p. 439). Such examples remind us that censorship is not only about what is banned from our schools but also how information is presented. Obscuring the reality of marginalized groups in official textbooks can certainly have significant ramifications for society because, as Inglis (1985) notes, "a curriculum is no less than the knowledge system of a society and therefore not only an ontology but also the metaphysics and ideology which that society has agreed to recognize as legitimate and truthful; it sets the canons of truthfulness" (p. 22).

As I reported in censorship studies (Shariff & Manley-Casimir, 1999), principals, teachers, secretaries, clerks, and other school employees often take it upon themselves to self-censor books and educational resources. Sometimes "offending" pages are torn out of books or blacked out. Hence it is not surprising, as Lankshear and Knobel (2006) observe, that educators transport this mind-set to online learning and expression. To address these uses of agency and discretion and begin to incorporate elements of trust and student empowerment, the type of professional development and teacher education model I recommend in Figure 8.1 is grounded in legal literacy and legal pluralism. This combination takes into account "cultural specificity" (Macdonald, 2006). When applied, the model draws on a range of educational theories that are largely informed by a critical perspective. Using the Critical Legal Literacy Model, prospective teachers, graduate students, and school administrators learn to assess critically their own agency and leadership approaches, question their own assumptions about student differences, and apply them to the legal literacy framework. This exercise helps them determine whether they in fact bring a hegemonic perspective to their teaching, supervision, and administrative duties, including discipline and punishment for the forms of expression that underpin bullying and cyberbullying.

PRACTICAL SOLUTIONS: ONLINE LIMITATIONS

Teacher education and professional development programs need to integrate and apply the foregoing approaches with more practical attention to digital literacies. Developing familiarity and confidence with digital literacies ought to be a key element of these courses. Media literacy experts can be called in to support such programs on an ongoing basis and work with prospective teachers and school administrators to identify online resources in a range of teaching subjects. Online educational initiatives might include:

- Hands-on Internet research strategies and links to useful resources;
- Blogs that discuss civil liberties such as freedom of expression, limits on free speech, and a range of current affairs and world politics;
- Legislation, policy information, and links to case law where pupils learn to contribute to policy development;
- Educational Web sites on a range of subjects such as art, architecture, history, and the natural sciences;
- Online writing competitions;
- Links to scientific and medical journals;
- Links on music and cultural information;
- Links to video games such as Second Life with a view to encourage team building and co-operation among online avatars and opportunities to deconstruct the objectives of violent online games.

Experts in digital literacies need to be invited to engage in hands-on practice with prospective teachers to guide them on how to develop resource databases of useful Web sites, so that slowly they can overcome the restrictive mind-set and integrate digital literacies as a normal part of their everyday teaching.

In Canada, the Media Awareness Network (www.mediawareness.com, "MNet") has developed teacher education programs that they license to school boards. These programs include introductions to constitutional and human rights law, as well as criminal justice issues relating to youth, all of which use the Internet interactively, so that teachers develop proficiency with it. This non-profit organization has also developed excellent interactive online resource lists that help young people critically assess their social relationships and attitudes online. For younger students, it has created an interactive game called "Privacy Playground: The First Adventure of the Three CyberPigs" and "CyberSense and Nonsense: The Second Adventure of the Three CyberPigs" (Media Awareness Network, n.d.).

For older students, they have also developed an interactive educational program that addresses online hate that has been licensed to approximately eighty school districts across Canada (Steeves & Wing, 2005). I am working with MNet to develop in-depth lesson plans for prospective teachers and high school students on children's rights, ethical online communication and moral codes of social communication, tort law and cyber libel, tort law and negligence in supervision, criminal law as it relates to online threats and harassment, and constitutional and international human rights provisions. The organization is also developing networks with the Canadian Girl Guides association and the Canadian Red Cross on antibullying education focusing on respect. In this connection they are launching an enormous public awareness campaign. MNet works with kids' help phone lines in various provinces across Canada and are members in PREVNet, an academic networking organization that brings together researchers interested in young people's social relationships, nationally and internationally. Other initiatives under consideration include online mediation among youth groups, and youth experts who work with adults to show them how to navigate the Internet.

We must engage young people in the rule-making aspects relating to responsible use of new technologies and work with them (on a consistent and supportive basis) to help them think critically about the consequences of their actions for the victims, their own education, and their families. In this context, the international work of TC2 (the Critical Thinking Consortium) directed by Professor Roland Case (as cited in Shariff & Johnny, 2007) is highly applicable. The consortium works with schools and teachers to infuse critical thinking into the curriculum, whereby students are presented with contentious scenarios and taught the tools to help them to make reasoned judgments about their actions, attitudes, and responses in specific situations. As Willard (2005) suggests, in the cyber-bullying context, it is of crucial importance that we provide the supports to help young people reconnect with their sense of ethics, so that they can think critically about the impact of their online actions and attitudes.

Similarly, in the United Kingdom, the Teacher Resource Exchange Web site (British Educational Communications and Technology Agency, n.d.-b) allows for exchange of online resources developed by teachers, as does the Becta online resource directory for teachers (British Educational Communications and Technology Agency, 2007). Awards are given to schools that incorporate and raise awareness of ways to integrate digital literacies in schools (British Educational Communications and Technology Agency, n.d.-a).

Moreover, the examples from the American Library Association in response to the proposed Deleting Online Predators Act of 2006 bill in the United States in Chapter 7 suggest that libraries can be instrumental in developing adult online proficiency. This expertise can, in turn, support children's use of online tools. The range of online educational resource guides is expanding every day as information technology experts join with educational pedagogues, librarians, and academics to develop improved access and proficiency on digital literacies.

It is not within the scope of this book to list all online resources because these proliferate on a daily basis. However, it is important to cite one important study by library scientists who engaged children in the development of a Web portal for peers. Large, Nesset, Beheshti, and Bowler (2006) embarked on a research study that investigated three challenges to developing Internet resources for classroom use. They wanted to determine how elementary school students use Web portals to find information in support of class-based projects. They also examined what constitutes an effective Web portal design for elementary school students. Finally, they wanted to know whether intergenerational design techniques could be used to design such a Web portal. The study used two intergenerational teams: one team comprising three researchers and eight Grade 6 students; the other team the same three researchers and six Grade 3 students. The teaching team under this project designed a low-tech Web portal prototype. The research was conducted in a public elementary school located in a middle-class suburb of Montreal.

Subsequently, the two low-tech portals were converted into working prototypes to search the Web for sites in English or French relating to Canadian history. The portals were evaluated by single-sex focus groups comprising children in Grade 6 and Grade 3. The researchers report that overall, these users responded positively to both portals and said they would choose to use them over other well-known portals such as Google or MSN if seeking information for a project on Canadian history. Drawing from a literature review of Web portal design that incorporated user-centered design methodologies, contextual design approaches, and learner-centered approaches, the designers developed a new methodological framework called "bonded design," because they believed this term encapsulated the essence of what all members of the design team experienced. The team included eleven individuals in one case and eight in the other. They were divided into two groups: the children and the adult designers. Each group brought special and unique expertise that was essential to the successful completion of the team's task. The children were "experts in thinking like children" (Large et al., 2006, p. 78) and represented the user community for which the two portals were being designed.

The researchers explain that adults frequently cling to the illusion that they understand how children think and behave. They suggest that this misconception arises from the fact that they were themselves once children or that they have children of their own through whose observation they can generate a child's view of the world. They wanted to test their hypothesis that emergence from childhood is irreversible and that if adults want to understand children, the best way to do so is to work alongside them as collaborators. The researchers explain:

> While the children were involved alongside adults as team members, each with an equal voice, not every voice sang the same song. The children were novice users. Of course they had a critical expertise – they understood how children think and behave – but they knew little about Web portals or the design process. In contrast, the adults had expertise in portal design and functionality but could not think like children. Furthermore, there can be no denying that it was the adults who set the agenda, designed the initial research plan, and determined such important details as the length, content, and organization of sessions. Although the atmosphere in the design sessions was relaxed and informal, when required, it was the adults and not the children who brought things to order.
>
> (Large et al., 2006, p. 78)

If considered in terms of adults' fear of losing control, this model illustrates that children need direction from adults even in situations in which the adults may not necessarily have a great deal of expertise. Nonetheless, the learning took place both ways:

> From the perspective of all team members – adults as well as children – the design process was evolutionary. By the final sessions, the adults had a better understanding of the children's perspectives, and likewise the children were much better informed about portal functionality, design, and working as a team. This introduces an irony: The children are involved in the process because they think as children and not as designers, but gradually as they acquire more knowledge they become potentially less representative of their peer group.
>
> Neither the children nor the adult designers alone, then, could have accomplished the design task facing them—to design two Web portals appropriate for young information seekers. *But when these two disparate groups were bonded in the design teams, they were able to draw upon their relative strengths and achieve something neither could do in isolation.*
>
> (Large et al., 2006, pp. 78–79; emphasis added)

These are the kinds of initiatives that I believe need to be considered. The strengths that each intergenerational team bring to the collaboration allow participants to develop a strong sense of bonding and mutual respect. The essence of the bonded design brought together by Large and his research team is a means of bringing together intergenerational members of a team that unites despite the diversity of its members. The team includes adult experts in design and children who are "experts" in the sense of knowing what online requirements children might have. The adults and children work together throughout the design process. The authors note that like cooperative inquiry, bonded design emphasizes an intergenerational partnership in working toward a common goal.

It also ensures that children play an active role in the Web design, giving them a sense of agency and confidence that they would not experience if they were merely evaluators or testers at the end of the design process. The researchers explain that bonding design also shares aspects of learner-centred design in that it provides a learning environment for all team members – children and adults alike. Learner-centered design assumes that everyone is a learner, whether a professional or a student. In designing Web portals for children, the team's objective was to make sure that the design incorporated the interests, knowledge, and styles of the child users for whom it was built. Although they shared reservations about the true equality of children alongside adults in a design team, they concluded that cooperative inquiry was the central focus in the involvement of children from the beginning to completion of the design process.

The researchers explain that bonded design is essentially situated between cooperative inquiry and informant design. It is dependant on the belief in the ability of children to work as partners in all aspects of the design process; however, it retains reservations about the extent to which full and equal cooperation can occur across the generational divide, and therefore, in these respects, some informant or instructive aspects are necessary from the adults involved in the design team. The researchers also report that the Web portals were created in a short period of time and that both were converted into working Web portals that can be used by children. In this sense, they note the efficiency of bonding design. Ultimately the researchers note that the strength of bonding design resides in the fact that it unites children and adults, novices and experts, in a shared experience, but retains their individual strengths and weaknesses and their different expertise in a cooperative venture.

This example of engaging both adults and children in developing online educational resources is in keeping with constitutional principles of equality and freedom of expression, as well as with international conventions of the rights of the child. It allows children the opportunity to engage and participate in developing online tools. Such empowerment gives them ownership, and with ownership comes responsibility – none of the children involved in the project would want to see it used for cyber-bullying or defamatory statements. This is one of many important initiatives. Teachers should get used to engaging with students in the development and creation of Web portals, online blogs, and discussion groups, so that they no longer feel excluded and so that youth no longer perceive cyberspace as their own private space. Teenagers will show much more respect to their teachers if they recognize their knowledge of information technology, their willingness to engage in online discussions, and their proficiency in helping them find resources. When students perceive that their teachers lack expertise and are afraid of the Internet, they will more likely be tempted to take advantage of the situation. If more adults make a conscientious effort to accept and actively use technology as a primary source of learning, with texts and books that complement such use, students will gradually gain confidence in their teachers' expertise and demonstrate greater respect.

RAISING STUDENT AWARENESS OF CENSORSHIP

Working with children to develop civic virtue and social responsibility is not limited to cyberspace. Moreover, although students might be aware of their free expression rights in cyberspace, they ought to know what resources are censored from their eyes in school settings. They ought to hear various (as opposed to only official) perspectives regardless of how controversial a topic might be. Lisa K. Winkler (2004) is a New York educator who agrees that we ought to ensure students can become responsible citizens, capable of meeting the complex challenges in society. She believes that in addition to teaching reading, writing, speaking, listening, and viewing, it is important that students also become aware of censorship in all its forms. Winkler uses mock trials and readings in which students are given permission to choose their own books, as well as short writing assignments to bring the issue of censorship into the classroom.

Petress (2004) agrees that in-class discussions about the motivations that lie behind censorship to encourage critical analysis by students is essential. Keene (2004) provides activities that go with the classroom discussions suggested in her book, *Who Said I Can't Read This?* Keene has developed units that feed off the resources provided by the American Library Association. The Book and Periodical Council of Canada launches an annual "Freedom to Read" week every February (Book and Periodical Council, 2004) when it publishes lists of challenged and banned books with their synopses. Discussions about censorship can begin with a currently controversial issue that makes students aware of all sides of the problem, such as discussion of banned music, books, controversial Web sites and movies, and the reasons for the controversy from all sides. Teachers can facilitate discussion and recommend readings that provide alternative or a range of perspectives on the issue.

As Foerstel (1994) noticed, as long as there are authors who have meaningful things to say, the horns of censorship will be raised, creating an enormous dilemma for schools. I certainly realize, however, that in some cases, censorship might serve useful purposes, such as when material that is harmful to society is restricted from use in the public education system (e.g., child pornography or hate-oriented thought that proliferates on the Internet).

However, there is much written about the health and educational benefits of introducing students to a range of opinions or sensitive and controversial issues (Bettelheim, 1989; Elbaz-Luwisch, 2004; Katch, 2001; Shariff, 2004). For instance, when children gain exposure to more than one perspective, they garner the knowledge they need to make informed decisions about their lives and, ultimately, how they express their views and attitudes toward others. Avoidance can merely perpetuate conflict as suppressed concerns fester and surface through explosive disputes (Elbaz-Luwisch, 2004; Herzog, 1995; Larson, 1997; Shariff, 1999; Shariff, Case, & LaRocque, 2001; Shariff, Case, & Manley-Casimir, 2000). In other words, the educational growth of children and the promotion of tolerance in society benefits from a school system that includes a wide-ranging curriculum, one that adequately acknowledges the realities, values, and culture of different social groups. The lived realities, oral traditions, cultures and religion, and gendered perspectives ought to be at the heart of development education if the educational beneficiaries are to be empowered toward self-sufficiency, democracy, health, and peace.

In discussing the censorship aspects as they play out in cyber-bullying controversies, I have conceptualized censorship as an act of power in an educational system that excludes certain groups. In the preceding chapters, I developed this understanding even further by considering how censorship plays a key role in cultural hegemony and control of student spaces. To that end, I have drawn on scholarly perspectives on pluralism and civil society that provide guidance on valuing and validating the histories, contributions, and cultures of students from diverse backgrounds.

I have also alerted educators to the fact that censorship is a legal issue that ought to be grounded more in substantive human rights and legal pluralism than in positivist policy approaches that can result in costly ramifications for school boards. I agree with the observation that we currently seem to be building "an architecture that unleashes 60 percent of brain [and] a legal system that closes down that part of the brain" (Lawrence Lessing, 2004, as cited in Lankshear & Knobel, 2006, p. 21). Lankshear and Knobel (2006) argue that closing down 60 percent of the brain is exactly the impact of current policy directions in education generally, as well as of official versions of "digital literacy" (p. 21). This is certainly true when zero-tolerance policy approaches and reactive censorship (withdrawing computer privileges, book banning, firewalls, etc.) are arbitrarily applied under pressure from some teachers and parents. A positivistic approach most often erupts in hotly debated controversies that divert the focus away from student concerns. With the help of substantive, critical, and legally pluralistic doctrines, the Critical Legal Literacy Model demonstrates that substantive law is an essential component of knowledge construction and education that caters to a pluralistic global society. The issues are presented and analyzed within the broader sociocultural context, using models and a guiding concept map that show greater promise of being ethical, educational, and legally defensible when censorship controversies erupt.

Using the Critical Legal Literacy Model, which could incorporate, for example, classroom approaches advocated by critical pedagogues (Apple, 2000; Kincheloe, 2005), prospective educators can begin to remove the layers of prejudicial attitudes that have developed as a result of years of censorship and reconstruct knowledge that is grounded in comprehensive legal, digital literacy, and critical perspectives. There is a now substantial amount of excellent literature on digital literacies, as well as a range of studies that review ways in which technology is used by children and adults (Leander, in press; Mazzarella, 2005).

My Critical Legal Literacy approach provides fewer opportunities for conflict and allows for incorporation of educational resources, hard-copy and digital curricular approaches that engage and validate the diversity, and ethical and cultural frameworks of their students. Although I do not suggest that use of this model would bring the desired results instantly, it will, over time, facilitate the process to break down hegemonic barriers. The model also addresses the fact that educational decision makers use agency when they select, censor, and punish students. In that connection, it will also help educators critically assess the forms of agency and knowledge construction they bring to their decisions about whether to discuss negative online or face-to-face discourse with their students. Regardless of whether the content of a student's offensive expression included sexual connotations about the teacher, this could be a teachable opportunity. For example, if I were the teacher whom Bram wrote about on Facebook, I would have students research the etymology and history of bullying, as well as school censorship controversies involving freedom of expression and supervision, and ask them to come to decisions about where the lines crossed over to become cyber libel and criminal expression.

Moreover, I would attempt to find out what fueled the anger that resulted in the comments made online. Was the student unhappy with his grade? Did he perceive unfair treatment? Was he having problems at home and taking out his frustrations this way? Where there is smoke, there's fire, and it is the source of that fire that needs to be addressed.

Given the litigious nature of school controversies among educators, students, and parents over free expression, supervision, privacy, and safety, it is imperative that teachers' knowledge construction is grounded in legal literacy that incorporates substantive and legally pluralist modes of law, critical pedagogy and critical media literacy, as well as theories of leadership, ethics, and social justice. Currently, I believe that many university teacher education and professional development programs lack coherent models that provide educators with the conceptual grounding they need for a wired and litigious world. Such grounding would facilitate recognition of the common elements and congruence between substantive legal principles, critical pedagogies, and ethical frameworks that incorporate the cultural and paradigmatic perspectives of a broad range of stakeholders.

When the law is studied from a legally pluralistic perspective, it becomes apparent that there are four normative archetypes: (1) explicit and canonical norms (manifest or patent norms), (2) explicit and inferential norms (allusive norms), (3) implicit and canonical norms (customary norms), and (4) implicit and inferential norms (latent norms) (McMorrow, 2007). Legislation, for example, falls under the category of explicit and canonical norms. Hence if the Deleting Online Predators Act of 2006 legislation discussed earlier is passed in the United States, such legislation could be described as canonical or patent. Judicial precedents, such as the landmark *Tinker* case on student expression rights (*Tinker v. Des Moines Independent Community School District*, 1969) or the controversial *Davis v. Munroe* case (*Davis v. Munroe*, 1999), might be considered allusive norms, commercial software laws customary norms, and general principles of law latent norms. However, many of these modes of law and the legal interpretation and application of law can intersect depending on the context and factual circumstances in each case. Hence, although these categories might be plotted on a graph, the application is immensely more complex; nonetheless, these categories constitute a frame of reference to evaluate how law emerges in myriad forms.

The point of elaborating a sociological typology of norms is not to provide a set of discrete compartments in which to pack away such legal artifacts as concepts, institutions, processes, methodologies, and the basis of legitimacy or legal authority itself. It is intended to expose and challenge our assumptions about what form these legal artifacts can and do take (McMorrow, 2007). At the risk of being tedious, I stress that institutional legal positivist thinking rests on a set of fallacious assumptions that law exists outside and separate from the way human beings choose to govern their behavior.[2] In contrast, the Critical Legal Literacy model acknowledges the inherent plurality, flux, and heterogeneity of all legal normativity.

Instead of accepting any a priori criterion for distinguishing between law and nonlaw, a critical legal pluralist understanding of law is conceptually consistent with learner-centered educational pedagogies, particularly those that are advanced from a critical pedagogical perspective (Apple, 2000; Giroux, 2003; Kincheloe, 2005). When a legal pluralist approach is combined with critical pedagogical perspectives, the combined practical value and application from an educational and policy development point of view becomes clear, as illustrated in upcoming examples. Suffice it to say at this juncture, that critical legal pluralism provides the best legal theoretical foundation on which to base legal research in pursuance of this goal:

From a critical legal pluralist perspective, what matters is not just what the Education Act states, or the latest judicial decision declares or even what principal or teacher says. Seeing the law that students live in the school setting as issuing from a simple and unified top-down structure of authority in this manner ignores other relevant normative orders, institutions and rules to which students are subject. Most obviously belonging to a particular religion may mean a student feels under the obligation to adhere to certain prayer rituals, port a certain form of dress, or adhere to specific dietary rules, depending of course on his or her interpretation of the obligations of the faith.[3] On the other hand, a child's parents may be outspoken social justice activists, and accordingly she may feel an obligation to challenge openly anything said in class that sounds to her as being slanted with capitalist bias. Further, maybe a child is from a background of normalized violence. He might be a former child soldier who has recently arrived as a refugee to Canada or she might have grown up all here life in group homes where she was subjected to sexual molestation. Of course, any one of these characteristics does not define a child's normative universe any more so than two normative worlds characterized by violence, or a certain religious creed, or a certain ideology, or a certain socio-economic status or a geographic location would necessarily resemble one another. From daily life, as informed by interpersonal relationships (be they with family, friends, teachers,

bus drivers, homeless persons, baby sitters, soccer coaches etc. and be they healthy or
pathological), exposure to literature as well as multimedia sources (like television, film,
music, and the web), we spin the filaments of our own everyday law.[4]

                                                          (McMorrow, 2007, pp. 12–13)

The most important step is acknowledging this plurality of legal norms,
institutions, and orders to which students are subject. This adjusted mind-set is
much more vital to changing the classroom than an elegantly composed statutory provision or stirring written court judgment. Understanding the particular-
ity of how students engage within social networking sites, as boyd and Jenkins
(Wright, 2006) have explained is key. If educators really take their responsibility seriously, they must ensure they remember the personalities of students
who engage in antiauthority online expression or peer-to-peer cyber-bullying.
Although teachers may burn with anger from the insults they read online, it is
important that they stop and remember the individual student and ask, what
are that student's gifts and insecurities, his or her fears and ambitions? It is
essential not only to learn how to teach them about a subject like math or history but also to help them to cultivate an ethical framework for thinking about
their interactions at school and online. Although many teachers believe this to
be a parental responsibility, their professional designation as "teachers" makes
it incumbent that they socialize children to develop a sense of right and wrong
and to treat each other justly.

By reorienting legal inquiry toward the decision-making processes of legal
actors, a critical legal pluralist perspective has the potential of shedding greater
light on what the law actually is and the manner in which it must be reformed
to be altered substantively. Given the task of determining effective international
policy objectives for addressing cyber-bullying, it is imperative that we understand what norms currently govern student behavior. Research into the classroom and cyberspace dealings between students is therefore not merely sup-
plemental to but constitutive of legal research on cyber-bullying. In the school
context, as I have always maintained, various modes of law, normative values
(ethics), and learning (attaining knowledge) are mutually inclusive – they cannot
be separated or compartmentalized and ought to be understood this way.

A CONCEPT MAP: POSITIVE SCHOOL ENVIRONMENTS

One of the legal standards identified in Chapter 5 (see also Table 8.1) is schools'
obligation to avoid tacit condoning of bullying and harassment such that they
create a "deliberately dangerous environment" for students and teachers. There
is a clear legal expectation, based on human rights and civil law decisions in
North America,[5] that schools are required to foster and sustain positive school
environments.

Moreover, throughout this book, I have emphasized that school environment
plays an important role in knowledge production and learning in the school

context. I have explained that when the lived realities and educational resources of some stakeholders are ignored, there is an impact on the school environment, whether it is physical or virtual (involving classmates cyber-bullying). Hence, what is learned from the Critical Legal Literacy Model can be transported into a concept map that informs the objectives of fostering and sustaining school environments that are welcoming and inclusive, thereby empowering all students to engage confidently in their learning. This could mean allowing pupils to explore the Internet but preparing them through discussion and dialogue to know when to avoid predators, when to avoid joining peers in joking that crosses the line to cyber-bullying and cyber libel, and preparing them speak up against cyber-bullying or discriminatory forms of expression.

One example of students who spoke up against cyber-bullying took place in the aftermath of the mass college shootings in Virginia, United States, in April 2007. Facebook was used by young people in two ways. The first was that thousands of young people reached out to the students of Virginia Tech University with their condolences. The exchanges helped them develop bonds and feel as though they were contributing something positive to a terrible situation. Others, however, began to attack an Asian student because the killer had been South Korean. This was quickly abated by the influx of responses from young people who protested the singling out and stereotyping of Asian youth on Facebook (Agence France Presse, 2007).

Cyber-bullying is reduced in an environment where selection of what is taught, discussed, and validated as learning is informed by a proactive educational approach that incorporates critical pedagogies, digital and media literacy, legal literacy, and relevant ethical frameworks. Such an approach is not built on assumptions but is incorporated through dialogue and engagement of students from all backgrounds. This is where social networking tools, as Jenkins and boyd (Wright, 2006) both observe, can have significant positive value. The research presented earlier (Large et al., 2006) confirms that the more involved students are in establishing the parameters and content of their own education, the more likely they are to engage critically in their learning.

I have discussed some of the common patterns that emerge when school environments are "poisoned" and when relationships among administration, teachers, parents, and students are not cohesive. I present a concept map that incorporates the Critical Legal Literacy approach. The concept map informs teacher education on bullying and cyber-bullying and illustrates the benefits of more proactive, rather than reactive, responses. The approach educators adopt ultimately determines whether the school environment will be positive and conducive to learning or poisoned and detrimental to learning (Figure 8.2).

The model (original in shades of red for reactive and green for proactive), illustrates that a reactive approach underpins suspensions, expulsions, censorship of student expression and use of technologies results in tacit condoning of discriminatory attitudes through blanket policies that ignore differences. Moreover, a reactive approach generally reduces student safety because it encourages

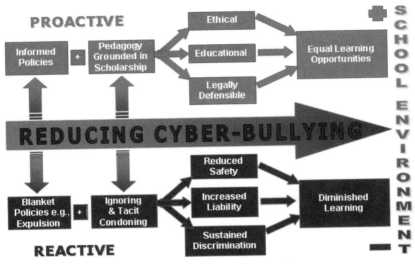

FIGURE 8.2. Concept map incorporating critical legal literacy.

racism, sexism, homophobia, and other forms of discrimination. A reactive approach can also be rooted in historically negative and fractured relations between administration and staff and a lack of common educational goals. There is no question that student learning in such an environment is impeded because students are distracted by the negative, hostile, and exclusionary messages they receive.

Zero tolerance provides no opportunity for dialogue, analysis of demeaning forms of expression, or consideration of all stakeholder perspectives. Students can be shown the impact of their expression on the teachers they decide to target, including their ability to work or find other employment and their feelings of frustration at not being validated as good teachers, which can ultimately affect their spouses and families. When school environments are more nurturing than hostile, teenagers such as Brad, Bram, Julia, and others discussed in earlier chapters might think more carefully before they post negative comments about teachers and administrators online. This is where the Stakeholder Model I have developed as part of the Critical Legal Literacy Model is also useful.

THE STAKEHOLDER MODEL

Figure 8.1 includes the Stakeholder Model within the Critical Legal Literacy approach. It is in the same box as "Trust and Agency." This is an important component of the Critical Legal Literacy approach. During my ten years of studying legal issues in education, I have developed a simple test for nonarbitrary balancing of competing rights in the school context. The test is modeled after the adjudication process that Canadian courts use in weighing and balancing

stakeholder rights to rule on questions of equality, freedom of expression, freedom of religion and conscience, and so on. This is how the Stakeholder Model
works.

The Stakeholder Model can be applied to a range of specific democratic challenges in schools that involve stakeholder conflicts. Although the model may
appear somewhat mechanistic, I suggest that it is a first step in helping educators
navigate stakeholder concerns regarding cyber-bullying and student expression.

Drawing from a combination of legal tests derived from U.S. and Canadian
jurisprudence on constitutional challenges, the Stakeholder Model guides an
understanding and appreciation of the perspectives that each stakeholder brings
to the issue. In Chapters 5 and 6, I mentioned several high schools that had
experienced a significant number of antiauthority postings about teachers and
school administrators by students at the schools. Consider the following case
example as applied to the Stakeholder Model.

Poisoned Environment

In one high school (High School X), more than 100 students had joined a
Facebook forum under the school name. Approximately twenty students were
caught discussing teachers, and out of those, four were narrowed down as
posting the most negative comments about teachers. When I met with administrators, what struck me was the history of deep divisions among staff within
departments, some of whom did not even speak to each other. There was resentment toward administration because it had changed so often, as well as resentment and mistrust toward the school board. Parents were competitive and
demanding because this school has a highly competitive academic program,
and the approach of older teachers was didactic. Moreover, the new administrators informed us that young teachers who joined the school quickly became
part of and were influenced by the cynical culture at the school.

Cyber-bullying was a symptom of this poisoned environment, where students
put into words the negative feelings their teachers conveyed and modeled. I
was invited to attend the school to give workshops for teachers and students
on cyber-bullying. I realized this would make no difference unless I was able to
address the deeper issues, specifically, the divided culture at the school. How
could I address the "horns of the dilemma"? This was a perfect time to draw
on the Stakeholder Model for help.

Step 1: Identify the Stakeholders

As I have emphasized throughout this book, although the media would have
people believe that cyber-bullying is limited to a battle between teachers and
students, or among students themselves, this assessment is inaccurate. If we take
the case of High School X, we realize antagonism among teachers at the school
and the administration went back many years, to when the school went from
being a private school to a public school taken over several times by different
school boards. Each time a new school board took over, administrative changes
were made. Promises made by the previous board were rarely carried out by

the next school board. Yet teachers remained at the school because it of its reputation as an institution of high academic stature. This fact made the school attractive to teachers and gave them a high stake in remaining at the school. Administrators came and went, in some cases because they could not handle the teachers' hostility. Students were of a high calibre; a significant number were in an international baccalaureate program. This made the school attractive to competitive parents who wanted their children to succeed academically. Using Step 1 of the Stakeholder Model, we can identify several stakeholders:

1. the current school board – elected trustees;
2. new administrators;
3. parents who support student free expression off-campus and those who do not, and parents who support suspensions as discipline and those who oppose it;
4. teachers who endorse use of social networking tools online and those who do not understand or use the Internet, teachers who engage in didactic teaching methods and support punitive measures such as suspensions and expulsions, teachers who prefer interactive teaching in which students are empowered and have a voice; and
5. students ranging from those who use social networking tools solely for personal purposes and those who use it as a discussion forum to express their views.

When student online comments were discovered at High School X, the teachers signed a petition demanding that offending students be asked to leave the school. The teachers' union endorsed their petition. Parents, on the other hand, felt their children were being unfairly punished and argued that the teachers were overreacting. The administration was caught in the middle. The media became involved when information was leaked out, resulting in dissonance and conflict. This is where Step 2 of the model became in useful. The key claims set out in Table 8.2 have emerged from the scholarship on media framing, my review of the range of media reports on cyber-bullying, case studies discussed in Chapters 5 to 7, interviews with school administrators and teachers under my research grants, and anonymous student surveys under my two research projects funded by the Social Sciences and Humanities Research Council of Canada, reported in Chapter 4. Some claims emerge from personal communication with teachers, administrators, and school board members from a range of schools as part of my ongoing research and consulting activities. They are also exemplified in the case of High School X where the problems appear to have existed for many years and where sensitivities are described as running deep.

Step 2: Validate Their Claims
Table 8.2 describes Step 2 of the Stakeholder Model, using High School X as an example.

TABLE 8.2. *Validating Stakeholder Claims*

	Media	School Board	School Administrators	Teachers	Parents	Students
Claim 1	Wants a sensational story that can be framed a certain way – the "battle"	Concerned about reputation and regaining control of the situation	Trying to balance demands of all stakeholders – parents, teachers, students, school board	Angry with students if comments have some validity and for sexually charged statements	Concerned about disruption to their children's learning	Need positive learning environment to succeed academically
Claim 2	Wants a story that that supports the teachers because they are angry	Has to meet parental expectations – does not want to reduce school's popularity or reputation	Concerned about reputation but also overwhelmed with work – no time to meet everyone's needs	Concerned about their marred reputation and the possibility of finding employment elsewhere	Concerned about fair treatment for their children	Pressured by parents to achieve academically
Claim 3	Wants a story with scapegoats – the students, technology, school administration	Wants teachers to know that the school board is listening and doing something	Concerned about gaining the trust of teachers and developing a cohesive, collaborative school climate	Already mistrust school board – cynical and angry about board response and unkept promises to do something	Concerned about their children's and their own reputations if publicized	Need avenues to express their feelings about the tensions within the school

(cont.)

TABLE 8.2. (cont.)

	Media	School Board	School Administrators	Teachers	Parents	Students
Claim 4	Wants a story about disruption to a bright student's academic achievement	Has policies on bullying and cyber-bullying – due diligence	Wants to ensure fairness in disciplining students, especially those graduating	Already mistrust administration – cynical and angry that they do not care	Concerned that teachers will mistreat their children if they stay	Need privacy; unsupervised – lack of adults in cyberspace; made mistakes – "just joking" – need to be given another chance
Claim 5	Wants to focus on the most negative comments – the behavior – without looking at the motivations	Has created a task force on cyber-bullying – due diligence	Wants to retain trust of parents	Determined to get revenge and be vindicated – looking for "blood," according to one administrator	Do not particularly want to uproot their children from school – especially if they are graduating	Not receiving enough attention from teachers; sense that teachers do not care because they are too busy fighting among themselves

Step 3: Critically weigh each claim against the other

It is always easier to weigh the rights and interests of stakeholders once they have been identified and their claims heard. It is the first two steps that most reactive policy responses overlook.

School Board Claims

In their haste to "control" the students, appease teachers or parents, and preserve the good reputations of their schools, school board officials often override the first two steps of the Stakeholder Model and focus only on the students. When the claims of other stakeholders are not heard or validated, the process is doomed to failure. Teachers and parents begin to lack confidence in the school board because their concerns are ignored. I have been contacted so often by frustrated parents of children who are victims of bullying and cyber-bullying. In every case, parents have come up against the "wall of defense" described in Chapter 6. Having antibullying policies and task forces in place is not enough. Similarly, teachers and school administrators who attend my graduate courses at McGill express frustration at the fact that often their school board policies are not supported with adequate training or time to implement initiatives to address bullying. If school board claims are applied to Step 2 of the Stakeholder Model, we find that from an administrative perspective, maintaining reasonable control and managing a crisis is a justified priority. The question that challenges this justification is whether prioritizing control of the situation ought to trump the educational concerns of stakeholders such as the students and their parents. This is the question that will determine how much weight the school board justifications carry.

School Administrator Claims

School administrators are often caught in the middle. The school board wants head teachers and principals to maintain the school's reputation and keep things under control. They want to avoid media attention at all costs. They have to keep parents happy. In cases in which academically proficient students are caught cyber-bullying, school administrators are required to make tough choices about how to discipline them. Should they support teachers who want the students suspended or expelled? Should they listen to parents who insist their child remain in school and be allowed to graduate? In all the chaos, do administrators create opportunities, or have the time, to hear the students' side of the story? How school administrators react can have an enormous influence on a negative or positive school climate. School administrators need to remember that over and above the logistics of juggling stakeholder demands, they are the school heads or principals of institutions of learning. Their priority ought to be the students. Students watch the reactions of their school administrators. On the basis of the legal standards identified in Chapter 7, it is arguable that cyber-bullying disrupts learning and also disrupts the educational mission of the school. When classmates or teachers are the subjects of cyber-bullying, there is also a nexus to the school. Administrators should always be cognizant of the fact that one clearly established legal responsibility of educators is to ensure that schools do not create a hostile or "deliberately dangerous" school environment. The obligation resides in the responsibility to ensure that school climates (physical or virtual) are conducive to learning. It is at this point that the administrative claims lose legitimacy. Zero-tolerance suspensions convey a sense of intolerance, a lack of caring, and a lack of responsibility. Removing the "problem child" from the school appears to absolve schools of responsibility to do more. However, this action in and of itself creates a hostile and chilled school climate. This is especially true when students notice that little action is taken to address peer-to-peer bullying or cyber-bullying. In this context, then, it is reasonable to ask whether suspension is a justifiable claim on the part of school principals and head teachers.

I have always argued that the only educational value of suspensions is that they teach and model intolerance. Educators argue that students need consequences. Students can experience the consequences of their actions through many other means, however. The lack of creativity within school systems globally to find other alternatives never ceases to amaze me. I would argue that if weighed on a scale against educational alternatives, school suspensions do not carry significant weight on the scale of legitimate claims.

Teacher Claims

When teachers who discover they have been defamed, demeaned, and libeled in the highly public forum of cyberspace demand consequences for the perpetrators, it is reasonable to agree that their claims are justified. Their claim for revenge in the form of suspensions and expulsions against students, however, is not justified and carries little weight. Such claims might be informed by dissatisfaction and disillusion with school board and administrative support in the past and a lack of confidence or trust in the way things are run at the school. Nonetheless, unless teachers refocus their attention on why they are there, unless they reconceptualize their role as educators, protectors, caregivers, and student mentors, I argue strongly that they are not justified in demanding harsh discipline. Suspensions are rooted in military models and boot camps. They are not grounded in educational pedagogies. Those responsible for the education and nurturing of future generations ought to remember this. Instead of demanding a ban on YouTube or calling for "forceful" action, educators could be searching for ways to address these issues by utilizing the infinite educational resources that technologies now provide. If teachers were able to overcome the mind-sets that Lankshear and Knobel (2006) argue hold them back, the possibilities for creative collaboration with bored and cynical students are infinite. If teachers can engage with and empower students to guide them in becoming familiar with new technologies, they have a greater chance of succeeding in overcoming the mindset and addressing cyber-bullying in more educational and empathetic ways. The resolution I present in Chapter 6, drafted by the

Canadian Teachers' Federation, begins to do this. The resolution is sufficiently comprehensive and seeks to learn more about how young people are using the technologies.

The predominant teacher responses, as evidenced by interviews with teachers (Shariff, 2007), suggests that when weighed on a scale against the types of online educational opportunities described earlier, teachers' demands for suspension or expulsion and their general lack of attention to peer-to-peer bullying among students carries little weight on the scale of legitimate claims. If we consider this from the perspective of English common law and Canadian obligations under tort law, the duty of care on teachers to be "careful and prudent parents" and stand in place of parents (in loco parentis) holds that there is an ethic of care and responsibility to exhibit concern, nurturance, and guidance of students. If teachers only hold out for punishment and revenge, it would seem that their claims fall widely short of a legal duty of care to their students.

Table 8.2 shows how important it is to communicate. If the school board is intent on hearing the teachers, trustees need to demonstrate this in ways that go beyond simply having antibullying and anti-cyber-bullying policies in place. Moreover, the teachers need to allow new administrators time to catch up and make a difference. They need to foster opportunities to develop relationships of trust. As educators, their claims for vindication are less valid than student claims for a learning environment that is less poisoned and more conducive to learning. This requirement, as established by law, is detailed in Chapter 7. Further, if teacher responsibilities are placed under the legal "duty of care" and "careful and prudent parent" doctrine, how many careful parents would not give their children a second chance if they had made a mistake? Yet again, student claims carry greater validity than teachers' hostile responses. Moreover, according to the courts, the test for cyber libel is whether an ordinary person who is not unduly sensitive would interpret the expression as truth. The reality is that some teachers may be unduly sensitive, and this sensitivity may also be reflected in the Ontario College of Teachers' survey (2007) suggesting that 84 percent of teachers report being cyber-bullied. This is perhaps why cases in which student comments were close to the truth have received such strong reactions.

For example, in one case, the teacher had openly declared she was a lesbian, yet her colleagues were extremely offended when the students described her online as a lesbian. Another teacher was chided for her accent. She was extremely annoyed by this, but in reality, she did have a strong accent. Rather than seeking revenge through suspensions, teachers ought to focus on how they can explain to students the impact of their online statements. As educators, it is their responsibility to communicate and open a dialogue with students about why those statements, no matter how close to home they might be, are hurtful. By opening a dialogue, I mean engaging students' respect and trust and listening to and hearing their perspectives. A teacher's first priority should be to determine whether it was the poisoned environment at the school that led to the online comments. If so, the next step is to seek student input as to how the learning environment might be improved. Find out what is missing, what teachers might be doing that upsets students, and how can they change some of their teaching approaches. Are students receiving opportunities to provide opinions? Are these opinions being validated?

The participation rights of children and adolescents are protected under the United Nations International Convention of the Rights of the Child. Canada and a range of European and Asian countries have signed a treaty that requires attention to provision, protection, and participation of students in their learning. If this is not happening, teachers should inform students that they have this right and work with them to develop ways to ensure their participation in classroom discussions, in developing codes of conduct, and so on. The problem is that few teachers have any knowledge of human rights or their implications for educational policy and practice (Shariff & Sarkar, 2004). Once students come to realize that teachers are genuinely interested in their well-being and learning experiences, they will be significantly more open to hearing why their online expressions should not cross the line to cyber-libel or defamation. As the Media Awareness Network (n.d.) has shown, when children and teenagers take leadership in addressing peer behavior, they can be very effective.

Moreover, if teachers were to pay more attention to peer-to-peer bullying and cyber-bullying and critically evaluate their own modeling of attitudes to children, some of them might realize that they have not been listening to their students – and that their students need avenues to discuss concerns that are bothering them.

I recall, for example, my own son who was frustrated with his math teacher in Grade 7. He was the only student in the class who was taking advanced Grade 8 math, and the teacher saw marking his assignments as a chore. This class was a cotaught classroom with two teachers in a middle school. One of the teachers was always late returning my son's marked assignments. She rarely paid him any attention in class, other than to ask him to teach students who had difficulty in math. One day after asking for his marked test back several times, he received a curt response from the teacher saying she had not graded it. In frustration, he uttered the words "f . . . you" under his breath. The other teacher heard him, and he was suspended. The school administration in this case handled the issue well. Although he still had to serve his in-school suspension, after being made aware of the issue, they invited him to meet with a visiting delegation of government officials from the Ministry of Education as an ambassador or leader in the school to show them around, answer questions, and ask them about certain policy changes they were planning to make. This showed that the school had confidence in his ability and provided him with an opportunity to take leadership. Although I do not suggest that he should not have received any consequences for uttering the "F word" I wonder what would have happened if the Internet had been available and he had a chance to unleash his frustrations with more words about his teacher?

Moreover, if I had not taken the time as a parent to find out the source of his unusual behavior, would he have received the leadership opportunity the school gave him? I wonder how many students do fall through the cracks when they are bored, disengaged, or frustrated with teachers in schools and cannot turn to parents. Accordingly, I suggest that when young people engage in this kind of expression online, it is definitely worth hearing their point of view before deciding on the consequences. Of course, there is also the teacher's perspective: she had a heavy workload, and this was extra work. Yet when we weigh and validate each claim, we can argue that students are at school to learn, and when the teacher is not doing an adequate job, then her claim is less valid than that of the student who is doing his best to learn.

In the same example, if we consider how the school administrators turned a negative into a positive learning opportunity, while also preserving the school reputation with the ministry officials, they fostered, at least at the school level, a proactive environment. It might be argued that there are other children who do not use this kind of language. We would all like to believe our children are not capable of using this kind of language, but we know in the back of our minds that they all use it, as do most adults under frustrating circumstances. What my son learned that day was that he has support both at home and at the school and that when he is bored or having difficulty with the teacher, he can always turn to someone instead of stewing about it himself. He also learned that using the "F word" has consequences but that the consequences he received were fair and appropriate.

In this section, I have walked through some of the considerations for applying the Stakeholder Model and took readers through the process of weighing and juxtaposing competing stakeholder claims to assess their respective validity. This nonarbitrary process has no room for reactive responses or band-aid solutions. I appreciate that when all stakeholders are making simultaneous and contradictory demands, a reactive response appears to be the only choice. However, I would urge educational policy makers to remember that the Stakeholder Model is worth undertaking to hear and grasp important claims and to bring together the voices of all stakeholders, collaboratively and cohesively, to create harmony. Arguably this sounds far too utopian, but I am not describing a panacea. Judges adjudicate complex cases using this process all the time. Although I agree that the outcomes of some judicial decisions are not always satisfactory, I proffer that at least the Stakeholder Model allows for a thoughtful and ethical assessment of the issues, bearing in mind the legal standards and responsibilities identified in Table 8.1, and the educational and ethical considerations that affect all stakeholders. There is one final step in the Stakeholder Model.

Step 4: Minimal Impairment of Rights

Once stakeholder claims have been weighed against each other, it is important for the decision makers involved to ensure that whichever policy decision is most validated, that decision or policy does not substantially infringe on the rights of certain stakeholders. For example, if the school decides to stay with a zero-tolerance policy and suspend only the students who make sexually libelous comments about teachers, this policy is justifiable. Why? Because it protects the interests of a greater number of teachers. However, the policy makers must then ensure that they consider whether any of the offending students are graduating soon, the extent to which the suspensions will affect their grades and chances of acceptance to college or university, and so on. In cases where a straight-A student receives a suspension of this sort, it may be worthwhile to consider an alternative consequence that does not affect the student's entire academic future. Although a defamatory expression can certainly have an impact on a teacher's reputation, it is important to remember that we are still dealing with an immature young person who needs to be educated as to why he or she should not behave this way. Young people deserve a second chance. Let me clarify this in more legal terms.

In cases of students' online expression that demeans teachers and school officials on Facebook, most school responses have been to suspend the students involved. Some of these students, like Brad Parsons, have protested infringement of their rights to free expression. Many parents agree. They believe that their school has no right to interfere with comments made from home computers in a private online conversation. The school might have a policy calling for zero-tolerance suspension. This might be supported by government legislation. Nonetheless, school officials have important decisions to make. They must consider whether the student comments were so harmful that they have a negative impact the entire school environment and learning of all students at the school or in the classroom. As the freedom of expression cases have ruled, schools do have the authority to intervene if the expression materially or substantially affects learning or if it interferes with the school's educational mission. In the case of sexually charged comments about teachers being pedophiles or masturbating in class, I would argue that such comments pose a risk to the greater good in several ways. They undermine the authority of the teachers or school officials in question. When students read the comments, they are likely to gossip and giggle in class. This disrupts their focus and learning and upsets the teacher. When the teacher finds out, his or her anger also has a significant impact that poisons the entire school environment.

Although I agree that schools have a responsibility to intervene and have specific postings that are blatantly insulting or abusive to teachers or other students, I do not agree with means that schools and some governments adopt, such as suspension policies, banning of technologies from the classroom, withdrawing computer privileges, or suspending students from school field trips they were eagerly looking forward to. This in my view does not minimally impair student free expression rights; it attempts to muzzle them completely. This is why the minimal impairment test is a crucial fourth step in the Stakeholder Model. It is incumbent on school officials to determine educational options to help students realize the impact of their statements. I argue for introduction of the circle sentencing approaches, for example, that many aboriginal communities use. Through this method, perpetrator(s) are brought to face their victims and hear their reactions and pain. Instigators must hear how their actions negatively affected the lives of victims' families and loved ones as well. In the case of antiauthority online defamation, they should hear from the teachers, their families, and other students who want to learn but find it distracting when these controversies take place. Similarly when peer-to-peer cyber-bullying is involved, the perpetrators should be made to face the victims' parents, their siblings, and anyone else who was affected.

CONCLUSION

Although I have argued that schools have a legal basis for extending their reach into cyberspace, I reiterate that actions such as censoring student Web sites, or searching e-mails, for example, are rooted in legally positivist approaches that do not provide the most effective means of preventing cyber-bullying. On the contrary, I recognize that school discipline policies are least successful when they merely serve as a reactionary mechanism to unwanted behavior. Schools have an obligation to monitor inflammatory student speech, but it is equally important to recognize that educators have a duty to cultivate an educational atmosphere that is consistent with the moral and political principles essential to expanding democratic values. In other words, when cyber-bullying becomes pervasive within a school, we cannot simply place the blame on students. Instead we must look at the systemic forms of discrimination that pervade the institutional setting and the school climate, revisit the values and beliefs that our schools and constitutional principles impart, and select educational measures to ensure that these values promote acceptance and respect among students.

As school landscapes evolve to keep up with changes in technology and society, it is important to consider the simple alternatives provided in this book, ones that are less costly than the calls for "battle," loss of children's lives through suicide, and positivist rules that attempt to force conformity. Although I have provided a number of models and a concept map that I believe show greater promise for addressing the policy vacuum and the enormous challenges that technologies bring, I reiterate that this book is not a "how-to" text. Rather, I hope it has provided readers with an adjusted lens that discloses rich context for discussion and dialogue about the definitional complexities and the biological, environmental, and systemic influences that shape and perpetuate the content of student expression in cyberspace. Furthermore, I hope it motivates readers to engage in a responsible process of analysis, which avoids reliance on reactive decisions that lead to the kinds of battles on which the media is always eager to report.

As noted by scholars such as Giroux (2003), school discipline is best achieved when it incorporates an element that aims to educate students about both moral and political principles. Giroux argues that "schools should provide forms of critical education in which ethics and values are used to teach students to keep the spirit of justice alive in themselves, embrace the need to be compassionate, respect the rights of others, and be self-conscious about the consequences of their actions" (p. 94).

I have also observed that adults need to become proficient and participate with young people in learning how to use the technologies that form such an important and prominent part of their lives. If adults do not take the initiative to do this, they will eventually be shut out – or, it could be said, censored – from the virtual worlds of their children and students. As I have already mentioned, students are increasingly forging social relationships and learning much of what they know through new technologies. It is incumbent on educators to engage with these technologies to develop interactive curriculum programs that are not restricted to class time. As I explained earlier, the potential for learning in the Digital Age is enormous. Consider, for example, some of the pedagogical suggestions recommended by Lankshear and Knobel (2006). They comment that the "digit" or "skill teaching" aspect of digital literacies is far less important than allowing room for social relationships to "emerge organically" (p. 20) through immersion in new technologies. They recommend the kind of Knowledge Producing Schools that are being developed on a school-by-school basis by Chris Bigum, Leonie Rowen, and Associates (Knowledge Producing Schools Web Site, 2005; Lankshear & Knobel, 2003). They also recommend James Gee's (2003) celebrated study of what video games have to teach us about learning and literacy in which he explores game playing as a sociocultural practice. Through this study, Gee tests what drives people to learn and keep learning, and how they achieve and grow in their learning.

In this book, I have attempted to provide an adjusted lens through which we ought to view the highly publicized issue of cyber-bullying. Elsewhere (Shariff, 2008), I have introduced the following metaphor and believe it is in order to recall it here: An artist has to take time away from his painting when the colors he is using become so blurred that he can no longer see them clearly. He takes time out to visit an optometrist. During his eye exam, the focus is no longer on what he sees but on *how* he sees. It is the adjustment to the lens through which he sees and interprets his surroundings that is the focus during that short visit to the optometrist (Esmail, 2007). Similarly, this book was written to help educators and policy makers to consider readjusting the lenses that seem to have blurred their policy and practice alternatives to such an extent that they need to refocus and reconceptualize the issues. The legally pluralistic perspectives, Critical Legal Literacy Model, Stakeholder Model, and the concept map all contribute to this adjusted lens and toward a reconceptualized approach to understanding the role of law in a digitized world.

Instead of seeing cyber-bullying as a problem and a battle that needs to be controlled and squelched, an adjusted lens will refocus our attention on what these symptoms tell us and how we can address the root causes that drive such expression. Research into empirical studies is necessary before the legal research approach we adopt to cyber-bullying will ever be as broad and balanced as it should be. In mapping legitimate anti-cyber-bullying policies, it is vital to bear in mind what Macdonald and Kong (2006) wrote in a recent article on law reform that opens this chapter:

A legal rule is legitimate only to the extent that it can capture people's imaginations and make them believe it is worth engaging with and participating in the normative framework proposed. Moreover, the legitimacy of a legal rule depends on a minimum functionality common to all rules: its capacity to effectively capture, shape, and refract parties' perceptions of problems. In brief, a legal rule ceases to be a command and instead becomes a hypothesis of action and interaction.

(p. 22)

If we want pupils to follow our rules, it is essential that we engage them and their desire to comply through interaction and agency. As the quote from *Vernon God Little* (Pierre, 2003) that opens this book suggests, our children's biggest cyber-"bullies" tend to be adults – from the harsh and intolerant zero-tolerance policies and legislation they implement to the tacit condoning of peer-to-peer bullying and cyber-bullying among kids to sexual predation. As McMorrow (2007) notes, the question of what is legitimate law for students must always be asked with their inalienable dignity in mind. Elsewhere (Shariff, 2008), I have provided numerous examples of how many children's lives are exploited by sensational news reports in the news media and on television. I direct readers to reconsider the quote from *Vernon God Little*, now that they have reached the conclusion of this book, as a reminder that we must realize adults carry the greatest share of the blame for all forms of cyber-bullying among youngsters. Moreover, unless we reconceptualize our approach from a legally positivist paradigm to a collaborative, substantive, and legally pluralistic approach, we can expect only minimal progress toward fulfilling educators' concerns to reduce cyber-bullying. Those that fall through the cracks will be children who need our help if they are to contribute to fostering a better world than the legacy we have left them.

It is time our schools took up their responsibility to do what they are mandated to do – educate, not punish, students. As this book has attempted to show, this will involve a collaborative effort on the part of all stakeholders, including government law and policy makers, Web providers, parents, the news media, school boards, teachers' unions, the judicial system, and the students themselves. Instead of turning all children who experiment with their freedom in cyberspace into *Vernon God Little* scapegoats and criminals who must be controlled, it is important that we work with the law to implement democratic and ethical responses that encourage young people's participation. It is time that we empower them to work with adults and peers toward inclusive and less demeaning forms of online interaction. To do otherwise ignores and jeopardizes their versatility, creativity, and potential to take leadership and engage in a digital world that will expand their minds. Stakeholders need to discard the burdens of a society that pays lip service to democracy and digital progress under the guise of intolerance, exclusion, and orthodoxy. The time to embrace the digital age and all its emerging legal and policy challenges in collaboration with our children is well overdue. Shared leadership with young people shows infinitely greater promise in advancing peaceful and inclusive relationships (both on and offline) than does the current "battle" on cyber-bullying between schools and kids.

REFERENCES

Agence France Presse. (2007, April 18). Foreign students don't fear backlash. *Gazette*, p. A4.

Apple, M. W. (2000). *Official knowledge: Democratic education in a conservative age* (2nd ed.). New York: Routledge.

Apple, M. W., & Christian-Smith, L. K. (1991). The politics of the textbook. In M. W. Apple & L. K. Christian-Smith (Eds.), *The politics of the textbook* (pp. 1–21). New York: Routledge.

Bettelheim, B. (1989). *The uses of enchantment: The meaning and importance of fairy tales*. New York: Vintage Books.

Book and Periodical Council. (2004). *Freedom to read week*. Retrieved August 26, 2007, from http://www.freedomtoread.ca/freedom_to_read_week/index. asp.

British Educational Communications and Technology Agency. (2007, August). *Becta Home Page*. Retrieved August 26, 2007, from http://www.becta.org.uk/.

British Educational Communications and Technology Agency. (n.d.-a). *Awareness of ICT in schools for School Improvement Professionals*. Presented at school improvement professionals event. Retrieved August 26, 2007, from http://events.becta.org. uk/display.cfm?cfid=662527&cftoken=63d05f972705-4b7df789-c05d-eae1-9848116 5ea7bbc6b&resID=29602.

British Educational Communications and Technology Agency. (n.d.-b). *Teacher Exchange Resource*. Retrieved August 26, 2007, from http://tre.ngfl.gov.uk/.

Elbaz-Luwisch, F. (2004). How is education possible when there's a body in the middle of the room? *Curriculum Inquiry, 34*, 9–27.

Esmail, A. (2007, August). Untitled paper presented at the Institute of Ismaili Studies, McGill University, Montreal, Quebec.

Foerstel, H. N. (1994). *Banned in the U.S.A.: A reference guide to book censorship in schools and public libraries*. Westport, CT: Greenwood Press.

Gee, J. P. (2003). *What video games have to teach us about learning and literacy*. New York: Palgrave/Macmillan.

Giroux, H. (2003). *The abandoned generation: Democracy beyond the culture of fear*. New York: Palgrave/MacMillan.

Golding, W. (1954). *Lord of the flies*. New York: Penguin Putnam.

Hart, H. L. A. (1997). *The concept of law* (2nd ed.). Oxford, England: Oxford University Press.

Herzog, M. J. R. (1995). School censorship experiences of teachers in southern Appalachia. *International Journal of Qualitative Studies in Education, 8*, 137–148.

Inglis, F. (1985). *The management of ignorance*. Oxford, England: Blackwell.

Katch, J. (2001). *Under deadman's skin: Discovering the meaning of children's violent play*. Boston: Beacon Press.

Keene, L. (2004). Who said I can't read this? *School Library Media Activities Monthly*, 21, 29–32.

Kincheloe, J. L. (2005). *Classroom teaching: An introduction*. New York: Peter Lang.

Knowledge Producing Schools Web Site. (2005). Retrieved August 19, 2007, from deakin.edu.au/education/lit/kps/.

Lankshear, C., & Knobel, M. (2003). *New literacies: Changing knowledge and classroom learning*. Buckingham, England: Open University Press.

Lankshear, C., & Knobel, M. (2006). *New literacies: Everyday practices and classroom learning* (2nd ed.). Maidenhead, England/New York: Open University Press.

Large, A., Nesset, V., Beheshti, J., & Bowler, L. (2006). "Bonded design": A novel approach to intergenerational information technology design. *Library & Information Science Research*, 28, 64–82.

Larson, C. L. (1997). Is the Land of Oz an alien nation? A sociopolitical study of school community conflict. *Educational Administration Quarterly*, 33, 312–350.

Leander, K. (in press). Toward a connective ethnography of online/offline literacy networks. In J. Coiro, M. Knobel, C. Lankshear & D. Lou (Eds.), *Handbook of research on new literacies*. Mahwah, NJ: Lawrence Erlbaum.

Macdonald, R. A. (2002). *Lessons of everyday law*. Montreal: Published for the Law Commission of Canada and the School of Policy Studies, Queen's University, McGill-Queen's University Press.

Macdonald, R. A. (2006, November 1). *Pluralistic human rights: Universal human wrongs*. Paper presented at the Dialogues on Human Rights and Legal Pluralism Workshop, Centre for Human Rights and Legal Pluralism, Faculty of Law, McGill University, Montreal.

Macdonald, R. A., & Kong, H. (2006). Patchwork law reform: Your idea is good in practice, but it won't work in theory. *Osgoode Hall Law Journal*, 44, 11–52.

Macdonald, R. A., & McMorrow, T. (2007). Wedding a critical legal pluralism to the laws of close personal relationships [Electronic version]. *European Journal of Legal Studies*, 1. Retrieved September 8, 2007, from http://www.ejls.eu/.

Mazzarella, S. R. (Ed.). (2005). *Girl wide web. Girls, the Internet, and the negotiation of identity*. New York: Peter Lang.

McDougall, A., & Philips Valentine, L. (1999). Selective marginalization of Aboriginal voices: Censorship in public performance. In K. Petersen & A. C. Hutchinson (Eds.), *Interpreting censorship in Canada* (pp. 334–350). Toronto: University of Toronto Press.

McMorrow, T. (2007). Lord of the bullies: Advocating a student-centred approach to legal research into cyber-bullying. Unpublished paper submitted for graduate course at McGill University, Montreal.

Media Awareness Network. (n.d.). *Media Awareness Network Web site*. Retrieved December 10, 2006, from http://www.mediawareness.com.

Montgomery, K. (2005). Imagining the antiracist state: Representations of racism in Canadian history textbooks. *Discourse: Studies in the cultural politics of education*, 26, 427–442.

Ontario College of Teachers. (2007). COMPAS State of the Teaching Profession [Electronic version]. *Professionally Speaking, the Magazine of the Ontario College of Teachers*. Retrieved August 28, 2007, from http://www.oct. ca/publications/PDF/survey07_e.pdf.

Petress, K. (2004). The role of censorship in school. *Journal of Instructional Psychology*, *32*, 248–252.

Pierre, D. B. C. (2003). *Vernon God Little*. London: Faber & Faber.

Shariff, S. (1999). *Managing the dilemma of competing rights: The case of the three books*. Unpublished master of arts thesis, Simon Fraser University, Vancouver, Canada.

Shariff, S. (2004). Keeping schools out of court: Legally defensible models of leadership to reduce cyber-bullying. Educational forum. *Delta Kappa Pi, 68*, 222–223.

Shariff, S. (2007). Unpublished research conducted as part of a three-year research project on cyber-bullying, funded by Social Science and Humanities Research Council of Canada. Shaheen Shariff, McGill University, Principal Investigator.

Shariff, S. (2008). *Cyber-bullying: Issues and solutions for the school, the classroom, and the home*. Abington, England: Routledge.

Shariff, S., Case, R., & LaRocque, L. (2001). Begging the questions: The court of appeal decision in the Surrey school board controversy. *Education & Law Journal, 11*, 85–111.

Shariff, S., Case, R., & Manley-Casimir, M. (2000). Balancing competing rights in education: Surrey School Board's book ban. *Education & Law Journal, 10*, 47–105.

Shariff, S., & Johnny, L. (2007). *Censorship! . . . or . . . Selection?: Confronting a curriculum of orthodoxy through pluralistic models*. Rotterdam, the Netherlands: Sense.

Shariff, S., & Manley-Casimir, M. E. (1999). Censorship in schools: Orthodoxy, diversity & cultural coherence. In K. Petersen & A. C. Hutchinson (Eds.), *Interpreting censorship in Canada* (pp. 157–181). Toronto: University of Toronto Press.

Shariff, S., & Sarkar, M. (2004). Investigating inclusion: From educational policies to practice. A project funded by the Social Sciences and Humanities Research Council of Canada. Unpublished research findings. Department of Integrated Studies in Education, Faculty of Education, McGill University, Montreal.

Shariff, S., & Strong-Wilson, T. (2005). Bullying and new technologies: What can teachers do to foster socially responsible discourse in the physical and virtual school environments? In J. Kincheloe (Ed.), *Classroom teaching: An introduction* (pp. 219–240). New York. Peter Lang.

Steeves, V., & Wing, C. (2005). Young Canadians in a wired world. Media Awareness Network Web site. Retrieved December 4, 2006, from http://www.media-awareness.ca/english/research/YCWW/phaseII/.

Willard, N. (2005). Educator's guide to cyber-bullying: Addressing the harm caused by online social cruelty. http://cyberbullying.org. Retrieved July 19, 2005.

Winkler, L. K. (2004). Celebrate democracy! Teach about censorship. *English Journal, 94*, 48–51.

Wright, S. (2006, May 26). MySpace and Deleting Online Predators Act (DOPA) [Electronic version]. *MIT Tech Talk*. Retrieved August 13, 2007, from http://www.danah.org/papers/MySpaceDOPA.pdf.

Notes

CHAPTER ONE

1. McMorrow notes, "Although Weil's (1977, pp. 153–154) remarks specifically address the context of war, she identifies the "empire of might" as weighing on all facets of human existence." Simone Weil, "The *Iliad*, Poem of Might."
2. See "The Grand Inquisitor" (Dostoyevsky, 1937). See also Belley (1998, p. 70), who notes that the fundamental value being extolled in this passage, the freedom of human conscience, is at the heart of R. A. Macdonald's legal thought. From this perspective, law can be imagined both as mould and as mirror of social interactions.
3. The irony of the boys' "rescue" from their isolation on the island is that they now return to a world just as violent and hostile to human dignity.
4. See Macdonald and Sandomierski (2006).

CHAPTER TWO

1. Eight to nine percent of elementary school children are bullied frequently (once or more a week) and 2–5 percent of students bully others frequently (Bentley & Li, 1995; Charach, Pepler, & Ziegler, 1995). Vaillancourt and Hymel (2001) found higher rates in a study of high school students (10–11 percent are bullied, 8–11 percent bully others). Other surveys cited by National Crime Prevention Council disclose similar results (Boulton & Underwood, 1992). Roher (1997) reports that out of 457 students surveyed, 20 percent reported more than one incident; 8 percent of the students questioned are bullied weekly or more often. In a recent U.S. survey of more than 15,000 young people in Grades 6 to 10, Nansel, Overpeck, Pilla, Simons-Morton, & Schedit (2001) found that 9 percent of students reported being bullied frequently, and more than 8 percent of students admitted to frequent bullying. In a recent study of junior secondary school students, Henderson and Hymel (2002) found that of 490 students from Grades 8 through 10 (50 percent female, 50 percent male), 64 percent of respondents indicated they had been bullied, 12 percent reported being victimized regularly (once or more a week), and another 13 percent admitted to participating in bullying regularly (once or more a week). The majority of respondents reported observing bullying at the school, but only 40 percent said they tried to intervene. See also DiGuilio (2001).
2. A bully was described as "a tyrannical coward who makes himself a terror to the weak," "[A] low-minded unscrupulous bully, notorious for his pro-Slavery

sympathies," or a "[R]uffian hired for purposes of violence or intimidation" (Dicey, 1863, p. 646).

3. Mooney, Creeser, and Blatchford (1991) found that 96 percent of the 308 seven to eleven year olds in their study reported teasing as the most frequent form of bullying they experienced. See also Boulton and Hawker (1997). Seventy-four percent of girls spend time on chat rooms and instant messaging (Berson, Berson, & Ferron, 2002); 14 percent of Canadian youth are harassed electronically, and 15 percent admitted harassing others electronically (Leishman, 2002).

4. Olweus (1993) first highlighted the difference between direct (open physical attacks) and indirect (social isolation and exclusion of victims) as bullying. Björqvist, Lagerspetz, and Kaukiainen (1992) went further to distinguish between physical aggression (hitting, pushing, kicking), direct verbal aggression (calling, threatening), and indirect aggression (e.g., telling tales, spreading rumors, deliberately excluding a person from activities).

5. Artz and Riecken (1997), Lanctot (2001), and Moretti (2002) reported violent acts as prevalent among males but on the rise among females. Schissel's (1993) analysis of trends in official Canadian youth crime rates disclosed a steady increase in the number of violent offences committed by females from 1970 to 1990. Tanner (1996) cites a 29 percent increase in the number of female youths charged between 1986 and 1990, cautioning, however, that this still only represented 18 percent of all youths charged during this time. Moretti (2002) reports that the gender gap in terms of the seriousness and physical nature of bullying and violence between boys and girls is narrowing.

6. Scholars in the field now recognize this discrepancy in the research, resulting in a recent conference that specifically focused on girls and violence. The conference objective was to gain a more accurate profile of girls and violence through a joint review of research by psychologists, sociologists, and criminologists who specifically study this perspective ("Vancouver Conference on Aggressive and Violent Girls," 2002).

7. See also Chamberlain and Houston (1999) and Katch (2001).

8. Although the research on prevalence of bullying is reported under a separate heading in this chapter, these statistics are important here because they relate to sexual harassment as a primary form of bullying in schools. See also Louis Harris and Associates (1993); Chamberlain & Houston (1999); and Tolman, Spencer, Rosen-Reynoso, and Porches (2001). Watkinson (1999) and Bowlby and Regan (1998) provide Canadian statistics that corroborate U.S. findings.

9. O'Connell and colleagues (1999) videotaped 185 bullying episodes by students in Grades 1–6 and observed that just over half (54 percent) contained a bully, a victim, and two or more peers. An average of four students was present during the episodes. Significantly, they found that the duration of the bullying increased as the number of peers watching the episode increased. In 54 percent of the cases peers simply observed the episode. In nearly 21 percent of the cases, peers physically or verbally joined in the bullying.

10. For example, Hamed Nastoh, Dawn-Marie Wesley, Emmett Fralick suicides; murder of Reena Virk; shootings at Columbine High School in Colorado and in Mayo, Alberta.

11. The parents abandoned the Dufour litigation after filing a Statement of Claim in the Vancouver Supreme Court Registry.

12. Seventy-five percent of Americans interviewed thought school shootings were likely to happen in their community.
13. These authors also agree that most young people who engage in crime are not dangerous. They engage in petty thefts or break and enter, or they play truant from school.
14. Providing U.S. statistics, he notes that in 1992 and 1993, seventy-six students were murdered or committed suicide at school – an average of about 38 a year. Six years later, sixty-nine students suffered school-associated, violent deaths (murder and suicide) in a two-year period. The number also decreased 40 percent from 1998 to 1999, from forty-three to twenty-six. DiGuilio argues that when compared with the rate of youth murders occurring outside the school context, in 1992–1993, young persons between the ages of five and nineteen were more than 100 times more likely to be murdered away from school than in school according to a report from the Office of Juvenile Justice and Delinquency Prevention.
15. This is a result of the baby boomers having children.
16. Doob, Marinos, and Varma (1995) observe, for example, that whereas previously schoolyard fights were simply reported to school administrators, they are now more frequently reported to police.

CHAPTER THREE

1. Article 2: A person who disturbs public order, endangers public safety, infringes on the rights of person and property or hampers social administration, which is harmful to the society and which, according to the provisions of the Criminal Law of the People's Republic of China, constitutes a crime, shall be investigated for criminal responsibility according to law; and if such an act is not serious enough for criminal punishment, the public security organ shall impose on him a penalty for administration of public security according to this Law.
2. Article 42: A person who commits one of the following acts shall be detained for not more than five days or be fined more than 500 yuan; and if the circumstances are relatively serious, he shall be detained for not less than five days but not more than ten days and may, in addition, be fined not more than 500 yuan:

   (1) writing letters of intimidation or threatening the personal safety of another person by other means;
   (2) openly humiliating another person or slandering another person by fabricating stories;
   (3) framing another person by fabricating stories in an attempt to make the person subject to criminal investigation or to penalty for administration of public security;
   (4) threatening, humiliating, or beating up a witness or his close relative or retaliating against either of them;
   (5) repeatedly dispatching pornographic, humiliating, intimidating, or other information to disturb the normal life of another person; or
   (6) peeping, secretly taking photos, eavesdropping, or spreading the privacy of another person.

3. Article 246: Those openly insulting others or using force or other methods or those fabricating stories to slander others, if the case is serious, are to be sentenced to three

years or fewer in prison, put under criminal detention or surveillance, or deprived of their political rights.

4. Although most of these case examples are taken from media reports that frame stories in a certain way, what is indisputable in all of them is the way in which young people perceive and use their online space. I deconstruct some of these cases later on to analyze ways in which the media puts a certain twist to our understanding of them. In the meantime, the facts regarding the positions generally adopted by various stakeholders – students, parents, politicians, and educators – are consistent across news reports.

5. The end of the article says he was expelled, whereas, he was in fact only suspended by school authorities.

6. See also G. S. Takach (1999).

7. In this case Pat Holly, a member of the First Nations, sent thirty e-mails accusing the plaintiff of grave robbing and committing crimes against his people during the course of her archaeology digs.

CHAPTER FOUR

1. The National Children's Homes (2005) survey found that nearly 30 percent of cyber-bullied students told no one. Seventy percent of the children in Grades 6–8 surveyed under my own research in Quebec (Shariff, 2007), said they did not believe it was the school's responsibility to intervene in bullying outside of the physical school property.

2. See also Stonebanks (in press) on the impact of residential schools on Canadian aboriginal peoples.

CHAPTER FIVE

1. Salkind (1990, p. 361) defines personality as "the pattern of behaviours and thought that characterizes individuals, distinguishes them from others and remains relatively stable throughout their lives." A longitudinal study supports these findings (DiGiulio, 2001). Researchers discovered that half of the children with behavior problems in the fourth grade (including fighting, stealing, or lying) were arrested by age fourteen. Of those, 75 percent were repeatedly arrested at least three times by the time they were aged eighteen years.

2. He found that 35 to 40 percent of children who were described as being bullies in Grades 6 through 9 were convicted of at least three officially registered crimes by age twenty-four. Only 10 percent who were not described as bullies ended up with convictions later in life.

3. Hall (1999) cites research that provided some evidence to suggest human aggression is biologically determined (Thiessen, 1976). Smith (1995) summarized a large body of literature examining genetic influences, concluding that they have little impact and that most aggression is shaped by environmental factors.

4. Cesare Lombroso in the latter part of the nineteenth century was known for measuring the skulls and ears of notorious male criminals but failed to establish a clear link. William Sheldon, a U.S. criminologist known as the father of somatotyping, was more successful in linking aggression to physique and temperament. There have also been numerous studies on the linkage between violence and the presence of the extra Y chromosome in men, but these are again inconclusive. Studies of identical

twins provide more concrete evidence that genetics is a potent predictor of aggression.

5. Hall (1999) cites a number of studies on the impact of hormones on aggression, including Berkowitz (1993), Mazur (1983), Thiessen (1976), Renfrew (1997), all of which find a link between hormones and environmental influences that result in aggressive behavior. Renfrew reports evidence that suggests a mediating connection between the male hormone testosterone and aggressive behavior.

6. Lanctot (2001) reports a correlation in the increase of aggressive tendencies in girls with the onset of early puberty, particularly as this plays out in their interactions with older boys. Moretti (2002) reports increased conduct disorder in girls around age sixteen.

7. Reena Virk, Jamie Dufour, and Dawn Marie Wesley (Shariff, 2003).

8. Prinsloo and DuPlessi (1998, p. 11) describe this as "awakening a positive attitude to fellow human beings and awakening a sense of ... social conscience" (as cited in DiGiulio, 2001). South African studies have found that for girls especially, the family is a formidable shaper of self-concept (Marjoribanks & Mboya, 1998).

9. Cited in Hall (1999), Glueck and Glueck's (1962) well-known study on the relationship between family environment and criminal or violent tendencies identifies a range of sociocultural influences that include hostile treatment and erratic punishment. Numerous others have found a correlation between child abuse, poor parenting, neglect, and aggression in children. James (1995) identifies three familial characteristics that consistently distinguish the development of violent tendencies in young people, especially those from low socioeconomic groups: (1) severe and erratic punishment bordering on abuse; (2) marital discord, including frequent observing of spousal abuse; and (3) a high level of parental irritability. James suggests a causal relationship between a hostile caregiver and aggression in children in later life.

10. This was true in the cases of Reena Virk, Jamie Dufour, Dawn-Marie Wesley, and other girls who engaged in extreme violence that were studied by 1997.

CHAPTER SIX

1. I wish to acknowledge and thank Myles Ellis, director of Economic and Member Service, of the Canadian Teachers' Federation for permission to publish this resolution.

2. The complainants include the Dufour family, who commenced civil litigation on behalf of their daughter Jamie Dufour but abandoned the case; Azmi Jubran's human rights case, in which the decision was appealed and ruled in favor of the school; Jane Forin, who joins Leanne Dufour and Nasimah Nastoh in raising awareness of the issues; twelve parents in Teulon, Manitoba, Canada, who made their children's experiences with the school public through the CBC National News; and Emmett Fralick's parents (Emmett also committed suicide). Similar sentiments have been verbally raised by many concerned parents at public forums on bullying that I attended, including a parent workshop held during the annual conference of the British Columbia Parent Advisory Council on May 3, 2002.

3. Personal communications received by parents Jane Forin, Nasim Nastoh, Jamie Dufour's mother, and Nancy Knight are among those that confirm a "wall of defense" – a term coined by Jane Forin of Courtney, British Columbia, Canada.

The pattern of denial is also evident in court documents filed in several actions against schools for failing to protect victims of bullying.

4. All information provided here with respect to the named cases of bullying (whether taken from publicly available court documents or cited with parental permission) is based on public information – either from the media or from the victims, their families, or both. No information has been used here without their permission. Neither the author nor the publisher accepts liability for information that might have been inaccurately reported by the media or for any false accusations contained in filed court documents.

5. Andrew Forin, who was not involved in bullying but filmed a bullying incident and was manipulated into selling it to the media, was suspended for making the school look bad. Azmi Jubran put up with three years of bullying before punching a perpetrator in the stomach. He was suspended, but his perpetrators were not disciplined. In one case, an Ontario boy was jailed for four months without bail for writing a story titled "Twisted" about retaliating against his perpetrators.

6. For example, in the wake of well-publicized cases of bullying in the last six years, blanket zero-tolerance policies have been widely adopted in schools as seemingly sensible and efficient ways to curb bullying. In Chapter 7, I explain why these policies are not as sensible or effective as they appear.

7. The sources of these personal communications with school administrators cannot be disclosed because of ongoing consultation to resolve some of the heated and sensitive issues currently underway at the school.

CHAPTER SEVEN

1. See Michel Foucault, *Discipline and Punish* (1995), on using panoptical surveillance in prison institutions for the disciplining of docile bodies.
2. See Fuller (1964).
3. Communications Act of 1934 (Wikipedia, 2007).
4. Retrieved from http://www.okhouse.gov/Committees/CommitteeReports/7017.doc. August 21, 2007.
5. Illinois Social Networking Prohibition Act (State of Illinois, 2007). Retrieved from http://www.ilga.gov/legislation/billstatus.asp?DocNum=1682&GAID=9&GA=95&DocTypeID=SB&LegID=29749&SessionID=51 August, 25, 2007.
6. Popular Web sites fitting this definition include MySpace (http://www.myspace.com/), Friendster (http://www.friendster.com/), and LiveJournal (http://www.livejournal.com/). This definition, however, could potentially cover a much broader range of Web sites. Many news Web sites such as Slashdot (http://slashdot.org/) and blogs such as RedState (http://www.redstate.com/) permit both public profiles and personal journals. Amazon (http://www.amazon.com/) allows personal profiles including photos, interests, and contact information. In addition, many media companies such as News.com (http://news.com) publisher CNET Networks (http://www.cnetnetworks.com/) permit users to create profiles displaying photos and other personal information, as well as sending e-mail to other members. Some popular chat services include ICQ (http://www.icq.com/), AOL Instant Messenger (http://www.aol.com/), and Yahoo! Chat (http://messenger.yahoo.com/chat).
7. For more information, contact P.Tsatsou@lse.ac.uk.

8. Retrieved from http://www.legifrance.gouv.fr/WAspad/UnTexteDeJorf?numjo=
   INTX0600091L.

CHAPTER EIGHT

1. ("Les Veilles Gardes: hypothèses sur l'émergence des normes, l'internormativité et
   le désordre à travers une typologie des institutions normatives," 1996, p. 233). See
   also Macdonald (1986). For a recent application of this normative typology to the
   laws of close personal relationships, see MacDonald and McMorrow (2007).
2. These assumptions are first, *centralism*: the belief that law can be traced to a single
   official institutional source. Second is *monism*: the belief that normative activity is
   coherent. Third is *prescriptivism*: the belief that law is a social fact existing above
   and apart from those it claims to regulate. Finally there is *positivism*: the belief that
   law can be identified on the basis of a specific test of validity. From a critical legal
   pluralist perspective, centralism, monism, prescriptivism, and positivism appear for
   what they are: a set of interpretive commitments, not universal truths; they represent
   beliefs not facts, which a critical legal pluralism invites us to reject.
3. McMorrow explains: "For example, a Roman Catholic kid's grandmother may give
   him fish sticks for lunch every Friday because in the pre-Vatican Council II faith she
   was brought up in, eating meat on Fridays was forbidden. Today the official position
   of the Church is different; nevertheless that child may believe that it is wrong to eat
   meat on Fridays because that is the norm at home. Or, perhaps he feels obligated to
   eat whatever grandmother makes him; thus, in deference to her authority, he does
   not complain even though he does not really like them."
4. See also Macdonald (2002).
5. I have presented some of this research in Chapter 6 and also at conferences at the
   University of Oxford in the United Kingdom, at the University of Grenada in Spain,
   and at the American Education Research Association Conferences in San Francisco
   (2006) and Chicago (2007).

REFERENCES

Artz, S. (1998). Where have all the school girls gone? Violent girls in the school yard.
Child & Youth Care Forum, 27(2).

Artz, S., & Riecken, T. (1997). What, so what, then what? The gender gap in school-
based violence and its implications for child and youth care practice. *Child & Youth
Care Forum, 26*, 291–303.

Belley, J.-G. (1998). Le pluralisme juridique de Roderick Macdonald: une analyse
sequentielle. In A. Lajoie & R. Macdonald (Eds.), *Théories et emergences du droit:
pluralisme, surdétermination et effectivité*. Montréal: Les Éditions Thémis.

Bentley, K. M., & Li, A. K. F. (1995). Bully and victim problems in elementary schools
and students' beliefs about aggression. *Canadian Journal of School Psychology, 11*,
153–165.

Berkowitz, L. (1993). *Aggression: Its causes, consequences, and control*. Philadelphia:
Temple University Press.

Berson, I. R., Berson, M. J., & Ferron, J. M. (2002). Emerging risks of violence in the
digital age: Lessons for educators from an online study of adolescent girls in the United
States. *Journal of School Violence, 1*, 51–71.

Björqvist, K., Lagerspetz, K. M. J., & Kaukiainen, A. (1992). Do girls manipulate and boys fight? Development trends in regard to direct and indirect aggression. *Aggressive Behavior, 18*, 117–127.

Boulton, M., & Hawker, D. (1997). Verbal bullying: The myth of "sticks and stones." In D. Tattum & G. Herbert (Eds.), *Bullying: Home, school and community* (pp. 53–63). London: David Fulton.

Boulton, M., & Underwood, K. (1992). Bully/victim problems among middle school children. *British Journal of Educational Psychology, 62*, 73–87.

Bowlby, B. L., & Regan, J. W. (1998). *An educator's guide to human rights.* Aurora, Canada: Aurora Professional Press.

Chamberlain, E., & Houston, B. (1999). School Sexual Harassment Policies: The Need for Both Justice and Care. In M. S. Katz, N. Noddings, & K. A. Strike (Eds.), *Justice and caring: The search for common ground in education* (p. vi). New York: Teachers College Press.

Charach, A., Pepler, D., & Ziegler, S. (1995). Bullying at school: A Canadian perspective. *Education Canada, 35*, 12–18.

Dicey, E. (1863). *Six months in the federal states.* London/Cambridge: Macmillan.

DiGiulio, R. C. (2001). *Educate, mediate, or litigate? What teachers, parents, and administrators must do about student behavior.* Thousand Oaks, CA: Corwin Press.

Doob, A. N., Marinos, V., Varma, K. N., & University of Toronto Centre of Criminology. (1995). *Youth crime and the youth justice system in Canada: A research perspective.* Toronto: Centre of Criminology, University of Toronto.

Dostoyevsky, F. (1937). *The Brothers Karamazov* (C. Garnett, Trans.). New York: Modern Library.

Foucault, M. (1995). *Discipline and punish: The birth of the prison.* New York: Vintage Books.

Fuller, L. (1964). *The morality of law: A reply to critics.* New Haven, CT: Yale University Press.

Glueck, S., & Glueck, E. T. (1962). *Family environment and delinquency.* Boston: Houghton Mifflin.

Hall, M. T. (1999). *Administrative discretion and youth violence in schools: An analysis.* Unpublished doctoral dissertation, Simon Fraser University, Burnaby, Canada.

Henderson, N. R., & Hymel, S. (2002). *Peer contributions to bullying in schools: Examining student response strategies.* Paper presented at the National Association of School Psychologists Annual Convention (Poster session), Chicago, Illinois.

James, O. (1995). *Juvenile violence in a winner-loser culture: Socio-economic and familial origins of the rise in violence against the person.* London/New York: Free Association Books.

Katch, J. (2001). *Under deadman's skin: Discovering the meaning of children's violent play.* Boston: Beacon Press.

Lanctot, N. (2001). *Violence among females from adolescence to adulthood: Results from a longitudinal study.* Paper presented at the Vancouver Conference on Aggressive and Violent Girls, Simon Fraser University, Vancouver, Canada.

Leishman, J. (2002, October 10). Cyber-bullying: The Internet is the latest weapon in a bully's arsenal [Electronic version]. *CBC News. The National.* Retrieved January 27, 2003, from http://cbc.ca/news/national/news/cyberbullying/index.html.

Les Veilles Gardes: hypothèses sur l'émergence des normes, l'internormativité et le désordre à travers une typologie des institutions normatives. (1996). In J.-G. Belley

(Ed.), *Le droit soluble: Contributions québécoises à l'étude de l'internormativité*. Paris: L.G.D.J.

Louis Harris and Associates. (1993). *Hostile hallways: The AAUW survey on sexual harassment in America's schools*. Washington, DC: American Association of University Women.

Macdonald, R. A. (1986). Pour la reconnaissance d'une normativité juridique implicite et 'inférentielle'. *Sociologie et Sociétés, 18*, 47–58.

Macdonald, R. A. (2002). *Lessons of everyday law*. Montreal: Published for the Law Commission of Canada and the School of Policy Studies, Queen's University by McGill-Queen's University Press.

Macdonald, R. A., & McMorrow, T. (2007). Wedding a critical legal pluralism to the laws of close personal relationships [Electronic version]. *European Journal of Legal Studies, 1*. Retrieved September 8, 2007, from http://www.ejls.eu/.

Macdonald, R. A., & Sandomierski, D. (2006). Against monopolies. *Northern Ireland Legal Quarterly, 57*, 610–633.

Marjoribanks, K., & Mboya, M. M. (1998). Factors affecting the self-concepts of South African Students. *Journal of Social Psychology, 138*, 572–580.

Mazur, A. (1983). Physiology, dominance and aggression in humans. In A. P. Goldstein & Syracuse University Center for Research on Aggression (Eds.), *Prevention and control of aggression* (pp. 145–155). New York: Pergamon Press.

Mooney, A., Creeser, R., & Blatchford, P. (1991). Children's views on teasing and fighting in junior schools. *Educational Research, 33*, 103–112.

Moretti, M. (2002, June). *Aggressive and violent behaviour in girls: Rates, risk factors and relevance for adjustment*. Paper presented at the Vancouver Conference on Aggressive and Violent Girls, Simon Fraser University, Vancouver, Canada.

Nansel, T., Overpeck, M., Pilla, R. S., Simons-Morton, B., & Scheidt, P. (2001). Bullying behaviors among U.S. youth: Prevalence and association with psychosocial adjustment. *Journal of the American Medical Association, 285*, 2094–2100.

National Children's Homes. (2005). *Putting U in the picture. Mobile Bullying Survey 2005*. Retrieved December 5, 2006, from http://www.nch.org.uk/uploads/documents/Mobile_bullying_%20report.pdf.

O'Connell, P., Pepler, D., & Craig, W. (1999). Peer involvement in bullying: Insights and challenges for intervention. *Journal of Adolescence, 22*, 437–452.

Olweus, D. (1993). *Bullying at school: What we know and what we can do*. Oxford, England/Cambridge, MA: Blackwell.

Prinsloo, E., & Du Plessis, S. (1998). *Socio-education 1*. Pretoria: Department of Educational Studies, University of South Africa.

Renfrew, J. W. (1997). *Aggression and its causes: A biopsychosocial approach*. New York: Oxford University Press.

Roher, E. (1997). *An educator's guide to violence in schools*. Toronto: Canada Law Books.

Salkind, N. (1990). *Child development*. Chicago: Holt, Rinehart and Winston.

Schissel, B. (1993). *Social dimensions of Canadian youth justice*. Don Mills, Ontario: Oxford University Press Canada.

Shariff, S. (2003). *A system on trial: Identifying legal standards for educational, ethical and legally defensible approaches to bullying in schools*. Burnaby, British Columbia: SFU Library. Doctoral Thesis.

Shariff, S. (2007). Unpublished research conducted as part of a three year research project on cyber-bullying, funded by Social Science and Humanities Research Council of Canada. Shaheen Shariff, McGill University, Principal Investigator.

Smith, D. J. (1995). Youth crime and conduct disorders: Trends, patterns and causal explanations. In M. Rutter & D. J. Smith (Eds.), *Psychosocial disorders in young people: Time trends and their causes* (pp. 389–489). Chichester, England/New York: Published for Academia Europaea by J. Wiley.

State of Illinois. SB1682. (2007).

Stonebanks, C. (In press). *The James Bay Cree.* Rotterdam, the Netherlands: Sense.

Takach, G. S. (1999). Internet law: Dynamics, themes and skill sets. *Canadian Business Law Journal, 32,* 1–83.

Tanner, J. (1996). *Teenage troubles: Youth and deviance in Canada.* Toronto: Nelson Canada.

Thiessen, D. D. (1976). *The evolution and chemistry of aggression.* Springfield, IL: Charles C. Thomas.

Tolman, D. L., Spencer, R., Rosen-Reynoso, M., & Porches, M. (2001, April). *"He's the man!" Gender ideologies and early adolescents' experiences with sexual harassment.* Paper presented at the American Educational Researchers Association Conference, Seattle, WA.

Vaillancourt, T., & Hymel, S. (2001, September). *Bullying is power: A look at bully-victim problems in British Columbia.* Paper presented at the First Annual B. C. Ministry of Education Research Symposium, Vancouver, Canada.

Vancouver Conference on Aggressive and Violent Girls. (2002, June). Burnaby, Canada: Simon Fraser University.

Watkinson, A. M. (1999). *Education, student rights, and the Charter.* Saskatoon, Canada: Purich.

Weil, S. (1977). *"The Iliad," Poem of Might.* In G. A. Panichas (Ed.), *The Simone Weil Reader.* New York: David McKay.

Wikipedia. (2007). *Description of the Communications Act of 1934.* Retrieved August 23, 2007, from http://en.wikipedia.org/wiki/Communications_Act_of_1934.

Cases

CHAPTER 1

Beidler v. North Thurston Sch. Dist., No. 99-2-00236-6 (Thurston Cty. Super. Ct., July 18, 2000).
Hill v.v. Church of Scientology of Toronto, 2 S. C.R. 1130 at 1175 (1995).
Robichaud v. Canada (Treasury Board), 2 S. C.R. 84 (1987).

CHAPTER 2

Dufour v. Howe Sound Board of Education (2000).
Jubran v. North Vancouver School Distr. No. 44, B. C. H.R. T.D. No. 10 (Q. L.) 221 (2002).

CHAPTER 3

Barrick Gold Corp. v.v. Lopehandia, O. J. No. 2329 (2004).
Bryson v. News America Publ'ns, Inc., 672 N.E. 2 d 1207 (Ill. 1996).
Colour Your World Corp. v. Canadian Broadcasting Corp., 38 O.R. (3 d) 97 (1998).
Cullen v. White, WASC 153 (2003).
Doe v.v. GTE Corp., 347 F.3 d 655, 660 (7th Cir. 2003).
Gould v. Regina (East) School Division No. 77, 3 WWR 117 (Sask.) (1997).
Hill v. Church of Scientology of Toronto, 2 S. C.R. 1130 (1995).
Hunter v. Board of Education of Montgomery County, 439 A. 2 d 582 (Md.1982).
I. M. L. v.v. State, 61 P. 3 d 1038 (Utah, 2002).
Newman et al. v. Halstead et al., BCSC 65 (2006).
Newton v.v. Vancouver, 46 B. C.R. 67 (1932).
Parmiter v. Coupland, 6 M.&W. 105 (1840).
Ross v. Holly (2004).
Stratton Oakmont, Inc. v.v. Prodigy Services Co., WL 323710 (N.Y. Sup. Ct., 1995).
Times v. Sullivan, 376, U. S. 254 (1964).
Vaquero Energy Ltd. v.v. Weir, ABQB 68 (2004).
Vitzelly v. Mudies Select Library Ltd., 2 Q.B. 170 (1900).
Wagner v.v. Miskin, 660 N. W. 2 d 593 (N.D. Sup. Ct., 2003).
Williams v.v. Eady, 10 TLR 41 (1893).

World Wrestling Fedn. Entm't Inc. v. Bozell, 142 F. Supp. 2 d 514, 534 (S.D. N.Y. 2001).
Zeran v. America Online, Inc., 958 F. Supp. 1124, 1134 (E.D. Va) aff'd, 129 F.3 d 327 (4th Cir. 1997).

CHAPTER 4

A. B. v. State of Indiana, No. 67A01-0609-JV-372, 2007 Ind. App. LEXIS 694 (Ind. Ct. App. Apr. 9, 2007).
Bethel School District No. 403 et al. v. Fraser, a minor, et al., 478 U. S. 675 (1986).
Beussink v. Woodland R-IV School District, 30 F. Supp. 2 d 1175 (E.D. Mo. 1988).
Emmett v. Kent School District No 413, 92 F. Supp. 2 d 1088 (WD Wash. 2000).
Garrity v. John Hancock Mutual Life Insurance Co., 18 IER Cases 981 (Mass. Dist. Ct. 2002).
Irwin Toy Ltd. v. Québec (Attorney General), 1 S. C.R. 927 (1989).
J. S., a Minor v. Bethlehem Area School District, 757 A.2 d 412, 422. (Pa. Cmwlth. 2000).
Lutes v. Board of Education of Prairie View School Division No. 74, 101 Sask R 232 (1992).
Morse v. Frederick, 551 U. S. ___ (2007).
New Jersey v. T. L. O., 469 U. S. 325 (1985).
People v. B. F. Jones, 62 Mich. 304 (1886).
People v. Carlos Overton, 20 NY2 d 360 (1967).
R. v. D. W., B. C. J. No. 627 (2002).
R. v. M. R. M., 3 S. C.R. 393 (1998).
R. v. Oakes 1, S. C.R. 103 (1986).
Singleton v. Board of Education, 894 F. Supp. 386 (D. Kan. 1995).
Sullivan v. Houston Independent School District, 307 F. Supp. 1328, 1340 (S.D. Tex. 1969).
Tinker v. Des Moines Independent Community School District, 393 U. S. 503 (1969).
United States of America, Plaintiff, v. Jake Baker, 890 F. Supp. 1375 (E. D. Mich. 1995).

CHAPTER 5

Davis v. Monroe County Bd. of Ed., 526 U. S. 629 (1999).
Jubran v. North Vancouver School District et al., No. 44 B. C. H.R. T.D. No. 10 (Q. L.) 221 (2002).
Robichaud v. Canada (Treasury Board), 2 S. C.R. 84 (1987).
Ross v. New Brunswick School District No. 15, 1 S. C.R. 825 (1996).

CHAPTER 6

A. B. v. State of Indiana, No. 67A01-0609-JV-372, 2007 Ind. App. LEXIS 694 (Ind. Ct. App. Apr. 9, 2007).
Lutes v. Board of Education of Prairie View School Division No. 74, 101 Sask. R 232 (1992).

CHAPTER 7

A. B. v. State of Indiana, No. 67A01-0609-JV-372, 2007 Ind. App. LEXIS 694 (Ind. Ct. App. Apr. 9, 2007).
Chamberlain v. Surrey School District No. 36, 4 S. C.R. 710, 2002 SCC 86 (2002).
Lutes v. Board of Education of Prairie View School Division No. 74, 101 Sask R 232 (1992).

CHAPTER 8

Davis v. Monroe County Bd. of Ed., 526 U. S. 629 (1999).
Tinker v. Des Moines Independent Community School District, 393 U. S. 503 (1969).

Index